African Americans and Political Participation

African Americans and Political Participation

A Reference Handbook

Minion K. C. Morrison, Editor

Foreword by U.S. Rep. Bennie Gordon Thompson

A B C · C L I O

Santa Barbara, California • Denver, Colorado • Oxford, England

Library of Congress Cataloging-in-Publication Data

African americans and political participation : a reference handbook / Minion K. C. Morrison, editor.
       p. cm. – (Political participation in America)
Includes bibliographical references and index.
   ISBN 1-57607-837-X (hardcover : alk. paper) ISBN 1-57607-838-8 (e-book)
 1. African Americans—Politics and government. 2. Political participation—United States. 3. United States—Race relations—Political aspects.   I. Morrison, Minion K. C., 1946– II. Series
  E185.A2538 2003
  323'.042'08996073—dc21
                            2003013700

07   06   05   04   03   10   9   8   7   6   5   4   3   2   1

ABC-CLIO, Inc.
130 Cremona Drive, P.O. Box 1911
Santa Barbara, California 93116-1911

This book is printed on acid-free paper.
Manufactured in the United States of America

Contents

Foreword: The Struggle for Participation

The African American political history is a much under-assessed experience. Although we are hardly bereft of studies of American politics and government, those studies rarely give full due to the independent and integrated role of African Americans. *African Americans and Political Participation* is a first of its kind and it is a welcome contribution. It pulls together the broad sweep of this experience, showing both its independent character and how it has been influenced by interaction with the general American population. It is a rare achievement, and one that I applaud.

The marvel of this volume is how well it captures the centrality of struggle by African Americans for the acquisition of first political rights and then participation. It has been a cardinal principle that in the absence of struggle, little power would be ceded to those who were deemed the servants to the American social and economic elite. The system of chattel slavery was designed to prove this fixed, almost castelike exclusion of African Americans. This volume carefully documents how this happened from the earliest time to the present, achieving the rare feat of an integrated, highly nuanced assessment of the mass of information dictated by such a long time frame.

Professor Morrison and his colleagues first provide a sketch of this community, showing how it has been disabled by slavery and its vestiges that continue in various guises—outright discrimination, selective racial exclusion, class discrimination, underrepresentation via voter dilution, and economic disparities. They reveal how the real life chances of African Americans are curtailed by disparities in education, health care, and a range of other socioeconomic indicators. The deftness of their analysis is all the more important now that a more invidious guise is upon us—the claims that we have achieved a color-blind, equal society. These claims notwithstanding, this analysis shows the deep continuing racial division in the United States that impinges on full participation for African Americans.

The balance of this volume copiously documents the various historical phases and patterns of the participation among African Americans. The authors show that while much remains to be done, tremendous progress in legal-formal and active participation has occurred since the first Africans arrived in the Americas by force. For example, they illustrate that first and foremost among this population there has been a tradition of resistance and protest participation. This strategy was often the only one available to them since the promise of universal freedom in the United States Constitution did not extend the franchise to most Blacks. Those who were slaves, the overwhelming majority of the population, were accorded the infamous three-fifths value. But incongruously this was only for the purpose of boosting the representation of their masters vis-à-vis the population in the non-slave North. In spite of all, however, the participation by resistance was very real. It was sufficient to keep the perpetrators of the system vigilant in trying to anticipate and control routine resistance and presumed threats of violence.

We all now know that this resistance was not sufficient to completely displace the system, but it provided a strategy that became a means of negotiation for change. Its results have been remarkable. In concert with allies, African Americans have moved beyond slavery to the institutionalization of political rights. These authors show how this condition obtains through abolition, civil war, a reconstruction, the challenges of ambivalence and backtracking on formal rights, and the most sustained social movement in this nation's history during the 1950s and 1960s. In short, once the system of slavery was replaced, this volume shows the ways and means that African Americans have engaged the political system for the acquisition of political resources.

By focusing exclusively on participation in public affairs the authors pull together the broadest amount of political history and theory on the subject to date. Their sweep is comprehensive, but with the added advantage of strong disciplinary political science theory and conceptualization. It allows the reader to fix African American political experience in the context of the broader American political system. This is especially welcome because it is virtually impossible to understand the two separate arenas without also understanding the ways in which they are intertwined. Indeed, it may be said that the two contexts are essential to each other. One can have little understanding of American politics without also having an understanding of the special place of African Americans within it, and vice versa. Meanwhile, much of our American experience with its almost unique articulation of boundless participatory democracy, has been dedicated to resolution of an anomalous restriction of that democracy for African Americans. The authors help us to appreciate the mass of evidence and information they cover, which links the races by constantly invoking political science theory for context and explication. The quality of this product is much better for this consistent application of theory to the evidence.

Consequently, while a good deal of this material is already known, the volume is nevertheless a discovery. In its comprehensive scope it is a discovery that there are patterns to the activity of African American participation that can be drawn together for the benefit of knowledge, reflection, and disciplinary enterprise. In a recent nation like ours, defined by advances in science and technology, knowledge can be fleeting. Our tendency to create and discard simply causes us to lose sight of details of our history. So, for many readers of this collection the mass of data will serve as a kind of documentary record of rarely known events, which together, provide the complete picture of the participatory efforts of African Americans. This knowledge can be deployed for a variety of purposes—to wit, educating citizenry in a democracy that can only be enriched by information; and, providing a base for reflection by activists for whom the vision of the democratic dream requires social change.

At the same time, the professional enterprise of African American politics is infinitely enhanced by this comprehensive volume. After all, the phenomenon of an enterprise for the professional study of African American politics remains a relatively new and contested arena. I recall in my college days in the mid-1960s that it was rare to find course options treating this material. And when one did find the option it was pieced together for lack of standard academic material. This absence of material related and continues to relate to the fact that many political science generalists contest the existence of such a subfield. Some of these argue that dedicating an area of specialization to one racial group is tantamount to balkanization, or worse, a variety of "reverse" racism. Yet, in such a charged atmosphere about what is appropriate activity for professional pursuit, African Americans as subjects often become residuals in general analyses. Their numbers are so small in samples that analysts can be indifferent to or unable to make statements about the observable differences in African American political behavior, for example. This highly focused analysis by Morrison and his colleagues, however, demonstrates both that the enterprise is certain, and that its dedicated focus does not obviate an integrated approach where the general system is brought into play.

As a contemporary public figure, I have been privileged to be a part of the phenomenon this volume documents so well. I believe that I am a product of and am sustained by the tradition of protest and resistance illustrated here. I find this comprehensive body of information confirming of my experience, and of utility as I continue as a public servant to my state, my country, and the African American racial community.

The New Reconstruction of the 1960s Civil Rights Movement

Many people argue that the single biggest boost African American participation has received in history was the civil rights movement in the 1960s. I have little disagreement with that conclusion, notwithstanding many necessary first steps that made a movement of its scope in the 1960s possible. In the general ebb and flow of participation for the group certainly the end to slavery was a major achievement. But as this volume clearly demonstrates, the end to institutionalized slavery did not result in immediate or full-scale participation or even the full elaboration of democratic rights. Major issues of citizenship, equal protection of the laws, and voting were left unresolved succeeding Lincoln's Emancipation Proclamation. Then even Reconstruction, the first formal period of participation when massive numbers of Black voters sent their own to political offices, hardly matches the range and depth of the participation that followed the movement of the 1960s. This latest period of resistance and protest represents the broadest and most successful assault on racial discrimination, segregation, and barriers to participation to date. At full steam, this movement challenged virtually every sector of the American society on account that it was tainted by racial discrimination and exclusion. And to the benefit of an American democracy with full integrity, many barriers came tumbling down.

I think of this contemporary period as the high watermark of the American experiment. This second "Reconstruction" whereby the society was brought to confront the fundamental contradiction of racial exclusion, resulted in the fullest flowering of participation since the Constitution was promulgated. Why do I think this? In the first place, the imperfections of the system were stark in the 1960s when it came to the integration of African Americans into the fabric of everyday life and access. This was especially clear in the South, where after 1876 the dictates of the emancipation were almost completely abandoned. The "ancien regime" was gradually restored by various means, including eventual sanction by state laws after 1890 and the Supreme Court in 1896.

But it was also the case that while whites in the North fought to abandon slavery, they did not necessarily practice equality toward the Blacks. The impact of this differential status in the North for Blacks was heightened because by the 1960s almost half of them had migrated from the South. Moreover, whites in the North sanctioned or tolerated the post-1876 restoration of the racially exclusive remnants of the Confederacy in the South.

This nadir for Blacks lasted a long time before the 1960s movement made a broad strike against the racial status quo. Its scope also swept the North, where Blacks had slowly made inroads with representation in the urban central cities they populated.

So the second Reconstruction really enveloped the entire country in a way that the first had not. When Blacks began to attain political representation in the 1960s, they did so in virtually all parts of the country. The most visible early examples of the national scope of the change occurred in the early 1970s when southerners Barbara Jordan and Andrew Young became the first Blacks to return to Congress from the South in almost 100 years. They joined their northern African American counterparts already representing central city districts like those in New York, Chicago, Detroit, and Philadelphia.

That was just the tip of the iceberg. The more interesting stories were occurring at lower electoral levels and in a range of other sectors in the society. Let me first speak of the latter. When Rosa Parks, Martin Luther King, and their cohorts challenged the segregated bus system in Montgomery and won, they set off a cycle of events that would ultimately change the landscape of American race relations. They demonstrated that seizing the opportunity to act could mobilize a cross section of American allies to their cause, and that they could be successful. In a matter of five years a full-scale challenge ensued against segregation, disfranchisement, and economic inequality. And the scope of the challenge broadened with every event of protest or resistance, with the effect that this racialized conflict became a general American one.

Allies and proponents could be found all across the society, and most importantly within the ruling coalition of the government. The Supreme Court, which had already declared "separate but equal" a dead federal policy, made a number of related decisions that made it impractical for virtually any public entity to continue practices of segregation. And the increasingly strong American executive gradually deployed the weight of that office to the passage of civil rights legislation. Segregationists and avowed racists found it more and more difficult to sustain the status quo. The examples of Mississippi and Alabama Governors Ross Barnett and George Wallace, who stood in the schoolhouse doors in the early 1960s to block the entry of African American students, represented the "last stand" for that sort of segregationist. The strong American presidency that supported civil rights significantly clipped the wings of these governors. Much of this resulted from executive support of three pieces of legislation between 1960 and 1965—the Civil Rights Acts of 1960 and 1964, and the Voting Rights Act of 1965.

What remained to complete this picture was the electoral arena. The second Reconstruction in this area actually preceded the arrival of Barbara Jordan and Andrew Young in Congress. It first evolved slowly with voter registration campaigns by local organizations buttressed by the likes of the NAACP, SNCC, and CORE in deeply segregated southern states of Mississippi, Alabama, and Georgia. By the time of the passage of the Civil Rights Act of 1964 registration was sufficient to elect a few Blacks to aldermanic posts. And when the Voting Rights Act passed, the rapid enrollment of Blacks allowed them to send multiple representatives to local offices. It was in the local sector where the most spectacular changes were occurring— Blacks became mayors, aldermen and women, municipal councilors, inter alia. The increases, while not proportionate, were indeed spectacular for the speed with which they occurred. Almost everywhere they were related to a significant mobilization of an African American constituency that voter registration had catapulted to a majority of the electorate. The positions these officials occupied were far beyond the number and range that Blacks acquired in the first Reconstruction. Moreover, they were nurtured in a political environment where racial group influence on the ruling coalition was perhaps at its historic peak.

It is in this period that my personal odyssey began as a public official. I was propelled to representation of a small local district in Mississippi. I, like perhaps a majority of American public officials, began there and accepted the challenge of representing a constituency at successively higher levels of responsibility until I assumed the office I hold today as congressman for a majority African American district in Mississippi. That means that in large measure the story recounted in this volume is my personal story—of a struggle to represent an African American district where a major responsibility is attending to the needs of many of my constituents who were too long isolated from the public goods they rightly deserved.

The Special Case of Mississippi in the Civil Rights Struggle and Beyond

I am exceedingly proud to play a small role in this new period of electoral participation, representing and giving voice to the hopes of that portion of my constituency that has been peculiarly bereft of influence in our political system. These are the sons and daughters of slaves in Mississippi, whose accident of birth in this particular region meant an experience of some of the most abject practices of racism in the history of the republic. This is a state that was long known as the least redeemed in the perpetration of a racial caste that rent African Americans completely powerless. It did so with a mix of local legal machinations, terror, violence, guile, and relentlessness. When the wave of the movement swept over the South, it was Mississippi that had the lowest voter registration rate, and the least access to the benefits of modern health, welfare, and education. And, it was perhaps the most rigorously segregated of all the states. So the challenge for Blacks in my state was always regarded as more difficult.

Indeed, changes did come later to Mississippi, but they did come. Despite our slower pace, the pattern for us was similar. Local people gradually organized small but visible efforts to try and integrate facilities or to register to vote. And with the help of civil rights leaders and foot soldiers from elsewhere, a campaign was soon afoot. The early days of our struggle were built around organizations like the NAACP and the SNCC that collaborated to an unusual degree to challenge segregation and disfranchisement. We organized and challenged in the streets perhaps as much as anyplace else, and surely perceived ourselves to be more bruised in the process. For example, the horrible symbol of the lynching of Emmitt Till was still fresh in our minds with the emergence of Aaron Henry and Medgar Evers as NAACP leaders in the late 1950s. And I personally recall the horrific events of the brutal beating of Fannie Low Hamer, and the assassinations of Medgar Evers and the three civil rights workers at Philadelphia. But the courage and conviction of these strong individuals laid the foundation on which we all stand today—citizens, voters, elected officials who make it possible for the likes of Jesse Jackson to aspire to the highest public office in this country.

This backdrop and the scope of its circumstances moved me to go into public affairs in Mississippi when I was just out of college. The political mobilization in Mississippi had been very rapid and broad. This least redeemed of states in race relations had organized perhaps the strongest Black political party that replaced the formerly segregated state Democratic Party with a now integrated entity; and, local towns and villages everywhere were engaged in political efforts. So, instead of heading off as many of my mates did to study law, I headed back to my hometown of Bolton, population 800.

Mobilization there was high. With two other Blacks I ran for alderman in 1969. Coming on the heels of the all-important Voting Rights Act, this majority Black town elected us as its first African Americans to political office in almost 100 years. Four years later I was elected mayor of that town with a full slate of African American aldermen and women. There has been no turning back since then. Once Blacks had the franchise restored in Bolton and elsewhere in Mississippi their political mobilization has been exceedingly high. And they have been equally successful in controlling or influencing local public affairs. It was largely they who elected me as congressman in a majority Black district in 1993.

So when I say that the story of this volume is partly my personal story, the recitation above of my evolution from small-town Black alderman to member of Congress illustrates my point. I was propelled to leadership on the wings of a largely African American constituency, whose continuous exclusion led to an enduring struggle to overcome. The achievement of what seemed improbable by this community shows the promise and the major flaw of the American democratic experiment—the system promises equality to all, but has persistently fell short in regard to African Americans. But our strivings in what I have termed the second Reconstruction have in many ways achieved more than at any other time in American history.

The Challenge of Representation as a Minority

Even as I record the degree of success in recent electoral politics for African Americans, I am fully aware that the promise remains unfulfilled. There are several dimensions to this. In the first place, while some gains have been made, nowhere near parity has been attained for this former slave community. There are major disparities between the races to be overcome on virtually every relevant socioeconomic indicator. Second, electing African American representatives in a majoritarian system still leaves uncertainty about the extent of influence for a racial minority. So long as Congress, for example, makes its choices largely by majority vote, it is a foregone conclusion that more general interests will be more persuasive in that body. Then, there is the major question about what representation means. Is it enough merely to have Black (or other racial representatives) fill legislative seats in districts where Blacks are concentrated? Or, are there some larger requirements, namely that those representatives reflect the distinct policy preferences of these communities that are routinely treated differentially?

I believe these are vital questions in contemporary American politics because we have not fundamentally addressed the problem of differential access for numerical minorities, and especially African Americans. This failure is a primary reason why Jesse Jackson felt compelled to run a major campaign for the presidency. His extraordinary campaigns made a fundamental critique of this flawed system, at the same time that he invited the entire American population to become a part of a "Rainbow Coalition" for resolution. Although Jackson did not become president, I believe he offered a sound model for more effective American democratic representation. His model continues to invigorate those of us who represent constituents whose status remains uncertain in the American democratic polity.

This important volume puts all of this into perspective. It is and will remain an important source of documentation of this continuing struggle. Moreover, in the thorough way in which it integrates history with the continuing story of African American struggles and strivings, it is a definitive source book for any serious student or practitioner of this racial group's political history and political future.

Bennie Gordon Thompson
U.S. Representative
Second District of Mississippi

Series Foreword

Participation in the political process is a cornerstone of both the theory and the practice of democracy; indeed, the word "democracy" itself means rule by the people. Since the formation of the New Deal coalition in 1932, the study of U.S. politics has largely been organized around the concept that there exist distinct "blocs" of citizens, such as African Americans, women, Catholics, and Latinos. This trend was reinforced during the 1960s when the expansion of the media and the decline of traditional sources of authority promoted direct citizen mobilization. And more recently, the emphasis on "identity politics" has reinforced the notion of distinct groups organized along lines of shared personal characteristics rather than common economic interests.

Although political participation is a mainstream, even canonical, subject in the study of U.S. politics, there are few midrange reference materials available on this subject. Indeed, the available reference materials do not include works that provide both a systematic empirical base *and* explanatory and contextualizing material. Likewise, because of the fragmentation of the reference material on this subject, it is difficult for readers to draw comparisons across groups, even though this is one of the most meaningful ways of understanding the phenomenon of political participation. The Political Participation in America series is designed to fill this gap in the reference literature on this subject by providing key points of background (e.g., demographics, political history, major contemporary issues) and then systematically addressing different types of political participation, providing both substance and context for readers. In addition, each chapter includes case studies that either illuminate larger issues or highlight some particular subpopulation within the larger group.

Each volume of the ABC-CLIO Political Participation in America series focuses on one of the major subgroups that make up the electorate in the United States. Each volume includes the following components:

- Introduction to the group, comprising a demographic, historical, and political portrait of the group, including political opinions and issues of key importance to members of the group
- Participation in protest politics, including marches, rallies, demonstrations, and direct actions
- Participation in social movements and interest groups, including involvement of members of the group in and through a wide variety of organizations and associations
- Participation in electoral politics, including a profile of involvement with political parties and voting patterns
- Participation in political office-holding, including elected, appointed, and "unofficial" offices from the local to national levels

The end of each book also includes an A–Z glossary featuring brief entries on important individuals and events; a chronology of political events salient to the group; a resource guide of organizations, newsletters, websites, and other important contact information, all briefly annotated; an annotated bibliography of key primary and secondary documents, including books and journal articles; excerpts from major primary documents, with introductions; and a comprehensive index to the volume.

Raymond A. Smith
Series Editor

Preface

This project opportunity seemed a daunting challenge when it was first presented to me. At the time I was in my customary state of overextension—too many projects, too many deadlines, and an unusual array of added professional responsibilities. Among other things, I was in the midst of a term as president of the National Conference of Black Political Scientists (NCOBPS), the professional organization of specialists studying politics among African descendants, principally in the United States. But the prospect of organizing a group of principal scholars in the field, many of them active in NCOBPS, to provide a comprehensive analytic overview of Black participation in American politics was enticing. After all, there was no such dedicated piece in the literature, although many people had provided good sketches, many among them historians. Yet, there has been a proliferation of research resulting in seminal monographic studies and articles in the past thirty years of which it seemed an ideal time to take stock. Perhaps the greatest flowering of study and publication about African American life in general and in politics especially took place just after the civil rights movement that culminated in the 1960s. Thus this project had a level of importance that it seemed apt to exploit—to pull together the best of what we knew at a time when the field of study had reached maturity. It was in this spirit that I agreed to the project and after some fits and starts arranged for a select group of professional political scientists to participate.

This edition focuses on the grand sweep of African American political participation from the enslavement period to the present time. It presents the range of theories that have been used, and description and analysis of the details of activities of Blacks to find spaces to exercise their will for political autonomy. This effort for autonomy has always been acted out in defiance, resistance, and bound by a kind of cultural communalism. The defiance and resistance was a product of the systematic relegation of Blacks to an unequal status and often total exclusion from bonafide membership in the larger American "democratic" body politic. And so Blacks found themselves formulating a way with the world at once defined by their cultural extended-family basis of existence, but which was also reinforced by a system that defined the group *en bloc* as outsiders. Today we observe the consequences of this monolithic status-structuring in the widespread perception by Blacks that their fates in the United States are intrinsically linked. In this context we are able to document the ways in which African Americans have mobilized political resources and allies for changing the fundamental exclusion of enslavement, and then how they have used their claims to human and civil rights to expand political participation. This volume documents these efforts and puts them within the framework of professional political science, in the end revealing how that very disciplinary framework has been expanded.

The scope of this project means that many, many hands and resources have been brought to bear in making the finished product. I am grateful to Ray Smith, the series editor, for having worked with spectacular diligence and efficiency in shepherding the project along. His gentle nudges kept us going amidst matters of health, deadlines for other projects, and the vicissitudes of changing plans of would-be contributors. Once our team was formed, however, it worked with good cheer and met schedules reasonably. I am especially grateful to Hanes Walton at the University of Michigan who agreed early on to dedicate some of his prodigious energy to a chapter. He stands alone in the scope of his achievement in the study of African American politics. Lawrence Hanks of Indiana University graciously accepted to participate after another colleague found that she had to suddenly withdraw. Larry's work in the field too is well known, he sharing with me an intense interest in politics among Blacks in the South. Byron D'Andra Orey, now at the University of Nebraska, accepted this project while at the University of Mississippi. As a young scholar with a busy research program and amidst moving to a new job, D'Andra never flagged in sustaining commitment to work, for which I am grateful. He was assisted by Reginald Vance of Southern University. And finally, I owe gratitude to one of my graduate students, Richard Middleton, IV, who agreed near the end of his doctoral work, to coauthor the final substantive chapter with me. I expect the experience has had the good benefit of helping to focus a major portion of his postdoctoral research on the subject.

I also owe a good deal to a number of graduate research assistants who performed a variety of tasks in helping to bring the project to conclusion. Kevin Anderson researched historical information for the chronology and the section on key people, laws, and terms. Gaurav Ghose developed much of the historical census data and tracked many sources for our use. Xi Zhou spent her first semester as a graduate student at Missouri negotiating her way through reams of sources on Afro-Americana, developing socioeconomic data sources, and preparing charts, graphs, and tables. She also started the complex task of acquiring publisher permissions. Monika Klimek arrived in time to complete the permissions and to work with the copyedited manuscript. I am grateful to them all for a substantial contribution to the project. They were all provided by the good offices of various Directors of Graduate Studies in the Department of Political Science at the University of Missouri.

Minion K. C. Morrison
Columbia, Missouri

1

Overview

Minion K. C. Morrison

The principal task in this work is to describe and analyze the participation of African Americans in American politics. This introductory chapter provides an overview of the African American population and an outline of African American political participation in American politics. First it describes the ways political scientists have characterized and attempted to explain the phenomenon of African American political participation. It then presents a historical demographic picture of the African American community, situated in the social environment of the United States. Next, it identifies and describes the resources that provide the foundations for their participation in the American democratic political process. This includes an assessment of socioeconomic resources and how they provide a base from which the group has bid for political allocations. Finally, it provides a comprehensive outline of the political activities in which African Americans have engaged from the beginning of the republic to the present. These activities form the basis for the later analytic chapters of this book.

The Differential Status of African Americans: The Long Shadow of Enslavement and the Continuity of Resistance

Although African Americans constitute one of the earliest population groups of the United States, they have always had a special status within the republic. The single most important factor that defined—and continues in some ways to determine that status—was the enslavement to which African Americans were subjected for about 200 years, as well as its residual effects. During that period, African Americans resisted, using innumerable methods to free themselves. Most sought options within the democratic framework of the United States, whereas others sought more independent solutions. These challenges, whatever the type, often had the effect of more fully elaborating the principles of the republic (Dawson 2001). Indeed, in part because of the enslavement of African Americans, the republic found itself in a profound crisis that led to and was ultimately resolved by a civil war.

Despite the end of slavery in the United States, the sociopolitical environment for African Americans has been fraught with continuing actual discrimination—the residual effects of a system originally based on their supposed genetic inferiority and of ambivalence about the universal freedom codified after the Civil War. For example, the postwar Reconstruction period, during which African Americans gained formal citizenship, was truncated, lasting a mere seven to ten years. Thereafter, although the constitutional provisions conferring full citizenship on African Americans remained intact, breaches of the law occurred everywhere. In the South, where most African Americans lived, there was little difference between their daily lives as free citizens and their former lives as enslaved persons. Throughout U.S. history, this population has at various times been subject to fundamental breaches of its full citizenship rights. At the same time, many practices of discrimination and racism have been so institutionalized as to have enduring residual effects without any compensatory measures. Ambivalence about such practices and how to address them has been equally detrimental; inconsistent or lackadaisical application of the law has created uncertainty and served to maintain the struggle for African Americans.

This uncertainty has been leavened only by enduring efforts, on the part of African Americans and their supporters in the general population, to resist discrimination and racism. They have worked to resolve the fundamental contradictions inherent in the group's status. On the strength of these efforts it is possible to track the growth and development of institutional political participation by African Americans.

The Study of African American Politics

A Preface to Theory: Racial Hierarchy and Political Challenge

An initial question we seek to answer in this volume is that of what African American politics is. It is, first and foremost, the study of racial politics in the United States—how this socially defined racial group has been relegated to a distinct unequal status on the basis of negative attributes assigned to the "race" (Nobles 2000; Omi and Winant 1994; Sears et al. 2000). The substance of this racialization has been the ascription of a lower hierarchical status to Blacks. Some scholars have termed this a kind of "outsider" status, because benefit allocations for Blacks were constrained by a set of routines outside the bounds of regular democratic participation. Barnett (1976, 13) has stated this clearly. "Blacks are external to the American ideological system and not effectively integrated into the political system. In structural terms, Blacks are qualitatively different from white ethnic groups. For white ethnic groups, there is no nationwide ideology that ranks specific groups. In contrast, racism is a pervasive ideology that ranks Blacks in a group below all others . . . assum[ing their] inherent genetic inferiority."

Barnett suggests that this racialization has caused the enduring "oppositional politics" among African Americans. Since this is a hierarchical system based on "a principle that ranks groups consistently and pervasively, *and is enforceable through social control,*" Blacks succeed largely by becoming agents for social change or challengers to the status quo. This thesis then leads Barnett to enumerate four characteristics of African American politics:

1. In a system where power is divisible between the races, all Blacks are perceived as powerless and exist in a political climate of "dependency," but with "a deep and serious concern with fundamental social change."

2. Black politics emphasizes change: "challenging [the system] in an effort to bridge black experience and the American creed . . . critici[zing] such fundamental aspects of the American system as capitalism, federalism, and states' rights."

3. The process of political activity (opposition) more often involves tactics such as social movements and reliance on charismatic leaders.

4. Ideology, defined as Black nationalism, is much more important in African American politics. "In this context, a combination of imposed collectivism, qualitative separation of blacks from all others, and the desire on the part of black politicians to destroy hierarchy between whites and blacks has led to the articulation of black nationalism" (Barnett 1976, 20–25).

Other general theorists of the field are in agreement with Barnett. Walton (1972a, 11), in a macroanalysis, said, "Black politics springs from the particular brand of segregation practices found in different environments in which black people find themselves." Walton and Smith (2000) extend this conceptualization, illustrating how racialization has defined the terms of Black struggle for "universal freedom." Barker et al. (1999) also argue that race continues to determine how African Americans are situated in the political community. Using a wide variety of statistical evidence, they demonstrate the disparity between races. Both discrimination and ambivalence about the full inclusion of African Americans seem to sustain the differentials. Like Barnett, Barker et al. argue that it is the persistence of the oppositional activity that exposes this system and maintains change as a national agenda. They also indicate that the relatively large size of this population makes it much more difficult to ignore, given its potential influence on outcomes in electoral politics.

In light of these general conceptualizations of what constitutes African American politics, what constructs have political scientists used to explain the phenomenon? The two oldest and most prominent theories are pluralism and elitism, the same theories used to characterize the general U.S. political processes.

Pluralism

Three theorists associated with pluralism (the group basis of politics) are Truman (1951), Dahl (1961), and Easton (1965). The pluralist model assumes democracy and asserts that power is everywhere, with accessibility to all members in the political community. Success depends on group organization and the ability of the groups to cross-cut in their alignments. The openness of the bidding process, it is argued, keeps players in the game and creates a degree of stability or equilibrium. The model presumes equality of the bidders in developing and expressing their preferences. Pluralists suggest that the relative unequal position of African Americans was due only to the lag caused by slavery. After the Civil War, in this view, the group was on a path toward greater participation in the political system, just like everyone else. Several euphemisms came to be associated with the supposed American society's pluralist absorption of African Americans—the "melting pot" (Moynihan 1965) and "assimilation" (Park 1950) being two of the more common. Many scholars (Pinderhughes 1987) have called into question whether this thesis can explain the peculiar hierarchical ranking of Blacks in the political system. In short, the principle of equality of opportunity among groups bidding for power has rarely been borne out for African Americans. They have more often encountered barriers to independent in-group organization and to voluntary membership in external organizations.

Elitism

Elitism is an explanation that goes back to Charles Beard's (1913) analysis of the elite characteristics of the "founding fathers." This theory suggests that power rests in the hands of a few individuals in society. Some of the euphemisms associated with it are "class" and "hegemony." In this view, elites control power through their command of the means of production and their control over labor. The founders of the republic, Beard argued, represented a high economic class set apart from the average citizen. They developed institutions to protect their position of power. These structural arrangements provided the foundations for an interlocking social, political, and cultural elite. This elite defined the terms of order and established what was acceptable public behavior (Dolbeare and Edelman 1979). Insofar as African Americans were not a part of the elite structure, they were powerless. Nevertheless, the elitists argue that the system was not entirely closed, allowing opportunities for members to circulate from lower to higher sectors in small increments over time. The increments, however, were never sufficient to change the essentially elitist character of the political system. Dolbeare and Edelman (1979), for example, illustrate how the elite functions today via a relatively small class of circulating economic interests that dominate banking, insurance, and higher levels of the government bureaucracy. This thesis is consistent with a number of analyses of African American politics that focus on both racialized powerlessness and class structure (Davis 1981; Jones 1972; Reed 1971; Robinson 1983).

Colonialism

A smaller number of scholars have used a colonial model to explain the status of African Americans. This conceptualization posits that the status of African Americans is determined by a kind of exploitation that is akin to the imperial exploitation used by Europeans who occupied Africa, Asia, and Latin America as colonies. This theory presupposes the occupation of land, control over labor, and hegemonic force. The exploitation ultimately leads to political powerlessness as the colonial power institutes an administrative apparatus through which its hegemony is guaranteed. This thesis looks very much like that elaborated by Georges Balandier (1965) in describing the colonial situation in Africa. He focuses on domination by a racial and cultural group of a different racial group, with the assertion of superiority by the former. Balandier suggests that the relationship that develops between these heterogeneous cultures is conflictual and antagonistic. However, the dominant society has both recourse to force and the ability to denigrate the culture of the racial group that it dominates (Balandier 1965). Carmichael and Hamilton (1967) adopted this theory to explain the position of African Americans. They argue that "the predication of decisions and policies on considerations of race for the purpose of subordinating a racial group and maintaining control over that group is what constitutes colonialism in the United States." They refer to overt—"individual acts against African Americans"—and covert discrimination—"the active and pervasive operation of anti-black attitudes and practices"—that allow white control over the ghetto communities: "Exploiters come into the ghetto from outside, bleed it dry, and leave it economically dependent on the larger society." According to this thesis, African Americans also bear all the psychological baggage that Balandier suggests leads to an inferiority complex among the colonized (Carmichael and Hamilton 1967, 6–17).

Conflict

Still another theoretical conceptualization is the conflict model, sometimes referred to as power theory. It focuses on the perpetual struggle for power between organized groups in a given political context (Jones 1972, Blalock 1967). In the racial context in the United States, the struggle for power is between African Americans and whites, the two major groups in conflict in the society. Power theorists argue that the ruling white population seeks to sustain its supremacy by limiting the acquisition of power by African Americans. The latter, on the other hand, seek to attain liberation within this structure, where they are hierarchically ranked below whites.

Social Dominance

Social dominance theory, which is related to both the conflict and colonial models, focuses on hierarchy in multiethnic societies. Sidanius and Pratto (1999) argue that all groups in diverse societies are organized into ranked hierarchies, with one or more dominant group enjoying power and privilege. The key to this conceptualization is that the hierarchies are routine and practically immutable.

The mechanisms and processes that establish and maintain the expected hierarchy can be informal—group-based associational patterns create and limit opportunities—or formal—political and economic institutions can promote the interest of dominant segments. But whatever the ordering dynamic, dominant groups implement the hierarchical order by using the structure of the society to their advantage (Sidanius and Petrocik 2000, 8–9).

This selection of theories, although not exhaustive, illustrates some of the principal efforts that have been made by social scientists to describe and assess the political activities of African Americans. Each of the theories reveals something—some more than others—of the dynamics of the struggle for universal freedom and the acquisition of political benefits. In the course of this historical analysis, it will be obvious how one or more combinations of these constructs may be deployed for illustrating African American efforts. Aside from classical pluralism, they all are able to account, more or less, for the constancy of racism, discrimination, ambivalence, and struggle in the African American political experience.

Who Are the African Americans?

Counting African Americans: The U.S. Census

Census taking in many parts of the world is a highly political process. It has been and remains no less so in the United States, where the census of the African American population has been one of the most politicized and perhaps least accurate among long-standing historical groups in the society (Nobles 2000). Exactly what the size of the population is and whether accompanying political representation, when achieved, has been appropriate are therefore enduring questions. The first census of the U.S. population, taken in 1790, reported data in terms of two racial categories—whites and Negroes. Yet the racialization of the population had a distinct meaning and implication for African Americans. Its meaning was that unless you had free status, you were not counted as an individual citizen. Instead each slave was counted as three-fifths of a person for the purposes of apportioning representation for slaveholders (Walton and Smith 2000). Free status, however, did not necessarily mean citizenship rights and representation. For example, "free" persons were often required to register their racial status or to have guardians, or they were treated as enslaved persons despite their free status (Berry and Blassingame 1982, 34).

The implication was that the first U.S. census treated the African American population as corporate and not individual entities. The enslaved population, which was not "listed in vital, land, military and other pre–Civil War records," was not counted (Lipscomb and Hutchinson 1994, 66). The first census to record information about the total African American population as individuals was taken in 1870, almost ten years after the Civil War. Its accuracy was highly suspect, given that many African Americans simply were not counted in the former Confederacy or maintained relationships of indenture to plantation owners.

This racialized history and the inaccuracies it generated makes it difficult to create an accurate demographic portrayal of African Americans over time. For a time a standard surmise was that African Americans constituted about 10 percent of the population, but no one really knew. African Americans themselves always argued that the population was far larger than official estimates suggested. Because the census count is used to apportion representation and has public policy consequences in this racialized society, the accuracy of census results has often been contested by African American leaders. Although the accuracy of the general count has improved remarkably over the years, the counting of African Americans remains controversial. This was especially true when the Census Bureau conceded that a sizable portion of this population group was not counted in the 1990 census. It has been estimated that almost 5 percent of the population was not counted in 1990 (Harrison 2001, 14–17). In spite of these difficulties, the early estimates of the population will be used here to develop as clear a historical profile as possible of the descendants of continental Africa in the United States.

The Black Community as a U.S. Minority Group

The African American population has historically been the largest identifiable minority group in the United States. Its special identity owes to its definition as a racial group, and the fact that the group's skin color also translates into a lower hierarchical ranking in the society increases its importance. Indeed, it was not until the 2000 census that the count of another group with a similar hierarchical ranking, Hispanics (35.3 million), exceeded that of citizens identifying themselves solely as African Americans (34.7 million). But even these numbers are subject to interpretation because of a policy change in how race was recorded in the 2000 census. For the first time, citizens were allowed to express racial heritage in multiple categories—and 6.8 million exercised the option; 1.8 million of them were combinations of African American and some other race category. Using the traditional socially defined race categories, this group of nearly 2 million Americans now claiming the "multi-racial/ethnic" category would be categorized as African American, thus maintaining that group's status as the largest minority group in the population.

As the data in Table 1.1 show, the U.S. population was relatively small in 1790, with just under 4 million people. The African American portion of that population was nearly 760,000, or 19 percent. The African American population, like the general population, was growing rapidly. The general population nearly doubled in twenty years and almost quadrupled in forty years. The trajectory for African Americans was similar, taking fifty years to quadruple. Thereafter this group's growth slowed considerably, taking forty years to double itself after 1840, a pattern that has largely continued to the present.

The overwhelming majority of the African American population was enslaved in 1790 (more than 600,000), and the balance were free people living in both the North and the South. Although the number of free Blacks grew for a time, by 1810 their numbers had decreased vis-à-vis the enslaved as the scope of servitude increased and as it became next to impossible to work one's way out of the system. Free persons in the deep South became almost extinct after 1810, either losing their freedom or being forced to leave the region (Franklin and Moss 1994, 149ff).

African Americans as a proportion of the general population is a slightly different story. As Table 1.1 shows, in 1790 their number constituted the largest proportion of the general population (19.3 percent) that it has ever been. Despite continuous and sometimes rapid growth over the next century and a half, this proportion has

TABLE 1.1 General Population and African American Population in the United States, 1790–2000

	Total Population	African American Population	Percentage
1790	3,929,214	757,208	19.3
1800	5,308,483	1,002,037	18.9
1810	7,239,881	1,377,808	19.0
1820	9,638,453	1,771,656	18.4
1830	12,866,020	2,328,642	18.1
1840	17,169,453	2,873,648	16.1
1850	23,191,876	3,638,808	15.7
1860	31,443,790	4,441,830	14.1
1870	39,818,449	4,880,009	12.7
1880	50,155,783	6,580,793	13.0
1890	62,947,714	7,488,676	11.0
1900	75,994,775	8,833,994	11.6
1910	93,402,151	9,827,763	10.7
1920	105,710,620	10,463,131	9.9
1930	122,775,046	11,891,143	9.7
1940	131,669,275	12,865,518	9.8
1950	150,697,361	15,042,286	10.0
1960	179,323,175	18,871,831	10.5
1970	203,302,031	22,580,289	11.1
1980	226,504,000	26,495,000	11.7
1990	248,710,000	29,986,000	12.0
2000[a]	281,421,906	36,419,434	12.9

[a] For 2000, the figure for the African American population includes those who combined that identity with another racial or ethnic category.

SOURCE: Data from U.S. Department of Commerce, *Statistical Abstract of the United States, 1992*; Census of Population, 2000, Bureau of the Census, 1992, 2001.

never again come close to its original size. The first significant decline in the population came when the abolitionist challenge to slavery was in high gear in 1840. By that time the proportion of African Americans had dropped to 16 percent. This decline continued for a century, falling to 9.8 percent in 1940, about one-half the proportion the Black population had been at the end of the colonial period. A gradual increase began in 1950 (10 percent) and has continued unabated through the 2000 census. However, in this fifty-year period the population has grown by a mere 2 percent.

Geographic Distribution of African Americans

The distribution of the population over time indicates much about the racial order as well as about the growth and development of the United States as a social and economic order. At the time of the census, African Americans were concentrated in the South. They remained so with little mobility until well after the Civil War. Most remained attached to the southern agricultural economy—a labor-intensive sharecropping system that left most of them in virtual peonage. Meanwhile, much of the rest of the country was rapidly industrializing, for which labor was increasingly needed. This served as a partial trigger for a massive migration of the African American population that started around the turn of the twentieth century. The contradictory market systems and the competition between them for labor, coupled with sanctioned segregation in the South, ultimately led to a redistribution of a large portion of the African American population from the South to the North. Equally significant, however, was the simultaneous urbanization of this previously rural population. The data in Table 1.2 show the distribution patterns for African Americans through the development of the United States.

The migration that was discernible as early as 1890 among Blacks continued through 1970, reaching remarkably high levels in all but the Depression years. As Table 1.3 shows, outmigration from the South rose from just under 3 percent between 1900 and 1910 to almost 11 percent between 1920 and 1930. It then dropped to 5 percent between 1930 and 1940, but then rose sharply to its highest point of 18 percent between 1940 and 1950. Although it was not to reach this level again, it remained near 14 percent in 1970, although at this point a reverse flow of migration southward also began, stabilizing the regional distribution with slightly over 50 percent in the South. Meanwhile, the migration of African Americans was outrunning that for whites moving from the South to the North by phenomenal rates. At its highest level, between 1940 and 1950, the ratio of Blacks to whites migrating out of the South was nine to one. This represented the most substantial movement of the African American population since its arrival in the United States, signaling a major shift in the group's location in the economy as well. Blacks were no longer the mainstay of the southern agricultural economy, which itself was no longer a traditional labor-intensive enterprise. In this period the population shifted from almost three-quarters in the South

TABLE 1.2   Regional Distribution of African American Population, 1790–2000 (Percent)

Year	Northeast	Midwest	Southwest	West	Total Population
1790	9		91		757,208
1800	8	.06	92		1,002,037
1810	7	1	92		1,377,808
1820	6	1	93		1,771,656
1830	5	2	93		2,328,642
1840	5	3	92		2,873,648
1850	4	4	92	.03	3,638,808
1860	4	4	92	.10	4,441,830
1870	4	6	91	.13	4,880,009
1880	3	6	90	.18	6,580,793
1890	4	6	90	.36	7,488,676
1900	4	6	90	.34	8,833,994
1910	5	6	89	.51	9,827,763
1920	7	8	85	.75	10,463,131
1930	10	11	79	1	11,891,143
1940	11	11	77	1	12,865,914
1950	13	15	68	4	15,044,937
1960	16	18	60	6	18,871,831
1970	19	20	53	7	22,672,570
1980	18	20	53	9	26,495,000
1990	19	19	53	9	29,986,000
2000	18	19	53	10	36,419,434

SOURCE: Data from U.S. Census, 1790–2000.

to almost one-half. The shrinkage of the southern population was by and large to the advantage of the Northeast and the Midwest, both regions where virtual transport pipelines developed for this movement. There was some movement to the emerging western states, but it was much smaller.

The shift in the population from the agricultural economy was largely to urban areas in the North and South. African Americans soon became one of the most highly urbanized populations in the country. Table 1.4 lists the major cities to which this migration flowed from 1910 to 1920. During this period northern cities in the Northeast and the Midwest were far and away the anchors for the African American population. The cities that had the largest draw by 1920—New York, Philadelphia, Washington, D.C., Chicago, Baltimore, and Detroit—continued to serve as the home of the largest

TABLE 1.3   Black and White South-to-North Migration, 1900–1970

	Race	Net Migration (in 1,000s)	Migrating Population (%)	Black-White Ratio in Proportion[a]
1900–1910	Black	–213	–2.8	
	White	–60	–0.4	7:1
1910–1920	Black	–572	–6.9	
	White	–626	–3.5	2:1
1920–1930	Black	–913	–10.8	
	White	–626	–3	3.6:3
1930–1940	Black	–473	–5.4	
	White	–482	–1.9	2.8:1
1940–1950	Black	–1689	–18	
	White	–553	–2	9:1
1950–1960	Black	–1512	–15.9	
	White	+330	+1	
1960–1970	Black	–1400	–13.7	
	White	+1800	+5	No Ratio

[a] No ratios are listed for the 1950s and the 1960s because net white migration was southward during those decades.
SOURCE: Adapted from Groh 1972, 48.

numbers of African Americans. At the same time, southern cities such as New Orleans, Birmingham, Atlanta, Jacksonville, and Houston underwent significant growth in African American populations as well.

African American Demographic Resources and the Political Process

Now that we have a general picture of the African American population and its movement, we can turn to the question of what its status has been over time and how this status translates for the purposes of political participation and inclusion. Historically, the status of African Americans vis-à-vis the general population has been differential. It began with the group's being defined as chattel (property) and has continued with its lower hierarchical ranking in the social order. Walton and Smith (2000) show that such a racialized hierarchy was

TABLE 1.4   Chief Urban Centers of African American Population in 1910 and 1920, in Rank Order by Region as of 1920

City	1910	1920	Increase	% Increase
North				
New York, N.Y.	91,709	152,467	60,758	66.5
Philadelphia, Pa.	84,459	134,229	49,770	58.9
Chicago, Ill.	44,103	109,458	65,355	148.2
Detroit, Mich.	5,471	40,838	35,097	611.3
Pittsburgh, Pa.	25,623	37,725	12,102	47.2
Indianapolis, Ind.	21,816	34,678	12,862	59.0
Cleveland, Ohio	8,448	34,451	26,003	307.8
Cincinnati, Ohio	19,639	30,079	10,440	53.2
Border				
Washington, D.C.	94,446	109,966	15,520	16.4
Baltimore, Md.	84,749	108,322	25,573	27.8
St. Louis, Mo.	43,960	69,854	25,894	58.9
Kansas City, Mo.	23,566	30,719	7,153	30.4
South				
New Orleans, La.	89,262	100,930	11,668	13.1
Birmingham, Ala.	52,305	70,230	17,925	34.3
Atlanta, Ga.	51,902	62,796	10,894	21.0
Memphis, Tenn.	52,441	61,381	8,740	16.7
Richmond, Va.	46,733	54,041	7,308	15.6
Norfolk, Va.	25,039	43,392	18,353	73.5
Jacksonville, Fla.	29,293	41,520	12,227	41.7
Louisville, Ky.	40,522	40,097	−435	−1.1
Savannah, Ga.	33,246	39,179	5,933	17.8
Nashville, Tenn.	36,523	35,633	−890	−2.4
Houston, Tex.	23,929	33,960	10,031	41.9
Charleston, S.C.	31,056	32,326	1,270	4.1
Total	1,060,510	1,508,061	447,551a	42.2

SOURCE: Smith and Horton 1995, 1505–1506.

enshrined in the Constitution with the "three-fifths compromise" on how slaves would be counted for the purposes of congressional apportionment. Barker et al. (1999) suggest that despite constitutional changes after the Civil War, ambivalence about racial equality has been constant. They argue that these two conditions have thus sustained the lower status position of African Americans. In short, African American corporate political status is a product of a range of resource deficits that reverberate throughout the social system. The group suffers a complement of dislocations in the total system, which has a significant impact on its ability to exercise potential influence and power in routine ways in the system. Hence, even after the formal admission of African Americans into the political structure, the system has functioned in such a way that the benefits of admission have been truncated for this group.

The following assessment of the inclusive social world of African Americans reveals how a combination of factors produces significant and continuous deficits for this group in comparison with the general population. Descriptive data are presented on the location of African Americans in the educational, health, economic, and social environments. The historical picture shows that African Americans deviate from the general-population norm on these factors. Continuing discrimination and a standardized lower hierarchical ranking have consistently resulted in an unequal sociopolitical status for African Americans and decreased their life chances. Their educational access and achievement have consistently been lower; their chances for gainful employment and economic progress have been fewer; their health care has been inadequate; they have resided separately from the general population in ghettoes; and they have been more susceptible to sanction in the criminal justice system. In fact this social and political isolation was so complete that the National Advisory Commission on Civil Disorders—known as the Kerner Commission, which studied racial rebellion in the 1960s—referred in its report (1968) to African Americans as constituting a separate and isolated society.

Residential Segregation

Social relations and the development of internal community are immensely affected by where people live. Hardly any pattern of existence has more affected the social status of African Americans than their segregation into racially defined living enclaves. During the period of slavery in the United States they lived in segregated places arrayed around a large plantation house and compound. Often they lived in relatively close proximity to whites, but in distinctly separate social spaces. The community that developed in these social spaces was also distinct. Slaves lived on subsistence disbursements while providing labor for agriculture. It was a design to maintain their subservience and dependence, and it was successful in maintaining residential isolation.

Although these minimal disbursements did not promote independent living among African Americans, residential segregation allowed a community to evolve. Considerable research has shown that there was indeed a flourishing cultural and social community of African Americans (Blassingame 1979; Gutman 1976). It was identified as such with patterns based on African memories with adaptations appropriate to the peculiarities of enslavement. This thriving community managed to retain some degree of self-control over the inchoate institutional forms in these racial enclaves. They even managed to sustain a degree of clandestine organization and resistance via what has been termed "hidden transcripts" for challenging systems of oppression (Aptheker 1942; Scott 1985).

It is ironic that the residential segregation of African Americans actually increased and became public policy after the end of slavery. In the South the Jim Crow era set in as the truncated Reconstruction ended (Woodward 1955). It revealed itself first in practices of separation, but almost everywhere in the region racial segregation had become law by 1890. The U.S. Supreme Court codified the policy in its 1896 decision in *Plessy v. Ferguson,* which sanctioned the segregation provisions of the South's post-Reconstruction constitutions. This decision became widely known as the "separate but equal" doctrine and led to the acceptance of segregation nationwide. Although the ruling was overturned in later Court decisions (such as *Shelley v. Kramer* 1948), its residual consequence has been the relegation of African Americans to separate housing sectors all over the country.

Residential segregation did not end at the plantations. A staggering degree of housing segregation characterized the African American population even as it moved from the plantations, ostensibly to a better life in the North and in southern cities. As Blacks moved to urban areas, segregation was "enforced through both legal and extralegal practices, which included violence, real estate marketing . . ., federal housing policies . . ., municipal zoning ordinances, school board policies that designated separate attendance zones . . ., and the activities of thousands of neighborhood organizations" (Jaynes and Williams 1989, 88). Table 1.5 offers a review of twenty years of the most intense African American migration, revealing the scope of the segregation. On an index in which pure random distribution in housing would be zero and total separation would be 100, the averages for major U.S. cities in 1960, 1970, and 1980 were 80, 81, and 77, respectively. In short, the level of segregation was so high that these

TABLE 1.5   Residential Segregation in Selected Metropolitan Areas with Large Black Populations, 1960–1980

Metro Area	1980 Population (in 1,000s)		Indices of Black–White Residential Segregation[a]			Interracial Contact Measures[b]			
	Total	Black	1980	1970	1960	% Blk for Wht	% Wht for Blk	% Wht for Wht	% Blk for Blk
New York	9,120	1,941	78	74	74	9	28	84	64
Chicago	7,104	1,428	88	91	91	4	15	90	84
Detroit	4,553	890	88	89	87	5	20	93	80
Philadelphia	4,717	884	78	78	77	7	28	92	70
Washington, D.C.	3,061	853	71	81	78	12	30	84	69
Baltimore	2,174	557	75	81	87	9	26	89	73
Houston	2,905	529	74	78	81	8	31	85	66
Atlanta	2,030	499	78	82	77	9	26	90	73
Newark	2,966	418	80	79	73	8	26	89	70
St. Louis	2,356	408	83	87	86	5	24	94	75
New Orleans	1,187	387	73	74	65	14	27	85	72
Birmingham	846	240	75	68	64	10	26	89	74

[a] Indices of dissimilarity with value of zero for random distribution and 100 for total separation.

[b] Potential interracial contact by 1980: percentage blacks in census tract of the typical white; percentage whites for blacks; percentage whites for whites; and percentage blacks for blacks.

SOURCE: Adapted from Jaynes and Williams, eds. 1989, 78–79. Reprinted with permission from National Academies Press.

residents almost never had opportunities for social relations outside their racial group. Thus when Hacker (1992) revisited the question of racial segregation almost twenty-five years after the Kerner Commission concluded that the nation existed as two racial societies, he came to the same conclusion.

Separate and Unequal Education

This housing segregation became a major dimension of another important factor of social relations—education. However, education was not just a matter of social relations; it was a cornerstone of virtually all other success in the democratic society. The promise was for free and universal education in this highly mobile and increasingly industrial nation. The special role of education as a means to better placement was even clear during slavery. Although education as a policy or practice was barred for slaves, in fact some of them always found the means to literacy—through stealth or with the connivance of members of the plantation households—and some were encouraged to acquire some level of literacy in order to perform their instrumental functions in the system (Bullock 1967, 10ff). After the Civil War, however, the promise of education for Blacks remained far from realized. The breach for them was almost complete for more than 100 years, often either as the denial of education or its provision in segregated settings with inadequate resources.

Initially finding the means, venues, and personnel for the education of African Americans after the end of slavery was a massive undertaking, not least because adults and children alike needed education. In some ways the pressures for adults to acquire some education were even greater, for the benefits of education could be immediately realized with better placement in the society. A system for the education of the freed African Americans moved along slowly after the Civil War. It did so both with the support of government and independent sources, largely benevolent and church organizations. Some of the first educational efforts were those for refugees who fled to the Union forces during the war. As this population grew, military officers sought the means for helping its members become able to lead independent lives. Philanthropists and churches responded and started modest efforts in educational training. The project was formalized in 1865 with the establishment of the Freedmen's Bureau, a part of whose function was the education of the newly freed. Church missionaries became an important source of personnel for the

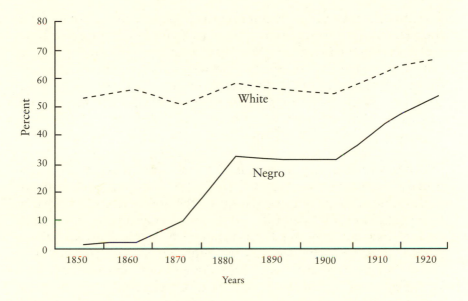

FIGURE 1.1 Percentage of White and Negro Children, Aged Five through Nineteen, Who Attended School in the Southern States, 1850–1920.

SOURCES: Charles S. Johnson, *The Negro in American Civilization* (New York: Henry Holt and Company, 1930), p. 232; and Bureau of Census, Census of Populations: 1920 (Washington, DC: Government Printing Office, 1952), vol. II; cited in Bullock 1967. Reprinted with permission of Harvard University Press.

schools that were partially sponsored by the bureau. "Fourteen southern states had established 575 schools by 1865, and those were employing 1,171 teachers for the 71,770 Negro and white children in regular attendance. . . . Louisiana, Virginia, and North Carolina . . . possessed half the schools, teachers, and pupils in the region" (Bullock 1967, 29).

Figure 1.1 shows how African Americans progressed in school attendance in the first seventy years after education for them was legalized. In 1850 about 5 percent of this group in the South attended some kind of school, whereas more than 50 percent of the white population was already attending school. The scope of the gap between the races actually increased during the war years and peaked in 1870. This was a time when the Freedmen's Bureau was most active in its promoting education for the freed population. However, general public education received its greatest boost from this effort, and it underwent an overall expansion. Hence the rate of African American school attendance never caught up or kept pace with that of the general population in this period. Attendance nonetheless rose steadily, except during the period of 1890–1910. That decline seems to be a result of the expansion of the Jim Crow system and the legal imprimatur brought with the 1896 "separate but equal" doctrine legitimated by the Supreme Court. The decline that leveled off in 1910 was then followed by steady progress through 1920. The greatest gains in African American school attendance have been made since then, and the gap between the races has decreased significantly.

The level of literacy among Blacks rose rapidly, considering the paucity of education before the war. By 1890, more than 40 percent of the African American population in the South was literate, compared with almost 60 percent of the whites. However, it was already evident that some parts of the former Confederacy were moving faster than others. The deep South states, which had larger populations of newly freed citizens, moved more slowly. Among these were Alabama, Georgia, Louisiana, and South Carolina. The worse record was that of Louisiana, an early initiator of public schools. As Table 1.6 shows, the gap between Blacks and the total population in 1890 was nearly two to one everywhere. However, the acquisition of literacy by Blacks underwent phenomenal growth over the next forty years, and in 1930 they were little more than ten points behind the general population in almost all of the southern states.

Although Blacks were gaining in literacy, they were not receiving an education equal that whites were receiving. A system of segregated and special education or "Black education" rapidly emerged. On the one hand, the separation of the races in the schools moved as rapidly as the overturn of Reconstruction. In consonance with the dominant view of a racialized social order, it was inevitable that the schools, too, would be separate. But the logic of the dominant belief in the genetic inferiority of Blacks also dictated that the standard liberal education was not suitable for the capacity or needs of this community. Therefore, in the education of African Americans, industrial and vocational training came to be emphasized. In addition to the presumption that Blacks were incapable of managing liberal education was the presumption that the newly freed had first to be taught the skills necessary for independent living, such as management of domestic affairs and economic subsistence.

All across the South, separate schools appropriate to the tasks at hand were developed, and a plethora of philanthropic resources were mobilized to sustain the project. However, the inferiority of the education provided to African Americans was hardly concealed. Often

TABLE 1.6   Literacy in the South among Persons Aged 25 Years and Older, in the General Population, and among African Americans, 1890 and 1930 (Percent)

			General Population Percent Increase		African Americans Percent Increase	
			1890	1930	1890	1930
Alabama	59.0	87.4	48.1	30.1	73.8	145.2
Arkansas	73.4	93.2	27.0	46.4	83.9	80.8
Florida	72.2	92.9	28.7	49.5	81.2	64.0
Georgia	60.2	90.6	50.5	32.7	80.1	145.0
Kentucky	78.4	93.4	19.1	44.1	84.6	91.8
Louisiana	54.2	86.5	59.6	27.9	76.7	174.9
Mississippi	60.0	86.9	44.8	39.2	76.8	95.9
North Carolina	54.3	90.0	65.7	39.9	79.4	99.0
Oklahoma	94.6	97.2	2.7	61.0	90.7	48.7
South Carolina	55.0	85.1	54.7	35.9	73.1	103.6
Tennessee	73.4	92.8	26.4	45.8	85.1	85.8
Texas	80.3	93.2	16.1	47.5	86.6	82.3
Virginia	68.8	90.8	32.0	41.8	81.0	93.8

SOURCE: Bullock 1967, 172. Reprinted with permission from Harvard University Press.

these schools were only public in name, and the source of their funding was maintained by special taxes levied on African Americans or via sponsorship from philanthropic sources. More often than not, the school buildings were either Black churches or constructed from resources provided by Blacks themselves (McMillen 1990). As W.E.B. DuBois (1969) noted, tax funds were diverted to other purposes, most having nothing to do with education.

There was great disparity between the expenditures for African Americans and those for whites. Bullock (1967) shows that the average expenditure for white children in the 1914–1915 school year was about $11 per pupil, compared with just $4 for African Americans. In the 1929–1930 school year the comparison was worse—about $42 for whites and $15 for Blacks. Black teacher pay mirrored the expenditures for children. Moreover, because of the special character of "Black education," these children actually spent far less time in school—68 percent of the time white children in Alabama spent in school, and a mere 59 percent of the time whites in Louisiana spent in school (Bullock 1967, 172ff). As a white Mississippi school superintendent stated, "Our public school is designed primarily for the welfare of the white children of the state, and incidentally for the negro children" (McMillen 1990, 73).

Higher education for African Americans was almost entirely a product of church and philanthropic organizations at the start. Beginning in 1865, schools that would ultimately become the first colleges for Blacks were established. They, too, were located largely in the South. The American Missionary Society was the most prominent sponsor in establishing these schools. It organized the establishment of Fisk University in Tennessee and Talladega College in Alabama, both in 1865. A string of other private, church-related, or church-sponsored colleges followed in virtually every southern state. Later, state colleges and universities for Blacks emerged, largely dedicated to agricultural and teacher education. The names of these institutions attest to their missions—among others, Jackson State Teachers' College; Tennessee State, Florida, and Alcorn (Mississippi) Agricultural and Mechanical Colleges; and North Carolina Agricultural and Technical College.

Thus African Americans began with serious deficits in one of the resources deemed most significant for advancement in society. These deficits became another part of an interlinked set of characteristics by which Blacks were allotted a negative hierarchical ranking in American society. Table 1.7 shows the continuing disparity in high school and especially college completion rates for African American men and women compared with whites. Although considerable improvements have been made in high school completion rates in the two age groups indicated, African Americans remain about ten percentage points behind their white counterparts, and their college attendance rate remains half that of whites, as it has since 1940.

Free Labor, Economic Dependence, and Job Discrimination

The economic picture for Blacks has hardly been encouraging either. Their wealth and earning power has perhaps been even more affected by their enslavement. As slaves, they were property and thus were unable to amass independent property of their own. When African Americans entered the economic system as free people after the Civil War, they were destitute. With rare exceptions, African Americans acquired freedom as homeless, jobless, and propertyless people. Most remained attached to and dependent on their former owners; this proved disastrous for any attempts on the part of Blacks to mobilize

TABLE 1.7 High School and College Completion, by Race and Sex, 1940–1998 (Percent)

	25 years and over				25–29 years			
	White		Black[a]		White		Black[a]	
Level/Year	Male	Female	Male	Female	Male	Female	Male	Female
Completed Four Years of High School or More[b]								
1940	24.2	28.1	6.9	8.4	38.9	43.4	10.6	13.6
1947	33.2	36.7	12.7	14.5	52.9	56.8	19.6	24.7
1959	44.5	47.7	19.6	21.6	66.9	67.4	40.6	38.6
1970	57.2	57.6	32.4	34.8	79.2	76.4	54.5	57.9
1980	71.0	70.1	51.1	51.3	86.8	87.0	74.8	78.1
1990	79.1	79.0	65.8	66.5	84.6	88.1	81.5	81.8
1996	82.7	82.8	74.3	74.2	86.3	88.8	87.2	84.2
1997	82.9	83.2	73.5	76.0	85.8	89.4	85.2	87.1
1998	83.6	83.8	75.2	76.7	86.3	90.0	87.6	87.6
Completed Four Years of College or More[c]								
1940	5.9	4.0	1.4	1.2	7.5	5.3	1.5	1.7
1947	6.6	4.9	2.4	2.6	6.2	5.7	2.6	2.9
1959	11.0	6.2	3.8	2.9	15.9	8.1	5.6	3.7
1970	15.0	8.6	4.6	4.4	21.3	13.3	6.7	8.0
1980	22.1	14.0	7.7	8.1	25.5	22.0	10.5	12.5
1990	25.3	19.0	11.9	10.8	24.2	24.3	15.1	11.9
1996	26.9	21.8	12.4	14.6	27.2	29.1	12.4	16.4
1997	27.0	22.3	12.5	13.9	27.2	30.7	12.1	16.4
1998	27.3	22.8	13.9	15.4	26.5	30.4	14.2	17.0

[a] Data are for Black and other races for 1940 to 1960; for 1970–1993, data are Black persons only.
[b] Beginning in 1992, high school graduate or more.
[c] Beginning in 1992, bachelor's degree or more.
SOURCE: Data from U.S. Census.

in order to enhance their economic or political status. Labor remained cheap as most Blacks continued to work on the same plantations, now as tenant farmers and sharecroppers. Illiterate, impoverished, and powerless, they were left to the whims of the white planters. Perpetual debt became the norm, leaving them bound to the plantations in perpetuity, never amassing any wealth with which to establish independence.

The free persons in the urban areas in the North and the South became worse off after emancipation. Some had occupied a niche that provided some independence in the prewar economic structure. They dominated some of the service trades such as barbering, catering, stable keeping and livery service, and tailoring. In the curious way that racial discrimination worked, Blacks who occupied the otherwise lower-status occupations actually became the upper stratum within their segregated world. However, in the North the major prewar surge in Irish immigration brought a new unskilled class that displaced the Blacks, while in the South Jim Crow displaced those who previously occupied positions of independence in the region (Meier and Rudwick 1966).

Economic dependence severely limited the ability of African Americans to leverage influence in politics to work toward changes in public policy. Blacks remained subject to economic reprisals, retaliatory terror, and total dislocation from shelter for the least breach of protocol in the post-Reconstruction racial order. It was in the economic realm that Blacks were and remained most vulnerable in making the leap to independence and ultimately political expression and influence. The data indicate that African American economic status vis-à-vis whites has always been one of comparative disadvantage, and that the disadvantage worsened in the Jim Crow era, as access to jobs was blocked. Moreover, once migration began and African Americans shifted from an agricultural employment base, ironically their status vis-à-vis whites took a precipitous decline. This condition became most evident during the Depression, when the economically vulnerable situation of Blacks was devastating.

African Americans and whites over time occupied essentially separate parts of the labor structure. Until the 1940s Blacks remained concentrated in farming, while whites occupied white-collar and service occupations, especially higher-status and skilled labor positions. Indeed, white dominance of these higher-status occupations increased over time. As the African American population left agriculture, it moved into service occupations, but largely in the unskilled category. The data show that when Blacks were concentrated in the agricultural sector, their employment was almost at parity with whites, although this fact obscures the degree of underemployment among Blacks. However, once Blacks became concentrated in the urban areas and became a part of the industrial labor force, the extent of the disparity between their employment status and that of whites becomes clearer.

Unemployment differentials between the two racial groups are similar. Table 1.8 shows unemployment rates by gender from 1955 to 1998. It reveals that unemployment among Blacks has remained about twice that of whites throughout this period and was at its highest levels through the mid-1970s and almost the entirety of the 1980s. The disparity was maintained even in years of economic prosperity. Table 1.9 shows the median family incomes of the two racial groups in roughly the same period (1950–1987). These data show that at no time during that period did the median income of African Americans exceed 62 percent of that of whites. Indeed, Black income remained stable, around 55 percent of white income, over this thirty-seven year period, notwithstanding events and economic conditions. This deep and enduring impoverishment of the African American community had consequences for all of the other sociodemographic categories discussed in this section. Blacks without sufficient income could not afford better housing, even in racially segregated enclaves, nor could they provide enhanced educational opportunities for their children.

Unequal Justice and Insecurity

Security is another social sector where African Americans experience a differential status. There is a wide disparity between the results obtained by African Americans in the criminal justice system and those obtained by whites. Historically, justice has been meted out differentially for the two groups at all levels and all across the country. Blacks have been much more likely, as a proportion of the population, to be arrested, charged, and convicted of more severe crimes and to receive harsher sentences. This unusually high level of engagement with law enforcement agents makes for a unique condition of insecurity in the daily life processes of African Americans.

These practices were most evident in the southern states during the period of slavery. The record is replete with accounts of the wanton abuse and often the murder of slaves. The "slave narratives" present gruesome testimonies of beatings, terror, and imposition of cruel

TABLE 1.8   Unemployment in the United States among Persons Aged 20
Years and Older, by Race and Sex, 1955–1998 (Percent)

	White		Black[a]	
Year	Male	Female	Male	Female
1955	3.3	3.9	8.4	7.7
1960	4.2	4.6	9.6	8.3
1965	2.9	4.0	6.0	7.5
1970	3.2	4.4	5.6	6.9
1972	3.6	4.9	7.0	9.0
1973	3.0	4.3	6.0	8.6
1974	3.5	5.1	7.4	8.8
1975	6.2	7.5	12.5	12.2
1976	5.4	6.8	11.4	11.7
1977	4.7	6.2	10.7	12.3
1978	3.7	5.2	9.3	11.2
1979	3.6	5.0	9.3	10.9
1980	5.3	5.6	12.4	11.9
1981	5.6	5.9	13.5	13.4
1982	7.8	7.3	17.8	15.4
1983	7.9	6.9	18.1	16.5
1984	5.7	5.8	14.3	13.5
1985	5.4	5.7	13.2	13.1
1986	5.3	5.4	12.9	12.4
1987	4.8	4.6	11.1	11.6
1988	4.1	4.1	10.1	10.4
1989	3.9	4.0	10.0	9.8
1990	4.3	4.1	10.4	9.6
1991	5.7	4.9	11.5	10.5
1992	6.3	5.4	13.4	11.7
1993	5.6	5.1	12.1	10.6
1994	4.8	4.6	10.3	9.8
1995	4.3	4.3	8.8	8.6
1996	4.1	4.1	9.4	8.7
1997	3.6	3.7	8.5	8.8
1998	3.2	3.4	7.4	7.9

[a] Black and other prior to 1972.
SOURCE: Data from Stanley and Niemi 2000, 405.

punishments on the plantations. Frederick Douglass's account of his
own floggings and abuse (Meyer 1984) is perhaps the best known.
There was rarely any hesitation to resort to violent means when the
law was not sufficient. Franklin and Moss (1994, 45) suggest that this
was in part responsible for the "exceptionally high" mortality rate

TABLE 1.9   Median Family Income, by Race, 1950–1997

	Median Income in Current Dollars				Median Income in Constant (1997) Dollars			
Year	All Families[a]	White	Black	Percentage of Black to White	All Families[a]	White	Black	Percentage of Black to White
1950	3,319	3,445	1,869[b]	54.3	20,332	21,104	11,449	54.3
1955	4,418	4,613	2,544[b]	55.1	24,367	25,443	14,031	55.1
1960	5,620	5,835	3,230[b]	55.4	28,013	29,084	16,100	55.4
1965	6,957	7,251	3,993[b]	55.1	32,649	34,029	18,739	55.1
1970	9,867	10,236	6,279	61.3	38,345	39,779	24,401	61.3
1971	10,285	10,672	6,440	60.3	38,300	39,741	23,982	60.3
1972	11,116	11,549	6,864	59.4	40,183	41,748	24,812	59.4
1973	12,051	12,595	7,269	57.7	40,979	42,828	24,718	57.7
1974	12,902	13,408	8,006	59.7	39,899	41,464	24,758	59.7
1975	13,719	14,268	8,779	61.5	39,180	40,748	25,072	61.5
1976	14,958	15,537	9,242	59.5	40,417	41,981	24,972	59.5
1977	16,009	16,740	9,563	57.1	40,656	42,512	24,286	57.1
1978	17,640	18,368	10,879	59.2	41,944	43,675	25,868	59.2
1979	19,587	20,439	11,574	56.6	42,483	44,331	25,103	56.6
1980	21,023	21,904	12,674	57.9	40,999	42,717	24,717	57.9
1981	22,388	23,517	13,266	56.4	39,881	41,892	23,631	56.4
1982	23,433	24,603	13,598	55.3	39,341	41,305	22,829	55.3
1983	24,674	25,837	14,561	56.4	39,761	41,635	23,464	59.4
1984	26,433	27,686	15,431	55.7	40,832	42,768	23,837	55.7
1985	27,735	29,152	16,786	57.6	41,371	43,484	25,039	57.6
1986	29,458	30,809	17,604	57.1	43,139	45,117	25,780	57.1
1987	30,970	32,385	18,406	56.8	43,756	45,755	26,005	56.8

(continues)

TABLE 1.9 (continued)

Year	Median Income in Current Dollars				Median Income in Constant (1997) Dollars			
	All Families[a]	White	Black	Percentage of Black to White	All Families[a]	White	Black	Percentage of Black to White
1988	32,191	33,915	19,329	57.0	43,674	46,013	26,224	57.0
1989	34,213	35,975	20,209	56.2	44,284	46,564	26,158	56.2
1990	35,353	36,915	21,423	58.0	43,414	45,332	26,308	58.0
1991	35,939	37,783	21,548	57.0	42,351	44,524	25,392	57.0
1992	36,812	38,909	21,161	54.4	41,839	44,238	24,141	54.6
1993	36,959	39,300	21,542	54.8	41,051	43,652	23,927	54.8
1994	38,782	40,884	24,696	60.4	42,001	44,277	26,748	60.4
1995	40,611	42,646	25,970	60.9	42,769	44,913	27,350	60.9
1996	42,300	44,756	26,522	59.3	43,271	45,783	27,131	59.3
1997	44,568	46,754	28,602	61.2	44,568	46,754	28,602	61.2

[a] Includes other races not shown separately.

[b] For 1950–1965, black and other races.

SOURCES: U.S. Department of Commerce, *Statistical Abstract of the United States* (Washington, DC: U.S. Government Printing Office, 1987), p. 436; U.S. Bureau of the Census, Current Population Reports, "Money Income in the United States: 1997" (Washington, DC: U.S. Government Printing Office, 1998), Series P-60, no. 200, 13–16, Tables B-1 and B-4.

among slaves (estimated to be above 30 percent after less than five years in the Americas). The situation was hardly better for free African Americans, who were subjected to violence and long periods of incarceration when accused or convicted of crimes. At the same time, these free citizens often could not successfully bring charges against whites, and they were permitted no role in managing or modifying the system.

Little changed when responsibility for the security of African Americans moved from the plantation owner to the state after the Civil War. Almost immediately, the system of justice, inchoate at the time, was applied differentially. The evidence suggests that African Americans were more often arrested, more likely to go to jail, and more often the subject of vigilante justice. Indeed, the postwar period saw a rapid increase in one of the most heinous crimes perpetrated against Blacks after the end of slavery—lynching. There were 846 lynchings between 1901 and 1910, and 754 of them were of Blacks. More than 80 percent of them occurred in the southern states, where the African American population was concentrated (Logan 1972, 348). Lynchings were carried out by mobs or terror organizations, often with the sanction of state officials, and despite major efforts, it was impossible to implement legislation against such acts (Holt 1982). In some states officials also drew revenues from incarcerated African Americans—what DuBois called "crime as a source of income for the state." Imprisoned African Americans could be leased as laborers. The practice was so widespread in Georgia, according to DuBois, that Georgia had "no regular penitentiary at all, but an organized system of letting out the prisoners for profit" (DuBois 1962, 698).

As the criminal justice system evolved, it became possible to look at aggregate data of incarceration rates by race and the type of crimes for which charges were brought. The story that these data tell deviates little from the differential treatment that African Americans have experienced in the justice system since the inception of the republic. In a study of arrests and imprisonment from the 1930s (when reliable data became available) to 2000, the disparity between African Americans and whites is striking, and it gets worse through time. As Table 1.10 shows, in 1935, at which time most Blacks remained on plantations in the South, the proportion of arrestees in the United States who were Black was 23 percent; the figure rose slightly, to about 25 percent, in the 1940s and remained there through the 1970s. The proportion jumped again in the 1980s and stabilized at nearly 30 percent. This means that at the time when Blacks were experiencing their most intense political mobilization during the civil rights

TABLE 1.10   Total Arrests and Homicide, by Race, 1935–2000 (Percent)

Year	Total Arrests		Arrests for Homicide[a]	
	White	Black	White	Black
1935	72.5	23.2	62.0	34.1
1940	72.2	22.8	55.7	40.1
1945	71.8	26.8	53.8	45.4
1950	72.6	25.9	53.2	45.6
1952[b]	72.8	25.3	55.0	44.3
1955	70.4	27.4	54.8	44.4
1960[c]	68.0	28.8	53.0	45.2
1965	68.2	28.4	50.8	47.3
1970	69.9	27.0	45.6	52.2
1975	72.2	25.2	49.0	48.6
1980	73.8	24.5	50.6	47.9
1981	72.9	25.5	49.6	49.0
1982	70.7	27.8	48.8	49.7
1983	71.1	27.3	49.0	49.6
1984	73.4	24.9	53.7	44.9
1985	71.7	26.6	50.1	48.4
1986	71.3	27.0	50.3	48.0
1987	68.7	29.5	45.8	52.4
1988	68.6	29.6	45.0	53.5
1989	67.3	30.8	42.2	56.4
1990	69.2	28.9	43.7	54.7
1991	69.0	29.0	43.4	54.8
1992	67.6	30.3	43.5	55.1
1993	66.9	31.1	40.7	57.6
1994	66.6	31.3	41.7	56.4
1995	66.8	30.9	43.4	54.4
1996	66.9	30.7	42.8	54.9
1997	67.1	30.4	41.9	56.4
1998	68.0	29.7	44.5	53.4
1999	69.0	28.6	45.9	51.8
2000	69.7	27.9	48.7	48.8

[a] Before 1978, homicide includes: (a) murder and nonnegligent manslaughter, and (b) manslaughter by negligence; as of 1978, homicide refers to murder and nonnegligent manslaughter only.

[b] Before 1952, information was available from the fingerprint arrest cards received at the Identification Division of the FBI in Washington. Thereafter, information is from police reports and is not comparable to previous records.

[c] During and after 1960, rural area was included.

SOURCE: Federal Bureau of Investigation, U.S. Department of Justice, *Uniform Crime Reports for the U.S.* (Washington, DC: U.S. Government Printing Office).

movement, they became much more susceptible to engagement with the criminal justice system. During this period Blacks were estimated to constitute 10 to 12 percent of the national population, which means that their arrest rate was wildly out of proportion to their representation in the population. The racial differentials are much wider in arrests for the more severe crime of homicide. The data in the table show that as early as 1935 Blacks accounted for 34 percent of arrests for homicide. Ten years later the proportion reached 45 percent, and since 1970 it has averaged well above 50 percent.

What is one to make of these circumstances, which involve not merely the law enforcement services but also the application of the law? Many scholars have long since determined that there are problems in the administration of justice that yield discrimination against Blacks. Historically, this differential application of enforcement against Blacks was related to their status as slaves. Later it was a product of the combination of police prejudice, white vigilantism, and the inability of Blacks to influence changes in personnel or policy. At the same time, the range of social problems that plagued this increasingly urban migrant population led to Blacks' committing more economic crimes to make ends meet. Whatever the crime, however, Blacks were much more likely than whites to be convicted and sentenced to longer terms when arrested for their crimes. Moreover, they were much more likely to be convicted of alleged crimes against whites. In the resolution of charges for crimes, Blacks have been less able to mount a defense at the bar of justice. Many have been unable to afford counsel or effective counsel of their choice, decreasing the likelihood of prevailing in court. This factor also has a role in the greater engagement of Blacks in the criminal justice system.

Blacks have long perceived that they are targets for illegal police surveillance and arrest. Perhaps the most revealing evidence to support this perception in recent years has to do with racial profiling. After years of charges, the state of New Jersey conceded that its highway authorities did indeed have standard practices of targeting African American and Hispanic motorists and charging them with sundry crimes and traffic violations. Since then, racial profiling has become a public policy issue for other police departments around the country.

The involvement of African Americans with the criminal justice system has a considerable impact on individuals, families, and the general community. A large number of those who are incarcerated are fathers, and their absence causes a loss in family income and access to growing children. At the same time, they often lose their ability to have any influence on the public policy system.

Differential Health: Life and Death Chances

Historically, the social resources of African Americans have been diminished by lack of, or inadequate, health care and high rates of mortality. In general, the availability of medical care for Blacks has been limited both because it is unaffordable and because of a paucity of medical personnel in the racially segregated residential enclaves. As a result, Blacks have less access to physicians and medicine, but at the same time they are least able to afford lifestyle choices that improve health, such as proper nutrition and preventive health care. This helps explains the greater incidence of preventable diseases that lead to a shorter life expectancy for African Americans.

This aspect of inequality, too, had its trajectory set in the system of slavery. African Americans on the plantations were instruments deployed to serve the interests of their owners. Because the supply of these instruments seemed limitless, the owners often made no provisions for slaves' health and welfare. The supply from Africa was steady, and the price was affordable. Hence enslaved persons could be worked until spent and then disposed of. If their work was unsatisfactory, they could easily be replaced. There was little incentive, at least while the importation of persons as chattel remained legal, to protect the health and welfare of African Americans.

After the Civil War, access to medical care became even less available and affordable. Most Blacks became sharecroppers and tenant farmers for their former plantation owners. But in their quasi-independent status as sharecropper, for example, they remained beholden to the plantation owners for their livelihood. Plantation owners assessed exorbitant charges for goods and services used by the sharecroppers. Moreover, the goods and services rarely met the needs of sharecropping families. Services beyond the most basic of needs, such as health care, often were simply not provided at all. And as Jim Crow practices became increasingly common, Blacks became more and more isolated from the services of physicians and from public benefits that could enhance a healthy lifestyle. "The sick had their wretched care. Public hospitals supported by public funds turn Negroes away or segregate and neglect them in cellars and annexes. White physicians often despise their clientele and colored physicians crowd into larger towns and cities to escape insult and insecurity . . . in the country and smaller towns" (DuBois 1962, 698).

Historically, the truncated life chances for Blacks begin at birth. The *Common Destiny* study (Jaynes and Williams 1989, 398ff) found that the infant mortality differential between African Americans and whites was about two to one in 1984—18.4 and 9.4 per 1,000, respectively. But there were major differentials between states and regions. For example, the highest infant mortality rates were in northern states where Blacks were densely concentrated in cities—Illinois (23 per 1,000) and Michigan (24 per 1,000). The early-life difficulties reflected in infant mortality rates ultimately have consequences for Blacks who survive into adulthood. They do not live as long, are more susceptible to diseases, and have less access to treatment. Heart disease and cancer are consistently the leading causes of death—and here, too, the differential between Blacks and whites is almost two to one. For Blacks between the ages of 45 and 54 in 1984, deaths from these two diseases were roughly 300 per 100,000, and for the next ten-year age cycle, the figure more than doubled. In the same period, the figures for whites (for whom the same diseases are the leading cause of death) were 200 and 400, respectively. The conditions of poor health are exacerbated by inadequate insurance or lack of insurance—and these are the households least able to lay out cash for immediate health services.

Today, few diseases have a greater impact on African American health than HIV infection and AIDS. HIV-AIDS is more prevalent and is increasing at a greater rate than most other diseases in the African American population. Although Blacks constituted 12 percent of the U.S. population in 2000, they accounted for almost 40 percent of the AIDS cases. Women are almost as vulnerable as men, since HIV infection evolved from being contracted principally by homosexual men to being transmitted heterosexually and via intravenous drug use. Women now constitute 28 percent of HIV infections, and Black women, many of whom are heads of households, constitute "68 percent of the women infected with HIV through June 2000" (Hearn and Jackson 2002, 163); their rate of infection is sixteen times that of white women. Since AIDS is incurable, it has a devastating and differential impact on African Americans.

When one calculates the combined impact of these socioeconomic factors, they clearly demonstrate a differential status for African Americans, the largest identifiable minority group in the nation until the 2000 census. Although many policies have been designed to alter the castelike conditions wrought by slavery in the United States and its residual effects, the lower status of African Americans has remained in most areas. It may thus be concluded that African Americans have significant deficits in these resources vis-à-vis the white population, and that the absence of resources leaves them with less ability to influence the political benefits structure or the allocations emanating from it. In the analysis that follows, I look specifically at political resources.

Political Processes: The Slavery Era to the Present

Race as Trump Card in Politics

Given the differential status described above, it is hardly surprising that African Americans as free citizens in the republic have rarely received equitable allocations from the political system. Without sufficient social resources, it is impossible to bid successfully in the political community. The civic society for African Americans remains incomplete insofar as they are unable to translate their interests in a routine manner via the regular channels of the social and political system. One of the advantages of the democratic-oriented states in the West, as Robert Putnam (1993) has argued, is that a plethora of reinforcing, cross-cutting organizations and alignments exist that sustain a robust civic life. These organizations are not all avowedly political either. However, because they exist in an environment with long-standing agreements about the stakes and the rules of the game, all manner of organized citizen activities are critical to sustaining the participant political process. This is an argument akin to the pluralist formulation. Nevertheless, one is not required to accept or reject the pluralist formulation to come to the conclusion that African American status as "universal" participants in the American democracy has rarely held up. Despite the fact that African Americans tend to be involved in far more organizations than whites (Morris 1975), this overorganization has not translated into a more equitable status in the society.

All the data presented so far indicates a differential status for African Americans by which they are assigned a lower hierarchical ranking in the society. This lower ranking has meant that African Americans suffer a stable and continuing inability to marshal the group's meager resources for regularized effective participation in the social structure. Elements of both race and class seem to contribute to this ranking system. However, repeatedly race seems to trump other variables, where the indelible mark of color determines the lower ranking of Blacks. This "linked fate," as Dawson (1994) calls it, makes it practical for institutional patterns of discrimination to take on an independent life, just as it makes it possible to measure citizens by color and target specific minority groups in practices such as racial profiling. Needless to say, the lower ranking is a distinct disadvantage in gaining access to the political process. If group organizations are barred from the standard bargaining process, then cross-cutting alignment is not applicable, and the benefits that flow from it are un-available—for example, the ability to align and form coalitions with others, to develop feelings of efficacy, and to support the system.

The Persistence of African American Political Challenge and Contention

Consequently, the history of African American politics is replete with extrasystem efforts to make correctives to the political order or to challenge it. This has given African Americans essentially an outsider status as they seek to act on and not within the routine mechanisms of the political system. This approach began with the arrival of Africans in the "New World" as enslaved persons and has continued since then, ebbing and flowing with the severity of their displace-ment from the promise of universal freedom. The discussion that fol-lows focuses on the frames of reference political scientists use to try to explain this phenomenon and on the nature of African American political strivings from the period of slavery to the present.

The lower hierarchical ranking of African Americans and their re-sistance to it have defined and determined the character of the group's existence in the American political community. During slav-ery African Americans were not considered a bona fide part of the po-litical process or even full human beings. Even after the principles of universal freedom had been accorded them, everyday life was still fraught with discrimination and social isolation. There was also am-bivalence in the implementation of the full rights of citizenship for these new community members. Hence everywhere there were barri-ers to political participation for African Americans, often perpetrated or at least sanctioned by the state.

However, African Americans always contested their status as slaves and, later, their lower hierarchical ranking in the social order. After the end of slavery, although the implementation of citizenship for Blacks was characterized by contradictions, from time to time the state also genuinely promoted full citizenship rights for the group. Therefore contestation has become the other frame through which African American political life must be explained. Vincent Harding (1983) has metaphorically characterized this strain of group resistance or oppositional disposition as a steadily flowing river, suggesting that oppositional politics for African Americans has been continuous through U.S. history.

The discussion below summarizes the arguments about and events related to political participation that will be analyzed in later chapters of this book. The most general conceptual themes are that African Americans have struggled to alter their lower hierarchical ranking in the political order through constant resistance, through an unceasing commitment to the implementation of the ideals of American democracy, and, when circumstances have permitted, through routine engagement in partisan politics as a minority interest group. The broad periods into which these activities can be divided are the colonial period, the period of U.S. slavery, abolition and the Civil War, Reconstruction, southern disfranchisement and the Great Migration, urban central city politics, the civil rights movement, and postmovement electoral politics.

Currents in African American Political Ideologies

African Americans have had a variety of ideas of their own that have guided their strategies for gaining inclusion in a racialized political system. In the face of racism, it has been easy to convert these strivings to ideologies—frames by which the environment is interpreted and negotiated in efforts toward liberation. Dawson (2001) has shown how these currents endure in a system in which hierarchical ranking remains constant and how they adapt to changes in the ways the hierarchy is sustained. A wide range of ideas have been prominent, most variations on two ideological themes: nationalism and integration. Nationalism places—and continues to place—a premium on group identity and membership. African Americans define themselves and make claims, as an oppositional entity, upon the power elite. Within the myriad ideas associated with nationalism, two strands have been prominent in African American politics—externally and internally oriented constructs. Those who have an external orientation often focus on struggle designed to obtain a homeland outside the territorial United States (Africa, say), whereas those who have an internal orientation focus on struggle as an identifiable group within the United States (Bracey et al. 1970; Cruse 1967).

Those within the integrationist current focus on struggling for full membership in the general political community. They seek to destroy the racialized hierarchy, in concert with others who are committed to universal freedom for African Americans. The ideology of integration is consistent with some pluralist arguments in its acceptance of the notion of cross-cutting linkages as critical to universal inclusion of African Americans. All of these currents, in their complex and myriad iterations, have endured as African Americans have engaged in political action in the United States. They sometimes operate together and sometimes separately, their ebb and flow dependent on the events in the general political environment. These patterns will be seen as the historical progression of African American political strivings as enumerated below.

The Politics of Slavery

The African American population began its sojourn in the United States just after 1600 in a status of servitude, although not yet formally as slaves. At that time most of the Africans who arrived were indentured servants. However, the status of these Blacks quickly devolved to a lower hierarchical ranking as the new community of European immigrants became more settled. The formal political definition of Blacks as an enslaved population was clear by the middle of the seventeenth century, however. The first colonies to institute slavery laws and regulations were Virginia in 1661 and Maryland in 1663 (Franklin and Moss 1994, 56–59). Fairly soon, everywhere in the southern part of the republic, where this population was concentrated, slavery became a regular, codified feature of life.

It is not known precisely how many Africans were brought to the Americas in the lucrative triangular trade in human beings from the west and central coastal areas of Africa (Williams 1961). Estimates are that 10 million to 25 million Africans (Curtin 1969; DuBois 1965), were removed from the continent—so many that continental Africa has never recovered, remaining one of the least populated areas in the world. The scale of the transfer of population was high enough to create major concentrations of African descendants throughout the Americas, from Canada to the southernmost tip of South America. In fact, the second largest political entity with an African-based population is in the South American republic of Brazil.

Despite the intent of enslavement to deny African Americans any role in the political system, their independent actions exerted influence on the system. The African American politics of slavery may be divided into two strands—the influence inherent in the development of an independent "slave quarter" community structure, and the direct individual and group acts of resistance exerted against the system.

The slave quarters, that is, the slaves' living quarters, was always partially under their control. Community life there was imbued with an identifiable cultural and structural expression. This provided the community some ability to take spontaneous and routine actions to defend its space and to replicate itself. But it also provided sufficient independence for slaves sometimes to influence their status as chattel or servants. John Blassingame (1979) has documented how memories from Africa helped slaves organize their independent spaces outside the plantation fields. They did so with a degree of integrity to African (and general) principles of social organization, given the circumscribed context. They also deployed aspects of this culture for resistance, such as infusing hidden messages in musical expression (Raboteau 1978).

Much of the independent character of these organized communities was not avowedly political. Instead, it consisted of the mundane day-to-day actions for survival and maintenance of some degree of human integrity. Among these were efforts to maintain family structure in the face of strictures against it or to provide protection and sustenance for children (Gutman 1976). Yet, in these peculiar circumstances, virtually any mundane act by a slave could become political, unleashing the full force of the law, extralegal violence, or terror.

However, there were efforts among slaves that constituted institutionalized patterns intended to effect change in their status. Many of these acts against "masters" must have been spontaneous or a matter of opportunity. But the frequency with which resistance was expressed by personal acts of violence or sabotage against masters indicates that the tactics had some efficacy. The repertoire of tactics included acts of violence against overseers in plantation households and in the fields (where most slaves were occupied). African Americans were widely known for the equivalent of job actions on the plantations, withdrawing their labor under the pretext of illness or by running away (Parker 1993). Starobin (1969) suggests that more than 2,000 successful runaways per month took place and that about ten times that number were unsuccessful. Acts of sabotage—theft, tool breakage, and arson—were used to effectively immobilize the one-crop, plantation economy. Such acts were committed so often that they led to the convenient mythology among plantation owners that these behaviors were indicative of the genetic inferiority of Africans—that they were lazy and shiftless. But not all political acts were directly aimed at the destruction of the plantation master. Sometimes they reflected the ultimate acts of desperate men and women who took their own lives or that of their children to rid themselves of the daily burdens of enslavement (Franklin and Moss 1994).

Some of the political resistance was highly organized, with the avowed aim of obliterating the system or of getting Blacks away from it. Much of the former efforts lay in rebellions mounted by slaves and in the general abolition movement, and efforts to get away are reflected in the highly successful Underground Railroad (Siebert 1968). As Aptheker (1942) has documented, rebellions were fairly frequent, a fact often lost in attention devoted to the two or three best-known events. The most famous of these was the Nat Turner revolt of 1831 in Virginia. Other well-known events—which, unlike the Turner revolt, never got under way—were the planned rebellions led by Denmark Vesey in Charleston, South Carolina, in 1822, and by Gabriel Prosser in Richmond, Virginia, in 1831. Although both of these events were betrayed before they were launched, they were characterized by a considerable level of organization.

Running away, or escape, was often aided and abetted. So rampant were escapes, organized and unorganized, that the infamous Fugitive Slave Act was passed in 1850 guaranteeing the return of slaves who were subsequently apprehended. All of the southern states had patrols and various other devices to stem the flow of runaways. The Underground Railroad, by far the best known means of escape, was a highly organized system operating under the tireless leadership of Harriet Tubman, who made numerous forays into the South to spirit away slaves (Franklin and Moss 1994, 187).

With time, such activities occurred in tandem with a growing moral argument for the abolition of slavery. Those who favored this position formed a successful movement in which orators, publicists, and religious leaders attacked the system of slavery as fundamentally opposed to human rights and Christianity. They represented one of the earliest coalitions of Blacks and whites who collaborated to undermine the system by attacking its foundation (Kraditor 1969; Quarles 1969). Among the leaders of the movement were some of those who went on to play defining roles in the transition from war to emancipation. The orator Frederick Douglass and the publicist William Lloyd Garrison established their own newspapers, which then became the chief vehicles through which their views were disseminated. Toward the end of the period of slavery, the persistent abolition movement aided in making slavery an issue of major public policy contention.

Parallel ideological strands of nationalism developed during the period of slavery. They were reflected in individual as well as organized efforts to remove African Americans from the United States to an African homeland and to organize communal efforts on the ground for African American freedom. Paul Cuffee's effort was one of the earliest in which an African American actually returned to Africa. His was consistent with a number of others, some of whom collaborated with the American Colonization Movement that returned some Blacks to Liberia (Shick 1977). Their arguments sought both to repossess the fundamentals of African culture and to bring "Christian virtues" to "benighted" Africa (Blyden 1971; Crummell 1971). These ideas served as the genesis for an enduring set of nationalist arguments with Africa at the center. At the same time, in the prewar period, the Negro Convention Movement emerged (Walton 1972b). It was the first quasi-political party to use a model of communal organization to demand political change in the United States. It, too, provided a model of an organizational pattern that has endured in the racialized political order.

Many scholars argue that the contradiction of institutionalized slavery in the democratic republic was so thoroughly exposed, partially by these efforts, that some sort of crisis was inevitable. Indeed, the nation had experienced major revolts by African Americans, and the arguments of the abolitionists were widely discussed. Equally important was the growing competition between the industrializing North and the agricultural South. The *Dred Scott v. Sandford* decision by the Supreme Court in 1857 seems to have brought things to a head in this regard, with the Court appearing to side with the South in the dispute. The Court declared that Scott was not even entitled to citizenship when he moved away to a territory where slavery was not practiced.

Soon afterward, the greatest conflagration since the Revolutionary War broke out—the Civil War. The South declared its secession from the Union in order to maintain the practice of slavery, which sustained its agricultural economy. The North, on the other hand, sought to preserve a more diverse, industrial-based economy, for which the labor market was sufficient. In effect, the question of slavery became the centerpiece of the war—the fight would likely determine the acceptance or rejection of enslavement for the American republic. There were other issues, to be sure, but for African Americans none was as important as the question of their enslavement. Some aspects of the period are discussed in more detail in chapter 2, which focuses on protest political actions among Blacks.

Reconstruction Politics

When the Confederate states lost the war, citizenship in the republic underwent a fundamental redefinition. This was a defining moment for African Americans. They became citizens and could now imagine the end to their lowly status as nonpersons. A wide range of new policies were adopted to secure their formal inclusion in the social and political system. These were best reflected in a number of constitutional and statutory provisions that secured the formal rights of citizenship. The Emancipation Proclamation, which freed those who had been slaves in the former Confederacy, was followed by three amendments to the Constitution that destroyed the system of slavery and served to redefine African Americans as regular members of the social and political community. The Thirteenth Amendment ended their enslavement; the Fourteenth provided them citizenship; and the Fifteenth provided them voting rights. The "Radical Republicans" in Congress also passed a series of accompanying statutory measures to further secure regular citizen status for the newly freed Blacks. These statutes, which guaranteed equality in social relations, economic pursuits, and security, included the Black Code Act (1866), the Kidnap Act (1866), the Peonage Act (1867), the Enforcement Act (1870), the Ku Klux Act (1871), and the Accommodation Act (1875) (Blaustein and Zangrando 1968, 229–243).

This legislation ushered in the Reconstruction period, during which formal participation by Blacks in the republic expanded dramatically. In its heyday, which lasted from 1865 through the early to mid-1870s, African Americans voted in large numbers and were elected to political office. During this time they made the first of their essentially one-party strategic alignments in the two-party system, in the Republican Party of Lincoln. They had a considerable impact on governments throughout the South, where the majority of African Americans were located.

Although the African American population was largely destitute and uneducated, it managed a remarkable degree of participation in a relatively short period. Across the South they ran as candidates for office and engaged in the formal political process as ordinary citizens, when allowed to do so. The Black population remained stable in the region, and in some instances it constituted a majority, such as in Mississippi, Louisiana, and South Carolina. Their numbers were almost at parity with whites in Louisiana and Georgia. In all of these states, African American participation was realized at all levels of government, including town, county, state, and federal offices.

Absent proportional representation in any state, the scope of the participation was considerable. It began in the requisite constitutional conventions in the former Confederate states, all of which had Black representatives. Thus Blacks had a hand in fashioning the local governments under which they would live in the reconstructed South. Franklin and Moss (1994, 238) have noted that the resulting constitutions "were some of the most progressive the South had ever known. Most of them abolished property qualifications for voting and holding office. . . . All of them abolished slavery . . . and extended [the ballot] to all male residents except [some] Confederates." Many Blacks went on to serve in the state legislatures and to hold office at the state level. Most of their activities focused on policy within the state, although in the latter days of Reconstruction, some moved away and acquired national standing in the Republican Party. However, this standing had little influence on their status within the state later on, after the integrated Reconstruction regimes had been dismantled.

The best information we have about participation and representation by Blacks is at the federal level, to which the first Blacks were elected to office in 1870. Among federal officeholders were two senators from Mississippi, the first serving in 1870 and 1871 and the second between 1875 and 1881. Generally most of those who were elected at the federal level served as representatives to Congress between 1870 and 1879, a period when multiple members served at the same time. However, a few African Americans served until 1901 who could be said to have been a part of the Reconstruction period. South Carolina had the most African American representation in Congress, having sent eight Blacks to Washington between 1870 and 1897. North Carolina had the second most, with four, followed by Alabama with three. Mississippi, Louisiana, and Virginia had the most significant differential between their African American populations and congressional representation; each sent only one congressman. The brevity of the Reconstruction period is underscored by the fact that much of this congressional representation was clustered between 1870 and 1875 (Barker et al. 1999, 258).

The best records for elected Black officials occurred in the states of South Carolina, Louisiana, and Mississippi. South Carolina's population had an overwhelming African American majority, and the group had developed some organization, foretelling their success in the electoral arena. The state had a sizable number of fairly well-to-do, literate Blacks, many among them mulatto. This enterprising group had organized statewide for the purpose of participating in public affairs. For a time they were rebuffed, but as the Radical Republicans in Congress pushed through the Reconstruction program in 1867, the importance of this group's prior organization of Blacks became critical. They were a majority and dominating force when the state convention was called in the same year, constituting seventy of the 124 delegates. The eight congressional representatives they sent to Washington were merely the highest level example of the scope of their ubiquitous presence in South Carolina politics, in one of the shortest Reconstruction periods in the region, ending about 1877. Holt has shown that "of the 487 men elected to the various state and federal offices . . . between 1867 and 1876, more than half were black" (Holt 1977, 1). Among these he has identified convention delegates, state legislators in both houses, U.S. congressional representatives, and almost all of the state-level executive offices, except the governorship (234).

The circumstances in Louisiana were more colorful. This state did not have an African American majority, but it did have a much more complicated political base than most other southern states. Because of its French legacy the state had an indigenous Creole population, and it also had a large number of immigrants from the North of various political persuasions. Its partisan division always had a respectable number of both Democrats and Republicans. Although the sizable Black population was comparatively underrepresented in Washington, it was not for lack of effort. One of its two elected representatives was not seated, nor was its elected senator, the famous P.B.S. Pinchback. Pinchback did, however, serve as the first Black state governor and in a variety of other high state offices. Moreover, three Blacks served as lieutenant governors between 1871 and 1877, which had the effect of giving individual African American leaders more power in Louisiana than elsewhere. In addition "scores of black men served in the General Assembly, which contained on the average about seven out of thirty-six in the senate and about half of the 101 members in the house" (Bennett 1967, 276).

Reconstruction in Mississippi was a limited success for its African American majority. This state elected two Blacks to the Senate in

Washington, more than any other state. However, the majority population did not control the state convention that rewrote the constitution, nor did it ever come close to controlling the state legislature. Of the 100 delegates to the state convention, only sixteen were Blacks. African Americans had considerable success in statewide offices, however: "One black served as Lieutenant Governor; five as Secretary of State; one each as Superintendent of Education, Librarian, and Secretary of Agriculture and Immigration; [and] two as Speakers of the State House of Representatives" (Morrison 1987, 38). Although African American success at the local level was nowhere near proportional to the population, Blacks in this state held a number of municipal and county positions. And in some places they completely dominated local affairs. For example, "in Issaquena County . . . [in the delta] there was a virtual hegemony of black officials. These new leaders controlled all but two elective offices. All the county supervisors were black, as were the 'members of the legislature, the sheriff, the clerks, the justices of the peace, and the constables'" (Morrison 1987, 38).

The current of ideas reflected by these leaders was deeply mired in the context of the times. They came to power at a time when the political alignment in the country was in flux and when government organization everywhere was in crisis. African American leaders were a part of the Republican Party alignment because of the party's role in demolishing the system of slavery. As such the congressional leadership of the party was the main ally of the new constituents in the South. But the South remained a contested battleground, and given the ambivalence in the executive branch of the national government, there were severe limits on what could be achieved in electoral politics. But the African Americans, many of whom had emerged from bourgeois circumstances, sought to penetrate the system and to work within it while espousing relatively moderate views. Most were conscious of the circumstances of their constituent base, the poor and destitute farmhands. In legislative activity they made an effort to represent these interests while also seeking to uphold the status quo for stable government.

Blacks who were involved in governance during this period faced a difficult task that, in hindsight, represented an inherent, unworkable contradiction. The marvel was that these individuals, so recently without any standing at all in politics, rapidly took the reins of power and succeeded in forging workable alignments and coalitions. Detailed aspects of this period are discussed later on, in chapter 2 (protest), chapter 3 (organizations), chapter 4 (elections), and chapter 5 (office holding).

Politics from Post-Reconstruction through the Depression

The betrayal of Reconstruction led to a rapid decline in political participation by Blacks. They went from near control of some districts to virtual disfranchisement. Reconstruction had itself been implemented ambivalently or lackadaisically. The Freedmen's Bureau had never quite succeeded in meeting the needs of a destitute population that had little wherewithal for bidding in the political process. The assassination of Lincoln left the presidency to a southern vice president whose goal seemed to be the restoration of the traditional power-holding class of plantation owners. The signal of the formal end of Reconstruction, however, was the controversial presidential election of 1876. It ended with the great compromise that sent the Republican candidate, Rutherford B. Hayes, to the presidency despite his having lost the popular vote. Much of the election controversy was focused in the South, where near anarchy reigned as the former white Confederates sought to regain their political standing and especially the removal of Union troops and military administration. Meanwhile, African American Republican partisans and their alignees were virtually under siege. The presidential poll in several southern states left both parties claiming victory, thus creating uncertainty about which of the candidates, Hayes or the Democrat Samuel Tilden, had won. Hayes won the day by striking a deal with the southern congressmen to remove the army and in effect to reconstruct the traditional power base (Logan 1972). That gave license to the former confederates to engage in an all-out effort to restore the ancien regime.

The restoration campaign occurred on all fronts, creating a period of intense struggle between the races for political ascendancy. It was a game that the former Confederates were destined to win because of the collaboration of the federal government or its ambivalence toward the protection of Black rights. The politics of the period, therefore, was a combination of legal and extralegal machinations against African American participation in politics. It ended not just with their political disfranchisement from roughly 1880 through the Depression, but also in their isolation from virtually every social resource in the society. The range of legal formulations, aside from the

Hayes compromise, included those of the Supreme Court. It declared an important body of civil rights statutes unconstitutional in 1880, and interpreted the Fourteenth Amendment as inapplicable to state actions (Logan 1972). This was a devastating blow to African Americans, for whom the equal protection of laws was now deemed to apply only in the federal realm, not to speak of the loss of protections for public accommodations and economic pursuits provided in the now "illegal" statutes.

These early legal formulations were accompanied by a range of equally effective extralegal tactics. African Americans who held office were forced into cooperation with the ascendant Democratic Party forces in order to maintain any semblance of representation, and sometimes the arrangements were accompanied by confrontations of considerable violence. In other cases, officials were subject to economic reprisals, harassed, or given ultimatums that forced them to leave. These tactics sometimes led to the murder of Black officials.

But attacks on elected officials were of no greater importance than the variety of extralegal tactics used against ordinary citizens in the African American community. During this period, terror became a major political force as the Ku Klux Klan and similar organizations emerged and used the cover of darkness and anonymity to perpetrate harassment, intimidation, and acts of violence against Blacks. These tactics were highly successful in creating widespread fear among a largely unarmed and dependent population. At the same time, the use of "dirty tricks" against Blacks in electoral procedure was widespread—removal of polling places, purging of voting rolls, and bureaucratic chicanery—all to the end of preventing the exercise of the vote.

This combination of factors had succeeded by 1890, when virtually all of the former Confederate states had new constitutions under advisement. When approved, these documents essentially repudiated the Reconstruction constitutions, leaving Blacks disfranchised everywhere. The Supreme Court's enunciation of its "separate but equal" policy in *Plessy v. Ferguson* in 1896 gave federal sanction to these practices. This period represented what Logan called the "dark ages of recent American history" (Logan 1972, 9).

The politics of African Americans in that period, however, was marked by both struggle and promise. For the first time, Blacks had developed an independent voice at the national level. A number of significant individuals emerged as spokesmen, and they often also served as high-level bureaucrats in patronage jobs. Almost all of those who served in these so called "Negro jobs" were cadre activists within the ruling Republican Party. Prominent among them was Frederick Douglass, the great abolitionist and orator, who was appointed in 1877 as the marshal of Washington, D.C., and in 1881 was appointed Recorder of Deeds for that city (Berry and Blassingame 1982, 161). John R. Lynch (1913), one of the former congressmen from Mississippi, remained in Washington and became a prominent lawyer, statesmen, and author.

Others took diplomatic posts, serving principally in two countries that came to be reserved as patronage posts for African Americans— the Black governments of Haiti and Liberia. Douglass was also among these, serving as the U.S. minister to the government of Haiti from 1889 to 1891. J. Milton Turner served as chief U.S. minister to the fledgling Liberian Republic from 1871 to 1879. Turner and Douglass were two of sixteen African Americans who served as diplomatic heads of mission before 1900 (Miller 1978; Skinner 1992).

Those who served in these capacities were a product of their time. They had the difficult task of negotiating a place for African Americans in a party that had the legacy of having obliterated slavery but that also had often done little to implement the universal freedom required by the constitutional amendments designed to secure full citizenship for Blacks. Indeed, it was a party that had forged an unsavory compromise with the South in order to maintain the presidency. In the process, the path to freedom was severely limited as southern whites completely undermined federal efforts to sustain African American participation in the region. In spite of these contradictions, the African American leaders occupying patronage posts refused to abandon the party, because remaining in them was seen as the best hope for fighting again a tide of complete reversal of the gains of Reconstruction. It was through their presence and influence that voices were heard in opposition to the racial hierarchy. That they failed in the end was a product of the scope of the forces arrayed against them or of silence from would-be allies.

Integration versus Nationalism: The Leadership of Washington and DuBois

It was in this period that one of the enduring currents in African American thought was writ in bold relief—that of integration versus nationalism. The debate on the issue brought into focus two of the most prominent thinkers in African American history—Booker T. Washington (1995) and W.E.B. DuBois (1989). Washington (Harlan

1972) had organized the prototype at Tuskegee after which the agricultural and industrial schools for Blacks would be modeled. He had gained wide influence among the white establishment by his views that African Americans should not aspire to full equality with whites; they should hone their skills as agricultural laborers, a natural complement for their talents and basic needs. The fame Washington earned from espousing such a view was that it offered an acceptable answer to whites of all political persuasions. It was attractive to those who believed in the genetic inferiority of Blacks, but also to those for whom the question of racial accommodation was vexing.

DuBois was Washington's opposite, proposing the full integration of African Americans into all aspects of American society. His goal was to have the full range of opportunities attendant to universal freedom made available the newly freed Blacks. DuBois's (Lewis 1993) every personal action was designed to model what he saw as the goal. In the first place, he argued that personal relations should be of an integrated nature, such as those obtained between himself and his white colleagues. As a scholar, his written analyses were dedicated to sustaining the same principle. He sought to show two things. That Blacks were the full equal of their white counterparts; and that the racialized American regime unceasingly violated fundamental human rights as well as those of the U.S. Constitution.

The two models were implemented to varying degrees, given the differential influence of their proponents in the centers of power. Washington was able to implement most of his strategies for accommodation for a national, but isolated African American community via largesse from white benefactors in government and philanthropic organizations. DuBois, on the other hand, worked to create an organization designed to obliterate the racial order in favor of equality. Around the turn of the century this organization, which began as the Niagara Movement, became the precursor to the National Association for the Advancement of Colored People (NAACP) (Kellogg 1967). The fledgling organization got its start across the border in Canada to avoid the strictures of racial segregation, and it enjoyed little of the support from government that Washington received. However, as will be seen, this NAACP enjoyed extraordinary success in the next period of African American politics.

Aspects of this low period of African American participation, when protests by Blacks as outsiders was the routine and when the foundations for social movements were laid with the emergence of national civil rights organizations, are covered in chapters 2 and 3.

Post-Depression Political Realignment:
The New Democratic Coalition

The NAACP Presages a National Movement for Civil Rights

The little-known and suspect NAACP was the signal of another major surge in the effort to rout racialized politics and ambivalence. Few could have predicted at the birth of the Niagara Movement in 1909 that such a "fringe" element of church leaders and left-oriented whites in collusion with African American intellectuals and activists would gain any advantage in light of "separate but equal" policy (Kellogg 1967). Yet their emergence signaled a turning point in an environment in which the contradictions of the racialized social order presented new opportunities. A migration of Blacks had started from the southern plantations, the country was on the cusp of a world war, and a cycle of economic difficulties emerged. The environment may have been ripe for social movement, or at least political realignment. World War I did come, creating new pressures for internal migration. And it was followed soon by the most catastrophic economic depression the republic had seen. This combination of factors led to a major realignment of the political forces in the political arena. After a long period of ascendancy for the Republicans, there was a fundamental shift in the alignment of African Americans, who now saw possibilities for achieving more of their political goals by aligning with a new, fairly diverse array of interests affiliated with the Democratic Party. The economic crisis provided a golden opportunity for the Democratic coalition to expand its base and to make overtures to African Americans. And besides, it could do so by making modest changes.

The activism within the African American community served as its own catalyst, however. The NAACP was getting its wings in making court challenges to formal and informal elements of Jim Crow that appeared to violate the Constitution (McNeil 1983). A. Philip Randolph was organizing a massive street protest (Quarles 1982). Marcus Garvey arrived on the scene espousing a brand of nationalism that hearkened back to some of the tenets of Back to Africa Movements of earlier periods (Garvey et al. 1986). Once again, the options of integration and nationalism set the parameters for the debate on the desired terms of participation. The apparent contradictory models, in short, belied the centrality of the focus on the acquisition of formal rights. These options remained central to the wide variety of groups and leaders who orchestrated the greatest mobilization in history of the African American community for political participation. It is a period that can arbitrarily be dated from about 1935 to the present. Because of the massive migration of African Americans from the South to the North, for the first time the mobilization for participation was nationwide and was both urban and rural.

Developing the Legalism Approach to Change

The new period was ushered in with the aggressive pursuit of the formal acknowledgment and protection of the legal rights of African Americans to full citizenship. The destruction of Reconstruction had been so complete and the Jim Crow practices so formalized that African American political participation was destroyed and the social segregation of Blacks was routine. So the efforts of the NAACP were to reestablish the basic fundamentals of citizenship. Their working assumption was that inherent in the Constitution were all the means for achievement of the goal. They also had an instinctual belief that there was a consensus in the general population supporting fundamental fairness for African Americans. So the NAACP chose as its chief strategy legal court challenges to what seemed patently unconstitutional practices. It set out to disqualify the "separate but equal" doctrine that was guiding social relations, and by extension its counterpart of disfranchisement. It was a long battle that was to last about a half century, but the potential success began to be apparent almost immediately, as the Supreme Court repeatedly accepted the NAACP's challenges for adjudication.

The foundation for the legal framework that was used so effectively by the NAACP after 1930 was apparent in two early challenges to the overt discriminations sanctioned by the practice of separate but equal. The first challenge came in 1908 when the NAACP was in its infancy. Berea College, a private school in Kentucky, voluntarily integrated by accepting African Americans for study at its campus on an equal basis. The state of Kentucky, however, had a law that stipulated that "whites and Negroes could not be taught together in any private school unless that school maintained separate buildings for each race at least twenty-five miles apart" (Blaustein and Ferguson 1962, 101). Berea's challenge to this state statute failed as the Supreme Court upheld the segregation statute (*Berea v. Kentucky* 1908). Seven years later came the infamous "grandfather clause," first instituted in Oklahoma, which disenfranchised African Americans by applying special voter registration restrictions for them because their grandfathers were ineligible to vote prior to 1866 (*Guinn v. United States* 1915). Although the NAACP did not have its legal arm fully established or funded until the 1920s (Tushnet 1994, 13), it used its modest influence to urge a legal challenge to the Oklahoma law (Hine 1979, 67). It was the U.S. government that presented the case, successfully arguing that the "grandfather clause" violated the Fifteenth Amendment. This success brought the failure of Berea into a new light and showed that well-tailored legal challenges had the potential to succeed.

Subsequently the NAACP made a frontal attack on the "separate but equal" policy as the causal agent for the social and political isolation of African Americans. It assaulted two practices, one social—school segregation (McNeil 1983; Tushnet 1994)—and the other political—the "white primary" (Hine 1979). In the education sector the challenge sought to disqualify the practice of providing inferior education for Blacks, which was indicated first and foremost by segregated schools but also by grossly inequitable allocation of public funding. In a series of cases after *Berea,* the Supreme Court gradually accepted the argument that the "separate but equal" policy did not constitute equality under the law. The Court disqualified the Missouri practice of dispatching African Americans to other states for education that the state routinely provided only for whites (*Missouri ex rel. Gaines v. Canada* 1938). Similarly, it disqualified the Texas practice of organizing a prima facie unequal parallel institution for the education of Blacks to prevent their being educated alongside whites (*Sweatt v. Painter* 1950). The Court finally completely overturned the principle of "separate but equal," declaring that it was "inherently unequal," in *Brown v. Board of Education of Topeka, Kansas* (1954).

The politics of legalism by the NAACP required a struggle at a variety of other levels, engaging large numbers of African Americans and others. In the first place, the organization also waged a public relations campaign via lobbying and the development of a cadre of support across racial lines. It was able to sustain its court challenges because of considerable support from a liberal and left-wing sector of the general population. These supporters provided money and important technical assistance. Meanwhile, in the South another part of the campaign ensued. The organization had a high degree of grassroots support (direct and sentimental) in this region where membership in the society was often officially barred. The direct state campaigns against the NAACP in Mississippi (McMillen 1990) and Alabama (Morris 1984) were but the most visible of widespread actions by southern states to root out the presence of the NAACP. Thus it was often an underground operation but one of sufficient strength to identify targets and sometimes to engage in public protests in support of legal action.

The current of nationalism espoused by Garvey was making its mark in urban places such as New York City as well as internationally. However, what was receiving the most attention in the United States was a groundswell of support for a movement of public protest and the use of routine electoral politics, especially in the central cities. Already, for example, routine electioneering was resulting in the reappearance of African Americans in Congress. Oscar De Priest was elected from Chicago (1929–1935) as a Republican, at the tail end of the African American alignment with the GOP. He was the first African American in the House in almost thirty years, reflecting Chicago's status as the largest concentration of recent African American migrants. He was succeeded by two other Blacks between 1929 and 1970, both Democrats. New York (Adam Clayton Powell in 1945) and Detroit (Charles Diggs in 1955) were not far behind (Barker et al. 1999, 258). But perhaps the single most important catalyzing national event was A. Philip Randolph's march on Washington. As a precursor to the street movement that was to come, Randolph proposed the march in 1941 to protest discrimination in hiring, precipitating an almost immediate response from President Franklin D. Roosevelt. An executive order was issued establishing the Fair Employment Practices Committee (Blaustein and Zangrando 1968, 356). Although this order was limited in scope, it represented a new level of influence by the new Democratic coalition that included an emerging African American voting bloc.

The New Democratic Coalition

The new Democratic coalition became much more solid through the World War II effort. When Truman assumed the presidency after Roosevelt's death, he initiated the broadest proposals of a civil rights nature since the Emancipation Proclamation. He established the Civil Rights Committee by executive order, which issued a set of civil rights proposals in 1946 in response to entreaties from civil rights forces. The overall initiative did not get through Congress, but Truman issued an executive order integrating the federal service, thus incorporating some of the committee's ideas (Blaustein and Zangrando 1968, 374). Later the Democratic Party avowedly acknowledged these new constituents at its national convention in 1948 with a civil rights plank. This precipitated the famous Dixiecrat revolt of southern Democrats, who followed Strom Thurmond out of the party (Ladd and Hadley 1978).

A Full-Blown Civil Rights Movement

The range of opportunities created by Supreme Court successes and the emerging civil rights coalition came to a head in a sustained social and political movement from about 1954 to 1970. It was the period of mobilization politics in the South (Morrison 1987) that yielded a groundswell of insurgency (McAdam 1982), which broke down many of the barriers of Jim Crow and disfranchisement. One of its major catalysts was the Montgomery Bus Boycott of 1956, which was built from a network of NAACP members. It also launched Martin Luther King Jr., who became the charismatic de facto leader of a broad coalition of forces that constituted the civil rights movement. Theirs was a campaign centered in the streets and in courthouses throughout the South for almost fifteen years. In the process the political currents evolved from integration to several varieties of nationalism, some making radical critiques of the American social order.

Although none of the currents were new, their deployment reached a new intensity and a high if sometimes fractured level of integration. The NAACP (Kellogg 1967) and the Urban League (Weiss 1974) remained the chief proponents of integration into the marketplace of plural interests, forcing the American polity to allocate to African Americans the benefits of the espoused democratic ideals. Legalism and lobbying remained their chief strategies. Martin Luther King Jr. and a smattering of other organizations, such as the Congress of Racial Equality (CORE) (Meier and Rudwick 1973) and the Student Nonviolent Coordinating Committee (SNCC) (Carson 1981), committed to developing a social movement, using the mobilization of Black and related forces to challenge the racial order. Many of these at the outset had goals not unlike those of the NAACP, but their focus on grassroots organization and mobilization led to very different tactics. Public demonstration and confrontation of authorities were more common. As events evolved, most of these groups developed a critique of the American democratic model, arguing that the prospects for the fundamental reallocation of resources to African Americans were not good. Some, like King, found institutionalized racism to be intractable (Fairclough 1987).

Some organizations, such as SNCC and the Black Panthers (Foner 1970), argued that capitalist democracy was inherently incapable of effectively integrating African Americans into the political system. The system thrived, they argued, on the existence of a reservoir of hierarchically lower-ranking laborers, African Americans. It was this combination of organizations and their complex of ideas and strategies that fueled the most important political mobilization of African Americans in the history of the republic.

As this conflict expanded and the general public became more engaged, changes began to occur in both the social and the political status of African Americans. A balance sheet of this period, which continues through the present, includes major legislation, court rulings with broader implications for civil liberties and civil rights, and the election of African American politicians in the South. These changes were the most substantive in 100 years for the restoration of African American rights. These gains, like those in periods of success in the past, remained the product of sustained struggle against avowed misapplication of the law from time to time and ambivalence about the rights of African Americans.

Allies in the White House and Congress

The changes wrought in the public law, all sanctioned by favorable Supreme Court interpretations, were some of the most far-reaching in history. They began with the establishment of a weak Civil Rights Commission in 1957 (see Blaustein and Zangrando 1968, 471) by a Congress controlled by the Democratic Party and agreed to by President Dwight D. Eisenhower. The commission was designed to collect information on voting irregularities but had no enforcement powers. Soon after that came the passage of the Civil Rights Act of 1960, the first of the Kennedy administration, during a time when the president enjoyed a majority in Congress. This legislation went further in authorizing federal monitors to settle disputes in the exercise of the franchise by African Americans and to compile information that could be used by the Justice Department in bringing court actions against violators of voting laws. Then in 1964 came the passage of the comprehensive Civil Rights Act (see Smith and Zangrando 1968, 524), noted most for its coverage of public accommodations in a broad range of social and educational spheres and the reaffirmation of voting rights as guaranteed by the Fifteenth Amendment. This legislation provided for significant sanctions against violators.

But it remained for another law, the Voting Rights Act of 1965, regarded by many as the single most important piece of legislation in this period, to specify enforcement and implementation strategies for a specific set of states in the South—along with Alaska—where irregularities had been documented (see Smith and Zangrando 1968, 567). Federal registrars were deployed to the region to implement the electoral registration of African Americans, resulting almost immediately in rapidly increasing registration rates.

These changes in public law were buttressed, indeed spearheaded, by the clearest executive support of African American political participation and social inclusion of any time since the Civil War. Despite a slim electoral mandate, President Kennedy issued civil rights speeches and took the remarkable step of publicly seeking the release of Martin Luther King Jr. from one of his numerous jailings. The Civil Rights Act of 1960 had his support, and he promised further actions. Amid tremendous turmoil in the streets, with protests and anti-Black violence and assassinations in the South, Kennedy oversaw the crafting of the Civil Rights Act of 1964. It was on the heels of the largest civil rights March on Washington in 1963 and the president's assassination that the legislation was passed the following year. Its passage was secured under the guidance of perhaps the strongest presidential proponent of civil rights in history, Lyndon B. Johnson. The following year, the even stronger Voting Rights Act was passed, and soon afterward, Johnson initiated his War on Poverty, a public policy companion to the array of legislation now on the books. Meanwhile, the intense mobilization continued from the "long hot summer" of 1964 through a cycle of race riots preceding and following the assassination of Martin Luther King Jr. in 1968.

The Southern Axis: Blacks with the Franchise

Social and political changes for African Americans soon became visible in many sectors. The limits of open public accommodation were everywhere being tested as Blacks challenged the Jim Crow system. But the greatest political changes seemed to be a product of specific acts designed to exercise the vote. It was perfectly obvious from the changes in voter registration that the huge concentration of African Americans in the southern states could have a major impact on elections in the regions. For example, in 1940 the disfranchisement of Blacks was almost complete in some states. Less than 1 percent of eligible voters case ballots in Mississippi, Alabama, South Carolina, and

Louisiana; less than 5 percent voted in Arkansas, Florida, and Georgia; and only in North Carolina and Tennessee did registrations surpass the 10 percent mark. By 1947 improvements had been made, but they were minimal; only Tennessee registered more than 20 percent of Blacks who were eligible to vote (Martin 1967, 18).

The progress of voter registration among African Americans in the South was very slow. Only 3 percent of them were registered in 1940. In five years registration barely reached 12 percent. By 1952 it reached 20 percent, but remained virtually flat until 1964. The civil rights movement mobilization had a major impact that showed up in voter registration attempts by 1963, and that showed in a substantial growth in enrollment of Black voters by 1964 (nearly 42 percent). Already these voters were having an impact on presidential politics because they voted overwhelmingly for Lyndon Johnson, who had given strong support to the civil rights agenda. With the Voting Rights Act in 1965 these figures began to climb rapidly. More than half of the eligible population of Blacks was registered by 1966. Nearly 70 percent of the population was registered by 1970. Registration dropped off somewhat in the mid-1970s, but climbed again in the presidential years when Jesse Jackson was a candidate (Jaynes and Williams 1989, 233).

A Second Reconstruction: Electoral Politics

The second great period in the election of Black officials in U.S. history began around the same time. Georgia appeared to be the first when Leroy Johnson was elected to the state senate in 1962. Johnson stood alone until two years later when two more Blacks were elected—another to the senate and one as a city councilman in Augusta. When Alabama entered the picture in 1964, it elected the widest range of officials to date, establishing what was to be a prelude to the most sustained electoral success of African Americans ever in the South. That year two Blacks were elected mayors of small towns, and others were elected as city council and school board representatives and justices of the peace. All of the southern states had elected African Americans to local and state offices by 1967, when the last holdouts, Mississippi and South Carolina, elected Blacks to local offices. There is some irony in the fact that it was in the two states that traditionally had the largest African American populations that the election of Blacks took the longest in this new period of mobilization (Civil Rights Commission 1967, 214ff).

The registration of African Americans and mobilization by other means continued apace in the South. The federal registrars were peculiarly successful in changing the patterns of discrimination that Fannie Lou Hamer (Mills 1993) and Unita Blackwell (Morrison 1987) described when they initially attempted to register in their towns. The high levels of registration among African Americans was changing the electoral landscape in virtually all of the former Confederate states, with the effect that the Democratic Party of the "solid" segregationist South was now finding it necessary to make its peace with Blacks, or face dissolution.

Nowhere was the struggle for the control of the party more dramatic than in Mississippi. A third party organization, the Mississippi Freedom Democratic Party (MFDP), challenged the credentials of the state Democratic Party at the national conventions of both 1964 and 1968. MFDP succeeded in removing those credentials in 1968, and then went on to negotiate a new version of the party, which was led by an African American for some years (Walton 1972b).

The scope of the mobilization soon expanded when, as during the post–Civil War Reconstruction, African Americans were elected as representatives to Congress. Representatives were elected in Texas and Georgia in 1973 and in Tennessee in 1975. There was then a relatively long gap before Blacks were elected in other states—Mississippi in 1987, Louisiana in 1991, and Alabama, Florida, the Carolinas, and Virginia in 1993. At the same time, high-profile large cities in the region—Atlanta (1973), New Orleans (1977), and Birmingham (1979)—all elected African American mayors.

The pattern was repeating itself all over the country in places where African Americans were concentrated. The greater share of early representation elsewhere in the country was in the election of members of Congress. Joining the group of representatives in Washington from constituencies in Chicago, Detroit, and Harlem were others from Philadelphia, Los Angeles, the border state of Maryland, Brooklyn, and Queens. Several states in fact sent several Black representatives. In a number of major cities, the concentration of African American led to the election of Black mayors; among the first were Cleveland, Gary, and Newark. By the late 1990s African Americans had determined or greatly influenced the election of Black mayors in virtually every major American city, including Chicago, Detroit, St. Louis, New York, Philadelphia, Baltimore, and Oakland. African Americans were also well represented in smaller places too. The range of offices held elsewhere easily matched those in the South, although the latter region was home to most Black officials. The total number of Black elected officials in 1970 was 1,469, and by 2000 it had risen to 9,040 ("Number of Black Elected Officials, by Year and Gender, 1970–2000" 2000). Such increases have been occurring steadily in a wide range of positions from the federal level (members of Congress) to the local level (such as on school boards). However, as substantial as these increases are, in none of the states with large African American populations or significant urban concentrations is representation anywhere near proportionate to the voting-age base. Fuller discussion of African American political organizations, elections, and offices are presented in chapters 3, 4, and 5.

Conclusion

The general overview provided in this chapter of the role of African Americans in the U.S. political process has illustrated how political scientists have organized their work in explaining the phenomenon, provided a demographic description of the community and its resource foundations, and surveyed its resultant political activities. The chapter also showed that African American politics is characterized by a continuing struggle against racism and discrimination and their residual effects. These efforts have been composed of a combination of resistance, a plethora of ideological currents, and political activism. The various phases of this drive for universal inclusion in the political process has been documented over the republic's several hundred years of history, showing its ebbs and flows amid general changes in the American political environment.

The balance of this volume will provide more detailed discussions of specific aspects of these political events and processes. In chapter 2, Hanes Walton discusses varieties of protest politics; in chapter 3, Lawrence Hanks provides a discussion of independent political organizations; in chapter 4, Byron Orey and Reginald Vance discuss electoral politics; and in chapter 5, Richard Middleton and I discuss African Americans in political offices.

References

Aptheker, Herbert. 1942. *American Negro Slave Revolts*. New York: International.
Balandier, Georges. 1965. "The Colonial Situation." In Pierre van den Berghe, ed., *Africa: Social Problems in Conflict and Change*, 36–57. San Francisco: Chandler.

Barker, Lucius, et al. 1999. *African Americans and the American Political System.* Saddle River, NJ: Prentice-Hall.

Barnett, Marguerite Ross. 1976. "Introduction." In Marguerite Ross Barnett and James Hefner, eds., *Public Policy for the Black Community,* 1–54. New York: Alfred.

Beard, Charles. 1913. *An Economic Interpretation of the American Constitution.* New York: Macmillan.

Bennett, Lerone. 1967. *Black Power, U.S.A.* Chicago: Johnson Publishing.

Berry, Mary Frances, and John Blassingame. 1982. *Long Memory.* New York: Oxford University Press.

Blalock, Hubert, Jr. 1967. *Toward a Theory of Minority Group Relations.* New York: Wiley.

Blassingame, John. 1979. *The Slave Community.* New York: Oxford University Press.

Blaustein, Albert, and Clarence Ferguson, Jr. 1962. *Desegregation and the Law: The Meaning and Effect of the School Desegregation Cases.* 2d ed. New York: Vintage.

Blaustein, Albert, and Robert Zangrando, eds. 1968. *Civil Rights and the Black American.* New York: Clarion.

Blyden, Edward. 1971. "The Call of Providence to the Descendants of Africa in America." In Okon Edet Uya, ed., *Black Brotherhood: Afro-Americans and Africa,* 83–95. Lexington, MA: D. C. Heath.

Bracey, John, et al., eds. 1970. *Black Nationalism in America.* Indianapolis, IN: Bobbs-Merrill.

Bullock, Henry A. 1967. *A History of Negro Education in the South.* Cambridge, MA: Harvard University Press.

Carmichael, Stokely, and Charles Hamilton. 1967. *Black Power.* New York: Vintage.

Carson, Clayborne. 1981. *In Struggle.* Cambridge, MA: Harvard University Press.

Civil Rights Commission. 1967. *Political Participation.* Washington, DC: Government Printing Office.

Crummell, Alexander. 1971. "The Relations and Duties of Free Colored Men in America to Africa." In Okon Edet Uya, ed., *Black Brotherhood: Afro-Americans and Africa,* 63–70. Lexington, MA: D. C. Heath.

Cruse, Harold. 1967. *The Crisis of the Negro Intellectual.* New York: William Morrow.

Curtin, Philip. 1969. *The Atlantic Slave Trade.* Madison: University of Wisconsin Press.

Dahl, Robert. 1961. *Who Governs?* New Haven, CT: Yale University Press.

Davis, Angela. 1981. *Women, Race, and Class.* New York: Vintage.

Dawson, Michael. 1994. *Behind the Mule.* Princeton, NJ: Princeton University Press.

———. 2001. *Black Visions.* Chicago: University of Chicago Press.

Dolbeare, Kenneth, and Murray Edelman. 1979. *American Politics.* 3d ed. Lexington, MA: D. C. Heath.

DuBois, W.E.B. 1962. *Black Reconstruction in America: An Essay toward a History of the Part Which Black Folk Played in the Attempt to Reconstruct Democracy in America, 1860–1880.* New York: Russell and Russell.

———. 1965. *The Suppression of the African Slave Trade.* New York: Russell and Russell.

———. 1969. *Black Reconstruction in America, 1860–1890.* New York: Meridian Books.

———. 1989. *The Souls of Black Folk.* New York: Penguin.

Easton, David. 1965. *A Systems Analysis of Political Life.* New York: John Wiley.

Fairclough, Adam. 1987. *To Redeem the Soul of America.* Athens: University of Georgia Press.

Foner, Philip, ed. 1970. *The Black Panthers Speak.* Philadelphia: Lippincott.

Franklin, John Hope, and Alfred Moss Jr. 1994. *From Slavery to Freedom.* New York: McGraw-Hill.

Garvey, Marcus, Amy J. Garvey, and Ann Jacques-Garvey. 1986. *The Philosophy and Opinions of Marcus Garvey, Or, Africa for the Africans.* Dover, MA: Majority Press.

Gutman, Herbert. 1976. *The Black Family in Slavery and Freedom.* New York: Vintage.

Hacker, Andrew. 1992. *Two Nations.* New York: Macmillan.

Harding, Vincent. 1983. *There Is a River.* New York: Vintage.

Harlan, Louis R. 1972. *Booker T. Washington: The Making of a Black Leader, 1856–1901.* New York: Oxford University Press.

Harrison, Roderick. 2001. "Numbers Running." *Crisis: Politics, Culture, and the Church* 19 (May/June): 14–17.

Hearn, Kimberly, and Lisa Jackson. 2002. "African Women and HIV Risk: Exploring the Effects of Gender and Social Dynamics on Behavior." *African American Research Perspectives: Occasional Reports* 8 (1): 163–173. Ann Arbor: University of Michigan Press.

Hine, Darlene Clark. 1979. *Black Victory.* Millwood, NY: KTO Press.

Holt, Thomas. 1977. *Black Over White.* Urbana: University Press of Illinois.

———. 1982. "The Lonely Warrior: Ida B. Wells-Barnett and the Struggle for Leadership." In John Hope Franklin and August Meier, eds., *Black Leaders in the Twentieth Century,* 39–62. Urbana: University Press of Illinois.

Jaynes, Gerald, and Robin Williams Jr., eds. 1989. *Common Destiny: Blacks and American Society.* Washington, DC: National Academy Press.

Jones, Mack. 1972. "A Frame of Reference for Black Politics." In Lenneal Henderson Jr., ed., *Black Political Life in the United States,* 7–20. San Francisco: Chandler.

Kaplan, H. Roy. 1977. *American Minorities and Economic Opportunity.* Itasca, IL: Peacock.

Kellogg, Charles. 1967. *NAACP.* Baltimore: Johns Hopkins University Press.

Kraditor, Aileen. 1969. *Means and Ends in American Abolitionism.* New York: Pantheon.

Ladd, Everett C., Jr., and Charles Hadley. 1978. *Transformations of the American Party System.* 2d ed. New York: W. W. Norton.

Lewis, David. 1993. *W.E.B. DuBois: Biography of a Race.* New York: Henry Holt.

Lipscomb, Anne S., and Kathleen Hutchinson. 1994. *Tracing Your Mississippi Ancestors.* Jackson: University Press of Mississippi.

Logan, Rayford. 1972. *The Betrayal of the Negro.* New York: Collier.

Lynch, John R. 1913. *The Facts of Reconstruction.* New York: Neale.

Martin, Robert. 1967. "The Relative Political Status of the Negro in the United States." In Harry Bailey Jr., ed., *Negro Politics in America,* 13–33. Columbus, OH: Charles Merrill.

McAdam, Doug. 1982. *Political Process and the Development of Black Insurgency.* Chicago: University of Chicago Press.

McMillen, Neil. 1990. *Dark Journey.* Urbana: University Press of Illinois.

McNeil, Genna Rae. 1983. *Groundwork.* Philadelphia: University of Pennsylvania Press.

Meier, August, and Elliott Rudwick. 1966. *From Plantation to Ghetto.* New York: Hill and Wang.

———. 1973. CORE: A Study in the Civil Rights Movement. New York: Oxford University Press.

Meyer, Michael, ed. 1984. *Frederick Douglass: The Narratives and Selected Writings.* New York: Modern Library.

Miller, Jake. 1978. *The Black Presence in American Foreign Affairs.* Washington, DC: University Press of America.

Mills, Kay. 1993. *This Little Light of Mine: The Life of Fannie Lou Hamer.* New York: Dutton.

Morris, Aldon. 1984. *The Origins of the Civil Rights Movement.* New York: The Free Press.

Morris, Milton. 1975. *The Politics of Black America.* New York: Harper and Row.

Morrison, Minion K. C. 1987. *Black Political Mobilization.* Albany: State University of New York Press.

Moynihan, Daniel P. 1965. *The Negro Family.* Washington, DC: Government Printing Office.

National Advisory Commission on Civil Disorders. 1968. Report of the National Advisory Commission on Civil Disorders. New York: Bantam.

Nobles, Melissa. 2000. *Shades of Citizenship: Race and the Census in Modern Politics.* Palo Alto, CA: Stanford University Press.

"Number of Black Elected Officials, by Year and Gender, 1970–2000." 2000. Joint Center for Political and Economic Studies. Available at http://www.jointcenter.org.

Omi, Michael, and Howard Winant. 1994. *Racial Formation in the United States from the 1960s to the 1990s.* New York: Routledge.

Park, Robert. 1950. *Race and Culture.* New York: The Free Press.

Parker, Freddie. 1993. *Running for Freedom: Slave Runaways in North Carolina, 1775–1840.* New York: Garland.

Pinderhughes, Dianne. 1987. *Race and Ethnicity in Chicago Politics.* Urbana: University Press of Illinois.

Putnam, Robert. 1993. *Making Democracy Work.* Princeton, NJ: Princeton University Press.

Quarles, Benjamin. 1969. *The Black Abolitionists.* New York: Oxford University Press.

———. 1982. "A. Philip Randolph: Labor Leader at Large." In John H. Franklin and August Meier, eds., *Black Leaders of the Twentieth Century.* Urbana: University Press of Illinois.

Raboteau, Albert. 1978. *Slave Religion.* New York: Oxford University Press.

Reed, Adolph, Jr. 1971. "Marxism and Nationalism in Afroamerica." *Social Theory and Practice* 1 (Fall): 1–39.

Robinson, Cedric. 1983. *Black Marxism.* London: Zed Press.

Scott, James. 1985. *Weapons of the Weak: The Everyday Forms of Peasant Resistance.* New Haven, CT: Yale University Press.

Sears, David, et al. 2000. *Racialized Politics: The Debate About Racism in America.* Chicago: University of Chicago Press.

Shick, Tom. 1977. *Behold the Promised Land.* Madison: University of Wisconsin Press.

Sidanius, Jim, and Felicia Pratto. 1999. *Social Dominance: An Intergroup Theory of Social Hierarchy and Oppression.* New York: Cambridge University Press.

Sidanius, James, and John Petrocik. 2000. "Communal and National Identity in a Multiethnic State: A Comparison of Three Perspectives." Unpublished manuscript, Feb. 2000.

Siebert, Wilbur. 1968. *The Underground Railroad from Slavery to Freedom.* New York: Arno.

Skinner, Elliott. 1992. *African Americans and U.S. Foreign Policy Toward Africa, 1850–1924: In Defense of Black Nationality.* Washington, DC: Howard University Press.

Stanley, Harold W., and Richard G. Niemi. 2000. *Vital Statistics on American Politics, 1999–2000.* Washington, DC: Congressional Quarterly Press.

Starobin, Robert. 1969. Lecture at University of Wisconsin, Madison, Wisconsin, March 10.

Truman, David. 1951. *The Governmental Process.* New York: Knopf.

Tushnet, Mark. 1994. *Making Civil Rights Law: Thurgood Marshall.* New York: Oxford University Press.

Walton, Hanes, Jr. 1972a. *Black Politics.* Philadelphia: Lippincott.

———. 1972b. *Black Political Parties.* New York: The Free Press.

Walton, Hanes Jr., and Robert Smith. 2000. *American Politics and the African American Quest for Universal Freedom.* New York: Longman.

Washington, Booker T. [1901] 1995. *Up from Slavery.* Dover, MA: Majority Press.

Weiss, Nancy. 1974. *The National Urban League.* New York: Oxford University Press.

Williams, Eric. 1961. *Capitalism and Slavery.* New York: Russell and Russell.

Woodward, C. Vann. 1955. *The Strange Career of Jim Crow.* New York: Oxford University Press.

2

Protest Politics

Hanes Walton Jr.

R esistance and oppositional activities have long characterized African American political participation in the United States. Protest politics has therefore been a defining feature of African American political expression. Since the Africans who arrived in the Americas came largely involuntarily as enslaved persons, they and their descendants have continuously struggled, first to abolish slavery and then to acquire regular citizen status within the social and political community. However, despite the abolition of slavery, its residuals of exclusion and discrimination have rarely allowed African Americans the comfort of universal freedom. Therefore much of the political activity associated with the group has occurred in the context of their opposition to unequal status. They have resisted what is seen as both the systemic and the individualized aspects of a racialized hierarchy that ranks them below others. This resistance has most often occurred via protest—public objections within and outside legal frameworks for interest articulation.

This chapter first details how political scientists misconceptualized the problem of African American protest. Then the discussion reviews analyses that have been especially useful in providing a framework for studying oppositional political behavior. In the analysis of protest as a vehicle for African American participation, this chapter provides a broad historical overview, beginning with the earliest participation and ending with the present. The phases considered include colonial and revolutionary America, slavery, abolition, the Civil War era, Reconstruction, the Jim Crow era of segregation, the social mobilization that began after World War I and culminated in a social movement in the 1950s, and the present-day clientage politics of neoconservatism.

Political Science and African American Protest

The Minimization of Protest as Political Activity

American politics has long been described as a group-based system. In this conceptualization of political activity, acts of political participation by both interest groups and individuals have been central. However, political science has seldom been able to conceptualize oppositional interest group protest activity as within the traditional bounds of political participation. This means that since its inception in 1885 and its subsequent institutionalization in 1903, political science as a discipline has rarely conceptualized African American political protest as either interest group politics or as a routine mode of political participation.

When the discipline has analyzed African American participation such as that of the 1960s, the participation has been seen as aberrant or as marginal to general theories of interest group politics or other explanations within the discipline. In the main this is because such protest expressions have been deemed more as acts of insurgency or deviations from mainstream political behavior. This conceptualization of the field where protest politics is minimized as a variety of participation has seriously undermined the role and the study of African Americans as political participants. The approach has had a particularly negative impact on the analysis of Blacks, because protest was frequently the only means of political expression available to them. They were long denied access to the routine structures and processes for articulation of their interests, and they opted for resistance and protest as a means of acquiring any political voice. This analytic minimization of protest as participation ironically increased the dearth of analysis of Black political participation after the Civil War. Despite the theoretical acquisition of universal freedom, protest remained the most effective means of political expression because of continued racial exclusion. The minimization of protest has characterized many methodological approaches in political science—traditionalism, behavioralism, rational choice, and new institutionalism. The traditionalist school defined African American protest politics as simply outside the American political process, essentially describing it as a civil rights social movement. By this view it was a more appropriate topic for sociologists than for political scientists (Truman 1951). The behavioralists, who used the individual as the unit of analysis, almost dismissed African American protest. They declared that protests reflected the work of disgruntled and radical fringe operatives that would quickly fade because they did not understand how the American political system worked (Walker 1991, 42–45; Wilson 1961, 291–303). The proponents of the rational choice model argue that the demands and other activities of African American protest groups and organizations are too particularistic and the strategies too uncompromising to succeed in a pluralist and gradualist democratic system, where political action has a rational, material base (Crowley and Skocpol 2001, 816; Skocpol et al. 2001). Finally, the new institutionalist school views both interest group politics and political participation as a form of civic volunteerism that engenders community engagement that sustains American democracy. In this approach, aggregated historical data are used to track the impact of civic engagement on politics. Unfortunately, in analyzing African American political engagement, the new institutionalists have severely limited the scope of the historical data, starting with the Civil War as its first instance, because prior information is too fragmentary. This ignores much of African American protest politics before the war. Aggregating data in this manner misses the vital texture of this formally excluded group.

All four approaches tend to interpret African American protest politics in two basic ways that fail to account for participation. First, African American political protest is explained as unconventional political behavior, thus easily dismissed. When not interpreted in this way, it is explained as a short-lived political insurgency, little more than a political fad. Both interpretations fail to situate African American protest politics in either of the general theoretical conceptualizations of the discipline—the interest group or political participation categories. Ironically, when protest is treated in these categories, it is seen not as routine group or lobbying politics, but as an ancillary or inchoate political resource development (Lipsky 1968). Such resource groups are seen as notoriously fractionalized and ineffective in influencing governmental outcomes. Largely, then, these conceptualizations leave African American protest politics bereft of a legitimate place in the political process, denying its important role as an independent force for reform and participation.

Protest as Parochialism

Let us look at some political scientists at work as they seek to explain the phenomenon of African American participation. Several scholars use such a narrow conceptualization of politics that African American protest is reduced to what they call a "single" and parochial political resource. Notwithstanding the African American organizational base and following routine political exclusion, protest is deemed to be outside the normal bidding process for public resources. In effect, this delegitimizes protest actions that seek redress of the fundamental rights and policy grievances that African Americans have against government. Perhaps unintentionally, this approach also renders unnecessary any governmental response to such protests. For example, James Q. Wilson (1961) said that African American protest activity must be conceived "as a problem of bargaining in which the basic problem is that Negro groups lack political resources to exchange." Michael Lipsky, using Wilson as a foundation, goes further in suggesting that it is the very nature of protest that makes for this problem: it is a result of protesters' having to appeal to four constituencies at once.

> As the concept of protect is developed here, it will be argued that protest leaders must nurture and sustain an organization comprising people with whom they may or may not share common values. They must articulate goals and choose strategies so as to maximize their public exposure through communications media. They must maximize the impact of third parties in the political conflict. Finally, they must try to maximize the chances of success among those capable of granting goals. The tensions inherent in manipulating these four constituencies at the same time form the basis of this discussion of protest as a political process (Lipsky 1968, 1144).

Lipsky concludes that "relatively powerless groups cannot use protest with a high probability of success. They lack organizational resources, by definition" (1157). He also notes that "the tensions which must be embraced by protest leadership may ultimately overwhelm protest activity" (1154), because African American protest groups are often rife with instability. In short, all the barriers that militate against this group's becoming a viable political resource re-

side within the African American community. There is little acknowledgment of the factors within the political system, the government, and the society that militate against the use of alternative
means of participation by African Americans.

Protest Voting: An Ineffectual Political Resource

Some scholars who studied African American voting behavior also
saw this kind of participation as essentially aberrant and ineffectual.
The work of William Keech is an example. His inductive and empiri-
cally based examination of African American registration and voting
in Durham, North Carolina, and Tuskegee, Alabama, while a different
approach, corroborates the earlier deductive findings of Wilson and
Lipsky (Keech 1968, 12–23). His study begins with the statement that
"various groups . . . have sought the vote on the grounds that it is an
important resource in the implementation of their preferences and
the recognition of their interests, as well as their worth as persons"
(3). Then he explores the following questions: "What is the impact of
the Negro vote on the outputs of a local political system, and what is
the relationship between the vote as a manifestation of formal political power and other forms and sources of social and political power?
Most importantly, is the vote able to achieve major social and economic of gains for the deprived group?" (7).

Basically Keech wanted to test whether the African American vote
was a useful and viable political resource. He determined this by separately measuring public- and private-sector outcomes. His conclusion was that nowhere is this activity seen as inherently important to
the general American political participation process. Even when his
empirical evidence at least partially contradicts this view, he persists
in seeing African American voting as ancillary to the broader American context. Here is what he found in the public sector:

> In Tuskegee, Negro votes have had a clear and direct effect on who is
> elected to public office, on street paving and garbage collection in Ne-
> gro areas, on recreation, Library and hospital facilities available to Ne-
> groes, and on who is chosen to appointive boards and civil service po-
> sitions . . . . Votes have been for the most part irrelevant to welfare and
> unemployment policy.
>
> In Durham, Negro votes have had a demonstrable impact on who is
> elected to public office, on the distribution of fire stations and recre-
> ation facilities and on the decision to have urban renewal. . . . Negro

votes have been irrelevant in street paving, welfare and unemployment policy. (Keech 1968, 78–79)

The impact of the vote on the private sector was even less, because it provided no relief for the continued effects of the past 300 years of racial discrimination (Keech 1968, 91–92). He concludes, "If social justice demands the eradication of the effects of past discrimination, the vote is even less useful" (101). In the final analysis, he agrees with Wilson and Lipsky that the African American vote is a "defensive" tool, or a resource with which to gain some specific group welfare benefits but not sufficient to substantively alter their differential status. "The most frustrating problem of the American Negro in politics is that even if elected policy-makers were responsive to Negro demands, it is not all clear that they have it in their power to eliminate the inequality with which three and a half centuries of discrimination have saddled the American Negro" (109).

The Pluralist Notion That Power Is Everywhere

The pluralist explanation also failed, despite its thesis that all groups possess the ability to influence government outcomes. Michael Parenti undertook a study of protest groups in city politics to determine whether, as pluralist theorists suggested, all groups did indeed have such access to power. He looked at the outcomes obtained by three African American protest groups in Newark, New Jersey, in three issue areas: housing, urban traffic, and electoral empowerment (Parenti 1970). He modeled his research on the pluralist approach used by Robert Dahl in *Who Governs?* (1961), a study of New Haven, Connecticut. Parenti found that the African American protest groups were thoroughly unsuccessful in all three issue areas.

Despite disproving the predictions of the pluralists, he nevertheless fell into the trap of Wilson and the others. He wrote that "the problem with most lower-strata groups is that they have few political resources of their own to exchange" (518). Expanding on Wilson, he continued:

NCUP's [Newark Community Union Project's] protest action failed to create the kinds of inducements that would have made it in the political leaders' interest to take positive measures. The withholding of rent payments, the street-corner demonstrations, the momentary disruptions of traffic and the feeble electoral challenge were treated by the politicians of Newark not as bargaining resources but as minor nuisances that were not to be allowed to develop into major threats. (528)

The Influence of Sociological Explanation on Political Theories

The conceptual problems noted above likely result from an overreliance on theories adopted by sociologists, who were wont to study African American behavior in the context of social movements. A host of sociologists argued "that collective behavior differs from everyday organizational and institutional behavior in that it arises in response to unusual situations . . . [such as] . . . periods of rapid social change or crises . . . [such as] . . . urbanization, modernization, industrialization, and natural disasters" (Morris 1984, 275). To this basic premise, sociologists have added that such behavior is:

> relatively spontaneous rather than planned; largely unstructured rather than organized; emotional rather than reasoned; nonrational rather than rational; and spread by crude, elementary forms of communication such as circular reaction, rumor, imitation, social contagious, and generalized belief rather than preestablished formed and informed communication networks. (Morris 1984, 276)

With this reasoning, political scientists did not have to go far to conclude that the oppositional protest activity of African Americans was aberrant and not conducive to attaining real influence in the political system. Lipsky does argue that protest could sometimes leverage modest influence by aligning with "third parties"(powerful interest groups) that "enter the implicit or explicit bargaining arena in ways favorable to the protesters" (Lipsky 1968, 1144–1145). In short, African American success was dependent on the sponsorship of institutionalized white interest groups.

An Alternative Model: Resource Mobilization

When these theoretical models strained to account for the civil rights movement activities of the 1950s and 1960s, a modified model emerged—"resource mobilization." This approach suggests that "it is the ability of groups to organize, mobilize, and manage valuable resources that determines whether they will be able to emerge in social protest" (Morris 1984, 279). Protests were not conceived of as actions by isolated individuals, but rather as actions by collections of contenders with similar political interests engaged in the democratic process. The political sociologist Doug McAdam began with the assertion that "social movements are *collected* phenomena . . ., [because] isolated individuals do not emerge, band together, and form movement groups. Rather . . . it is within established interactional networks that social movements develop" (McAdam 1982, 15).

He was among the earliest to use this approach, which he called the "political process model" of mobilization (McAdam 1982). He conceptualized the model as having two basic features. First, "a social movement is held to be above all else a *political* rather then a psychological phenomenon." Second, "a movement represents a continuous *process* from generation to decline, rather than a discrete series of developmental stages" (36). The factors that drive this process are the presence of local contentions, an activated indigenous leadership, a heightened perception of grievances, and one or more events that precipitate a crisis. McAdam then proceeded to analyze recent African American political "insurgency" to illustrate the viability of the model.

Another political sociologist, Aldon Morris, quickly followed, showing the importance of indigenous resources and organization for the initiation of movements. He asserted that "indigenous resources are far more likely to be crucial in the early phases of movements, because outside resources tend to be sporadic and highly conditional, in most cases coming in response to pressure from indigenous movements already under way" (Morris 1984, 283). Moreover, deliberate action is important because "the presence of indigenous resources within a dominated community does not ensure that a movement will emerge. . . . [M]ovements are deliberately organized and developed by activists who seize and create opportunities for protest. Social activists . . . play creative roles in organizing and developing movements; they must redirect and transform indigenous resources in such a manner that they can be used to develop and sustain social protest" (Morris 1984, 283).

But activities and indigenous resources are not enough. The dominated group must develop "tactics and strategies that can be effectively used in confrontations with a system of domination." Such tactics and strategies enable "masses of people to generate widespread disruption of a social order. It is the widespread disruption of a society that generates the collective power of masses used by dominated groups in their struggle to redistribute power" (Morris 1984, 283). And although there is no formal bureaucratic structure through which this action is directed, Morris adds the concept of "movement centers," staging areas where important events occur and from which they are dispersed by "loosely organized groups." He sees the Student Nonviolent Coordinating Committee (SNCC) and the Southern Christian Leadership Conference (SCLC) as the equivalent of the requisite intermediate organizations for "mobilizing and coordinating protest by large numbers of people" (Morris 1984, 285).

These findings show the significance of protest activity to a general theory of African American participation within the confines of the American political community. Morris and his colleagues discovered that protest is not only a vital means of acquiring goods, but it is also a critical means of socialization of the community. They show that the manifestations of political protest in the civil rights movement politically socialized African Americans into an ever-evolving movement for universal freedom (Morris, Hatchett, and Brown 1989, 282ff). From this point of view, protests are much more than spontaneous and ephemeral acts; they serve the long-term function of training citizens for participation within the context of their given state. Protests are therefore fundamental to the participation of African Americans. It is this perspective of resource mobilization that guides the analysis of protest as a political activity by African Americans. The analysis below shows that this protest has been enduring in a political system in which the implementation of universal freedom has often been incomplete or, at times, completely undermined for African Americans. As such, protest and contentious action have been the only resort for meaningful political expression.

African American Protests: Colonial, Slavery, and Abolition Periods

This section documents African American protest politics from the colonial period to the present. Contrary to the conventional perspectives described above, here African American protest politics are conceptualized within the framework of interest group politics. The conceptualization begins with the simple assumption that African American protest and social movements are the foundation for fairly conventional interest group politics. Because these inchoate groups are viewed within the ambit of standard American interest groups, they are fundamentally linked to other political processes, and hence they are limited by, connected to, and interconnected with the general political system. Hence this analysis focuses on the origins, evolution, and linkage of these "unconventional" politics to the more conventional politics of interest group behavior. A policy dimension is also included to further clarify the essential nature of this expression to the American democratic process.

Political protest as defined here may be an individual or a group-based act and may be formally or informally organized. This definition includes social movements "understood as a group of persons organized in a sustained, self-conscious challenge to an existing, [sociopolitical] system and its values or power relationships." Individual or group actors may function as intraracial or interracial units, and they usually seek right-based policies, material-based policies, or both (Walton and Smith 2002, 89–90).

Protests in Colonial and Revolutionary America

There was considerable African American political protest in colonial and revolutionary America, despite the small numbers of free Blacks at the time. In both periods, African Americans were composed of two demographic groups that formed soon after the arrival of the first Africans in the American colonies. Within seven years after their arrival in Jamestown, Virginia, in 1619, the twenty Black indentured servants were given their freedom (Walton and Smith 2002). However, Virginia and Maryland led the way in establishing "perpetual servitude" for people of color, in 1661 and 1664, respectively. Most of the other colonies soon followed in establishing slavery as a sociopolitical system (Bennett 1985, 28–29). By the time this new system was completed, there were two African American population groups: those who were free and those who were slaves. By 1860, the free African American population numbered nearly half a million and the enslaved population just under 4 million.

Both groups faced similar exclusion and discrimination. Indeed, the status of the "free Blacks" was linked almost from the beginning to that of their enslaved kinsmen. John Hope Franklin has written:

> One looks in vain at the entire miserable period from the writing of the Constitution to the outbreak of the Civil War to find any indication

that the Founding Fathers, the fledgling government of the United States, or the great leaders of the nation in the first half of the nineteenth century pursued a policy looking toward any semblance of citizenship or equality for free black Americans. The terrible truth is that by the beginning of the Civil War the status of free black persons had deteriorated to the point that they were pariahs of the land, unwanted, virtually helpless, and with no substantial basis for relief or redress of grievances under the Constitution. (Franklin 1995, 28)

Despite the technical distinctions between the two groups, the similarity of their realities led both to engage in political protest from the colonial period to the Civil War. The freed men tended to engage in formally organized interest group politics insofar as they could get access to routine political structures. In the main their protest activity was aimed at their local colonial government. During the revolutionary and colonial periods their individual and social movement protests or interest group politics were aimed at the duly constituted local, state, and national officials. These efforts sometimes did result in certain public policies directed to the African American community.

Extant documents from colonial and revolutionary America reveal the scope of both individual and group political protests. Table 2.1 shows that from the colonial era to the 1830s free men and women of color engaged in at least twelve different types of political protest. There were numerous protests for freedom in both the North and the South, for obvious reasons.

All whites agreed that the free Negro must be kept in check. First and foremost of the controls required that he carry a certificate of freedom. . . . A Negro without "free papers" was treated, as a rule, as a runaway slave. Even with his paper credentials in order, a free Negro risked servitude if he fell behind in his taxes, incurred debts, or was arrested as a vagabond. (Fishel and Quarles 1967, 127)

Blacks could not testify in court against whites, were subject to curfews, and could not carry firearms. Almost always they were socially segregated, being relegated to reserved "Negro" sections in pews in church and in public transportation, and they could not reside in some states. Despite considerable engagement in craft trades in cities, they were denied membership in most trade unions. Therefore, as the data show, African Americans engaged in protests against all of these forms of discrimination and legal disabilities. In addition, these free men and women of color consistently protested against the institution of slavery, as it bound the majority of their family members and racial kin to servitude.

Table 2.1 also reveals that these acts were both individual and group based. Among these protests were written petitions, prayers, and memorials sent to a variety of authorities. We have a partial picture of policy outcomes: some petitions met with success, while the vast majority were simply turned down or denied. The political system seldom responded positively to these initiatives.

An illustrative sampling of these political protests, documented over nearly a 200-year period, reveals something of their character. First, women were perhaps as active as men. In 1827, an African American woman named Naval Matilda issued a protest demanding rights for Negro women. It was an eloquent statement for women's rights. Secondly, H. Ford Douglas, a critic of Abraham Lincoln, described how the state of Illinois would not allow him "to testify in a court of justice, where a white man is a party." In order to change this law, Douglas "went to prominent Republicans, and among others, to Abraham Lincoln and Lyman Trumbull, and neither of them dared to sign that petition, to give me the right to testify in a court of justice" (Fishel and Quarles 1967, 212–213). This reveals that while the scope of denial was broad indeed, African Americans often had a keen sense of political interest and an awareness of important figures in positions of power. For example, the entreaty to Lincoln seemed well placed in light of the rising stock of this future president.

Protests by Slaves

But the portrait of African American political protest sketched in Table 2.1 is only half the story. Table 2.2 summarizes the different types of political protest made by African American slaves between 1741 and 1841. Unlike free men and women of color, slaves engaged in only three types of political protest in colonial and revolutionary America. They protested for freedom and exhorted others to engage in uprisings or rebellions against slavery. At the same time, a smaller group of African Americans protested against freedom and informed on some of those who planned and attempted slave uprisings and rebellions. The Denmark Vesey rebellion in South Carolina in 1822 was suppressed as a result of such a betrayal. And in each instance of betrayal, the slaves who informed were richly rewarded. One informer "was rewarded by the state of South Carolina with $1,000. The in-

TABLE 2.1   Political Protest by African American Free People, 1661–1837

Colony/State	Year	Number	Type	Response
New Netherlands (New York)	1661	2	General freedom	Granted
Virginia	1676	1	General freedom	N/A
North Carolina	1773	1	General freedom	Denied
Massachusetts	1773	1[a]	Against taxation without the vote	Granted
Massachusetts	1787	MP	Equal educational facilities	Denied
Massachusetts	1788	MP	Against kidnapping and slave trade	Denied
South Carolina	1791	MP	Against court discrimination	Granted
South Carolina	1793	23	Against poll tax	Denied
South Carolina	1794	34	Against poll tax	Denied
Pennsylvania	1797	4	Against slavery and fugitive slave law	Denied
Pennsylvania	1800	MP	Against slavery and fugitive slave law	Denied
Virginia	1810	1	To purchase freedom for slaves	N/A
Virginia	1811	1	To purchase freedom for slaves	N/A
Virginia	1815	1	To purchase freedom for slaves	N/A
N/A	1827	1	For women's rights	N/A
New York	1808	1	Against slavery	N/A
Massachusetts	1808	1	Against slavery	N/A
New York	1809	1	Against slavery	N/A
Massachusetts	1829	1[a]	Against slavery	N/A
Pennsylvania	1813	1	Discriminatory laws	Granted
South Carolina	1823	1[b]	Discriminatory laws	Granted
Illinois	1858	1[a]	Discriminatory laws	Denied
New York	1813	1	Inferiority concept	N/A
Connecticut	1837	1[a]	Inferiority concept	N/A

MP, mass protest

[a] Data from Fishel and Quarles 1967, 37, 115–117, 138, 147, 212.

[b] Data from Blaustein and Zangrando 1991, 86–90.

SOURCE: Data from Aptheker 1951, 1–95, except as noted above.

former himself was freed and given an annual pension of $50, which was raised in 1857 to $200" (Aptheker 1943, 75).

Table 2.2 shows that, in addition to the various types of protests by slaves, such protests occurred in both northern and southern states and that they were just as continuous as protests by free men and women of color. Although these documented protests come primarily from Massachusetts and Virginia, they also occurred elsewhere in New England and in every southern state. Throughout the colonial and revolutionary periods and until the pre–Civil War era, slaves continued to petition local and state governments and Congress for their freedom. After 1836 their petitions before Congress were placed under the gag rule. As such they were tabled and no longer read aloud. Although "the gag rule was repealed in 1844" (Walton 1972, 143), at best the reading of a petition was just that, a reading without any action. Indeed, it can be seen that all of these protest petitions were denied except those coming from informers. Routinely informers were rewarded, and rebellions and uprisings by slaves were vigorously suppressed. What these data reveal is that both demographic groups of African Americans from the colonial era to 1830 consistently engaged in a variety of political protests given the political context of the day. And the data show only protests for which some documentation has survived. Many protests went undocumented, or the documentation has not survived. "The slave revolts and insurrections definitely attest to this reality" (Walton 1972, 19). But as some historians have pointed out, numerous slaves engaged in "day to day resistance to the slave institution . . . [by] running away" (Bauer and Bauer 1942, 388ff). So rampant were such occurrences that eventually the Fugitive Slave Law (1850) was passed as a means for searching for and returning runaways to their workplaces. There were also many acts of sabotage and disguised work slowdowns and stoppages. Hardly any of this sort of political protest was systematically recorded and documented. Even so, the surviving documents show unmistakably that protest was widespread.

Rebellions and Formal Organizations for Abolition

African American political protest took two new directions in the 1830s—the most substantial rebellion by slaves in the United States and the first organized effort by free persons. Although political protest by the free men and women of color received mixed responses, those of slaves were rarely acknowledged. Policy outputs to

TABLE 2.2   Political Protest by African American Slaves, 1741–1841

Colony/State	Year	Number	Type	Response
New York	1741	2	For freedom	Denied
Massachusetts	1743	MP	For freedom	Denied
Massachusetts	1773	4	For freedom	Denied
Massachusetts	1774	MP	For freedom	Denied
Massachusetts	1777	MP	For freedom	Denied
Connecticut	1779	2	For freedom	Denied
Kentucky	1834	1[a]	For freedom	Denied
Louisiana	1841	1	For freedom	Denied
Virginia	1793	1	Rebellious uprising	N/A
Virginia	1800	MP	Rebellious uprising	Suppressed
Virginia	1802	1	Rebellious uprising	Suppressed
North Carolina	1810	1	Rebellious uprising	Suppressed
Virginia	1810	1	Rebellious uprising	Suppressed
Virginia	1812	1	Rebellious uprising	Suppressed
South Carolina	1793	1	Against rebellions and insurrections	Acted upon
Virginia	1802	1	Against rebellions and insurrections	N/A
South Carolina	1822	1	Against rebellions and insurrections	Acted upon
Virginia	1824	1	Against rebellions and insurrections	Acted upon

MP, mass protest

[a] Data from Fishel and Quarles 1967, 113.

SOURCE: Data from Aptheker 1951, 1–150, except as noted above.

Primary Cases: Public Scripts of Protests during Slavery

Blacks Petition the Massachusetts Legislature in 1773

Sir, The efforts made by the legislative of this province in their last sessions to free themselves from slavery, gave us, who are in that deplorable state, a high degree of satisfaction. We expect great things from men who have made such a noble stand against the designs of their *fellowmen* to enslave them. We cannot but wish and hope Sir, that you will have the same grand object, we mean civil and religious liberty, in view in your next session. The divine spirit of *freedom,* seems to fire every humane breast on this continent, except such as are bribed to assist in executing the execrable plan.

We are very sensible that it would be highly detrimental to our present masters, if we were allowed to demand all that of *right* belongs to us for past services; this we disclaim. Even the *Spaniards,* who have not those sublime ideas of freedom that English men have, are conscious that they have no right to all the services of their fellowmen, we mean the *Africans,* whom they have purchased with their money; therefore they allow them one day in a week to work for themselves, to enable them to earn money to purchase the residue of their time, which they have a right to demand in such portions as they are able to pay for (a due appraizement of their services being first made, which always stands at the purchase money). We do not pretend to dictate to you Sir, or to the Honorable Assembly, of which you are a member. We acknowledge our obligations to you for what you have already done, but as the people of this province seem to be actuated by the principles of equity and justice, we cannot but expect your house will again take our deplorable case into serious consideration, and give us that ample relief which, *as men,* we have a natural right to.

But since the wise and righteous governor of the universe, has permitted our fellow men to make us slaves, we bow in submission to him, and determine to behave in such a manner as that we may have reason to expect the divine approbation of, and assistance in, our peaceable and lawful attempts to gain our freedom.

We are willing to submit to such regulations and laws, as may be made relative to us, until we leave the province, which we determine to do as soon as we can, from our joynt labours procure money to transport ourselves to some part of the Coast of *Africa,* where we propose a settlement. We are very desirous that you should have instructions relative to us, from your town, therefore we pray you to communicate this letter to them, and ask this favor for us.

In behalf of our fellow slaves in this province, and by order of their Committee.

Peter Bestes,
Sambo Freeman,
Felix Holbrook,
Chester Joie.

For the Representative of the town of Thompson.

SOURCE: Aptheker 1951, 7–8. Reprinted with permission from Kensington Publishing.

the latter were for the most part nonexistent. This helped to inspire the free men and women of color to organize with the specific aim of abolishing the slavery system. Thus, almost simultaneously, African American free men and women created a national organization in 1830 to coordinate, centralize, and structure the political protests of individuals and small groups. They sought to put pressure on the fledgling state and national governments. However, since slaves had no chance to develop such organizations, their political protest took the form of a major rebellion in South Hampton, Virginia, led by Nat Turner on August 21, 1831 (Tragle 1971). Contextual restraints forced the emergence of these two distinct strategies. Free men and women of color sought to build a national organization, while slaves moved from petition to "violent destructive . . . revolts and insurrections" to attain their freedom and liberation from oppressive local and state governments (Walton 1972, 19).

The Nat Turner Revolt:
A Case Study in Political Protest

The prelude to the major revolt led by Nat Turner consisted of the numerous slave petitions to colonial and later state governments that went unanswered. Some of the individual runaways, and especially those who were a part of the organized Underground Railroad, met with some modest success, but clearly not enough (Franklin and Moss 1994). Indeed, these individual day-to-day acts of resistance were absorbed by the system of slavery. The institution persisted even in the face of both moral and political arguments for abolition. Hence, slaves resorted to another form of political protest from time to time: insurrection and revolt.

Of the numerous revolts rumored or attempted, the Turner rebellion is the most noted and discussed (Aptheker 1943). Historians John Hope Franklin and Alfred Moss write: "This slave . . . was a mystical, rebellious person who . . . had already begun to feel that he had been selected by some higher power to deliver his people from slavery" (Franklin and Moss 1994, 147). Marxist historian Herbert Aptheker tells us:

> Six slaves . . . started out in the evening of August 21, 1831, on their crusade against bondage. Their first blow—delivered by Turner himself—struck against person and family of Turner's master Joseph Travis, who were killed. Some arms and horses were taken, the rebels

pushed on, and everywhere slaves flocked to their standard. . . . Within twenty-four hours approximately seventy slaves were actually acting in the rebellion. By the coming of August 23rd at least fifty-seven whites—men and women, and children—had been killed, and the rebels had covered about twenty miles. (Aptheker 1971, 88)

White Historian Thomas Wentworth Higginson reveals that when "the number of adherents had increased to fifty or sixty, Nat Turner judged it time to strike at the county seat, Jerusalem . . . [there] . . . he could . . . find arms, ammunition, and money" (Higginson 1971, 58). Prior to reaching Jerusalem, which was three miles away, Turner and his band had to pass the Parker Plantation, where several of his men wanted to recruit some friends for the rebellion. "Nat Turner objected, as the delay might prove dangerous; he yielded at last, and it proved fatal" (Higginson 1971).

An alerted and small white militia overcame the few rebels at the gate to the Parker Plantation. However, when a reinforcement of slave rebels came back from the "Big House," they repulsed the small militia—which fell back until reinforcements came over from Jerusalem. This larger group forced Turner's band to scatter and hide under the cover of night. At daylight the group recovered and went to another plantation, only to meet strong resistance there. Later that morning they met another group of white militia that further scattered and dispersed the Turner group. The group was never able to regroup, despite Turner's successful escape. It was not to last, for he was captured six weeks later, on October 30. A "court convened at Jerusalem, November 5th, 1831, for his trial, and he was hanged at one o'clock on Friday, November 11, in Jerusalem, Virginia" (Drewy 1971, 74). In the end, "fifty-three Negroes were apprehended and arraigned. Seventeen of the insurrectionists were convicted and executed, twelve convicted and transported, ten acquitted, seven disdained and four sent on to the Superior Court" (Crowell 1971, 98). Needless to say, the rebellion caught whites in South Hampton County temporarily off guard, and therefore accomplished fleeting liberation for a few slaves. But this fleeting liberation eventually resulted in death for most of the participants.

The hanging of Nat Turner and the others did not signal the end of the affair. Local slaves and free men and women bore consequences for sometime to come. Since general hysteria gripped the state and the surrounding region, murder and violence were visited upon African American communities, both slave and free. In this process a great many innocent Blacks also lost their lives for no other reason than their race. Secondly, this violence gave rise to new laws that placed enormous legal inhibitions on both the African American free and enslaved populations. It further restricted their movements, especially to gather in large numbers for any reasons. Often free persons had their efforts to obtain reading and writing skills interrupted, as well as the right to carry firearms. Even many of the emerging semi-independent African American preachers were denied the right to preach.

The backlash to the Turner revolt also invigorated the southern colonization movement that sought to return Blacks to Africa (Drewy 1971, 171–173). One southern apologist for the bunker mentality that emerged in the wake of Turner's 1831 revolt, says: "The emancipation of the slaves in 1865 was not a result of fear of servile insurrection . . . servile insurrection tended to delay rather than quicken emancipation" (Drewy 1971, 186). And his concluding proposal was that even with emancipation, "it will be best for both races that the Negro be transported beyond the limits of the United States" (Drewy 1971, 194). By this view African Americans were deemed never to be acceptable for full membership in the American democracy, which was the special preserve of the dominant population of European descendants.

Thus in the short run at least, violence as a protest device ended much like petitions, prayers, resolutions, memorials, and pleas: with limited results and responses from the state and national government. In part this outcome motivated reformers and abolitionists to heighten their consciousness for a moral and humanitarian challenge to the institution of slavery. They did so by embarking on a moral and political crusade for abolition. It was this crusade that in part propelled the nation toward the Civil War.

Political Protest: National Organizations and Abolition

Mutual Aid Societies and Churches

Well before 1830, some African Americans started to organize at the local levels in the country. On April 12, 1787, they formed the Philadelphia Free African Society "in order to support one another in sickness, and for the benefit of their widows and fatherless children." Shortly thereafter, "similar societies were found . . . in Newport,

Boston, and New York. These maintained a steady correspondence and members exchanged visits" (Aptheker 1951, 18). In the same year the "Negro Masonic Order" was granted a charter from the lodge in London. Next came the "Boston African Society" in 1796.

In addition to these mutual aid societies, African Americans also began forming churches at the local level. "First among these were Negro Baptist Churches which appeared in Virginia by 1775 and in Georgia by [1788], . . . the latter being founded by George Liele in Savannah, Georgia. Following the Baptists, was the African Methodist Episcopal Church, which achieved its independence in 1816" (Aptheker 1951, 67). Other fledgling organizations also began to appear, almost all limited to the local level.

These locally based and evolving organizations addressing mutual aid and religious concerns would eventually evolve into political organizations. The first such broad organizational effort occurred on September 20, 1830, when a pioneering National African American Convention was held in Philadelphia. It organized "for the purpose of comparing views and of adopting a harmonizing movement of emigration, or of determination to remain in the United States" (Aptheker 1951, 200). This formative convention led to the "first annual national . . . convention . . . which . . . met in 1831 and four more times during the 1830s, three times in the 1840s, twice in the 1850s; in the sixties it reorganized itself into the National Equal Rights League. Although the meetings of the national organization were only occasional, those of many of its subsidiaries were regular" (Walton 1972, 144).

The Negro Convention:
The First National Organization

The formative Convention of 1830 (from which the subsidiaries emerged), adopted an organizational framework. It "called for the establishment of a permanent National Convention . . . [organization] . . . with permanent state and local auxiliary units to consider programs and policies to aid or change the . . . African American's condition in America." To link and connect these federated units, the 1830 Convention asked that "regional offices . . . [be] . . . set up in each state, and these, in turn, elected delegates to state Conventions at which a permanent state governing body was elected. . . . The state delegate also elected a delegation to go to the national body to discuss . . . and work out some kind of overall national strategy to eliminate the problem facing" African Americans. Finally, these delegations to the National Convention would elect "for a one-year term a national president, secretary and other officers, to attend to the national organization and its business for that particular year" (Walton 1972, 144).

Besides this structural characteristic, "the national body had roving secretariats to work with state and local areas that did not have organizations or could not afford to establish them." Thus, in 1831, with the birth of the first annual convention, African Americans now had a formally organized effort to lobby and pressure local, state, and national governments. "In addition, the Convention founded a series of organizations, known as the Phoenix Societies, in the urban areas of the North . . . [and] . . . These local societies made proposals to improve the moral welfare of blacks and to instruct them in literature and the mechanical arts" (Foner and Walker 1979, xi–xii).

This first organization was the precursor to many other organizations, almost all dedicated to ending slavery one way or another. It was not long before the National Convention Movement was superseded by a variety of other organizations. Because of factionalism in the annual National Convention over strategies and tactics, in 1835 African Americans from Pennsylvania withdrew from the National Convention. They then formed the American Moral Reform Society, which "set up its own constitution, and published its official organ, *The National Reformer*," and adopted the principles of Garrisonianism, "which advocated moral persuasion and pressure resistance, as the means to end slavery" (Foner and Walker 1979, xii). The central purpose of this new abolitionist body was "to extend the work of the Phoenix Society." And when the National Convention ceased meeting in 1836 for seven years, the Moral Reformists stepped into the vacuum on the state and local levels.

The Philadelphia organization soon sought a national base for continuing its efforts in favor of abolition. By September 1840 this state and local movement met in New Haven, Connecticut, and broadened its scope to create the National Reform Convention of Colored People. A New Yorker, David Ruggles, was selected as leader. This movement now had a national organization and no competition from the dormant National Convention Movement. The absence of competition was short lived, in the ever-increasing aggressive organizing campaigns among African Americans. The organization quickly ran into trouble because of its limited moral approach to the problems of slavery and of racial discrimination faced by free men and women of color. There was growing senti-ment for other strategies.

Third-Party Electoral Protest

Among some organizers, electoral politics was adopted as a more mil-itant approach. The Liberty Party, founded in 1840, attracted many of these organizers. Although the new party was not an African American organization, it was an avowed antislavery third party. It focused on elections as an alternative to moral suasion, then seen as the sole strategy adopted by the successors to the National Conven-tion (Walton 1969a, 38–79). The Liberty Party subsequently attracted a great following among African Americans. Several of them became delegates to the party's organizing political convention, and more than 7,000 African Americans voted in the 1840 presidential elec-tion. These activities turned out to be a great stimulus to the forces that had been involved in the National Convention, eventually lead-ing to the reactivation of the dormant group. The National Negro Conventions then held meetings in 1843, 1847, 1848, 1853, 1854, and 1864 (Walton 1972, 144–145). The reactivated 1843 Convention and its now broader campaign for African American improvement ul-timately spelled the demise of the Moral Reform Society and its ex-clusive dedication to abolition.

This realignment contributed to a revitalization of a plethora of lo-cal affiliate organizations in the states that had also fallen dormant. Their reemergence presaged what became a trend in the localization of protest and other political efforts for African Americans. Virtually all of these local conventions continued their fundamental concern with al-tering the slave status of African Americans. Philip Foner writes that during "the 1830's and early 1840's . . . societies of the free black ap-peared in New England and the Middle States and in the great western centers of Detroit, Chicago, and Cincinnati. State Conventions were held annually in the western states of Ohio, Illinois, Michigan and In-diana" (Foner and Walker 1979, xii). Table 2.3 shows that the number of state conventions of African Americans increased as the number of National Conventions decreased over the decades. This empirical evi-dence suggests that the sporadic nature of the national organization did not prevent African Americans from organizing and lobbying state and local governments over four decades. Once the foundation was laid, the commitment to ending slavery and discrimination was so strong that the local efforts proceeded under their own steam.

TABLE 2.3   Number of African American National and State Conventions
in Antebellum America, 1830–1865

	National Conventions	State Conventions
1830–1839	7	4[a]
1840–1849	3[b]	13
1850–1859	2	25
1860–1865	1	9

[a] Refers to the meetings of the American Moral Reform Society.

[b] Refers to the meetings of the National Convention Movement and excludes the 1840 meeting of the National Reformed Convention of Colored People.

SOURCE: Data from Foner and Walker 1979, 1980.

Abolition Protest and Third-Party Organizations: Success or Failure?

The abolitionist era saw two types of organizing within the African American community. First, the 1830 National Negro Convention Movement represented a *top-down* approach to organizing the African American community. Its purpose was to lobby the American federal government for a redress of their grievances. The second approach grew out of the first one. With the rise of the moral reform societies there emerged a *bottom-up*, grassroots approach to national organizing. These two major approaches would come to characterize the way African Americans organized to protest their conditions in American society thereafter. But the strategic contribution these organizations made to African American protest politics was that the activity now had a structure. This also made for a structural approach to the political, economic, and social dilemma of the African American community. It was to be borne out in the era of abolitionism.

So what did this activity look like on the ground? These national and state conventions usually did much of their lobbying via petitions, memorials, speeches, and prayers. They and their local auxiliaries petitioned four groups: Congress, state legislatures, the white public, and the African American community. They sought to have *influence* on five major issues: suffrage rights, equality, abolitionism, education, and colonization. "Other issues too received a hearing, such as the establishment of farmer and manual schools, support for black organizations (such as the church and literary and benevolent) along with the black press. Economic concerns loomed high on the agenda of the state Convention" (Foner and Walker 1979, xv).

Put differently, the political context in which African American free people and slaves found themselves shaped the lobbying agenda and demands of the conventions. As the context changed, the targets of action also changed. Some examples of changes in law or policy that elicited fairly different foci in lobbying include the Fugitive Slave Law (1850), the *Dred Scott* decision of the Supreme Court, and state laws like Ohio's Black Laws.

The Source of Race Leadership: Protest Spokespeople

The contextual issues naturally gave rise to leadership spokespersons. Race leadership sprang from both free and enslaved people, virtually all of it centered on the elimination of the inequalities inherent in slavery, racial exclusion, and discrimination. Some of the expressions of these early leaders are revealed in the data in Tables 2.1 and 2.2. Initially they were not necessarily community based, but instead reflected the entrepreneurial efforts of a few notables who felt called to act.

The next stage for race-based leadership was group and community based. It began with the mutual aid and benefit societies in sundry localities in urban areas of the North. These societies tended to blossom simultaneously with the rise of African American Baptist and Methodist churches. Nevertheless, it was these early mutual aid societies that transformed and enlarged the leadership base from individual and small-group, sporadic, and transitory efforts to more stable actions and broader community organizations.

Preachers, Pamphleteers, and Polemicists

But long before the rise of the National and State Conventions there were African American protest spokespersons outside the churches and mutual aid societies. These political activists also worked individually, but through the use of protest pamphlets. Like Thomas Paine during the Revolutionary War period, some African Americans became successful protest pamphleteers, thus attaining considerable renown and leadership status. Existing pamphlets indicate that such leaders existed from 1790 until 1860. The pioneering work of librarian and writer Dorothy Porter Wesley reveals that this group included such individuals as Absalom Jones and Richard Allen, Nathaniel Paul, William Hamilton, Hosea Easton, William J. Watkins, and Daniel Coker (Wesley 1969, 1971). Recent studies have shown that Maria Stewart, David Walker, Martin Delany, and Henry Highland Garnet were also in this group (Walton 1969a, 80–92).

Perhaps the best known of these pamphleteers was David Walker, who produced a very forceful and provocative document directed to the attention of African peoples everywhere, but especially those in the United States. His was a direct call for revolt among the enslaved. The document attracted a considerable amount of attention among both African Americans and whites. Indeed, it is widely believed that Walker's mysterious death soon after the appearance of the document was the product of foul play. In short, what pamphleteering gave to African American activists was another means of speaking to the race question absent an organizational base in either the community-based organizations or in the abolitionist movements.

African American Autobiography: The Slave Narratives

Pamphleteering would eventually give way to a larger population of writers known as the "slave autobiographers." Published narrative stories in this genre, of often escapees from enslavement, gave exposure to the horrors of the system and often inspired the escape of others. Many of these individuals, with the backing of the abolitionist movement, became elegant spokespersons for the African American community. Two of the best known among these orators were Frederick Douglass and Maria Stewart. Once Douglass was in the limelight, he propelled himself to the forefront of the antebellum leadership group. He went on to become a major spokesperson for the race through the Civil War, Reconstruction, and the post-Reconstruction era. Indeed, Douglass is an interesting example of how important the racial spokesperson could be. He later became arguably the distinguished African American leader of his era, escaping enslavement, educating himself, and wielding significant power. Douglass achieved this continuing leadership role not only because of his use of the written and spoken word but also because of his move from the written word to an organizational base. He became active first in the National Negro Convention organizations and later was instrumental in transforming them into the National Equal

Rights League. He eventually held various leadership positions in the ruling Republican Party as a domestic government functionary and as a diplomat. His narrative that started it all remains one of the most outstanding pieces of American prose, widely used in composition courses around the country.

Although both pamphlets and autobiographies were important, they offered distinct approaches to leadership. Recent scholarship has shown that the autobiographies written by former slaves were at times under the influence and control of white abolitionist leaders. These documents often followed a familiar structure. They recited the story of the experience under slavery primarily to convince a white audience of the moral deficiency of the system. In contrast, the protest pamphlets were under the sole control of the African American writer, and were written primarily for an African American audience.

These striking differences in proprietorship also led to striking differences in the nature of the racial leadership to emerge from these two genres (Newman et al. 2001). The autobiographers were far more likely to become a part of the moral suasion group seeking abolition within coalitions, while the more independent pamphleteers were far more likely to issue nationalist exhortations for a presumed self-reliant and independent race-based community.

Like the organizational approach to protest and lobbying politics, the pamphlet and autobiographical approaches were duplicated through the late nineteenth and into the twentieth century. Indeed two of the most influential exponents of these combined traditions are W.E.B. DuBois through his enduring 1903 essays, *The Souls of Black Folk,* and James Baldwin through his essays such as his 1955 *Notes of a Native Son* (Lewis 1994, 2000).

The Colonization Movement: Preface to a National Platform

However, the limitation of this period of pioneering organizing was that it was still local and was limited to urban areas. The bounds of these groups continued to be fairly localized. But a major change in the political context came with the rise of the colonization movement and the appearance of the American Colonization Society. This effort was national in orientation and required the development of significant networks for successful dissemination of information. African Americans who were either in favor of or opposed to this

African repatriation effort were forced to expand beyond the narrow confines of their urban bailiwicks. This immediately contributed to the development of organizations of a more regional and national scope (Harris 1972; Miller 1975). New African American men and women could now come forth by advocating a position on the issue of emigration. The organizing strategies developed in this context on the eve of the Civil War provided a virtual tool kit for organizations of protests through to Reconstruction.

The Institutional Church: Leadership, Protest, and Lobbying

The most enduring independent organization in the African American community is the church. Its roots extend back to independent efforts at religious expression during slavery, and continue through to what remain the most prominent separate congregations today, the Baptist and Methodist churches. These church organizations, even the inchoate ones that operated during slavery, in responding to the everyday realities of African American life, were forced to expand their roles and functions far beyond the religious. They found themselves immediately responding to a wide range of needs from their parishioners that were a direct product of racism, exclusion, and discrimination. Pushed by the tenets of Christianity that taught both obedience and liberation, the churches often became organized tools of resistance and sometimes rebellion (Harding 1969).

From its inception to the present the institutional church within the African American community has struggled with its religious role and mission vis-à-vis its role as an institution of resistance. Despite the conservative theological interpretations that some church leaders have always made, the resistant church has been prominent in social change because of its influence on the actions of its adherents. The most significant antebellum rebellion by slaves, that of Nat Turner, was in part church based. It will be recalled that Nat Turner was a minister. He was largely inspired by the precepts of Christianity that he believed required him to act to eliminate the evil system of slavery. He was merely one in a long line of minister leaders of great influence in protest politics in African American communities.

In the 1960s Reverend Martin Luther King Jr. faced the same pressures and conditions to keep the church focused on an otherworldly mission. He, however, moved to have the African American church take up a mission of resistance to segregation and desegregation (Walton 1971). In his efforts he found significant opposition from Reverend Joseph Jackson, the influential head of the decentralized National Baptist Convention, who wanted the church to stay out of protest politics because it detracted from the religious mission.

The African American church is distinct from many of the prominent national Christian denominations, insofar as the former is much more decentralized. In the nature of these independent and segregated denominations, they are inherently locally based organizations. In the main, they are neither national nor state based, but grassroots organizations. It is in these local communities that the omnipresent racialized conditions of life play out, and because the church is the closest independent institution to those circumstances, its has enormous impact and influence on the resolution of or lifting of the burdens of daily problems. So the constituency of the church brings its problems every Sunday or Saturday, and as many times a week as possible. But the gatherings are also sources of information and the sites of opinion formulation. This diverse and widespread organization becomes both a leadership source and a base for that leadership. The church has sent and continues to send a vast array of emissaries into the leadership circle. Moreover, the influence of the institution has expanded far beyond its locally based nature.

Many church leaders with political influence have transcended their local bases to become significant national leaders and spokespersons on racial matters. Adam Clayton Powell rose to national prominence from his constituent base at the Abyssinian Baptist Church in Harlem to become a long-serving congressman and national protest leader. Martin Luther King Jr. emerged from the Dexter Avenue Baptist Church in Alabama to assume the most exalted protest leadership position among African American leaders during the civil rights movement. Andrew Young and Jesse Jackson were but two of the many other clerics associated with King who attained great political leadership. And Malcolm X, too, while a Black Muslim cleric, also reflected the high influence of clerics as protest leaders, who sprang first from a localized base to national leadership.

Insofar as religious affiliations and the influence of those organizations remain so high among African Americans, the church maintains stable local and national political influence. To wit, they provide a continuing wealth of leadership talent for political work.

Witness the efforts of the Reverends Jesse Jackson (1984 and 1988) and Al Sharpton (2004), to seek the ultimate political prize in the United States—the presidency. In short, this sector far outlives many other protest and lobbying organizations that ebb and flow in the varying political contexts.

Legalism as a Protest and Lobbying Technique

Reconstruction: Abbreviated Universal Freedom

So far the discussion and analysis have been on the evolution and creation of protest leaders and organizations through different contextual forces and environmental changes among two groups of African Americans, free people and slaves. The next part considers how these realities gave birth to racial protest leadership in and outside of the church. After the Civil War, the Thirteenth, Fourteenth, and Fifteenth Amendments gave African Americans a legal basis for citizenship and dissolved the artificial distinctions between free people and slaves. All were now citizens. This change in the political context ushered in the Reconstruction era, during which these new citizens were permitted to participate on a nearly equal footing with all other American citizens.

The Reconstruction period of regularized African American participation lasted ever so briefly, roughly between the end of the war in 1865 and the presidential election of 1876. Although the betrayal of Reconstruction began soon after the assassination of Lincoln, it was virtually sanctioned in the 1876 election. Candidate Tilden won the popular vote, but was unable to prevail in the Electoral College vote. In the course of negotiations and deal making, candidate Hayes succeeded in securing the support of the southern states and eventually prevailed. But the price was a deal that effectively ended the presence of the federal militia in the former Confederate states and any aggressive pursuit of sustained rights for African Americans.

This "Compromise of 1877" set in motion a set of policies and practices that ended the privileges and rights of these new citizens. In a matter of ten or so years these practices were codified all over the South, ushering in an era of disenfranchisement, a phase between 1890 and 1901 that reduced African Americans to second-class citizens. It was accompanied by the most intense segregation of the races (Jim Crow) ever encountered in this country.

Protest through Legal Challenges to Political Exclusion

In response to the Jim Crow system, African American leaders and their organizations fashioned a new technique to protest and lobby against segregation. That technique was *legalism*. It can be defined as the use of reality-based or test cases in the judicial system, particularly the federal courts, to challenge the constitutionality of the formally instituted laws of segregation. This approach aimed to demonstrate that within constitutional law and its codified statutes, second-class citizenship could not be sustained. Ultimately legalism was designed to substantiate the view that African Americans were entitled to all the rights, liberties, and privileges of any other citizen in the American democracy (Walton 1972, 147–153). The National Association for the Advancement of Colored People (NAACP) was the organizational structure that developed a program based on legal challenges to expose the unconstitutionality of segregation. An integrated coalition of social activists, scholars, and religious people met in Niagara Falls, Canada, in 1905 to form an association anchored around protest. The version of protest to which the organization evolved was the legal one. Beginning in 1915, the NAACP pursued test cases in every area of American life except interracial marriages, and it continues such pursuits today (Walton 1972). The organization succeeded in some areas, but met defeat in others.

In addition to the preference for legalism, the organization was also well known for its lobbying activities. In areas where there was no clear body of constitutional law, the NAACP sought to get legislation passed. Lynching is one of these areas where the organization ran a well-organized campaign designed to get antilynching legislation enacted.

The "Grandfather Clause"

The NAACP challenge to the racial social and political order was comprehensive, and it established the legal foundations on which many court tests were based. "The Association declared that one of its primary goals was the destruction of the various schemes designed to disfranchise blacks. Its leaders planned to show . . . clearly the unconstitutionality of all of the subterfuges used to destroy the rights and privileges to blacks delineated in the Fourteenth and Fifteenth Amendments" (Hine 1979, 67).

The organization supported a successful early challenge of limits placed on the franchise through the "grandfather clause." This was a statute many of the southern states instituted after 1890 that limited the franchise to those whose ancestors voted just after the Civil War. In Oklahoma, where the challenge originated, the state established a requirement that these ancestors must have possessed the franchise after January 1, 1866. The NAACP supported the federal government's claim that this law was in violation of the Fifteenth Amendment; the Supreme Court agreed in *Guinn v. United States* (1915).

The "White Primary"

This started a string of challenges related to the exercise of the franchise by Blacks. Soon after the grandfather clause was declared unconstitutional, southern states sought to bar African Americans from the franchise by declaring that the Democratic Party was a private organization that reserved the right to select its members. African Americans were systematically barred from membership in these parties, and thus unable to participate in the all-important primary elections. The primary elections turned out to be critical because the South, where the majority of Blacks lived, was a one-party dominant region. And, most whites were affiliated with the Democratic Party. Therefore winning in the Democratic Party primary was where the real election was settled (Key 1949).

The NAACP challenged this practice, and as became its custom, used every piecemeal victory as a stepping stone to the next legal challenge until the total victory was won. In an initial challenge the association lost when the Supreme Court accepted the argument that primaries did not constitute elections, giving Blacks no relief from effective disfranchisement (*Newberry v. United States* 1922). Nevertheless, five years later, in *Nixon v. Herndon* (1927), the Court decided that the states could not legally sanction any rules that barred Blacks from participating in primaries. There remained loopholes, however, and soon the southern states removed any regulatory authority for primaries from the government, placing it all in the hands of the "private" party organizations. Once again the NAACP challenged. Despite the previous rulings, in *Grovey v. Townsend* (1935) the Supreme Court appeared to backtrack. Political parties were permitted to establish such exclusionary rules, being thereby recognized as private organizations. Finally, however, in *Smith v. Allwright* (1944) the Court provided a comprehensive victory outlawing what was dubbed the "white primary" on the grounds that the exclusion of African Americans was a violation of the Fourteenth Amendment. The reasoning was that insofar as primary elections were so central to the overall electoral process, racial exclusions were tantamount to denying the right to exercise the franchise.

Challenging Segregated Education

One of the areas in which leaders and supporters of the NAACP felt they had their greatest success was education. In a series of cases that challenged the earlier "separate but equal" doctrine (*Plessy v. Ferguson* 1896) the organization finally succeeded, after almost sixty years, in having this policy reversed in public schools. The Supreme Court had earlier made *Plessy* applicable to schools when it rejected the efforts of Berea College, a private institution, to integrate its student body (*Berea College v. Kentucky* 1908). It thus took some time before the NAACP realized any success in its challenges to school segregation. An important victory occurred when the Court ruled that the state of Missouri, which ran a two-tiered but not equal educational system, was obligated to provide the same education for African Americans as whites. So in the absence of a separate law school for Blacks, the Court ruled, Missouri had to admit them to its only law school, located at the previously all-white University of Missouri (*Missouri ex rel. Gaines v. Canada* 1938).

The NAACP further challenged separate institutions that were far from equal—specifically, the Texas Southern Law School established for Blacks to prevent the integration of the University of Texas Law School. Once again the association attained a victory when the new law school was declared unequal to that of the University of Texas, which then had to accept Blacks (*Sweatt v. Painter* 1950). But there was still substantial school segregation. The ultimate victory came four years later, when the Court fundamentally broke with the separate-but-equal doctrine, arguing in *Brown v. Board of Education of Topeka, Kansas* (1954), that separate but equal was inherently unequal, thereby reversing the *Plessy* decision.

Legalism ultimately had a central weakness. It was an elite, not a mass effort. Essentially it was a technique by which lawyers established important principles of law by protesting interpretations of the Constitution. However, while many cases were won, that did not guarantee implementation. Southern states often ignored Supreme Court rulings, actively resisted them, or slowed or selectively implemented them. Noncompliance or massive resistance to Supreme Court rulings made legal rights simply abstract, while second-class citizenship continued to be a reality for Blacks. For example, a turning point in school integration came in the South only as the grassroots civil rights movement got off the ground, combined with President Eisenhower's dispatch of federal troops to Little Rock, Arkansas, in 1957 (Burk 1985, 174–204). Thus, in spite of its successes, legalism as a protest tactic alone could not get the implementation of policy changes that physically altered the social order. Soon, it became obvious that more was needed.

The Rise of Protest Demonstrations, Boycotts, and Political Violence

A revival of conventional protests was in the offing. In the wake of World War I, the NAACP led several silent mass demonstrations down Fifth Avenue in New York City, but this tactic was the exception rather than the rule for the organization. Hence, it took a new organization to emphasize protest demonstrations on the local level. The first major example was Marcus Garvey's United Negro Improvement Association. This mass nationalist movement had members all around the world, but New York City was its base. It was also the venue for most of Garvey's public marches and demonstrations, designed both to exhort the race to mass action and to target issues for complaint. Many of the mass protest demonstrations, for example, were used to publicize and advance the associated Back to Africa component of Garvey's program. Often the issues of complaint remained locally based. (For more detailed analysis, see chapter 3.)

The A. Philip Randolph March on Washington

Soon, however, local efforts began to be translated to a national audience. Several leaders and organizations attempted the mass mobilization of the African American population by articulating a common understanding of racial conditions. And they also urged a cohesive strategy for resolution. In 1941, Asa Philip Randolph called for a march on Washington to protest President Franklin D. Roosevelt's failure to provide an executive order banning discrimination in industries with federal contracts. Randolph proposed a first-of-its-kind mass march that would immobilize the government. And the threat was sufficient to exact a positive decision from a government that had previously ignored conventional entreaties for a public policy to alleviate the effects of discrimination against Blacks in the federal service. This strategic decision encouraged President Roosevelt to sign Executive Order 8802, creating the Federal Employment Practices Commission (FEPC), forestalling the promised mass march. Later a march on Washington movement was formed to force President Harry Truman to desegregate the armed forces. Truman's signing of such an executive order left the fledgling march on Washington movement without a goal, and so it never developed as an organization and faded from the scene (Garfunkel 1959).

Just before World War II the Congress of Racial Equality (CORE) formed. This was an organization that developed out of the pacifist Quaker Fellowship of Reconciliation. The new CORE was to be dedicated to the attainment of racial equality via activist means to counter the legalistic approach associated with the NAACP. Like the Quaker parent group, CORE "had an interest in pacifism, trade unionism, and cooperative communities; inspiration derived from Gandhi's example in India; opposition to the capitalist system" (Broderick and Meier 1965, 210). The organization entered this revitalized protest phase with a series of sit-ins at restaurants in downtown Chicago in 1943. The stated aim was to desegregate these eating establishments so that they would be available to African Americans troops scheduled to be sent overseas. Limited success with the sit-in demonstrations led CORE to develop a somewhat more general campaign in 1946 to desegregate interstate bus lines (Walton 1971, 27–28). A small, integrated group tested its ability to travel as such on public conveyances (Greyhound and Trailways buses) over a two-week period through some border and upper southern states. They were often arrested along the way, but they succeeded in getting a court ruling that effectively desegregated the buses. The Supreme Court in *Morgan v. Virginia* (1946) upheld integrated bus riding in the South. Basically the South ignored the ruling (Davis and Graham 1995, 83–84). But this revitalized a movement for mass protest demonstrations.

Marching in the Streets: Mass Mobilization Protest

By the mid-1950s the mass political protest movement became an important supplement to the tactic of legalism. The first major example came from a bus boycott in Baton Rouge, Louisiana, in the summer of 1953. "The official leader of the boycott was the Reverend T. J. Jemison, pastor . . . of one of the largest black churches in the city. When white drivers refused to allow blacks to sit at the front of the bus," an almost 100 percent effective seven-day boycott reversed that policy (Morris 1984, 18). This was followed by a similar event in Montgomery, Alabama, that completely changed the protest landscape. The boycott in Montgomery began in late 1955 when Rosa Parks, a local activist, refused to vacate a seat in the white seating section of a city bus. The boycott continued for a full year, and before it was over had catapulted a local Baptist minister, Martin Luther King Jr., to the forefront of a national mass movement. The mobilization of the Black community in the city effectively ruined the public bus transport system and culminated in a Supreme Court finding that segregation on the buses was illegal (Lewis 1978, 79). A similar bus boycott began in the winter of 1956 in Tallahassee, Florida, and ended only with the Court ruling in the Montgomery case (Morris 1984, 19).

What Montgomery contributed to this new period was a set of tactics and the mobilization clergy leadership that ultimately transcended the local issues to become national. It illustrated how significant transformation could occur on the crest of a wave of new opportunities and political realignments that were sensitive to civil rights and racial discrimination. The movement served to bring Martin Luther King Jr. to international attention while allowing him to form an organization of clergymen that Morris says became the "decentralized arm of the movement"—the Southern Christian Leadership Conference (SCLC). King deftly used this affiliation as the means of developing the most sustained and successful mass mobilization ever realized by African Americans in this country. The movement was sustained largely on a clever adaptation of nonviolent direct action campaigns at targeted sites of gross discrimination and abject segregation throughout mostly, but not exclusively, southern venues.

The first nationalizing efforts to come out of the Montgomery bus boycott was the 1963 March on Washington, in which more than 200,000 people marched from the Capitol to the Lincoln Memorial. There Martin Luther King ignited the crowd with his famous "I Have a Dream" speech leading this signal event of protest. It presaged a period of massive mobilization in which local events were writ larger for the media and attention the national campaign generated. This effort combined mass protest, boycotts, a church base, and a race spokesman with a unique philosophy that challenged local as well as national authorities.

Thereafter important protest events took place in virtually every southern state through the 1960s, leading to remarkable changes in public behavior, judicial activism in favor of civil rights and civil liberties, and statutory laws favoring desegregation and political enfranchisement emanating from executive and legislative coalitions. For example, in 1960 African American college students in Greensboro, North Carolina, challenged segregated lunch counters; in 1962 James Meredith successfully challenged the segregated white university system in Mississippi; and in 1965 a march in Selma, Alabama (in which a white civil rights volunteer was murdered) advanced voting rights (Williams 1987).

Political Violence: Assassination, Riots, and Rebellion

Political violence as a tactic and technique has a long and spotty history in the African American experience. Theorists, exponents, and advocates of this strategy had long been active and vocal in the United States. The Nat Turner rebellion certainly falls into this category. But there have been instances during and after slavery when political violence in the form of riots was a feature of action or reaction by African Americans. Sometimes African Americans initiated riotous acts as a means of altering egregious aspects of their status. But perhaps more often, riots occurred as a result of external attacks on concentrated African American communities or individual acts against their number that resulted in mass acts of retaliation.

Riots have occurred all over the country, but they were perhaps more frequent in the urban North after free Blacks migrated there. Significant incidents occurred between 1815 and 1835 in New York, Pennsylvania, Michigan, and Ohio (Franklin and Moss 1994, 165). Perhaps the most serious riots before 1900 occurred in New York City in 1863. These so-called draft riots "began as a protest against conscription [but] more than 100 African Americans, many of whom were children, died in the violence" (Painter 2000, 646). After 1900 a rash of riots occurred during and around the period of World War I. After the riot in East Saint Louis, Illinois, in 1917, came the "Red Summer" of 1919, during which more than twenty-five riots occurred across the country. The one in Chicago was probably the worst among them. "Thirty-eight people had been killed, including 15 whites and 23 blacks; of the 537 injured, 178 were white and 342 were black. . . . More than 1,000 families, mostly blacks, were home-less as a result of the burnings and general destruction of property" (Franklin and Moss 1994, 351).

Race Riots in the Civil Rights Era

During the mobilization of the 1960s, riots came to be conceived as fundamental to the general crisis in race relations. After the assassination of Martin Luther King, civil rights leaders could declare that violence was both rational and ordained in the racist American society that systematically used violence to repress Black people. For example, Malcolm X had argued there was a justified role for violence even in an era of nonviolence. At times, he suggested, it acted as a counterweight to racist acts of violence, and at other times as an incentive for positive action on civil rights demands. Riots, like other techniques, had some impact and influence in spurring legislative action, despite the normal limitations of violent activity (Clarke 1969; Malcolm X 1965).

Riot activity "in the 1960s was perhaps the most considerable and most sustained of any non-war period in United States history. . . . There were fourteen [riots] in the summer of 1964 . . . 44 events in [1966] . . . Then [by] September [1967] over 160 riots" occurred. In all these instances there were deaths, sometimes in high numbers (thirty-four in the 1965 Detroit riots alone), and property damage estimated at $35 million (Morrison 1989, 98). The data in Table 2.4 provide a sample of twenty-six randomly selected cities where there were urban riots of varying intensity between 1963 and 1968 (Button 1978). Riot activity took place in virtually all areas of the country, although more occurred in the Northeast and the Midwest. Many cities had multiple events in this period—six in Detroit and Cleveland, and five each in Philadelphia, Pittsburgh, and Des Moines.

The measure of riot intensity used in the table is based on the following scale adapted by Jim Button (1978): Cities given a score of zero when there was missile throwing, crowds numbered under 125, and fewer than 15 arrests occurred; a score of one when there was in addition serious property damage, arson, crowds of up to 250 persons, up to 30 arrests, and up to 15 injuries; a score of four when the violence, looting, arson, and property damage are substantial, when crowds number up to 500, and where there are more than 75 arrests and 40 injuries. A score of twelve reflects major violence and property damage, deaths, crowds numbering over 400, and more than 65

TABLE 2.4   Race Riot Characteristics in Twenty-six Cities, 1963–1970

	1967 Riot Intensity	Number of Riots, 1963–1968	Overall Severity of All Riots, 1963–1968	Number of Riots, 1969–1970	Overall Severity of All Riots, 1963–1970	Catalyst in Most Severe 1967 Riot[a]
Birmingham, Ala.	1	4	5	0	5	1
Oakland, Calif.	0	3	1	1	1	1
New Haven, Conn.	4	2	5	0	5	1
Wilmington, Del.	3	3	8	0	8	1
Tampa, Fla.	10	1	10	0	10	1
Des Moines, Iowa	1	5	3	1	4	5
Wichita, Kans.	2	2	3	0	3	5
Cambridge, Mass.	2	4	5	0	5	4
Detroit, Mich.	16	6	21	3	26	1
Minneapolis, Minn.	2	3	2	0	2	3
Kansas City, Mo.	1	1	1	1	1	5
Omaha, Neb.	1	4	5	2	8	2
Newark, N.J.	18	2	20	1	23	1
Albany, N.Y.	2	1	2	0	2	5
Buffalo, N.Y.	11	2	11	0	11	2
Rochester, N.Y.	4	2	15	1	15	1
Syracuse, N.Y.	3	3	4	1	1	5
Durham, N.C.	1	1	1	0	1	5
Cincinnati, Ohio	11	3	14	0	14	1

Cleveland, Ohio	1	6	25	1	25	2
Dayton, Ohio	1	3	3	1	3	4
Philadelphia, Penn.	1	5	19	2	19	2
Pittsburgh, Penn.	0	5	13	1	13	2
Nashville, Tenn.	2	5	13	1	13	2
Houston, Tex.	3	1	3	1	3	1
Milwaukee, Wisc.	12	12	12	0	12	5

[a] Catalysts are coded as follows: 1, killing, arrest, interference, assault, or search of Blacks by police; 2, interracial rock throwing or fight, no lethal weapons; 3, issues related to civil liberties, public facilities, segregation, political events, and housing; 4, inflammatory speech by civil rights or Black Power leaders; 5, no apparent catalyst, or catalyst unknown.

SOURCE: Adapted from Button 1978, 17–18. Reprinted with permission from Princeton University Press.

arrests. The riot intensity scale shows that in this sample the most intense riots occurred in the larger cities in the North—Detroit, Newark, Buffalo, Cincinnati, and Milwaukee, with Tampa as an outlying southern city.

The Context of the 1960s: Civil Rights Organization and Social Movement

The ever-changing political context in the 1950s and 1960s ushered in a new group of organizations that used social movement tactics to shape outcomes in the area of civil rights. The Montgomery Improvement Association became the forerunner of a great variety of local organizations. The SCLC became the archetype for a number of other national organizations. Although many of them deviated considerably from the SCLC, its ethos of activist protest remained a significant foundation. Soon after the SCLC was formed, the local Freedom Summer Movement began in Mississippi, a state that eventually combined all of its major state civil rights organizations into a confederation. Still earlier, the Louisiana Deacons for Defense appeared, espousing violent self-defense (Cruse 1967, 361). At the national level the Student Nonviolent Coordinating Committee (SNCC) was formed, staging innovative sit-ins, wade-ins, pray-ins, and jail-ins. CORE was also revived and sponsored a series of high-profile protests against segregated public conveyances and facilities in the deep South, which drew a spectacular backlash of white violence. Other new organizations, such as the Black Panther Party, also emerged. As the contexts of racial exclusion began to shift, some of the organizations joined forces in an ideological critique of the capitalist system and sought to coalesce around the movement for "Black Power." This effort was in part designed to find a mass base out of the remnants of organization and anger from the riots in the wake of Dr. King's assassination, and to build on the new voting rights of Blacks in the South. The latter-day SNCC was in the forefront of some of these efforts, as were the Malcolm X movement and the Black Panthers.

The movement attracted attention on largely white campuses, where sizable numbers of African American students were now enrolled. Many of these students organized and protested for Black Studies programs as a means of ending their cultural and academic isolation in these new settings. In the process a variety of coalitions were formed in the interest of social change that emanated from the universities. Alignments were formed, for example, between African American and white leftist student organizations that resulted in common protests against "the establishment"—authority figures in these institutions and their supporters. At the same time, many of the post–civil rights efforts linked up with international causes—the Vietnam War and the fight against apartheid in South Africa being two major ones.

Before the movements of the 1960s were over, the older protest and lobby groups such as the NAACP and the National Urban League (NUL) converged with the more recent groups, such as the SCLC, SNCC, and the revitalized CORE. The joint efforts between the conventional and legalist activists and the street protesters led to considerable success in legislation and practical changes in the segregated social order. Although the street protesters used their mobilization skills, these efforts were now joined by the high degree of bureaucratic organization the NAACP had developed after long years of working in the court system and lobbying in the halls of Congress. This enabled Roy Wilkins of the NAACP, for example, to focus the confreres on specific legislative proposals and the development of coalitions of supporters to get the bills through Congress and signed by the president. Protest, as Wilkins told his latecomers, needed to have specific legislative and legal goals (Wilkins 1994). The legislative achievements of that time for African Americans were the most extensive in since the Civil War amendments of the 1860–1870 period. In terms of national legislation, the civil rights movement achieved the 1964 Civil Rights Act, the 1965 Voting Rights Act, and the 1968 Fair Housing Act, making the 1960s one of the most successful of all protest and lobbying eras. The Civil Rights Act became widely known for its focus on accommodations, although its coverage was broad indeed, making it practically impossible to legally justify any acts of racial exclusion. It covered "voting, public accommodations, public facilities, education, and fair employment practices . . . [establishing both] the Equal Employment Opportunity Commission and the Community Relations Service" (Blaustein and Zangrando 1968, 525). The Supreme Court forthwith upheld the constitutionality of the Civil Rights Act in a series of public accommodation test cases in the still mostly segregated South. Title VI and Title VII of the act are particularly important. Title VI bars discrimination from any entity that receives federal financial assistance, with specification about withdrawal or denial of funding for cause. Title VII focuses on employment, barring discrimination hiring, firing, or terms of service. It also specifies penalties similar to those in Title VI. This new practice of allowing federal intervention in order to protect citizens was new, and its consequences in public accommodations and the workplace exacted significant changes. The Voting Rights Act, because it dealt with voting, had the most important effect on the political disfranchisement of Blacks in the South. This legislation forced the states to take affirmative measures to enroll African American voters; when states failed to do so, federal registrars were dispatched to ensure compliance. Moreover, the law required these specified states to submit proposed changes in their voting laws and provisions for federal approval (Blaustein and Zangrando 1968). The act had a profound and rapid effect in adding Blacks to the voting rolls, and eventually it facilitated their election to public offices in the region. The 1968 Fair

---

Voices of the 1960s: The Black Panther Party

Black Panther Party Platform and Program, October 1966

What We Want
What We Believe

1. We want freedom. We want power to determine the destiny of our Black Community.

We believe that black people will not be free until we are able to determine our destiny.

2. We want full employment for our people.

We believe that the federal government is responsible and obligated to give every man employment or a guaranteed income. We believe that if the white American businessmen will not give full employment, then the means of production should be taken from the businessmen and placed in the community so that the people of the community can organize and employ all of its people and give a high standard of living.

3. We want an end to the robbery by the white man of our Black Community.

We believe that this racist government has robbed us and now we are demanding the overdue debt of forty acres and two mules. Forty acres and two mules was promised 100 years ago as restitution for slave labor and mass murder of black people. We will accept the payment in currency which will be distributed to our many communities. The Germans are now aiding the Jews in Israel for the genocide of the Jewish people. The Germans murdered six million Jews. The American racist has taken part in the slaughter of over fifty million black people; therefore, we feel that this is a modest demand that we make.

4. We want decent housing, fit for shelter of human beings.

We believe that if the white landlords will not give decent housing to our black community, then the housing and the land should be made into cooperatives so that our community, with government aid, can build and make decent housing for its people.

5. We want education for our people that exposes the true nature of this decadent American society. We want education that teaches us our true history and our role in the present-day society.

We believe in an educational system that will give to our people knowledge of self. If a man does not have knowledge of himself and his position in society and the world, then he has little chance to relate to anything else.

6. We want all black men to be exempt from military service.

We believe that Black people should not be forced to fight in the military service to defend a racist government that does not protect us. We will not fight and kill other people of color in the world who, like black people, are being victimized by the white racist government of America. We will protect ourselves from the force and violence of the racist police and the racist military, by whatever means necessary.

7. We want an immediate end to POLICE BRUTALITY and MURDER of black people.

We believe we can end police brutality in our black community by organizing black self-defense groups that are dedicated to defending our black community from racist police oppression and brutality. The Second Amendment to the Constitution of the United States gives a right to bear arms. We therefore believe that all black people should arm themselves for self-defense.

8. We want freedom for all black men held in federal, state, county and city prisons and jails.

We believe that all black people should be released from the many jails and prisons because they have not received a fair and impartial trial.

9. We want all black people when brought to trial to be tried in court by a jury of their peer group or people from their black communities, as defined by the Constitution of the United States.

We believe that the courts should follow the United States Constitution so that black people will receive fair trials. The 14th Amendment of the U.S. Constitution gives a man a right to be tried by his peer group. A peer is a person from a similar economic, social, religious, geographical, environmental, historical and racial background. To do this the court will be forced to select a jury from the black community from which the black defendant came. We have been, and are being tried by all-white juries that have no understanding of the "average reasoning man" of the black community.

10. We want land, bread, housing, education, clothing, justice and peace. And as our major political objective, a United Nations–supervised plebiscite to be held throughout the black colony in which only black colonial subjects will be allowed to participate, for the purpose of determining the will of black people as to their national destiny. (Foner 1970, 2–4)

Housing Act was much less successful, although it did allow the Department of Housing and Urban Development to investigate the many complaints it received about discrimination in housing, but it could not initiate them.

The Montgomery Bus Boycott: A Case Study

Segregation always encouraged its own opposition. Even as Booker T. Washington at the Atlanta Cotton Exposition in 1895 was embracing it, African Americans in the audience cried. And despite the widespread impact it was destined to have, there was fundamental opposition to the *Plessy v. Ferguson* decision even within the Court. Justice John Harlan issued a strong dissent to the separate but equal doctrine, saying: "Our Constitution is color-blind, and neither knows nor tolerates classes among citizens. In respect of civil rights, all citizens are equal before the law. The humblest is the peer of the most powerful" (Blaustein and Zangrando 1968, 309). As the doctrine of separate but equal became institutionalized in American social and public life, African Americans opposed, resisted, and defied this new orthodoxy. They did so in big and small places, with subtlety and boisterousness, and in fits and starts, but they did so continuously. There were heroic figures, martyrs, and sometimes tricksters in these efforts to defeat or manage the condition of segregation. But sometimes there were victories. As protests became more and more organized in local communities, these victories were at first isolated, or appeared to be, such as those of Tallahassee, Florida, and Baton Rouge, Louisiana. The victory in Montgomery, Alabama, was different, however, almost from the beginning. It rapidly transcended its local stage, creating a national movement.

Montgomery brought together several critical forces, activating other community elements that had not entered the protest stream. Rosa Parks, a Montgomery Fair department store seamstress, became the catalyst. Her actions created a space for the emergence of a new social philosophy that brought together, among others, new leadership, a rising student movement, the old-line civil rights organizations and their warriors from battles of the 1930s, 1940s, and early 1950s, and independent social activists. This merger would also benefit from the drive for independence in Africa and Asia as well as the rising Black Muslim religion in the urban African American community (Lincoln 1962). When Parks refused to give up her seat to a white man on December 1, 1955, these drifting and floating forces converged, effectuating the coming of age of a widespread and effective social movement. The model of Montgomery and its impact would be felt for the remainder of the civil rights movement. "Word of Mrs. Parks's arrest began to spread even before the white bus driver called the police. One passenger on the bus told a friend of Mrs. Parks's about the event, and that friend . . . immediately called the home of longtime black activist E. D. Nixon, a past president of Montgomery's National Association for the Advancement of Colored People (NAACP) Chapter and the most outspoken figure in the black community" (Garrow 1986, 13).

On hearing about the arrest, "Nixon called the home of a white lawyer, Clifford Durr, one of the city's few racial liberals. Durr . . . called the station and learned the charges . . . and . . . immediately called Nixon back and related the details." Then Nixon, Durr, and his wife went to the city jail and secured Mrs. Parks's release by posting a $100 bond.

Before they arrived at the jail—and in the great tradition of the NAACP—Nixon and the Durrs "discussed the possibility of Mrs. Parks being a test case. They knew how strong her character was and they had seen a strengthened self-confidence in her the past few months . . ." (Garrow 1986). Other potential test cases where the individuals had problems of character were dropped in favor of Mrs. Parks, who had impeccable character. She also agreed to the proposition.

Black leadership in the town moved immediately to involve the Women's Political Council, an organization founded in 1946 to pursue equity in the system of segregation. An activist member, Jo Ann Robinson, nearly single-handedly organized a citywide boycott of the Montgomery City Bus Lines. With a test case in the making and a planned boycott being organized, Nixon knew that mass protest would succeed only if they could obtain the enthusiastic support of Montgomery's Black ministers. Several of them immediately agreed to consider the boycott protest. Among them were Ralph David Abernathy and his friend, the new pastor at the Dexter Avenue Baptist Church, Martin Luther King Jr. The initial meeting was held at King's church. With this initial meeting, it quickly became apparent that a new organization would have to be formed to mediate personal rivalries and competition between existing leaders and organizations. Therefore, on December 5, 1955, King, as a relatively recent arrival, became president of the Montgomery Improvement Association (MIA).

This organization then coordinated and directed the boycott of the city bus lines and other aspects of the campaign. An important part of the strategy was a legal suit, filed on February 1, 1956, challenging the city's policy of segregation (Fairclough 1987, 478). So as the highly organized and very effective daily boycott campaign continued, the parallel action in court moved along with it. It was a long campaign indeed. Because of the defiance and intransigence of white city leaders, the bus boycott dragged on for a year, but the MIA persevered. Relief finally came on November 13, 1956, when the Supreme Court declared that Montgomery's bus segregation laws were unconstitutional. The MIA officially ended its bus boycott on December 20, 1956 (Fairclough 1987, 479). In the end, the success of this campaign owed to the fusion of three well-wrought protest tactics: legalism, the boycott, and a mass mobilization street protest.

The organization was not finished with this local victory, which had after all been nationalized in the widespread media attention it had received. King immediately rode the crest of the wave of success to directly inveigh against nationwide racial discrimination, and galvanize support for a national campaign. He did so by joining with the national leadership of the NAACP to plan a national mass meeting in Washington, D.C., at the Lincoln Memorial. They did indeed hold this meeting, which was held in the form of a "Prayer Pilgrimage" on May 17, 1957. This also provided an occasion for a call on the administration in Washington, a model for future movement protest and lobbying. A meeting was secured with Vice President Nixon on June 13 after President Eisenhower refused to meet with the African American leaders (Fairclough 1987, 39; Burk 1985, 84). By September 9, Senate Majority Leader Lyndon B. Johnson of Texas succeeded in getting congressional approval for the first Civil Rights Bill in more than a century. Fifteen days later, President Eisenhower sent federal troop to uphold the Supreme Court's ruling of the desegregation of public schools in Little Rock, Arkansas. And finally, on June 23, 1958, President Eisenhower capitulated and met with the African American leaders.

Why did a local campaign in a relatively small southern city assume such momentous importance in the most successful social movement among African Americans in history? Perhaps first and foremost was the emergence of a national leader in the person of Martin Luther King Jr., who had tremendous charisma and skill. He soon developed a regional protest organization, the SCLC, in order to harness widespread protest activity. But more important than this decentralized organization was the new strategy and philosophy of nonviolent civil disobedience. Montgomery wedded mass politics to the old strategy of legalism, and thus passed into legend as a module for movement action.

The Rebirth of the Clientage Leader:
The Post–Civil Rights Era

Efforts among African Americans that have achieved social transformations (such as Black abolitionism, the National and State Convention movements, Black Reconstruction, and the movement led by King) have always been accompanied or succeeded by those who reap the benefits of these successes in conventional political activity. Sometimes these conventional efforts have had a distinct conservative cast, at least in reference to the ideas from which new spaces were forged in the first place. Political scientist Matthew Holden has conceptualized this category of leaders as "clientage" leaders (Holden 1973; Walton 1985, 265–266). Simply put, these leaders are chosen and appointed by the white community for the representation of the African American community. Perhaps the best-known example of this variety of leadership was Booker T. Washington, who historian David Lewis tells us was an invention of his white patron, the railroad magnate William Baldwin (Lewis 1994). Such leaders often act as a cover for whites who seek to circumscribe the influence of African Americans in public affairs (Walton 1969b, 3–10).

After the civil rights thrust of the 1960s and 1970s, this reality emerged with a new wave of African American conservative protest leaders. In the 1980s the Reagan administration and the Republican Party became the sponsors of such a clientage effort by reconstituting a small cadre of African Americans within the right wing of the GOP, the then ruling partisan coalition. At the Fairmont Conference in December 1980, Ed Meese, President Reagan's attorney general, let it be known publicly that Republican political appointments and positions would be given to those African Americans who embraced the conservative ideology and to those willing to roll back the so-called liberal achievements (Walton 1988, 170–174; Smith 1983, 195–225). "Once selected blacks were brought in and made a part of the new conservative movement, they were given funds, access to leading white conservative magazines, publishers, and television and radio shows to promote their philosophy. Suddenly, they were everywhere. Overnight they were challenging the black civil rights leaders" (Walton 1988, 172). This new interest group attacked all of the civil rights achievements, affirmative action, and government programs that assisted the African American community. They articulated the view that such programs were detrimental to the African American community, and they sought to create the perception that this was actually consistent with general African American public opinion. In reality, however, their task was to provide a smoke screen for the articulation of a conservative Republican political program in the hope of generating favorable opinion among African Americans. The initiative appeared to remain on course through the successor George Bush administration when the conservative Fairmont Conference attendee Clarence Thomas was appointed to the Supreme Court. Other carefully placed individuals inside the governmental bureaucracy appeared to have the responsibility of turning back policy gains of African Americans by reducing federal programs targeting African Americans and by selectively neglecting civil rights regulations (Walton 1988).

Although the interlude with the Clinton administration did not follow this trend, it often left intact executive orders that had been issued by Reagan. Among the most significant measures in this regard was one that placed control over some civil rights regulations within the executive budget office, which reduced congressional oversight. Thus the "Reagan revolution" has had a lasting influence that is being perpetuated today in the George W. Bush administration with conservative appointees, many of them African Americans (Walton and Smith 2002). In short, the Black conservatives in the recent Republican administrations appear to have reinvigorated the role of the "clientage" official in several ways. They have created a public space for Black intellectual conservatism, they have been appointed to high bureaucratic offices, and they specifically take public policy positions in opposition to special protections for minority rights or the need for such protections (Dawson 2001, 281–302). African American leaders outside this group are largely relegated to the status of government critics.

Conclusion

As this analysis has shown, African Americans have engaged in interest group and lobby politics since colonial America. Spurred into mobilization and action by their contextual dilemmas, protest and lobby organizations have taken numerous forms, formats, and structures. They have also deployed a vast array of protest and lobbying tactics, techniques, and procedures. Such tactics often began as single and small group petitions, evolving into large-scale marches and demonstrations like those seen from the mid-1950s to the early 1970s. Often the political structures and organizations through which African Americans have made their efforts have been conceptualized as being concerned only with rights protection and thus were omitted from study samples as aggregate empirical analyses became prominent in political science analysis, or they were considered to fit somewhere outside the most general theories of political science. The fallacy of aggregate analyses is well illustrated by the work of Jack Walker (1991), who argued that he was conducting a national survey of interest groups in Washington. Yet in order to eliminate bias, the survey was drawn from the *Washington Information Directory,* which happened to exclude most African American organizations, which could not maintain national offices with a central administrative staff. For example, the oldest organization, the NAACP, for years had only one person in Washington, Clarence Mitchell. Yet his success in the direction of that office from 1950 to 1978 was such that he became known as the "101st Senator" (Watson 1990).

This analysis has shown that African American political activity has been far broader than civil rights efforts and that its oppositional protest character is well within commonly accepted means of political expression in democratic societies. Donna and Charles Hamilton support this view. They argue that African American civil rights organizations have had a "dual agenda" all along. Among African American interest, lobbying, and protest groups, they write, "then and now, there have *always* been two agendas—civil rights and social welfare." Their findings are based on an analysis of the appearances of African American interest groups at congressional hearings from the New Deal to the present (Hamilton and Hamilton 1997, 3).

Finally, the conceptualization of protest as outside the confines of normal political expression has allowed the discipline to miss the essential aspect of the enterprise in a racialized society in which formal participation was systematically denied to African Americans. Thus protest became the functional means for entering any expression into the political arena. Moreover, it was the base from which practically every formal political organization and leader emerged when participation was regularized in the ebb and flow of postslavery enfranchisement.

References

Aptheker, Herbert. 1943. *American Negro Slave Revolts*. New York: Columbia University Press.

———. 1951. *A Documentary History of the Negro People in the United States*. New York: Citadel Press.

———. 1971. "The Turner Cataclysm." In John Duff and Peter Mitchell, eds., *The Nat Turner Rebellion*. New York: Harper and Row.

Baldwin, James. 1955. *Notes of a Native Son*. Boston: Beacon Press.

Bauer, Raymond, and Alice Bauer. 1942. "Day to Day Resistance to Slavery." *Journal of Negro History* 27 (October): 388–449.

Bennett, Lerone. 1985. *Before the Mayflower*. New York: Penguin Books.

Blaustein, Albert P., and Robert L. Zangrando, eds. 1968. *Civil Rights and the American Negro: A Documentary History*. New York: Clarion.

———. 1991. *Civil Rights and African Americans: A Documentary History*. Evanston, IL: Northwestern University.

Broderick, Francis, and August Meier. 1965. *Negro Protest Thought in the Twentieth Century*. Indianapolis, IN: Bobbs-Merrill.

Burk, Robert. 1985. *The Eisenhower Administration and Black Civil Rights*. Knoxville: University of Tennessee Press.

Button, James. 1978. *Black Violence: Political Impact of the 1970s Riots*. Princeton, NJ: Princeton University Press.

Carmichael, Stokely. 1971. *Stokely Speaks: Black Power Back to Pan-Africanism*. New York: Vintage Books.

Clarke, John Henrik, ed., assisted by A. Peter Bailey and Earl Grant. 1969. *Malcolm X: The Man and His Times*. Toronto: Collier Books.

Crowell, John. 1971. "The Aftermath of Nat Turner's Insurrection." In John Duff and Peter Mitchell, eds., *The Nat Turner Rebellion*. New York: Harper and Row.

Crowley, Jocelyn, and Theda Skocpol. 2001. "The Rush to Organize: Explaining Associational Formation in the United States, 1860s–1920s." *American Journal of Political Science* 45 (October): 813–829.

Cruse, Harold. 1967. *The Crisis of the Negro Intellectual from Its Origins to the Present*. New York: William Morrow.

Dahl, Robert. 1961. *Who Governs?* New Haven, CT: Yale University Press.

Davis, Abraham, and Barbara Hill Graham. 1995. *The Supreme Court, Race, and Civil Rights*. Thousand Oaks, CA: Sage.

Dawson, Michael. 2001. *Black Visions: The Roots of Contemporary African American Political Ideologies*. Chicago: University of Chicago Press.

Drewy, William. 1971. "The Southampton Insurrection." In John Duff and Peter Mitchell, eds., *The Nat Turner Rebellion*. New York: Harper and Row.

Fairclough, Adam. 1987. *To Redeem the Soul of America: The Southern Christian Leadership Conference and Martin Luther King Jr.* Athens: University of Georgia Press.

Fishel, Leslie, Jr., and Benjamin Quarles, eds. 1967. *The Negro American: A Documentary History*. Glenview, IL: Scott, Foresman.

Foner, Philip, ed. 1970. *The Black Panthers Speak*. Philadelphia: Lippincott.

Foner, Philip, and George Walker, eds. 1979. *Proceedings of the Black State Conventions, 1840–1865*. Vol. 1. Philadelphia: Temple University Press.

———. 1980. *Proceedings of the Black State Conventions, 1840–1865*. Vol. 2. Philadelphia: Temple University Press.

Franklin, John Hope. 1995. "Race and the Constitution in the Nineteenth Century." In John Hope Franklin and Genna Rae McNeil, eds., *African Americans and the Living Constitution*. Washington, DC: Smithsonian Institution.

Franklin, John Hope, and Alfred Moss Jr. 1994. *From Slavery to Freedom*. 7th ed. New York: McGraw-Hill.

Garfunkel, Herbert. 1959. *When Negroes March: The March on Washington Movement in the Organizational Politics for FEPC*. New York: The Free Press.

Garrow, David J. 1986. *Bearing the Cross: Martin Luther King, Jr., and the Southern Christian Leadership Conference*. New York: William Morrow.

Hamilton, Dona Cooper, and Charles Hamilton. 1997. *The Dual Agenda: The African American Struggle for Civil and Economic Equality*. New York: Columbia University Press.

Harding, Vincent. 1969. "Religion and Resistance Among Antebellum Negroes, 1850–1868." In A. Meier and E. Rudwick, eds., *The Making of Black America*. Vol. 2. New York: Atheneum Press.

Harris, Sheldon. 1972. *Paul Cuffee: Black America and the African Return*. New York: Simon and Schuster.

Higginson, Thomas Wentworth. 1971. "Nat Turner's Insurrection." In John Duff and Peter Mitchell, eds., *The Nat Turner Rebellion*. New York: Harper and Row.

Hine, Darlene. 1979. *Black Victory*. Millwood, NY: KTO Press.

Holden, Matthew, Jr. 1973. *The Politics of the Black Nation*. New York: Chandler.

Keech, William. 1968. *The Impact of Negro Voting: The Role of the Vote in the Quest for Equality*. Chicago: Rand McNally.

Key, V. O., Jr. 1949. *Southern Politics*. New York: Knopf.

Lewis, David Levering. 1978. *King: A Biography*. 2d ed. Urbana: University Press of Illinois.

———. 1994. *W.E.B. DuBois: Biography of a Race, 1868–1919*. New York: Henry Holt.

———. 2000. *W.E.B. DuBois: The Fight for Equality and the American Century, 1919–1963*. New York: Henry Holt.

Lincoln, C. Eric. 1962. *The Black Muslims in America*. Boston: Beacon Press.

Lipsky, Michael. 1968. "Protest as a Political Resource." *American Political Science Review* 62 (December): 1144–1158.

Malcolm X. 1969. "Racism: The Cancer That Is Destroying America." In John Henrik Clarke, ed., assisted by A. Peter Bailey and Earl Grant, *Malcolm X: The Man and His Times*. Toronto: Collier Books.

Malcolm X, with the assistance of Alex Haley. 1965. *The Autobiography of Malcolm X*. New York: Grove Press.

McAdam, Doug. 1982. *Political Process and the Development of Black Insurgency, 1930–1970.* Chicago: University of Chicago Press.

Miller, Floyd. 1975. *The Search for a Black Nationality: Black Emancipation and Colonization, 1787–1863.* Urbana: University Press of Illinois.

Morris, Aldon. 1984. *The Origins of the Civil Rights Movement: Black Communities Organizing for Change.* New York: The Free Press.

Morris, Aldon, Shirley Hatchett, and Ronald Brown. 1989. "The Civil Rights Movement and Black Political Socialization." In R. Siegel, ed., *Political Learning in Adulthood.* Chicago: University of Chicago Press.

Morrison, Minion K. C. 1989. "Racial Violence and Racial Mobilization in the United States 1960–1980." In Sophie Body-Gendrot and Jacques Carré, eds., *Ville et violence dans le monde anglophone,* 97–114. Clermont-Ferrand, France: Université Blaise-Pascal.

Newman, Richard, et al., eds. 2001. *Pamphlets of Protest: An Anthology of Early African American Protest Literature, 1790–1860.* New York: Routledge.

Painter, Nell. 2000. "Rodney King, Police Brutality, and Riots." In Jonathan Birnbaum and Clarence Taylor, eds., *Civil Rights since 1787,* 645–649. New York: New York University Press.

Parenti, Michael. 1970. "Power and Pluralism: A View from the Bottom." *Journal of Politics* (August): 504–519.

Skocpol, Theda, et al. 2001. "Patriotic Partnership: Why Great Wars Nourished American Civic Volunteerism." In Ira Katznelson and Martin Shefter, eds., *Shaped by War and Trade: International Influence on American Political Development.* Princeton, NJ: Princeton University Press.

Smith, J. Clay, Jr. 1983. "A Black Lawyer's Response to the Fairmont Papers." *Howard Law Journal* 26: 195–225.

Tragle, Henry, ed. 1971. *The Southampton Slave Revolt of 1831.* Amherst: University of Massachusetts Press.

Truman, David. 1951. *The Governmental Process.* New York: Knopf.

Walker, Jack L., Jr. 1991. *Mobilizing Interest Groups in America.* Ann Arbor: University of Michigan Press.

Walton, Hanes, Jr. 1969a. *The Negro in Third Party Politics.* Philadelphia: Dorrance.

———. 1969b. "Blacks and Conservative Political Movements." *Quarterly Review of Higher Education Among Negroes* 37 (October): 3–10.

———. 1971. *The Political Philosophy of Martin Luther King Jr.* New York: Greenwood Press.

———. 1972. *Black Politics.* Philadelphia: J. P. Lippincott.

———. 1985. *Invisible Politics: Black Political Behavior.* Albany: State University New York Press.

———. 1988. *When the Marching Stopped: The Politics of the Civil Rights Regulatory Agencies.* Albany: State University of New York Press.

Walton, Hanes, Jr., and Robert Smith. 2002. *American Politics and the African American Quest for Universal Freedom.* 2d ed. New York: Longman.

Watson, Denton L. 1990. *Lion in the Lobby: Clarence Mitchell Jr.'s Struggle for the Passage of Civil Rights Laws.* New York: William Morrow.

Wesley, Dorothy Porter, ed. 1969. *Negro Protest Pamphlets.* New York: Arno Press.

———. 1971. *Early Negro Writing, 1760–1837.* Boston: Beacon Press.

Wilkins, Roy. 1994. *Standing Fast: The Autobiography.* New York: DaCapo Press.

Williams, Juan. 1987. *Eyes on the Prize: America's Civil Rights Years, 1945–1965.* New York: Viking.

Wilson, James Q. 1961. "The Strategy of Protest: Problems of Negro Civic Action." *Journal of Conflict Resolution* 5 (September): 291–303.

3

Civil Rights Organizations and Movements

Lawrence J. Hanks

Political participation is best conceptualized as a continuum. At the minimum level of participation, individuals may think or talk about politics. At its maximum level, an individual may serve as head of state for a country. At various points along the continuum, citizens may vote, run for office, write letters, protest, join political action committees, and provide resources in numerous ways. However, in U.S. history, only twice has African American participation been close to universal for sustained periods. Just after the Civil War, between 1865 and 1876, the Reconstruction period included widespread formal African American participation, executed largely through the organized national Republican Party. This period was followed by what is regarded as the nadir of formal participation, from 1876 through the 1930s (Logan 1972), when most Blacks were disfranchised. The second sustained period of participation has occurred since the Voting Rights Act of 1965, when all African Americans have been equally protected players in the activities of politics in the United States. Outside of these two periods, state-sanctioned barriers often severely repressed the traditional political participation of the mass of African Americans. Thus most of African American political action has focused on becoming full players in American politics (Hanks 1987, 1–34), and most of this activity has taken place within the structure of independent community organizations, civil rights organizations, and social movements.

This chapter focuses on the participation of African Americans in such organizations, spanning the era of slavery to the present. The organizations discussed represent the major thrust of political activity during their particular eras. For activities during the period of slavery, the discussion focuses on the African American church and religious leadership, especially Richard Allen and the African Methodist Episcopal Church. It then turns to the first national organization, the Negro Convention Movement. For activities during the nadir, the National Association for the Advancement of Colored People (NAACP), the National Urban League (NUL), the Nation of Islam, and the Marcus Garvey movement are discussed. Next, for the civil rights movement era, the Congress of Racial Equality (CORE), the Southern Christian Leadership Conference (SCLC), and the Student Nonviolent Coordinating Committee (SNCC) are covered. For the post-movement period, the chapter discusses the Nation of Islam, and a case analysis is presented of the Million Man March in Washington, D.C., in 1995. For each of these subjects, the analytical framework will consist mainly of the following elements: origins, constituents, issues and goals, strategies, major constraints and facilitators, achievements and failures, factions, and the future.

The common thread that runs through these organizations and groups is the desire to empower the African American community, although with differing styles. During the period of slavery they sought to end involuntary servitude. During the postnadir era, the challenge was the unequal application of the law. The civil rights movement used direct action to secure voting rights, access to public accommodations, and equal protection of the law. Thereafter the focus has been trained on persistent inequality in public policy. Despite shared goals, styles and tactics have varied. Among the groups are conservatives, moderates, and radicals; integrationist and nationalists; and advocates of nonviolence and of self-defense.

African American Organizations in the Context of U.S. Interest Groups

The Prominence of Groups in U.S. Politics

In American politics little is more important than organizations. The range of diversity in the social fabric and the sheer magnitude of the geographical landscape in the United States produces a large number of organizations. Not all of these are avowedly or principally political. However, their existence as social entities is prominently associated with the advancement of some interest in a large and often impersonal setting. That leads to a landscape with a bewildering array of organized activity. This activity sustains a fluid participant social culture, which outsiders often see as "over-organization." Myrdal (1944, 952) noted this: "America has an unusual proliferation of social clubs, recreational organizations, lodges, fraternities and sororities, civic improvement societies, self-improvement societies, occupational associations, and other organizations." But the activities of these groups can easily be translated into civic action. Indeed, most of the organizations use their social, cultural, or religious base, inter alia, as the means for exerting influence on the political system. In short, these are often the building blocks through which political allocations are sought.

The prevalence of so many organizations and their activities have had a great impact on theories about interest group politics. Perhaps the dominant explanatory model of political action in the United States centers on the role of such pressure groups. It is widely held that they are the fundamental tools by which American society achieves the most admired and emulated democratic government in contemporary history. The "group" thesis of politics (Truman 1951) posits a plethora of interests that are organized in a highly participant society and bid against each other for welfare benefits. It is assumed that the openness of the system allows everyone to bid equally and that the chances of success depend on the effectiveness of the organization.

Moreover, the social bases in the society are structured such that the interests of different groups often overlap, producing a kind of equilibrium in the system. In short, the group basis of politics—often identified as pluralism—suggests that everyone has an equal chance of getting his or her interests represented and that there are no perpetual losers (Dahl 1961). Rather, everyone has the possibility of becoming a member of an infinite array of formulations and reformulations of interests in the marketplace. Much of this fluidity is associated with the anti-class bias in American politics that does indeed sometimes have an effect of social leveling among bidders in the political process.

Interest groups are distinct from political parties. They operate at a lower level and are best known for articulating interests that have been formulated at the local or base level of interest specification. The evidence suggests that almost 80 percent of these groups are organized around business and professional interests, and the remainder are associated with relatively particularized issues (Walker 1991, 1–60). Truman referred to such groups as those with shared attitudes that they used to make claims for public allocations. Graham Wilson (1990, 1) follows this line of argument, defining interest groups as "organizations, separate from government though often in close partnership with government, which attempt to influence public policy." They carry out their functions by lobbying political representatives, orchestrating public relations campaigns to create a favorable climate for their ideas and interests, and sometimes sponsoring litigation as well as direct protest action. Moreover, they are essential in helping to fund the very costly political campaigns that characterize the political process in the United States. Thus it is easy to see why these entities are regarded as so fundamental to the democratic process as it has evolved in the United States.

Resource Poor, But Superorganized African Americans

The group basis of politics and its pluralist assumptions have rarely worked as outlined above for African Americans. As was noted in chapter 1, the pluralist assumption that the system is open to all groups is patently false in reference to African Americans. This is a group that, unlike most of the organized groups of other immigrants, was formally barred from participation of any kind for long periods of American history. During other periods the group's rights to participation were observed in the breach or applied differentially. The absolute barriers were most prominent during slavery and for almost 100 years after the Reconstruction era. The group's formal organizations have been severely hampered, limiting their ability to generate sufficient resources to catch up with organizations that have never known such barriers.

Walton and Smith (2000, 120) compare the resources of two prominent African American organizations, the NAACP and the NUL, with other general interest organizations. The two groups hardly compare in membership or annual budgets. The NAACP, with its 450,000 members in 1995, had an annual budget of $11.9 million, and the NUL, with 118 affiliates, had a $24 million annual budget. Compare that with the AFL-CIO, with 14 million members and an annual budget of $63 million; or the 2.9 million Mothers Against Drunk Driving, with a $43 million budget; or the Sierra Club, with 600,000 members and an annual budget of $89 million. Indeed, these relatively old African American organizations barely did better in membership and funding than some recently established social equity groups—for example, the National Gay and Lesbian Task Force, with 15,000 members, boasted a $1 million budget in 1995.

Despite the relative resource poverty of African American organizations, there certainly is no shortage of them, a factor also related to the racialized circumstances in the United States. Myrdal also noted this. Compared to whites, he wrote,

> Negroes seem to have an even relative number of associations. In Chicago in 1937, when the total Negro population of the city was less than 270,000, there were over 4,000 formal associations, the membership of which was wholly or largely Negro. In Natchez, Mississippi, where the Negro population was about 7,500 there were more than 200 Negro associations uncovered in one week in 1935. This characteristic of the Negro community becomes even more striking when it is realized that generally upper- and middle-class people belong to more associations than do lower-class people. (1944, 952)

Although Myrdal saw this as pathological, he did not fail to see that the phenomenon was partially explained by the strivings of an excluded community. Many of the organizations mirrored white organizations from which Blacks were barred. And despite the social or cultural purposes espoused, few could avoid the dual role of trying to alter the nature of segregation and discrimination. Deriving as they did from a racialized society, they were inherently political. The proliferation of avowedly political organizations has been and remains similar.

The Local Character of Organizations and the Enduring Civil Rights Agenda

Despite the national condition of racial exclusion and discrimination, Blacks have more often been forced to organize at the local level because the risks and costs of national organization were higher. Before the relatively brief Reconstruction period and after it ended, Blacks lacked the mobility for even interregional linkages, let alone national ones. At the same time, legislation and extralegal practices were employed to diminish the prospects of such organization. One example is the Fugitive Slave Law, which denied freedom even to runaways found in free territories. Another example is that in the post-Reconstruction South, Blacks were barred from membership in the NAACP (Morris 1984, 40–77). Even under these conditions, however, there is a long historical record of local organizations seeking to establish and sustain links on a national scale. They were much aided in this effort by their singleness of purpose, namely, removing racial barriers to participation.

The scope of organizations within the African American community makes it difficult to examine more than a small selection of the most important among them. However, in a selective sampling of political organizations, some general characteristics emerge. Almost all of these groups, whatever their stated purposes, had to confront the racialized society. This first agenda historically led organizations to "seek ambiguous, intangible goals . . . —equality, freedom, dignity, pride, legal rights, etc." (Walton 1972, 171). This set of goals remains a priority even in the post–civil rights movement era, in which protection of formal rights has been substantially improved. For example, at the height of electoral success in 1976, more than 1,000 officials and politicians still identified rights-based issues as of foremost importance (Walton and Smith 2000, 119).

Analysis of a sample of about 200 current organizations (Estell 1994) illustrates the predominance of civil and political rights among African American organizations. As shown in Table 3.1, more than a quarter (26 percent) of the organizations can be deemed to have a political or civil rights orientation. The proportion increases to 50 percent if one counts the professional organizations (second most often identified), more than three-quarters of which were created because of exclusion from parallel white organizations. Invariably a first-order agenda item for the latter is the attainment of equal rights to practice their profession or craft. Their missions always refer to efforts to increase their numbers in the profession and to secure equal access to jobs and treatment. Also a comparatively large number of organizations are dedicated to women's issues (12 percent), and virtually every women's organization has an avowedly political or civil rights agenda—advancement of women in a gendered and racialized environment. Another 9 percent of the organizations are religious in nature, perhaps the oldest and traditionally most significant source of

TABLE 3.1   Categorization of Selected African American Organizations

Organization Type	Number	Percent
Civil Rights/Political	58	26
Professional	54	24
Women	26	12
Religious	20	9
Africa	20	9
Education	13	6
Media	12	5
Business and Labor	12	5
Miscellaneous	8	4
Total	223	100

SOURCE: Data from Estell 1994, 449–496.

African American political leadership. Finally, another 9 percent are dedicated to the advancement of Africa, but with distinct civil rights or political agendas.

The African American Church and Religious Leadership

Origins and Constituents

Churches were perhaps the earliest formal Black organizations. They were inevitably political, being controlled by African Americans in an otherwise dependent environment. The origins of the churches and religious leadership derived from the enslavement environment. The Africans were encouraged to embrace Christianity while all their original cultures and religious traditions were denigrated. The church grew from plantation-sanctioned worship gatherings, led by men who subsequently became the leaders in the slave quarters. However, the activities of these organizations was never limited to their religious roles. The churches became major centers for social, cultural, and political activity. They also rapidly became reservoirs for contesting servitude via an encoded communications system (Blassingame 1979, 41–76; Raboteau 1980, 212–288). Over time the church became the major venue for development and transmission of organizational skills and networks for social and political action.

Although individuals belong to a variety of faiths, the African American church may be defined as those national religious institutions whose members are predominantly African Americans. The overwhelming majority of the congregants are found in the Protestant churches because the southern-based and servile population was required to affiliate with the predominant denominations of the region. Most were Baptist and Methodist, hence the historical preferences of African Americans. Organized commitments to the Baptist faith appear to have been the earliest—one in Virginia in the 1750s (the so-called African Baptist), and the Silver Bluff Baptist Church in majority-Black South Carolina in the 1770s (Lincoln and Mamiya 1990, 23).

Eventually all of the major African American religious institutions participated in the formation of the Congress of National Black Churches, Inc. (CNBC). The members of this national body are the African Methodist Episcopal Church, the African Methodist Episcopal Zion Church, the Christian Methodist Episcopal Church, the Church of God in Christ, the National Baptist Convention USA, Inc., the National Baptist Convention of America, and the Progressive National Baptist Convention, Inc. These seven conventions represent approximately 80 percent of America's African American population (McKinney et al. 1997, viii–xi.). (See Table 3.2.)

Issues, Goals, and Strategies

The primary issue for the African American church has been how to effectively provide a place for the spiritual growth and the ultimate spiritual salvation of its members—"being in the world, and not of the world." This goal remained constant whether the church was dealing with the dehumanization of enslavement, postwar state-sanctioned discrimination, the civil rights mobilization, or persistent inequality. As such, these religious institutions continue to generate active support and intense religious commitment and expression.

Yet the social and political roles the churches have played retain high priority. The churches and their ministers were prominent in the fight for the abolition of slavery, and they have remained prominent ever since. With their high moral authority and their closeness to African American constituents, ministers have enjoyed a level of influence unparalleled in formal and informal leadership positions. Today they maintain a widespread presence as high-profile municipal, congressional, and even presidential contenders (notably, for example, Jesse Jackson).

TABLE 3.2   Black Church Membership, Estimates, 1989

Denomination	Number (millions)	Percent
Black Baptists	11.1	46.8
National Baptist Convention USA, Inc.	7.5	31.6
National Baptist Convention of America	2.4	10.1
Progressive National Baptist Convention	1.2	5.1
Black Methodists	4.3	18.2
African Methodist Episcopal	2.2	9.3
African Methodist Episcopal Zion	1.2	5.1
Christian Methodist Episcopal	0.9	3.8
Church of God in Christ	3.7	15.6
Other Black Congregations	1.4	5.9
White Protestant and Catholic Churches	2.0	8.4
Total	37.9	100

SOURCE: Adapted from Lincoln and Mamiya 1990, 407. Reprinted with permission from Duke University Press

The church seeks to influence the political process in numerous ways. Chief among them are providing political information for its members, encouraging political participation among its members, and serving as a hub for political activity (Frazier 1974; Lincoln and Mamiya 1990). The ministers in these congregations have predominated as political leaders, making the church a center of public affairs activity. They easily mobilize their individual congregations into political forces. In short, in these highly decentralized churches congregants follow the lead of their ministers, the most visible leader in their ambit. In a similar vein, the ministers and other church leaders have had a unique role in African American political strategy formation.

Major Constraints and Facilitators

Two schools of thought, the activist and the apolitical, have been prominent in the African American church regarding the role of political participation. The activist school essentially argues that "God helps those who help themselves." From this point of view, it is the responsibility of Christians to serve as vessels to manifest God's goodness and activism on Earth. In this long tradition of activism, church leaders are among the most prominent African American activist political spokesmen. They have used the pulpit and their congregations to sketch an oppositional stance about the racialized status of Blacks, thus placing a political stamp on their organizations. Prominent activists include Richard Allen, Absalom Jones, and Henry McNeil Turner (Appiah and Gates 1999, 76, 1060, 1900); Vernon Johns (Branch 1988, 1–26); Martin Luther King Jr. (Washington 1968); Jessie Jackson (Reed 1986); and Al Sharpton (Klein 1991). Although none of these leaders were elected officials, there is also a long tradition of ministers as elected officials, particularly in the period after 1930, when national Black representatives returned to Congress. Among the ministers were Adam Clayton Powell (New York, 1945–1967), Andrew Young (Georgia, 1973–1977), William Gray (Pennsylvania, 1979–1991), and Floyd Flake (New York, 1987–1997).

The apolitical school argues essentially that political activity is not appropriate for good Christians. These inactive church leaders suggest that time is better spent helping the poor, keeping religious injunctions, and supporting the spiritual activities of the church. Proponents of the apolitical school are more often than not found among smaller congregations and are not affiliated with the major conventions.

It follows that the activist school of thought facilitates political activity while the apolitical school curtails it. The notion of the African American church as an agent of social change has always been present. This was evident from the time that Richard Allen withdrew his Black parishioners from the balconies of segregated white churches to found the African Methodist Episcopal (AME) denomination. That essentially political act boldly set the agenda for the mainstream denomination and has never ceased to be an element. The tradition blossomed during the post–World War II civil rights movement. Aldon Morris (1984) has argued persuasively that the African American churches, and the southern African American churches in particular, were crucial to the movement's success. They provided the foot soldiers whom Martin Luther King led in southern mobilization.

Achievements, Continuing Challenges, and Prognosis

The major political achievements of the African American church are arguably its provision of political leadership and its historical role as an organizational hub. The churches and their ministers usually supplied the first organizational capacity for African Americans, even before slavery ended. The presence of the churches as organized entities and the modicum of independence they enjoyed provided an arena for challenge and socialization for civic engagement. It was often the only such outlet. The scope of this achievement is easily revealed in the postwar civil rights movement. There the churches functioned as political, social, and economic units to address the needs of the African American collective. In this period they organized voter registration campaigns, served as venues for rallies and demonstrations, built public housing, and offered a vast array of social services. Their comprehensive scope gave them access to virtually all aspects of the lives of their communicants.

In spite of the oasis of hope offered by the church, its role as a political agent is mitigated by persistent challenges. Perhaps the greatest challenge is the external conservative and racialized political system within which the church operates. Despite the continuous activism of the churches, change occurs slowly. Many of their challenges remain the same—largely the integration of their congregants into the routine benefits from public coffers. In other words, the religious sector's claims to "righteousness" endow it with no greater ability than any other sector to alleviate social problems. Indeed, with the strong bias favoring the separation of church and state, the churches also endure an extra burden when bidding in the public arena. Then there are routine issues that in African American church organizations (as in all organizations) have an exaggerated effect because of its heavy leadership role. Internally, the church has its own conflicts about leadership, such as questions about morality and the crises of faith. These get writ large because the church often executes many social service or other public functions that are insufficiently attended by state and local offices.

The seven conventions represented in the Congress of National Black Churches reflect a diversity of religious traditions in the African American community. And with the political impact of those religious institutions outside of this Congress (Black Muslims, Catholics, etc.), it becomes clear that religion has provided much sustenance for African Americans during the quest for political equality. However, there are new institutions assuming some of the same roles. In the past thirty years the greatest growth has been among the Pentecostal Church of God in Christ denomination. It is less avowedly interested in political mobilization, but does assume many of the social services roles. Also in the last twenty years African American mega-churches, televangelists, and ministers have arisen, advocating a holistic approach to religion and spirituality. Ministers who are decidedly activist in meeting the total needs of their parishioners lead them. Prominent among these ministers are T. D. Jakes (Jakes 1999), Frederick K.C. Price (Price 1999), Creflo Dollar (Dollar 1999), Eugene Rivers (Rivers 2001), Barbara King (King 1995), and Johnnie Coleman (Coleman 2000).

The African American church has always had the saving of souls as its primary mission, but with an added twist. Given the history of disfranchisement and racial exclusion of African Americans in the United States, one readily understands the expanded role of the church for the enhancement of political participation. The African American church appears destined to continue to have a role in this mission.

Richard Allen and the AME Church: A Case Study

The first denomination organized by Blacks was the AME Church. Its founder, Richard Allen (1760–1831), was born a slave but worked to purchase his freedom. He then spent most of his adult life as a preacher. In 1816 he was consecrated the first official bishop of the AME Church. The AME foundations and teachings were directly derivative of the John Wesley Methodist movement in England. African Americans affiliated with the Wesleyans early. When Wesley sent Anglican priest Thomas Coke to speak to the American public in December 1784, AME prime mover Richard Allen attended. (A history of the church is available at http://www.amecnet.org) Just two years later "the Methodist Episcopal Church acknowledged 1,890 African American members, representing approximately ten percent of its total membership" (Lincoln and Mamiya 1990, 50). The current AME Church refers to Allen as one of the "Four Horsemen," or founders of the church. The others are Daniel Payne, William Quinn, and Henry Turner.

The AME Church organized in response to "stultifying and demeaning conditions attending membership in the white controlled Methodist Episcopal churches." This contributed to a common thread in this and similar African American distinctive denominations. "Unlike most sectarian movements, the initial impetus for black spiritual and ecclesiastical independence was not grounded in religious doctrine or policy, but in the offensiveness of racial segregation and the alarming inconsistencies between the teachings and the expressions of faith" (Lincoln and Mamiya 1990, 47). The immediate cause of the founding of the AME Church is that in 1787 the St. George's Methodist Episcopal Church in Philadelphia segregated its white attendees from African Americans, requiring the latter to sit in the balcony section. Further restrictions later led to the establishment of an abolition group in the city, the Free African Society. As the leader of the Methodist branch of the society, Richard Allen led his group and four others to eventually withdraw from St. George's Church. They formed the African Methodist Episcopal Church in Philadelphia in 1816.

Constituents

The constituents can be divided into two, pre– and post–Civil War groups. Prior to the Civil War, Richard Allen was perhaps the best-known leader. For all practical purposes, the church functioned outside the South, for obvious reasons. Richard Allen focused his attention on injustices African American parishioners faced in white-dominated Methodist churches around the North, and he was active in the Underground Railroad. Until the Civil War, the church's constituents were any African American Methodists who were willing to separate from the white-dominated mother church and affiliate with Allen's organization. The church drew a positive response wherever Allen and his missionaries traveled, spawning rapid growth. Some support was also offered by white liberals, although the AME remained separate from the control and influence of the white churches (Campbell 1995, 21). The second base for the prewar church was the population of escapees from southern plantations who had fled to the cities of the North or to Canada. Allen's own home was a central transmission site along the escape route (Campbell 1995, 21).

In the postwar period, the church came to be more animated by the issues of church teachings and the constitutional idea of the universal rights of men. This development elicited a political and legal focus from the Black church leaders, which generated an even larger constituency. The church developed a new set of constituents—freedmen in the South, especially those who were displaced after the short-lived Reconstruction.

Issues and Goals

The political issues and goals of the church have changed drastically over its 200-year history, as its constituent bases and opponents changed over time. Initially the church and Allen were reactive: political issues followed from the segregation that arose in the parent church. The church first focused its attention on expanding past the Allegheny Mountains to centers of the African American population. For example, William Quinn surreptitiously led expansion into two slave states, Kentucky and Missouri. This occurred despite the Fugitive Slave Act, which required runaways to be returned and which restricted even free African Americans (Smith 1922, 17). Then Daniel Coker, a fiery preacher and later the first AME African missionary, used the Christian scriptures to demonstrate that the social order was unjust, adopting a Jeffersonian-style argument (Campbell 1995, 24).

The African American supporters of the abolition movement also had their origins in this church. Allen and other AME leaders used the church and the Free African Societies, along with the Negro Convention Movement (a Black quasi-political party of which he was a founder), as platforms for advocating the abolition of slavery. This provided the early foundation for the use of church doctrine as the basis for declaring slavery inconsistent with Christian principles and thus immoral. And their activities were not tepid:

> Bethel Church (the Mother Black Church in Philadelphia) among others, served as a station on the Underground Railroad. Many of the four thousand members of the first AME church in Charleston, South Carolina, were deeply involved in the 1822 slave insurrection led by Denmark Vesey. The church was burned to the ground by the outraged whites who had never felt comfortable with its presence. (Lincoln and Mamiya 1990, 52)

But Allen and his cohorts did not end the argument there. They also put the church, and Allen in particular, at the forefront of the resistance to the American Colonization Society, which advocated "returning" Blacks to Africa for settlement in Liberia. The church leaders spoke out against colonization, arguing that it involved shipping people off to what was essentially a foreign land, with no provisions for future inhabitation (George 1973, 174–175). Another example of the strong political stance the church took in this period is reflected in the work of the church newspaper editor, Benjamin Tanner, an AME bishop. Between 1868 and 1884—years coincident with the failing Reconstruction—Tanner used the *Christian Recorder* as a platform for decrying the violations of African American civil rights and for taking a guarded stance against the American Colonization Society's scheme for Liberia (Seraile 1998, 38–42). He went on to argue strongly for racial solidarity as a means for achieving progress for Blacks in light of continued racial exclusion (Logan and Winston 1982, 577).

After the Civil War, the issues shifted from abolition and colonization to socioeconomic and political equality, education, and expansion in the South. The church then became less active. However, its benevolent work and its schools advanced each of these goals. By 1900, education among the Black masses was advanced by thirty-two secondary schools and colleges that the church helped establish (Baldwin 1983, 106). In 1856, the church founded the first African American college in the United States, Wilberforce University, and over time it went on to found a string of colleges and junior colleges throughout the South (Lincoln and Mamiya 1990, 53). The AME Church thereby expanded rapidly into the region, becoming the largest denomination in the South in the postwar years. However, with the emergence of the NAACP and the NUL, the church seemed to take a less active stance in the political arena. Instead it retreated to its religious activities, letting the void be filled by these new organizations.

Strategies, Achievements, and Constraints

In trying to achieve its goal of abolition and freeing the enslaved, the church adopted a twofold approach. It openly advocated abolition through reasoned argument, appeals to religious doctrine, and exhorting the ideals of the "Founding Fathers." Secretly (at least in the South) it helped organize and run the Underground Railroad. In the Reconstruction and post-Reconstruction eras, secular church elements came into greater prominence by taking public stances on rights issues. An example was the church newspaper, the *Christian Recorder,* which had circulated before the Civil War but was outlawed in the South and often condemned in the North (Seraile 1998, 20). However, when Benjamin Tanner took over the editorship after the Civil War, the paper became a widely circulated platform for condemning lynching, living conditions, and other problems affecting African Americans. For example, Tanner strongly supported a national civil rights bill in 1872, arguing that it would abolish discrimination. He also wanted amend the bill to prohibit school segregation (Seraile 1998, 47).

The AME Church largely failed in its early mission of convincing through reasoned argument of the need to abolish slavery and create equal rights. Given the times, this is not surprising. However, it did succeed in the creation of churches run by African Americans for members frustrated with the segregated white churches. At the AME Church's General Convention of 1908, the statistical report noted that there were 800,000 lay members (Smith 1922, 260). The Black-run churches formed an outlet for abolitionist sentiments that could not be expressed earlier. The church also succeeded in its activity in the Underground Railroad, assisting to transport about 80,000 people into free states.

In the post-Reconstruction era to the World War I era, the church led a largely successful fight against the colonization efforts in Liberia, arguing that native-born Americans should not be transported to foreign shores to start over. Likewise, the church's newspaper continued its role of informing the public of violations of civil rights, opposing colonization, and encouraging government action. Although this activity waned with the emergence of the NAACP and the civil rights movement, the church remained a solid base of foot soldiers for political mobilization in the later period.

The early church faced a number of important constraints, which, in retrospect, did not bode well for its future. In the first place, missionary zeal was required to open churches in relatively neutral states, and utmost secrecy was required in the South. The church had few allies beyond some liberal white churches and northern abolitionists. Even these faltered after Reconstruction.

Factions and Prognosis

Like many of the Protestant churches in America, the AME Church, born of a schism in the parent church, later underwent its own. Control emanated fairly consistently from the top, and a policy disagreement led to a split in 1840. These policy and personality conflicts precipitated the breakaway First Colored Methodist Protestant Church (Baldwin 1983, 81). Similarly, there were other rival denominations of Methodists. They often discussed union, but they remain separate to this day (Smith 1922, 370).

The AME Church is currently the largest African American Methodist church in the United States. Its base of support and lay membership seem fairly constant, growing about the same as the overall population growth rate. The church now has over 2.2 million members. Although the church remains involved in missionary and benevolence activities, its historical political role is now more muted.

The Back to Africa Movement

For as long as descendants of Africa have been in the "New World," most have remained interested in and curious about Africa and have thought of the "motherland" with a certain hopefulness. This view is inspired both by an awareness of having arrived in the West against their will and by the reality of long-term outsider status. But in African American culture there are also vestiges of Africa that serve as markers and reminders of the heritage. Notwithstanding a massive effort to divest Blacks in the Americas of their cultural heritage, many of its features survived. These Africanisms—such as in language, dance, music, approaches to religion, and cookery—along with the racialized conditions in the Americas provide a foundation for a yearning for Africa among Blacks. Similarly, Africa has animated many white leaders and organizations. For reasons both benign and insidious, they have seen Africa as the means for managing the "race problem" in the United States.

In any case, African Americans and whites have expressed this sentiment in a variety of schemes for a return to Africa. One could reasonably argue, therefore, that the Back to Africa Movement started when the status of Africans in America deteriorated from that of indentured servants to that of slaves. The movement gained focus when large numbers of manumitted Blacks began to reside in the various states and colonies. They looked to Africa as a means of attaining freedom. On the other hand, whites who believed that Blacks could not be integrated or that they were inferior viewed their return to Africa as desirable (Appiah and Gates 1999, 79).

Such views have consistently been expressed from colonial times to the present. One of the early exponents was Paul Cuffee, who transported some Blacks to Africa long before the Civil War. Perhaps the best known effort is the resettlement project of the white–dominated American Colonization Society (ACS), which transported thousands of Blacks to Liberia, clear up to the Civil War. In the early twentieth century, around the time of World War I, Marcus Garvey (1887–1940) had another Liberia scheme. His example influenced many such projects during the student movement of the 1960s, when Blacks resettled in small numbers in Guinea, Ghana, and Tanzania.

Proponents and Constituents

A number of individuals stand out in the Back to Africa Movement. Chief among them are Paul Cuffee, David Walker, Martin Delany,

Henry Highland Garnet, Alexander Crummel, Edward Wilmot Blyden, Henry McNeal Turner, and Marcus Garvey. The dominant organization was the predominantly white ACS. A lesser-known repatriation group was the African Civilization Society associated with Garnet. The following are case vignettes that illustrate this enduring movement.

Paul Cuffee (1759–1817), a wealthy son of a slave, was one of the most significant African American leaders and businessmen of his time. His leadership included strong protests against slavery and the racial exclusion that free Blacks experienced in the North. He was also committed to the repatriation of some Blacks to Africa and the establishment of the Christian faith there in the process. Cuffee earned his wealth in shipping and commerce. His assets of an estimated $20,000 in 1817 made him the wealthiest man in Westport, Massachusetts, and the wealthiest Black man in the country. Despite his economic status, he struggled, unsuccessfully in the end, to prevent the disfranchisement of Blacks in Massachusetts (Franklin and Moss 1994, 98). Meanwhile, Cuffee, whose efforts influenced the ACS, advocated mass emigration of Blacks to Africa as an escape from racial discrimination in the United States. Likely because of his strong Quaker religious experiences, he sought their return (to Sierra Leone) not only to get beyond American racism, but also to bring Christianity to the indigenous populations. He made two trips to Sierra Leone. The first was between 1810 and 1812 and did not actually involve repatriations. Later, in 1815, he resettled a total of thirty-eight people (Appiah and Gates 1999, 543). His work had a major impact on the development of the ACS, which in just a few years later repatriated perhaps 12,000 Blacks to Liberia (Franklin and Moss 1994, 169). His efforts also contributed to the enduring notion of repatriation among a small but visible minority of African Americans.

David Walker (1785–1830), who was born free and spent much of his adult life in Massachusetts, articulated a strong African-centered concept of racial solidarity. His formulation was not so much a back to Africa construct as one designed to attain the liberation of African peoples everywhere. Indeed, he is known as the father of Black nationalist theory because he offered the clearest construct of racial solidarity at the time (Stuckey 1972, 7). He is primarily known for his *Walker's Appeal . . . to the Colored Citizens of the World,* a hard-hitting and provocative call to arms for racial salvation. Long before Malcolm X, he urged slaves to revolt and pursue their freedom by any means necessary. He sought racial equality in the United States, a return to Africa, and independence for African nations. The document brought Walker both renown and notoriety. Many Blacks found the message attractive, while whites in the South found it so provocative that a price was placed on Walker's head.

Martin Delany (1812–1885) was born shortly before the death of Paul Cuffee, and later he would expand on Cuffee's ideas of repatriation. Delany wore many hats—"editor, author, physician, abolitionist, black nationalist, colonizationalist, and army officer" (Logan and Winston 1982, 169). This was an exceptional set of achievements for the son of an enslaved father and a free mother from West Virginia. He soon left the South and resided in Pittsburgh, Rochester (New York), New York City, and Ontario (Canada). Delany is widely known for his antislavery pamphlets and for stressing African heritage and self-reliance, further formulating a strong construct of Black nationalism. During the 1840s, he strongly opposed the repatriation efforts of the ACS, viewing them as a form of forced exile. However, he eventually changed his mind and in the 1850s began to advocate emigration, becoming one of its strongest spokesmen. He first proposed South America as a suitable site for the relocation of African Americans, and he made reconnaissance trips to Central America as well as to Hawaii (Logan and Winston 1982, 171). Later, after attending the emigration conferences between 1854 and 1858 and visiting Alexander Crummell, a fellow emigrationist resident in Liberia, Delany added Africa as a site (Appiah and Gates 1999, 1955).

Henry Highland Garnet (1815–1882) was a minister, abolitionist, and Black nationalist. Like David Walker, he acquired a reputation for militant espousal of universal Black rights. Nowhere were these views espoused as strongly as in his famous 1842 "Address to the Slaves of the United States of America" at the Negro Convention held in Buffalo, New York. He invoked Christianity to call for a slave insurrection. The convention came within one vote of endorsing his ideas, and Garnet gained renown as a proponent of radicalism. He founded the African Civilization Society and became its president soon after his return from Jamaica in 1856. The society had two goals: the establishment of Christianity and the creation of an agrarian economy that would compete with and undermine the slave economy of the American South (Appiah and Gates 1999, 813). His leadership skills and political activism also gave him an advantage with the white power structure as the Civil War got under way. Garnet became a strong war proponent and an active recruiter of Black soldiers for the Union effort. He remained active thereafter in Republican politics and was rewarded with a ministerial diplomatic appointment to Liberia (Hutchinson 1972).

Alexander Crummell (1815–1882) was born free in New York and served a full life in the Christian clergy and missionary service in Africa. He was one of the two most active Black advocates of African repatriation, specifically to Liberia. He came to be closely affiliated with the ACS and its repatriation efforts. Crummell subsequently took Liberian citizenship and made several trips back to the United States to encourage emigration to Liberia and to raise money for the fledgling nation's causes. Much of his argument for repatriation and nationalist thinking was acquired in his roles in the abolition movement and in the Negro Conventions in the 1940s. The ideas that drove his missionary work and the emigration perspective are set out in several books. In 1861 he published *The Relations and Duties of Free Colored Men in America to Africa;* in 1862 he published *The Future of Africa.* In these works he argued that Blacks around the world shared a common experience of racial discrimination and that emigration would provide opportunities for alleviating some of these circumstances and uplifting Africa. As Crummell's ideas evolved, he put education, hard work, and the Protestant ethic ahead of politics—much like Booker T. Washington. But the uses that education and moral training served for Crummell were akin to Du Bois's notion of a talented leadership class, steeped in liberal ideas (Scruggs 1977).

Edward Wilmot Blyden (1832–1912) was a pioneer of nationalist and Pan-Africanist thought. He was born in the West Indies, came briefly to the United States, and then went to Liberia. He took up residence there and became an ardent proponent of Black emigration. He encouraged descendants of Africa around the world to embrace African history and culture and to return to their ancestral home. He did so himself by remaining in Liberia for much of his life. He served the country in several posts in education, politics, and diplomacy. He was president of the University of Liberia for a time, held several cabinet-level positions, and served as the nation's ambassador to Britain and France. He was a prolific writer-theoretician and lobbyist, formulating ideas that would be central to Black Nationalism and urging emigration to Liberia. Much of the latter work culminated in 1850 with the support of the ACS idea for a new "colony" in Liberia—a state comprised largely of free persons of African descent. In 1861 he made the first of seven trips to the United States to argue for emigration to Africa, remaining wedded to the idea long past the heyday of repatriation (Lynch 1967).

Henry McNeal Turner (1834–1915) was one of the more complex figures in the early Back to Africa Movement. He too was a clergyman, largely in the AME Church. But he also served as a college president (the AME-run Morris Brown College in Atlanta), and a government bureaucrat. He was, however, best known after the failure of Reconstruction when he became a rabid nationalist, repudiating earlier conservative and white apologist views. After having grown disenchanted in 1870, he advocated Black migration to Haiti in 1871 and proposed a federal reserve for African Americans in New Mexico in 1874. When he became vice president of the ACS in 1876, his advocacy for returning to Africa had two planks; the first held that returning would highlight and draw attention to African American accomplishments, and the second, that African Americans could Christianize Africans. During the 1890s he made four trips to Africa promoting emigration, again long past the movements heyday (Redkey 1969).

The American Colonization Society (ACS) (1816–1963) was formed with the express purpose of encouraging free African Americans and those manumitted to emigrate to Africa. Its emergence captured the wave of a widespread debate about the disposition of the "race problem," as objections to slavery mounted. Many felt that the best way for Blacks to realize their dream of universal freedom was to move to Africa, because rampant U.S. racism would never cease. Often these proponents of emigration perceived this stance as supportive of African American aspirations for freedom without the perennial contestation attendant to U.S. exclusion. Others supported emigration because of their belief that Africans were inferior and caused a lag on progress in the Americas. Indeed, there were perhaps many proponents of emigration who held parts of both of these views.

At times the ACS program appeared to be a U.S. government project (Marinelli 1964). There was congressional support for providing part of its financing, and Abraham Lincoln as well as former presidents James Madison and James Monroe were proponents and ACS members. Supreme Court Justice Bushrod Washington was the organization's first president. In 1808 the U.S. Congress authorized $100,000 to buy a tract of land in Africa. The ACS made a purchase of some land on the West African coast on December 15, 1821. It was called Liberia for the "liberty" it signified for the returnees, a name that a much larger territory was eventually to assume. Its capital, again in a nod to its American provenance, was called Monrovia for President Monroe, who had been a party to the arrangements.

During the nineteenth century the ACS sponsored the emigration of perhaps 12,000 African Americans, most within the first ten years of the organization's founding. Franklin and Moss (1994, 169) also suggest that perhaps no more than 15,000 Blacks returned altogether.

The movement ultimately failed to repatriate large numbers, and it never captured widespread interest among Blacks, despite the very prominent Black spokesmen for the plan. The ACS did succeed in establishing a community of African Americans in Liberia who became a ruling minority reminiscent of the European colonial presence elsewhere in Africa. These Americo-Liberians and their descendants (Shick 1980) dominated politics and society in Liberia until 1980. Nevertheless the movement never found a means to transport a sizable portion of the African American population to Africa. Moreover, no related scheme since has even come close to the minuscule emigration attained by the ACS.

Major Constraints and Achievements

The Back to Africa Movement, in the early period and beyond, was seriously constrained by the strivings of African Americans to gain regularized status as a part of the republic. The attraction of the democratic promise with its emphasis on freedom and equality has been profound among African Americans. Such ideals fired their visions as they did the Europeans and fueled their hope that with continued resistance and demands, conditions would get better. Indeed, there was some evidence of improved conditions just after the Civil War with the abolition of slavery and the passage of the Thirteenth, Fourteenth, and Fifteenth Amendments.

But there was still another argument for staying: too much had been invested in the building of the republic—the investment of time, sweat, and blood largely as free laborers. The financial cost of leaving for most was absurdly prohibitive. Meanwhile, the enduring movement had been propelled by the continuous uncertainty about the achievement of the goal of regularization. Despite the abolition of slavery, most of the freed men and women were left in a state of virtual peonage. They had no land, jobs, or schooling, conditions that racists sought to maintain. Moreover, the political participation guaranteed to Blacks by the emancipation and other legislation quickly evaporated in the South, where most Blacks resided. The breach of civil rights, widespread discrimination, and social segregation thus signaled to many Blacks that progressive change was not inevitable or would be too slow. Some whites of goodwill agreed with this conclusion and supported efforts to return Blacks to Africa.

Perhaps the major achievement of the Back to Africa Movement is the ideas its exponents generated, which have sustained a nationalist tradition based on racial solidarity. Although the move to relocate to Africa dissipated after the Civil War, ideas about racial solidarity or a collective identity inherent in the African background and in the racialized experience have flourished. Practically all of them are based on ideas introduced by the early exponents, although the notion of a return to Africa is replaced by a focus on race pride, Black beauty standards, and race-based institutions within the general American population.

Marcus Garvey: A Case Study of a Back to Africa Movement

The Scope of Garveyism

Marcus Garvey (1887–1940) is arguably the major icon for the Back to Africa Movement (Cronon 1955). Although he was by no means the first to argue for a return to Africa (he regularly attributed his ideas to the mid-nineteenth century Black thinkers), he did so with a grandiosity that exceeded those before him. His quest to make it possible for African Americans to return to Africa was a part of his overall vision for the Pan-African self-actualization of African peoples. His vision, known as Garveyism, included an emphasis on Black economic independence and empowerment, Black self-determination, and the establishment of a Black nation on the African continent, specifically in the territory of Liberia (Jacques-Garvey 1969). Garvey attained widespread attention and popularity among Blacks around the world, and indeed, he liked to say that his vision was designed to appeal to the some 600 million Blacks in the world (Jacques-Garvey 1969). The Garvey tentacles stretched throughout the major Black population centers in the United States, colonial Africa, and the Caribbean. His thought has been a major influence or backdrop for Black nationalists ever since, including for the "father of African nationalism" Kwame Nkrumah, who was Ghana's first president (Birmingham 1998). Although Garvey is identified as a great Back to Africa Movement leader, he almost alone among the major proponents never set foot on African soil.

Garvey was born in St. Ann's Bay, Jamaica, in 1887. He grew up in a West Indian tradition that emphasized English common school education but that also made him aware of racial discrimination early.

The result was that when he moved to New York City in 1916, he was already primed for exploring Black Nationalism in a way that African Americans had not visualized. His innovative views on the subject developed despite the influence the conservative self-reliance ideas of Booker T. Washington had on him. Garvey lived and traveled in Central America from 1910 to 1912, and at the end of 1913 he went to Europe. In 1914, after attending classes in London, he returned once again to Jamaica and started the United Negro Improvement and Conservation Association and the African Communities League (later to be known as the United Negro Improvement Association—UNIA). In 1917 he established the New York division of the UNIA, and renounced assistance from white organizations or beneficiaries (Lyons 1971, 150–152). These remained the organizational arms of the movement from New York City until his deportation from the United States in 1927.

Constituents

Garveyism had several constituent bases, which might be thought of as a series of concentric circles. The first was the larger Black community, for which Garvey provided the ideas of Black Nationalism and self-help. The second was the smaller group of the Black public for which the UNIA provided direct services or contacts, largely in New York City. The third was the even smaller group of African Americans who sought to immigrate to Liberia, and for which Garvey's Black Star Line shipping company offered the most opportune prospects. The fourth was the UNIA dues-paying members who adopted Garvey's ideology. They could be found in far-flung places around the world.

Issues and Goals

Although the Back to Africa projects in general often had only the goal of emigration to Africa (largely to Liberia), Garvey supplemented this idea with larger plans for improving conditions for the Black American public as well. His "Back in Stride" article in a 1938 edition of the *Black Man* magazine carried an explication of his goal and the goal of Black nationalists in general. He wrote that Black "striding" would be feasible through universal Black cooperation and that self-reliant Blacks would improve not only themselves but also whites in America (Spady 1985, 14).

Beyond the abstract goals of the overall project, Garveyism also contained practical goals that were rooted in the membership services, business enterprises, and the Liberian emigration project (Lewis 1988, 67–75). Membership conferred a wide spectrum of apparent benefits and obligations. Membership services included encouraging financial independence, death benefits funds, policy debates, scholastic activities, and even the creation of a paramilitary force to combat KKK and white racist activity where it existed. Members were also expected to contribute substantially to the organization's operations. The UNIA established business enterprises as well, of which the most well known was the Black Star Line shipping company. The Negro Factories Corporation was also established and was responsible for the creation of small local businesses (Lewis 1988, 67–70). The third goal was the Liberian experiment, which aimed to transport some portion of dispersed African descendants back to the motherland.

The Liberian experiment was the best known and perhaps most misunderstood portion of the program. In an editorial in *Negro World,* Garvey expressed the concept this way: "It does not mean that all Negroes must leave America and the West Indies and go to Africa to build up a government . . . but remember that our success educationally, industrially, and politically is based upon the protection of a nation founded by ourselves. And that nation can be nowhere else but in Africa" (Lewis 1988, 71–72).

Liberia was deemed a viable choice for linking African Americans to the motherland because this African nation had managed to escape the wave of European colonial expansion from the 1880s onward. He also thought that the few other independent African nations were too far or too impractical as a migration destination (indeed only independent Ethiopia was available).

Strategies

The Garveyism approach envisioned African Americans as a self-reliant people. Garvey wanted them to be self-supporting and unobliged to outside contributors, particularly white contributors, for the survival of the organization. The standard approach he sought for funding the UNIA was through profit-making enterprises (the

Black factories), membership fees, and community donations. Garvey did not direct the operations of the businesses created by the Negro Factories Corporation; these were in fact locally directed. However, the UNIA expected to benefit if they succeeded—most of them did not.

Garvey and the UNIA also developed two communication tactics to spread their influence: public speaking and publication. He did not branch out to the traditional Black political leadership, which he often attacked as inept or worse (Moore 1974, 210). He rather derived his influence from the grassroots support. Typically, Garvey's speeches "contain this psychological encouragement, this exhortation to cast aside passivity and negation and take one's destiny actively into one's own hands" (Lewis 1988, 79). *Negro World* magazine was Garvey's prime publication instrument from 1918 to 1933, until it was supplanted by the *Black Man* magazine in 1933. He also ran other magazines and newspapers during this period (Lewis 1988, 80–82). Garvey and his activists placed great emphasis on getting these publications to the "man on the street."

Perhaps the most visible strategy for Garvey was the flamboyant mass parades that were held in New York City and elsewhere to rally support. Members from around the nation would march in colorful clothing, showcasing Garvey in military regalia. He adopted this uniform after the first UNIA convention (where he became the "provincial president of Africa") (Appiah and Gates 1999, 818). The groups marching through Harlem were especially visible and attracted huge crowds. With their placards, uniform dress, and military formations, they were a powerful tool that increased the personal recognition of Garvey and sentiment for his programs. This process was repeated in the UNIA conventions with the same results. For example, the first convention in New York City in 1920 reportedly drew 2,000 delegates, representing twenty-five countries (Lewis 1988, 86).

At still another level of strategy, Garvey articulated a fully elaborated doctrine of a Black God in the image of Black people. This was, of course, consistent with his program for a self-sustaining Black national community. He created the African Orthodox Church with a doctrine of a Black God and Christ (Lyons 1971, 158). This fully appropriated image then became the source by which Garvey could elaborate a racially defined conception of beauty in Blackness to reverse the self-hatred bred by the denigrating stereotypes perpetrated by whites.

Major Constraints and Facilitators

Among major constraints on Garvey and the UNIA were the mainstream press, opposition Black groups, and the fragility of the "bootstrapping" approach toward increased Black opportunities. The press in particular ridiculed Garvey at first as a dangerous clown and later, during the 1930s, as a Black fascist. This was not helped by Garvey's own statement in 1937 that "we were the first Fascists . . . Mussolini copied Fascism from me . . ." (Lyons 1971, 139). Opposition from the press meant that he had to appeal directly to the grassroots either through his own publications or public speaking. He had already demonstrated his unwillingness to deal with the existing political structure.

Garvey ironically attracted considerable condemnation over his tactics and goals from other prominent African American organizations and leaders. W.E.B. DuBois became an outspoken critic of Garvey, labeling the ideas crackpot and escapist. He believed that Garvey was deluding his followers with utterly unrealistic visions. Likewise, since Garvey was opposed to trade unionism, he also attracted the ire of A. Philip Randolph and others who would later help form African American–based unions (Lyons 1971, 160–161).

Then there was the factor of Garvey's "liaison" with the right-wing, racist Ku Klux Klan. He deemed this a strategic move to advance the Back to Africa plan, despite the racist dogma that inspired KKK support for emigration. The organization invited Garvey to its Atlanta headquarters in 1922 and he accepted. The payoff appeared to result when the race-baiting senator and former governor of Mississippi Theodore G. Bilbo introduced legislation in 1938, supported by Garvey, to fund the deportation of 13,000,000 African Americans to Africa (Foster 1974, 418). Although these efforts were designed to facilitate Garvey's goals, they turned out to be a serious constraint. He was roundly criticized by the traditional African American leadership and came under great suspicion at the grassroots level for consorting with an avowedly racist terror organization.

Two social forces, the Great Migration and World War I, made Garvey's ideas more acceptable in the African American community. The ascendancy of the Jim Crow system of segregation and the concomitant disfranchisement in the South caused a great migration of Blacks to the North. They occupied the central cities in residentially segregated enclaves. Then the acceleration of industrialization facilitated by the war provided job opportunities that induced thousands more

Black southerners to migrate. Their urban concentration provided an independent energy for community development and mobilization. But so did the discrimination visited upon Black veterans who came home to experience heightened discrimination, including lynchings, after having fought to secure democracy for Europeans. These conditions facilitated UNIA membership (Appiah and Gates 1999, 818). Many urban laborers and veterans became adherents of Garvey and the UNIA.

Achievements, Failures, and Legacy

When looking at the successes and failures of Garveyism, three immediate goals of the UNIA are appropriate units of analysis—membership, the business efforts, and African emigration. The membership services had some successes in that they effectively organized African Americans at the grassroots level who had not been swept up by the church movements or the NAACP. For those who were particularly impatient with the slow pace of civil rights changes, Garveyism seemed to offer a ready solution. Garvey suggested that discrimination and repression could be resolved by withdrawing from the system and developing independent Black institutions. Unfortunately for those who participated, this mandated the use of considerable amounts of time and money in support of the UNIA, ultimately a poorly conceived and poorly run organization. However, the ideas of self-sufficiency would inspire later Black nationalist activists.

The goal of entrepreneurship was a massive failure, although the efforts became important symbols. Most of the businesses were poorly run, devouring large amounts of membership capital while providing little in return. The Black Star Line was a spectacular failure that ultimately led to Garvey's decline. The Liberian expeditions were also abysmal failures, largely because of the farcical attempts at sailing—the ships were prone to accidents and mechanical problems. The flagship *Yarmouth,* for example, ran aground twice and had extensive mechanical problems on all three of its voyages to the West Indies (Smith-Irvin 1989, 6). These failures were compounded in 1923 when Garvey was convicted of mail fraud in the soliciting of stock for the shipping company. He was sentenced to five years imprisonment but was subsequently deported to Jamaica, the Garveyism dream in tatters (Cronon 1955, 103ff).

Perhaps the most important achievement of Garveyism is its ideological legacy for contemporary Black Nationalism in the

United States and elsewhere. Kwame Nkrumah and Nnamdi Azikiwe, among others in Africa, and the Black Muslims, Malcolm X, and the Black Panthers in the United States all built on his ideas (Clarke 1974). Garveyism offered an alternative to the integrationist reform philosophy of the NAACP and the NUL via a self-reliant political and economic life separate from the white mainstream. Although the UNIA virtually disappeared in 1949 (Spady 1985, 98–99), Garveyism served as a profound inspiration to Black nationalists in the 1960s and 1970s. The legacy can be seen in cultural changes and adaptations such as the revival of traditional African apparel, the appropriation of African names, and the adoption and creation of cultural events based on West African cultural practices (Cruse 1967, 420–448, 544–565).

The National Association for the Advancement of Colored People

Origins and Constituents

The NAACP was founded on February 12, 1909, with the 1908 race riot in Springfield, Illinois, as a backdrop. The National Negro Committee (renamed NAACP in 1910) issued a call to discuss racial justice. Among members were white liberals (including Mary Ovington White and Oswald Garrison Villard), and prominent African American activists (including Mary Church Terrell, Ida B. Wells-Barnett, and W.E.B. DuBois). The latter had set the agenda with the Niagara (Canada) Movement in 1905 calling for Black enfranchisement, educational opportunities, desegregation, and racial equality. In many ways these have remained the purposes of the NAACP, the largest organization of its kind dedicated to civil rights of African Americans.

The NAACP has always been a diverse organization, notably with whites in its hierarchy. Indeed, of the sixty people who issued the 1909 call to discuss racial justice, only seven were African Americans (Appiah and Gates 1999, 1388). In time, membership and leadership became predominantly African American. Moreover, the NAACP's emphasis on issues faced by African Americans also delimited them as the organization's chief constituency. Yet it continued to model the racial ideal of integration with its white members and in its efforts to develop transracial coalitions (Appiah and Gates 1999, 1388). Current estimates are that the NAACP has approximately 400,000 members in some 1,800 chapters.

Issues, Goals, and Strategies

After its founding the NAACP sought to achieve racial justice via a nine-point program of principles. These principles, which are listed below, covered the gamut of African American citizenship rights to the provision of legal aid. In essence, the early NAACP sought to secure the rights embodied in the Thirteenth, Fourteenth, and Fifteenth Amendments—freedom, citizenship, and the right to vote:

- Equality of the Black Vote
- Equal Access to Education
- Equality Before the Law
- Access to Jury Service
- Banishment of Lynching
- Desegregation of Public Transport
- Desegregation of Community Services
- Equal Right to Employment
- Abolition of Color Designations (adapted from Broderick and Meier 1965, 63–64)

The primary strategies of the NAACP have been legal action and lobbying. The legal strategy principally involved court challenges to breaches of constitutional guarantees embodied in the three amendments and statutory laws passed just after the Civil War. This strategy had broad constitutional reach but often focused on provisions in the Fourteenth Amendment—the "due process of the law" and "equal protection of the laws" clauses. The legal challenges were comprehensive, falling into generally six major categories: education, housing, voting rights, employment, public accommodations, and civil and criminal rights.

The lobbying strategy was equally comprehensive. The organization sought to influence lawmakers and government officials to make decisions favorable to its major goals. This strategy was also outlined in the NAACP's 1919 annual report, which noted that the provision of information to private and government officials would be a key factor in creating a favorable climate for its issues. Its campaign against lynching in the 1920s was an example. Among other things, it was designed to "reach the heart and conscience of the American people." But there was as much emphasis on organizing and fundraising. These resources would be used to educate the public and the government with "the facts," and then hold them accountable by "watching them" (Broderick and Meier 1965, 65). These strategies remained effective from the organization's inception through the 1970s, when landmark court decisions and legislation accompanied the post–World War II civil rights movement.

With state-sanctioned discrimination now largely in the past, the NAACP has had to diversify its strategies. Current efforts reflect the internal-external dimension of the challenges facing African Americans. The internal challenges are those that can be addressed primarily from within the Black community. The external challenges are those that are addressed primarily from outside of the community. Internal strategies focus on programmatic efforts such as campaigns against African American youth violence (such as "Stop the Violence, Start the Love") and support for academic excellence among these youths (such as ACT-SO EXCEL). External strategies include protests against residual segregation, the Confederate flag, and recruitment to the federal judiciary and lobbying for such issues as legislative reapportionment and economic empowerment (the Economic Reciprocity Plan, and the Fair Share Corporate Partners are examples). In essence, the NAACP has added targeted public policy and welfare issues to its strategies, some of which involve traditional direct action techniques of boycotting, demonstrations, and media exposures.

Major Constraints and Facilitators

The NAACP was founded when there was perhaps the widest gap between American democratic rights and Blacks' access to them. At the time, the denial of these rights to Blacks remained almost systematic, which constituted a serious constraint for the fledgling NAACP. However, this chasm also served as a major facilitator for those seeking racial justice. The inchoate NAACP sought to challenge and expose these breaches. Later, with a firm organizational footing, much of the NAACP's work provided the foundation for the broadest social movement ever seen in the United States in support of African American civil rights. The victories achieved from the earlier legal and lobbying challenges now facilitate the welfare and direct public policy challenges that currently dominate NAACP activities.

Achievements and Challenges

Between 1909 and 1954, the NAACP was undoubtedly the most effective African American civil rights organization. It successfully challenged the systems of segregation and disfranchisement. Both the lobbying and legal strategies became very effective combined tools that achieved a virtual revolution in the way courts, public policy makers, and legislators interpreted and then restored African American rights. Through its lobbying and information campaigns, the NAACP created a climate for racial justice that was backed up with successful challenges to the legal armature for racial discrimination and exclusion. Its work led to a Supreme Court decision that effectively destroyed the base for disfranchisement (*Smith v. Allwright* 1944), and culminated in the case that declared the "separate but equal" policy of segregation inherently unequal (*Brown v. Board of Education* 1954). The groundwork was laid for the 1944 and 1954 decisions with the successful challenge to the grandfather clause in 1910 that barred southern Blacks from voting if their ancestors had not voted before emancipation (*Guinn v. United States* 1915). Then during the 1920s, Ida B. Wells-Barnett, via the NAACP, led the charge against lynching (Holt 1982). That effort was followed by organizational campaigns against discrimination in unions, the armed forces, and the defense industries. These and later successful lobbying efforts through the 1960s were led by Clarence M. Mitchell Jr. at the NAACP bureau in Washington. He saw through passage of the major civil rights statutes, including the Civil Rights Acts of 1957 and 1964, the Voting Rights Act of 1965, and the Fair Housing Law of 1968 (Appiah and Gates 1999, 1388–1391; Watson 1990). Table 3.3 lists selected cases in which the NAACP was involved between 1935 and 1995.

Having achieved its goal of providing constitutional protections, the NAACP faltered before it shifted to younger leadership. This shift did not come easily. The organization underwent considerable financial difficulties and took missteps in board and executive leadership recruitment (Smith 1996, 91–94). Today it has revamped its leadership hierarchy, bringing in a new generation of young men and women who are more focused on welfare issues. Julian Bond, a leader of the student movement in the 1960s, is now at the helm of the NAACP board. His executive director is Kweisi Mfume, a former congressional representative from Maryland. They have sought to revitalize the organization by focusing on employment and education issues that now plague a community whose differential status belies its legal equality. To this end, the organization has launched major ini-

TABLE 3.3 Selected Cases Sponsored by the NAACP Legal Defense and Educational Fund, 1938–1991

Year	Case	Ruling
Education		
1938	*Missouri ex rel. Gaines v. Canada*	Barred states from requiring Blacks to matriculate at out-of-state professional schools to avoid integration.
1950	*McLaurin v. Oklahoma State Regents*	Blacks could not be isolated for instruction in formerly all-white schools.
1950	*Sweatt v. Painter*	Establishment of Texas law school for Blacks that was not equal to segregated white law school found unequal.
1954	*Brown v. Board of Education of Topeka, Kansas*	"Separate but equal" schools declared inherently unequal.
1958	*Cooper v. Aaron*	Arkansas governor barred from interfering with Little Rock school integration.
1971	*Swann v. Charlotte-Mecklenburg Board of Education*	School busing ordered to obtain desegregation.
1973	*Adams v. Richardson*	Enforcement of desegregation provision for all schools receiving federal funds.
Housing		
1948	*Shelley v. Kraemer*	States barred from enforcing racially restrictive housing covenants.
1971	*Turner v. Fouche*	Georgia property requirement for jury and school board service invalidated.
Voting Rights		
1944	*Smith v. Allwright*	Exclusion of Blacks from Democratic Party (white primary) invalidated.
1969	*Allen v. State Board of Elections*	Blacks permitted to organize a write-in campaign per Voting Rights Act of 1965.
1977	*United Jewish Organizations of Williamsburgh v. Carey*	Racial considerations permitted in order to prevent minority voter dilution in electoral district reapportionment.
1986	*Thornburg v. Gingles*	At-large elections in North Carolina diluted Black voting strength, violating the Voting Rights Act.

(continues)

TABLE 3.3 (continued)

Year	Case	Ruling
1991	Houston Lawyers Association v. Attorney General	The Voting Rights Act applies to state judicial elections.
Employment		
1940	Alston v. School Board of City of Norfolk	Black teachers must be paid salaries equal to white teachers.
1963	Simkins v. Moses H. Cone Memorial Hospital	Hospital discrimination in patient admission and staff privileges invalidated.
1971	Griggs v. Duke Power Co.	Tests for employment or promotion with a discriminatory outcome must measure only aptitude for the job.
1975	Franks v. Bowman Transportation Co.	Workers denied jobs because of race are entitled to retroactive seniority benefits.
Public Accommodations		
1946	Morgan v. Virginia	State segregated seating requirements on interstate buses invalidated.
1955	Holmes v. Atlanta	Segregation at public parks and beaches invalidated.
1956	Gayle v. Browder	Montgomery, Ala., city bus seating segregation invalidated.
1964	Willis v. Pickrick Restaurant	L. Maddox, later governor of Georgia, required to serve Blacks in his restaurant.
Civil and Criminal Rights		
1940	Chambers v. Florida	Convictions of four Blacks overturned because confessions were coerced.
1947	Patton v. Mississippi	Exclusion of Blacks from juries barred.
1964	McLaughlin v. Florida	Criminalization of interracial sexual relations invalidated.
1971	Clay v. United States	Muhammad Ali conviction for refusal of military service on religious grounds overturned.
1972	Furman v. Georgia	Death penalty outlawed as "cruel and unusual" punishment in 37 states.

SOURCE: Data from NAACP Legal Defense and Educational Fund (www.naacpldf.org).

tiatives on legislative redistricting to guarantee that the Black vote is not diluted; on voter registration to mobilize Black constituents to participate in the electoral arena; and on employment and criminal justice issues to try to sustain sufficient infrastructure for local community development. This new stage is a work in progress that continues to be undergirded by the traditional strategies of legalism and lobbying (Smith 1996, 87–125).

The Future

Despite many changes in the structure of civil rights issues, the NAACP is still regarded as the preeminent African American civil rights organization. It remains the largest and has over ninety years of experience, respected leaders, and a diversity of strategies for reorganized goals. Despite the leadership and financial difficulties it experienced during its recent transition (Smith 1996, 87ff), its survival seems secure. However, its reorganization and reorientation come at a time when there is a significant realignment of political forces in the country. The New Deal Democratic coalition has been disrupted with the ascendancy of a coalition of more conservative forces anchored around the Republican Party. This new coalition challenges many of the assumptions of the liberal civil rights alignees that contributed to the long string of NAACP successes in winning rights for Blacks. It remains to be seen how successful these alignees will be in winning support for the welfare issues of impoverished racial enclaves in the nation.

The National Urban League

Origins

The National Urban League (NUL) and its affiliates were founded in 1910 in New York City. This was perhaps a natural location for its urban mission, with 90,000 Blacks concentrated in Manhattan (although not yet in Harlem) (Brisbane 1976, 64). Most of the Blacks in New York City were a part of the recent migration from the Jim Crow South. They sought jobs, housing, and a variety of social services in their new and strange environments. Indeed, the large Black concentration in New York illustrated all of the promise and peril of this relocated population (Weiss 1974).

The increased African American presence in New York and its blighted existence inspired action. William H. Baldwin, president of the Long Island Railroad, initiated a series of interracial meetings of community leaders over five years (1905–1910) to deal with the ensuing social and economic problems. They were conscious of the effect that unresolved problems could have if left to simmer (such as the 1863 New York Draft Riots). In 1906 the Committee for Improving Industrial Conditions of Negroes in New York City was established. Still another committee of leaders, also led by Baldwin, was formed in 1910: the Committee on Urban Conditions Among Negroes (Brisbane 1976, 64). Because there were so many women in this migrant population, an additional committee was formed to focus specifically on gender issues. The League for Protection for Colored Women was set up by Frances Kellor, a white immigrant. Given the close working relationships attained by these groups and the similarity of their goals, in 1911 they merged to form the National League on Urban Conditions Among Negroes (NLUCAN). The name was shortened to the NUL in 1920 (Dickerson 1998; Strickland 1996). The NUL has always attracted an upper- and middle-class interracial leadership. It may be broadly cast as integrationist, although with a continuing core of African American middle-class activists and professional social workers (Moore 1981, 145).

Constituents

Initially the forerunners of the NUL focused on New York City. However, after 1911 its constituency widened when the NUL began to set national goals. Originally it targeted the Black workforce and the unemployed. This proved both controversial and limiting. On the one hand, the NUL met resistance in job placement from established institutions and labor unions. On the other hand, the migrants' problems included much more than just jobs. Thus the organization branched out to assist African American New Yorkers in the areas of the home, education, community activities, and recreation (Brisbane 1976, 65). Soon this broader agenda saw the NUL expand to other major industrial cities in the North.

World War I and the decade that followed brought national employment issues to the fore as Black migration increased. The NUL once again shifted its agenda to focus on the Black migrant workers who were filling vacancies created by white conscription. By then the NUL was already operating successful decentralized local branches (referred to as affiliates) in major northern cities. Affiliates had considerable leeway in defining programs for their local constituency. As the organization grew after World War I, it also began to tackle issues of labor discrimination that affected Black families in the armed forces and labor unions. Often these concerns strayed from an exclusive urban focus as the NUL evolved.

The constituency for the NUL expanded and contracted, depending on the saliency of issues affecting Blacks. For example, during the 1950s and 1960s the constituency expanded to include African Americans in the South generally as civil rights issues became paramount. The league worked in partnership with the other mainstream civil rights organizations, especially the NAACP. Whitney Young, the leader at the time, was so deeply engaged that he came to be regarded as one of the prime movers in the activist civil rights campaign. Then from the 1970s into the 1990s, the league refocused its primary attention on the conditions of urban African Americans. As the scale of the movement diminished, the NUL left the primary responsibility for civil rights action to other organizations. This provided more time to focus on escalating urban issues, for which the NUL was more suited—eliminating urban blight through social services, education, and other service-oriented programs.

Issues, Goals, and Strategies

The "mission of the Urban League movement is to enable African Americans to secure economic self-reliance, parity, and power and civil rights" (www.nul.org). This mission is described as having three components:

- Education and Youth—ensuring that our children are well-educated and equipped for economic self-reliance in the twenty-first century.
- Economic Self-Sufficiency—helping adults attain economic self-sufficiency through good jobs, homeownership, entrepreneurship, and wealth accumulation.
- Racial Inclusion—ensuring our civil rights by eradicating all barriers to equal participation in the economic and social mainstream of America. (www.nul.org)

Meanwhile the NUL describes its strategies as involving the following methods: "The Urban League Movement carries its mission at the local, state, and national levels through direct services, advocacy, research, policy analysis, community mobilization, collaboration, and communications" (www.nul.org). In general, however, the organization is best characterized by its low profile as a bureaucratic, behind-the-scenes player in engaging corporate boards and government bureau heads to support urban African American community development. Within this general context, local affiliates have a good deal of freedom to seek their goals by generating support from business and government entities within their official municipal or regional boundaries.

Major Constraints and Facilitators

Initially the factors that constrained the NUL from expansion and achievement of its objectives were a lack of funding and of community salience. Early funding was provided by wealthy white founding patrons, many located in the New York City area. As the achieving goals—training, education, and employment—could cost considerable amounts of money, a large and steady supply of cash was needed for success. This has made the NUL more dependent on developing external sources of support from patrons and corporate entities. When these funding forces lag, so do the programs of the NUL. A second constraint has been the relatively low-key approach and presence of the organization. Its processes and actions have often been regarded as slow and conservative, an approach that sometimes preserves the status quo.

Throughout its history, the NUL has been beset by three factional conflicts: African American versus white leaders in the league; advocates of the original mission versus those in favor of expanding the mission; and the national secretariat versus local affiliates. However, the outcome of the debates about mission did succeed in moving the NUL into the forefront of issues germane to the corporate African American community. The most trying time came in the 1950s as leader Lester Granger provoked internal debates with board members about mission expansion. This conflict spilled into the public and thus became a public debate (Moore 1981, 151). Before Granger's arrival, the overwhelmingly white board was not primarily focused on civil rights but on more practical issues, most likely because it devoted most of its attention to urban problems in the North rather than to southern segregation. Ultimately, the old guard was overthrown. NUL President Richard Dowling was replaced by Theodore

Kheel, who represented the new forces (Moore 1981, 164–188). This change lay the foundation for the emergence and eventual ascendancy of Whitney Young, who could then confidently move into the southern civil rights campaign.

Some of these constraints have also constituted significant strengths. The interactions and linkages that the NUL have developed with the corporate structure allow it a degree of entrée that few other African American organizations enjoy. Its training programs have sometimes been well funded and have had access to some of the best resources for human skills development. Similarly, when many African American leaders or militantly activist organizations have been excluded from corporate access, the NUL's entrée has more often than not been preserved. In short, it has provided another voice in the complex dynamics of the American environment.

Achievements and Failures

The NUL may be judged on both its generic goals and those that evolved during the civil rights era. The founding NUL seemed based on ensuring an orderly society, with routine social controls and supports for African Americans. It sought the calm integration of African Americans into urban society while mitigating dislocation and conflict with whites. The league did succeed in developing policies for educational advancement, in finding employment for migrant workers, and in easing social dislocations for the new Black city dwellers. However, its success was limited to the relatively small number of communities, first in the New York City area, and then in those where affiliates developed. The scale of the urban problems for Black migrants could hardly be addressed by the limited scope of NUL projects. Thus, for example, when the widespread blight of the cities and their urban Black residents was publicly acknowledged, it took a national effort like President Lyndon Johnson's War on Poverty to attain a scale of action even remotely sufficient. However, the skills within the NUL's personnel made the organization a natural conduit for implementation of some of the urban poverty programs.

Other failures of the NUL relate to its inability to respond effectively or rapidly to the mobilization of African Americans in the civil rights movement or to locate in the South—in the urban South, the NUL encountered the color bar (Moore 1981, 213). As the civil rights mobilization was mounting, the NUL lagged in joining forces, trapped in a struggle to replace an older guard of leadership. When the shift did occur, however, Whitney Young came to the helm and fully engaged the NUL in the movement campaign.

The Future

The NUL and its affiliates are still quite active, fulfilling their original roles in improving the socioeconomic lives of African Americans. Moreover the organization has relatively stable funding and leadership. The interracial leadership conflicts of the 1950s and 1960s have eased, and the organization has moved through the civil rights era with a strong leadership. It has once again undergone transition and refocused its traditional urban agenda, and it enjoys broad alliances with corporate entities. As the number of affiliates has grown to more than 150, most of which are essentially stable, there is reason to believe the NUL will continue to have a role in aiding the general participation of African Americans, especially in the urban areas.

The Nation of Islam (Black Muslims in America)

Origins

Many strands of Black nationalism flow from the seminal ideas of the early Back to Africa thinkers and Marcus Garvey. The "Black Muslims in America" represent one religious strand that focuses on the United States as the site for the national Black community. It was loosely based on Islamic teachings and adopted many of the outward symbols of the faith and subscribed to the teachings of the Koran. However, the founders clearly distinguished themselves in arguing that the group emerged out of the particular conditions of African descendants in the United States (Lincoln 1994). This particularity led the group to focus on a national Black community that was separate, self-determinant, and economically independent. Wallace D. Fard founded the Black Muslims around 1930 in Detroit, Michigan, after breaking away from a related sect. He immediately starting working toward his vision, preaching salvation and self-determination, concurrent with his independent job as silk salesman in Detroit's Black neighborhoods. His following soon grew from small meetings in private homes to an audience requiring rental of a large hall (Appiah and Gates 1999, 1399–1400).

The movement grew and fissured, spawning two other prominent leaders, whose work, however, cannot be separated from the parent organization: Malcolm X and Louis Farrakhan. The former broke away and developed a Pan-Africanist-oriented group, although one defined almost entirely by the personal ambitions of Malcolm X. The Farrakhan organization, as a result of a complex evolution that saw the parent body orient itself more toward orthodox Islam, broke away, hewing to the original orthodoxy propounded by Fard. The popularity of Malcolm X and Farrakhan became such that their strands of the faith are central to understanding the Black Muslim movement in the United States.

Constituents

The appeal of the Black Muslim organization was not universal, but it was always broader than its relatively small membership would suggest. It was by and large a northern movement, which appealed to some of the most desperately displaced urban African American migrants. It also had a certain amount of appeal to politically left-oriented college students and young professionals, many of whom never acquired membership in the organization. Its formal membership, estimated variously at 10,000 to 100,000 members, was made up of young to middle-aged, lower- to working-class, urban African Americans. But there is much broader sentimental support for the Black Muslim organization within the general African American population. This could be seen in the throngs that appeared when Malcolm X made public appearances and who attended Farrakhan's 1995 Million Man March (Alex-Assensoh and Hanks 2000, 322–323).

Issues, Goals, and Strategies

Like other groups, which seek to empower the African American collective, the general goal of the Nation of Islam is to create a vibrant African American community, free of the residual effects of enslavement. Its major goal is to overcome white supremacy and create a self-determinant, economically self-sufficient, separate African American community. The sect sees inequality and the devastated sense of self-esteem within the African American community as the problem. Poverty is the result of centuries of state-sanctioned enslavement, discrimination, and modern-day institutional racism. But there is an equally powerful problem in the lack of personal self-awareness and esteem, whereby Blacks collude in their psychological disablement and self-destruction. This analysis was critical in the special appeal the movement had in prisons, where the teachings of the Koran became a basis for self-redemption for many incarcerated young Black men. Indeed, one among them was Malcolm X, who became one of the sect's most outstanding leaders.

This combination of problems thus structured a set of strategies for the idealized independent African American community: race pride, discipline, and entrepreneurship to facilitate economic self-sufficiency. With a decided adoption of conservative Islamic tenets, the Nation of Islam stresses structure, marriage, a strict diet, hygiene, marital fidelity, prohibition of drugs and alcohol, and strict traditional roles for women (Lincoln 1994).

Major Facilitators

Support of the Nation of Islam was facilitated by some of its more conservative tenets. For those who were drawn to the capitalist foundations in some versions of Black nationalism, notably that of Garvey, the Black Muslim program for capitalist entrepreneurship was appealing. For them even the American capitalist economic system was a model for emulation. Second, the emphasis on race pride had a mass appeal for the way it reinforced an African American cultural community. Third, the apparent ability to rehabilitate drug addicts, prisoners, and others deemed to be incorrigible lags on the community's progress was profoundly attractive. The sect set high standards and goals for membership, and many subjects professed rehabilitation as they joined the regimented lifestyle associated with converts.

Support of the Nation of Islam is constrained in many ways. In its original iteration it purported to be apolitical, shunning participation in American politics. At the same time, it offered little in the way of extracting political benefits from a system it designated as racist and exploitative of the Black community. This was glaringly suspicious to traditional Black leaders who were engaging in the most intensive mobilization of resistance among Blacks in history. Meanwhile, the Black Muslims have always been hampered by the original tenet that whites were "devils" who originated as an error of scientific experiment. The view is widely held as racist and untenable, even by many of those sympathetic to the sect. Within the Black community itself the restrictive roles for women in the Nation of Islam is viewed as untenable, especially in light of the historically activist tradition among African American women. Finally, like a number of nationalist organizations, the program of self-help is woefully inadequate for addressing the complex and widespread forces that impinge on equity for African Americans.

Achievements and Failures

The Nation of Islam has had a major impact in several areas. First and foremost, it has devoted a great deal of energy to the development of self-assessment and personal responsibility on the part of its adherents. The organization directly addresses what its considers the low self-esteem of Blacks and sets a high standard of behavior to alter this status. It has been notably successful among some of the most dysfunctional parts of the racialized community, such as male prisoners and drug addicts. Historically, the Nation's regime of positive image building, purpose, discipline, and organizational loyalty have yielded unprecedented positive results.

Second, the Nation of Islam serves as an exceptional example of the potential for African American economic development. The relative independence that the Nation developed for itself with successful small business enterprises and land served as a model of what could be attained by pooling resources and reinvestment in a racially exclusive community. By 1945, for example, members of the Nation of Islam had pooled their resources and bought 140 acres of rural farmland in Michigan, and later acquired other real estate. Among these are more than 100 temples throughout the United States. Many of the latter operate grocery stores, bakeries, and other small businesses in the African American community (Appiah and Gates 1999, 1400).

Third, the organization spawned two leaders whose derivative religio-nationalist ideas won widespread sentimental support, even as the general population found them controversial at best. The ideas and activities of Malcolm X and Louis Farrakhan brought perhaps more African American attention and support for the ideas of the Black Muslims than the parent organization alone could have achieved. Indeed, today almost the entire public face of the Black Muslims in America is viewed through the lenses generated by Malcolm X and Farrakhan.

Yet the factions have been a major hindrance to the achievement of an unqualified success among the various strands of the Black

Muslims. There have been two major schisms, both involving break-away efforts by the most visible leaders within the sect. The first involved the departure of Malcolm X in 1964 after a dispute with the parent body's leader, Elijah Muhammad. The second occurred in 1978, when Louis Farrakhan split with Wallace Deen Muhammad, then leader of the parent body. While each of the splinter groups drew wide sentimental public support from African Americans, the parent group languished. Despite sentimental support, the fissures have left the formal membership base of all of the factions significantly diminished. As such, the leaders do not have an assured formal base for goal implementation.

Malcolm Little (later "X") was one of perhaps thousands of prisoners who found inspiration in the Nation of Islam's philosophy. After his prison conversion and release, he rapidly rose through the ranks of the organization. In the early 1960s it was Malcolm's oratory and persona that added renewed vigor and immense visibility for the Nation of Islam. He soon became impatient with Elijah Muhammad's apolitical philosophy, and eventually he became uncomfortable with the notion of whites as devils. His unease was exacerbated by allegations of Elijah Muhammad's impropriety in fathering children out of wedlock. Malcolm left the organization in 1964 and founded the Organization of Afro-American Unity. He was assassinated in New York's Audubon Ballroom on February 21, 1965, and members of Muhammad's faction were convicted for the crime. Malcolm's death left his personally inspired organization foundering.

The next major split occurred after the death of Elijah Muhammad in 1975 (Clegg 1998). Muhammad's son, Wallace Deen Muhammad, was named "Supreme Minister." He announced that whites were no longer viewed as evil and could be admitted to membership. At the same time, the group's name was changed to the World Community of Islam in the West, and still later it became the American Muslim Mission. This decision created friction that led to several splits, the major one being the 1978 departure of the organization's national spokesman, Louis Farrakhan. Although Wallace D. Muhammad pushed the Nation toward the orthodox Islamic Sunni sect, Farrakhan's group continued to embrace Black nationalism, separatism, and other tenets of the original Nation of Islam. However, Farrakhan's support of Jesse Jackson during his 1984 presidential campaign and his sponsorship of the Million Man March in 1995 demonstrated a willingness to engage in politics, a major deviation from traditional Nation of Islam ideology (Dodds 1997). Although Farrakhan continues to attract widespread sentimental support, he remains largely outside the structure of the traditional African American leadership group.

Despite the broad symbolic support the Nation of Islam has in the African American community, it has been unsuccessful in gaining formal membership among Blacks. The strict and conservative religious requirements have proved to be a difficult sell to the average African American. Although the group has also been successful in providing role models for African American entrepreneurship, it has been far less successful in motivating others to follow. Rarely has Black business entrepreneurship been argued to be within the compass of the Black Muslim business sector.

The Million Man March: A Case Study

The Million Man March was the brainchild of Louis Farrakhan and Benjamin Chavis, who was briefly the executive director of the NAACP. The march called for one million Black men to gather in the nation's capital for a day of atonement and focused discussion of their responsibility within the community. After the establishment of organizing committees in over 300 cities, many estimates are that nearly a million African American men congregated in Washington, D.C., on October 16, 1995 (Walton and Smith 2000, 130). It was the single largest gathering of African Americans in U.S. history, far exceeding the 1963 March on Washington. (The Million Woman March, a complementary event, subsequently drew 1.5 million in Philadelphia on October 25, 1997 [Appiah and Gates 1999, 1311–1312].)

Constituents, Goals, and Strategies

The Million Man March had a wide appeal for an ideological cross-section of the African American male population. It was composed almost exclusively of African American men (most were middle-class and educated) who traveled to Washington (Walton and Smith 2000, 131). However, millions more watched and joined in the spirit of the day via radio and television. Although there was a major dispute about women formally being barred from participation, Maya Angelou and Rosa Parks were among the women who spoke at the event (Appiah and Gates 1999, 1311–1312).

The overarching goal of the march was to draw attention to the social conditions of African Americans through its male "household heads." Although the broad purpose of the march was to draw attention to social and economic problems plaguing African Americans, Farrakhan focused primarily on the need for the individual African American male to take responsibility. Men were called upon to work to make themselves "whole." Once they were whole, they would move on to bring order to their families, their communities, and ultimately the nation. Although the general focus was internal (that is, African American men organizing themselves, other individuals, and institutions), Farrakhan and other speakers articulated few specific strategies for action (Appiah and Gates 1999, 730).

Major Facilitators and Achievements

The Million Man March was facilitated by what the leaders characterized as the continuing inequities that existed among Black Americans in society. Almost thirty years after the landmark legislation of the civil rights movement, African Americans still lagged behind the average white American in virtually all indices of social mobility. Moreover, in virtually all areas of downward mobility, African Americans continued to be overrepresented.

The march clearly showed the potential for organization among African American men. On a single day, African American men across the socioeconomic and ideological spectrum came together to express their dismay with the status quo. Most of them organized in their local communities and provided their own funds and logistical arrangements for the event. They had done so in a highly focused grassroots effort through churches and a vast array of other local venues. Surveys taken during and after the event revealed that they "were middle-age, married, and Christian . . . 31 percent identified themselves as liberal, 11 percent as nationalist, and 4 percent as socialist (20 percent used some other ideological label) . . . 86 percent were registered to vote, 55 percent had lobbied a public official. . . ." They were an extraordinarily active and informed group, with major issues on their minds that were not exploited by the march. Although a large number (88 percent) reported an interest in the moral focus of the event, an equal number were interested in self-determination and community unity (85 percent) and economic development (76 percent) (Walton and Smith 2000, 131).

Major Constraints and Failures

The goals of the Million Man March were constrained by the scope of the challenge it seemed to undertake without clear focus. There was not a clear organizational structure, nor has any evolved to harness the more than 300 local entities that sent marchers. Farrakhan also was unable to mobilize allies among most traditional African American leaders. The absence of most of the civil rights leadership and elected officials from the march was a weakness. Indeed, many of these leaders attacked Farrakhan as a "racist, sexist, anti-Semitic, homophobic demagogue" (Walton and Smith 2000, 130). The sentiments were deeper, however. There were serious objections to the "nationalist" project and the veneer of the Islamic faith as the modes for tackling the intractable problems of racial differentials. Most of the leaders who opposed him were committed to the pursuit of liberal-based approaches to partisan politics and electioneering. The focus on men also alienated many Black women, who saw this as sexist and inconsistent with the collaborative efforts between men and women in the struggle for civil rights.

The Southern Christian Leadership Conference

Origins

The Southern Christian Leadership Conference (SCLC) was founded in 1957 as a minister-led civil rights organization dedicated to wiping out segregation in the South. It was led by Martin Luther King Jr., who came to symbolize the civil rights movement. The SCLC was founded essentially to respond to the 1955 Montgomery bus boycott, a mass action against the segregated city bus transport system. As the relatively new minister of a local congregation, King was quickly tapped to provide leadership to the community-inspired protest (Fairclough 1987, 16–17). After the successful resolution of the boycott when the Supreme Court struck down bus segregation, the organization of ministers was launched in January 1957, and a month later it became the SCLC (Wynn 1974, 105). The membership was almost entirely male clergy. However, Ella Baker, a former labor and NAACP organizer, was the organization's first executive director. She also ran the Crusade for Citizenship, a related voter education campaign (Appiah and Gates 1999, 165). King became the SCLC's first president, quickly making the SCLC virtually synonymous with him, and served until his assassination in 1968.

Constituents, Issues, and Goals

Consistent with the focus on discrimination and disfranchisement in the southern states, the initial core constituency of the SCLC was Blacks in that region. But it was only a matter of time before King's voice became a central interpreter of the national agenda for racial inclusion. His charisma and powerful Christian-centered messages had an immediate appeal for all Americans interested in racial justice.

After the victories of the rights-focused movement, King's messages shifted to opposition to economic exploitation and warfare. These were seen as equally illustrative of differential treatment of African Americans, together with an expanded constituency of other impoverished classes. This caused him to greatly expand the audience to which he addressed his appeals, even as he made a more fundamental radical critique of the system of racial exclusion. The clergymen membership then became the conduits for spreading information to, and developing, foot soldiers in their church congregations. They could easily confront a racist Mississippi school principal, or an exploitative Chicago landlord, or a perpetrator of the Vietnam War like a secretary of defense. In this regard, the SCLC developed and maintained a national African American constituency despite its historical roots as a southern organization.

The goals of the SCLC differed little from the overall goals of the other major groups such as the NAACP and the NUL. All of these organizations focused on goals of equal opportunity, equal protection of the law, restoration of the franchise in the South, voter mobilization, and other activities to empower African Americans. It was widely believed that the destruction of the system of segregation and the right to vote would be sufficient evidence of the successful attainment of their goals.

Strategies

The SCLC had a number of strategies, and they mirrored those of the other major civil rights organizations. However, it was distinct in its adoption of nonviolent confrontation as the vehicle for most of its actions. This tactic evolved from Christian precepts and the combined thoughts of several philosophers and activists. However, King relied most on Christianity and the ideas of Mahatma Gandhi in structuring the campaigns of nonviolent protest and disobedience. Thence the SCLC became the primary purveyor of the principle of nonviolence as protests escalated across the South through the 1960s (Garrow 1978, 1–3).

Major Constraints and Facilitators

The SCLC had both major advantages and disadvantages, most re-lated to the visibility of its leader. To its advantage was the national consensus that the program of nonviolent change was preferable to more radical programs offered by SNCC and CORE. This consensus, for example, persuaded the Kennedy administration to seek ways to respond to King's demands, despite the surveillance of King and the SCLC by the FBI (Garrow 1981; O'Reilly 1989). Even so, the consen-sus trumped all else, generating the greatest general support for civil rights in American history.

The greatest constraints on the SCLC were the death of its leader and the shift in movement focus to questions of welfare equity. Al-though the SCLC has continued since King's death, it has rarely achieved anywhere near the success it enjoyed under his leadership. This is due in large measure to King's dominant position in the orga-nization. The financing of the organization is one telling example. During his life King generated more than half of the funding for the SCLC, but since his death the funding base has largely evaporated. Similarly the post-King SCLC has not effectively shifted as the nature of the civil rights struggle has changed. Although King's early efforts contributed significantly to the development of equal opportunity, today the major obstacles are inequality of results or inequities in re-source allocations to Blacks—issues for which the old tactics do not work as well.

Achievements and Failures

The achievements and failures of the SCLC, not surprisingly, are con-sistent with those of its leader. During his tenure, King had led all of the major SCLC projects. They constituted a series of high-profile protest campaigns centered mostly on southern cities, but they also included national campaigns and issues. Table 3.4 presents a chronological listing of the most important SCLC or SCLC-related projects. The Montgomery bus boycott represents the start of this organizational effort. And in many ways it was the most successful, becoming a model for succeeding campaigns in the region. It was followed by a series of activities suited to the King methods but in which the SCLC had a marginal or collaborative role—for example, the 1960 Greensboro sit-ins and the 1961 Freedom Rides. The SCLC had a tangential role in Greensboro, and it led a conference to reorganize the Freedom Riders and teach them techniques of nonviolent resistance (Peake 1987, 87). Both of these efforts were successful in moving toward desegregation. The first major setback for the SCLC was the Albany, Georgia, bus station sit-in, although again the organization was on the fringes of the campaign. This 1961 experience exposed some of the weaknesses of the nonviolent direct approach. For example, the Albany police arrested protesters in large numbers, filling up the jails, but without violence. The result was that the city officials preserved the status quo and remained unwilling to desegregate the bus stations (Garrow 1978, 215–218).

In contrast to this failure, the Birmingham campaign and the 1963 March on Washington were major successes. They thrust the SCLC and King into the national spotlight. In Birmingham the SCLC goaded Police Chief Bull Connor into displaying police brutality on national television, generating great national sympathy for desegregation efforts. The March on Washington generated a nationwide audience for the desegregation goals and the nonviolent strategy of King and the SCLC. It was the occasion for King's "I have a Dream" speech, which catapulted him to the forefront of civil rights leadership nationwide. The SCLC then became the "decentralized arm of the Black church" (Morris 1984), providing the foot soldiers for every King project thereafter (Garrow 1978, 284). The 1965 Selma March (in the face of southern white resistance) to promote passage of the Voting Rights Act then under consideration in Congress, effectuated all of the elements of the nonviolent strategy. There were masses of marchers, a cross-section of America, who when they finally peacefully crossed the Selma Bridge represented the SCLC's proudest moment. It was then hard to imagine that the Voting Rights Act would not succeed—and, in fact, the bill was enacted later that year.

The SCLC did not enjoy any major successes thereafter as King shifted focus to issues of poverty and general human rights. He ultimately understood that public accommodations and voting rights did not necessarily lead to equality. After gaining these victories, King turned to urban poverty and de facto segregation in the North, in

TABLE 3.4   Martin Luther King Jr. and the SCLC: Major Organizational and Associated Campaign Events

Date	Place	Events
Dec 1955	Montgomery, Ala.	Year-long bus boycott
May 1956	Tallahassee, Fla.	FAMU bus boycott
Jun 1956	Birmingham, Ala.	Citywide protests against segregation led by Rev. Fred Shuttlesworth
Jan 1957	Atlanta	SCLC founded; King elected chair
Feb 1958	South	"Crusade for Citizenship" campaign
Feb 1960	Greensboro, N.C.	First student-led lunch counter "sit-in"
Apr 1960	Raleigh, N.C.	SNCC organized
Oct 1960	Atlanta	King leads department store sit-in
May 1961	South	CORE-led Freedom Rides campaign devolved to SNCC, with King as coordinator
Nov 1961	Albany, Ga.	Widespread desegregation campaign over eight months
Apr 1963	Birmingham, Ala.	Citywide campaign of nonviolent direct action
Aug 1963	Washington, D.C.	March on Washington, with King as principal orator
Mar 1964	St. Augustine, Fla.	Citywide direct action campaign
Jan–Mar 1965	Selma, Ala.	Citywide SCLC/SNCC voting rights campaign
Jun 1965	South	SCOPE (summer voting rights campaign)
Jan–Aug 1966	Chicago	First urban "Freedom Movement" campaign for housing
Apr 1966	Chicago	SCLC calls for Vietnam withdrawal
Feb 1967	Chicago	King publicly denounces Vietnam War and joins antiwar movement
Jul 1967	National	"Operation Breadbasket" formed
Sep–Nov 1967		"Poor People's Campaign" initiative developed
Mar–Apr 1968	Memphis	Sanitation workers strike campaign
April 4, 1968	Memphis	King assassinated

SOURCE: Adapted from Fairclough 1987, 477–489. Reprinted with permission from the University of Georgia Press.

Chicago in particular. He took the organization to that city in 1966 to call attention to the urgency of the disparity of Blacks and others in the urban inner-city core ("war on the slum"). He experienced considerable difficulty in marshaling foot soldiers or generating sympathy for this essentially race- and class-based initiative. Indeed, aspects of the reception had all of the attributes of the racist resistance encountered from southern whites.

After the Chicago campaign King increasingly shifted from a civil rights focus to broader economic issues and the war in Vietnam. He argued that overcoming systemic poverty would require a redistribution of America's wealth. And he argued that Vietnam represented a violation of the rights of an impoverished people seeking to throw off the shackles of colonialism. In 1967, he organized the Poor People's Campaign within view of the White House designed to pressure lawmakers into focusing on issues of economic justice. Despite being roundly criticized by his usual allies in government, King took the SCLC to Memphis to support low-paid garbage workers, and he was assassinated there on April 4, 1968 (Appiah and Gates 1999, 1099).

Factionalism was kept to a minimum in the King-led SCLC, but figured into the post-King organization. King was insistent on moving the SCLC on to issues of economics and human rights, while some members resisted. At the same time, clearly some other young clergymen, such as James Bevel and Jesse Jackson, had ambitions of their own (Garrow 1986, 584–586). Nevertheless Ralph Abernathy, King's chief lieutenant, succeeded him as president of the SCLC and finished the essentially failed Poor People's Campaign. Joseph A. Lowery became the SCLC president in 1977 and served until 1998, struggling for part of that time against the first U.S. presidential administration (Reagan's) since King's death that was avowedly opposed to a civil rights agenda. Martin Luther King III succeeded Lowery as SCLC president in what has been a turbulent transition that has further weakened an already much-diminished organization. It is not entirely clear what the present goals are, and hence the SCLC's future is uncertain.

The Student Nonviolent Coordinating Committee (SNCC)

Origins

The Student Nonviolent Coordinating Committee (SNCC) was founded in 1960 as a spin-off from the SCLC. It was a response to the sit-in movement emerging among Black students at southern colleges and universities. King, for example, observed the critical role that students played in a succession of boycotts and protests after Montgomery, especially a bus boycott in Tallahassee and the lunch counter sit-in in Greensboro. Lunch counter sit-ins made great theater and drew press coverage, the importance of which King immediately understood. Such actions were fundamentally consistent with King's evolving ideology of nonviolent protest. Moreover, the students were also interested in facilitating local community organization and leadership to focus on political mobilization via voting.

King was initially motivated to develop SNCC as a support base for students, but also to harness their energy for the growing SCLC southern campaign. Indeed, the early movement among students lacked any central organizing unit, although clearly there was loose communication as the number of actions increased. To facilitate some organization, Ella Baker, in her capacity at the SCLC, convened a conference of student activists at Shaw University in North Carolina over April 15 to 17, 1960 (Grant 1998). There a committee was formed to coordinate the sit-in protests and other aspects of student work.

King clearly viewed this committee as a means of creating an auxiliary of the SCLC, whereas Ella Baker encouraged the students' independent thinking (Carson 1981, 19). Early on, SNCC did work in tandem with the SCLC. The staff worked in Atlanta in an old SCLC office and under the SCLC label. For a considerable time the organization, as its name implied, used the tactics of nonviolence that were so central to King's ideology. However, the students always preserved their independence and could never be said to be under King's control (Oppenheimer 1989, 45–46).

Constituents

SNCC itself was composed almost exclusively of students at the outset. Most of them were active members of some civil rights protest campaign, not a few of which were NAACP sponsored or inspired. And most of these early members were students at the segregated public and private Black colleges throughout the former Confederate states. As the goals of the campaign evolved, SNCC, like other civil rights organizations, expanded its base to include white students from an inchoate parallel movement. By 1964 a broad collection of American students from the South and the North collaborated in perhaps the most diverse student movement in history to contest southern segregation in a summer campaign in Mississippi. That publicly aired campaign revealed the excesses of a racialized society in a way many Americans had never encountered. And it helped to galvanize public opinion in opposition to the system.

The SNCC constituency evolved over time, but it is most associated with the southern towns and villages where racism was most widely and virulently practiced. This natural constituency was composed of poor and largely uneducated Blacks for whom voter registration or any semblance of equality had never been known. As SNCC gained more media exposure and as its ideology evolved, it sought to develop a broader portfolio of issues related to similarly situated classes of interests. Although it still focused primarily on African Americans, it developed issues to appeal to allies in the white left-wing student movements, the anti–Vietnam War coalition, socialist movements, and the anticolonial struggles in Africa. By the time the organization dissolved, it was concentrating almost exclusively on issues in the large urban areas of California and the Northeast. Its constituency became more and more circumscribed, appealing to a small base of African American radicals and white supporters.

Issues, Goals, and Strategies

SNCC had a very simple statement of purpose devised at the initial conference at Shaw University. It affirmed that nonviolence was the primary mechanism for achieving the committee's goals and that nonviolent resistance would appeal to the human conscience where violent resistant might not (Carson et al. 1991, 119–120). The most immediate goals were the continuation of the sit-in movement and cooperation with other African American civil rights organizations on direct action projects. Later goals included the expansion of African American voter registration, especially in Mississippi (Mississippi Freedom Summer), "Black Power" or office holding, and later a radical critique of American society that implied the use of violent resistance.

During its ten-year life span, SNCC took diverse approaches. Its first major approach was to further develop and coordinate the lunch counter sit-ins, within and between cities of the South. John Lewis perhaps put it best when he referred to SNCC as being "built on the foundation of confrontation—disciplined, focused, aggressive, nonviolent confrontation" (Lewis 1998, 181). The first campaign in which SNCC exerted itself as a loosely organized group of student associates took place in Rock Hill, South Carolina. There, in 1961, it entered an ongoing sit-in campaign of college students during which it exhibited its militant commitment to the exclusion of all other concerns—its members opted for month-long jail terms. This was to become a trademark of the new organization, which was fully evident in several later efforts. The goal of militant direct action was soon followed by its other major goal—voter registration. The aim was to register as many Blacks as possible in rural southern towns, where they were often a majority of the voting-age population. A third set of goals resulted from a leftist ideological critique of liberal democracy. The aim was to alter the differential status to which Blacks and other isolated groups were relegated in the capitalist society. As such SNCC became involved in issues such as African decolonization and U.S. involvement in Vietnam, and it fundamentally altered its position on nonviolence as a tactic.

Major Constraints and Facilitators

In the early days SNCC was greatly advantaged by its quasi-auxiliary status to the SCLC. This provided a basis of financial and administrative support. Ella Baker, a highly skilled administrator and organizer, was especially useful to the group's administrative and ideological development. At the same time SNCC also enjoyed support and nurture from the other major African American civil rights organizations, at least for a time. Similarly, like the SCLC, SNCC was especially effective in mobilizing public opinion because of the attention its actions drew from the press. This also generated an independent share of philanthropic resources for the organization.

However, from the start, and especially as the militant direct action style of SNCC evolved, some skepticism about the student organization constrained its support. For example, in the early 1960s SNCC was not entirely favored by more conservative elements of the civil rights movement. Its direct style was seen as too confrontational. Moreover, several conservative African American ministers also accused SNCC members of mismanaging finances as a means of derailing their efforts (Garrow 1986, 196). The general skepticism prompted the leadership of the organization to meet with the NAACP and NUL in March 1962 to look for avenues of cooperation. Instead, SNCC came away with the perception that both organizations were hostile and would only seek to advance their own agendas (Garrow 1986, 197).

The later SNCC severely challenged many of its early supporters. As the organization drew further away from the nonviolent approach associated with King and became more committed to a radical critique of American society, support dwindled. The Kennedy administration, which sought to channel the direct action program of SNCC to voter registration, found itself exasperated at the organization's relentless confrontational pursuit of this goal. Moreover, SNCC's increasing attacks on the government as hypocritical diminished Kennedy's support. The attacks on the Vietnam War, a strong position in favor of the rights of Palestinians, and the expansion beyond American issues in the South together prompted withdrawal of support by government and some philanthropists. By 1967 almost all external support had dried up, with some perceiving SNCC as a communist front organization (Carson 1981, 215ff).

Achievements and Failures

SNCC's activities can be divided into phases: sit-ins, voter registration, community leadership development, "Black Power," and "New Left" politics. The Greensboro sit-in was a catalyst for anxious Black college students in the South who wanted to contribute to the social change movement they saw emerging. Greensboro and later duplicates of it were stunning public relations successes, and SNCC members immediately recognized the social movement potential. Shortly after the wave of sit-ins there, SNCC joined a lunch counter sit-in at Rock Hill, South Carolina, in early 1961, demonstrating their bravura. Then in May of the same year the organization joined and then effectively took over the Freedom Rides campaign. This effort to desegregate interstate bus transport systems had been initiated by the Congress of Racial Equality (CORE), and featured integrated groups of passengers who sought to integrate bus depots and associated accommodations in cities in the deep South. The demonstrators were immediately and violently set upon by masses of whites who supported segregation. CORE was close to abandoning the effort because of the violence perpetrated upon demonstrators with little or no protection from law enforcement agencies. SNCC, however, took over and continued the campaign, demonstrating an ability to provoke a crisis atmosphere with a small cadre of dedicated workers (Carson 1981, 37). Although they were bruised and bloodied, the attention they drew to their cause was extraordinary.

In this vein SNCC also participated in major King campaigns at Birmingham and Selma. But at the 1963 March on Washington, John Lewis, then SNCC chairman, created a crisis because of what was deemed the militant tone of his remarks. Conservative African American leaders, particularly clergymen, threatened to withdraw unless the militant aspects of the speech were toned down. Lewis went on to give perhaps the hardest-hitting indictment of American racism (Levy 1998, 22–23). Several years later the desegregation of these facilities was achieved all over southern communities, and comprehensive civil rights and voting laws had been passed. The techniques used by SNCC in these early campaigns subsequently became a model for the sit-in campaigns throughout the region.

The voter registration phase was consistent with the initial interests SNCC members evinced in community organization. But it was also urged upon the group by the Kennedy administration, which partially underwrote the project in an effort to channel the student movement. In spite of partial government support, SNCC went on to develop a strong community organization program aimed at registering Blacks as a means of empowering them to take control of their affairs. At the same time, the organization escalated its attacks on the "hypocrisy" of the federal government in collaborating with southern segregationists and racists. Moreover, the expectation that the focus on voting would be a more tranquil affair proved to be completely in error. SNCC opted to establish its voting effort in the heart of the deep South—Mississippi. By September 1961 local workers were organizing in McComb, a town in the southwestern part of the state whose white population met them with unabashed violence, mass arrests, and murder. But the students pressed on in Mississippi for another three years, facing some of the worst violence in the history of the civil rights campaign (Dittmer 1994; Payne 1996). Their activity also probably shattered the complicity of silence on the part of the federal government about the atrocities that accompanied the system of racial exclusion in the South.

In Mississippi as well as in Georgia and Alabama, the organization worked out its highly successful community leadership development project. Before SNCC left Mississippi, a confederation of civil rights organizations had been formed, which was effectively run by SNCC; an inchoate political party movement was well along and eventually replaced the traditional white Democratic Party; and the most intensive concentrated assault on segregation, the "Long Hot Summer of 1964," had been executed. Mississippi was never the same, not least because an independent cadre of local leaders had been developed to sustain the attack on the system (Dittmer 1994). In Albany, Georgia, a long-running campaign in the trenches contributed to the development of the same kind of indigenous leadership base. In Lowndes County, Alabama, a political party effort similar to that in Mississippi was formed, although with less obvious success, as discussed below (Carson 1981).

The next phase was "Black Power." This is best illustrated by the effort to establish what became known as the Black Panther Party in Lowndes County, Alabama. It was the brainchild of Stokely Carmichael, one of a number of SNCC leaders in the 1960s. Carmichael sought to use this majority-Black county as a demonstration of the possibilities for political control wrought by successful voter registration. With intensive political education and voter registration in one small place, the aim was to generate a cadre of local leaders to wrest power from whites. And it was to be done via the ballot box. Despite the intensive work, the expected rapid transfer of power did not occur when a slate of Black candidates was fielded for office.

The failure of the effort, however, did not sully the project for Black mobilization for political control. Indeed, Carmichael developed the concept of "Black Power" into a kind of mantra in a 1966 march through Mississippi (organized by James Meredith, who had earlier been the first Black to enter the University of Mississippi). Carmichael and Hamilton (1967) later articulated this notion of Black Power as essentially the effort to organize group-based politics not unlike that successfully use by some white ethnic groups to achieve power. This project enjoyed considerable success among Blacks who used it in mobilizing majority constituencies that after 1967 began to elect large numbers of Blacks to political office. However, the concept was derided by most whites and by some African Americans as being separatist. This tag was attached to SNCC sometime before the organization articulated the view that whites could best contribute to the improvement of civil rights for African Americans by working within white communities. This approach did indeed have the effect of diminishing the interracial character of SNCC and in virtually splitting the core SNCC leadership into two camps (Carson 1981; Dittmer 1994).

This division in the organization had an impact on the success of its "New Left" politics. The conglomeration of student groups, human rights activists, pacifists, and socialists formed the group dubbed the New Left. SNCC had well established its bona fides as a part of this coalition by 1965, having objected to the escalating conflict in Vietnam and by siding with a number of powerless international groups. Equally important to this construct was what SNCC members called a radical critique of the capitalist system. Their assessment was that a major cause of African American displacement, like that of colonized people, was not only race but also class. This combination of powerful forces thus made African Americans natural allies of downtrodden peoples everywhere, race notwithstanding. In the Carmichael and Hamilton (1967) text, a theoretical model was offered that explained the African American situation as a colonial one. The authors argued the conditions of dominance by an external hegemonic force obtained in relations between African Americans and whites in the United States. Although in this argument race and class combined for an international movement, ironically Black nationalist ideals began to be adopted as organizing tactics for the local organization. Leadership passed from Stokely Carmichael to H. Rap Brown, who further solidified the nationalist perspective. Sometime before that, even "nonviolent" had been removed from the organization's name—it became the Student National Coordinating Committee.

Factions

SNCC was fraught with factional conflict virtually from its inception. As Andrew Young notes in his autobiography, "The Southern-born SNCC students like John Lewis were steeped in religion, but many of the Northern students, black and white, were drawn to SNCC for political reasons" (Young 1998, 398). Sellers and Terrell (1973) noted the tendency after 1964 for some to divide themselves into "floaters," favoring abstract intellectual discussions over meaningless subjects, and "hardliners," favoring adoption of the style and actions consistent with black power. And there were continuous discussions about the role of whites in the organization. Some thought their presence detracted from the "Black agenda," while others were skeptical about their commitment. Although SNCC started as a relatively integrated body, over time most white members left, leaving SNCC near the end of the 1960s essentially a revolutionary African American political organization. In its nature as a relatively small organization dependent on a committed cadre of students, intellectual discussions questioning organization's purposes and goals were pervasive.

At practically every project interval such debates occurred and were usually consequential, often resulting in a shift in leadership.

Factional leadership can be broken down into four eras. The formative years were 1960 to 1963, when first Ella Baker and then James Forman were critical leaders. That period was followed by the one with the most productive work in direct action and community development when John Lewis led SNCC between 1963 and 1966. The years of strong ideological focus on Black Power and nationalism was led by Stokely Carmichael from 1966 to 1967. The final period was under H. Rap Brown's leadership, between 1967 and 1970, focusing on nationalist power politics. This continuous state of searching may well have contributed to the ultimate demise of the formal organization.

Conclusion

Political participation has always been an integral part of the African American quest for equality. From the codification of slavery in Massachusetts in 1641 to the appointment of Colin Powell as secretary of state in 2001, political participation has played a major role in the strategy for full inclusion in the American dream. Although there is growing realization that political participation must be accompanied by social capital and economic wherewithal, there continues to be a major appreciation for the role of politics in determining the life chances of citizens in general and of African Americans in particular.

Throughout the various stages of African American history, there has been a diversity of thought on the best strategy to facilitate success. Nonetheless, there was a general consensus regarding the problem (Black oppression and inequality), the cause of the problem (discrimination and unequal treatment under the law), and the ultimate goal (an equal opportunity to optimize the group's full potential). Although there is still the shared goal of an equal opportunity to optimize one's potential, African American conservatives and liberals differ on the cause of their inequality as well as on the prescriptive measures required to make equal opportunity possible.

African American conservatives believe that the causes of inequality are primarily internal. Racism is virtually dead, they say, and it is not tolerated by the criminal justice system; African Americans must stop blaming outside forces and accept responsibility for their own success or failure (Loury 1995; McWhorter 2000; Steele 1991; Williams 1995). African American liberals acknowledge the progress that has been made in the post–civil rights era, yet they argue that race still matters and manifests itself traditionally as well as in institutional forms. Proponents of this perspective point to the external causes of African American inequity such as a conservative political system, even while working on internal challenges (Bell 1989; Dyson 1996; Robinson 2000; West 1994).

The best-known organizations seeking African American actualization today are those that have long experience. They tend to be more centralized and have strong membership or financial ties with whites. Their members are middle-aged or older, with higher socioeconomic status, and they more often have religious affiliations. CORE, the NAACP, the NUL, the SCLC, and the African American churches fit this profile. The weaknesses of the Nation of Islam and the demise of organizations like SNCC and the Black Power movement would seem not to fit this mold, and thus confirm the general assessment about organizational experience (Barker et al. 1999, 192–209).

The selected organizations that have formed the basis of this discussion have had significant roles in securing change in race relations and in securing African American participation in U.S. social and political institutions. The analysis has demonstrated how the various features of these organizations have been determined by the ebb, flow, and variations in the patterns of discrimination against African Americans. Despite the variations, there has been a consistency of purposes for most of these organizations—universal freedom and access for Blacks. Since that overarching goal has not been fully achieved, independent community and civil rights organizations will continue to have an important role. The scope of that role can be gauged by the length of time it took to demolish state-sanctioned segregation in the United States. Segregation effectively began in 1641 with the institutionalization of enslavement in Massachusetts. It effectively ended when a 1969 school desegregation case (*Alexander v. Holmes Board of Education*) implemented the famous dictum of "all deliberate speed" associated with the *Brown* case in 1954. That took 328 years.

References

Alex-Assensoh, Yvette, and Lawrence J. Hanks. 2000. *Black Multiracial Politics in America*. New York: New York University Press.

Appiah, Kwame Anthony, and Henry Louis Gates Jr. 1999. *Africana: The Encyclopedia of the African American Experience*. New York: Basic Civitas Books.

Baldwin, Lewis V. 1983. *Invisible Strands in African Methodism: A History of the African Union Methodist Protestant and Union American Methodist Episcopal Churches, 1805–1980*. Metuchen, NJ: Scarecrow Press.

Barker, Lucius, et al. 1999. *African Americans and the American Political System.* Saddle River, NJ: Prentice-Hall.

Bell, Derrick. 1989. *And We Are Not Saved: The Elusive Quest for Racial Justice.* New York: Basic Books.

Birmingham, David. 1998. *Kwame Nkrumah: The Father of African National-ism.* Athens: Ohio University Press.

Blassingame, John. 1979. *The Slave Community: Plantation Life in the Antebel-lum South.* New York: Oxford University Press.

Branch, Taylor. 1988. *Parting the Waters: America in the King Years, 1954–64.* New York: William Morrow.

Brisbane, Robert H. 1976. *The Black Vanguard: Origins of the Negro Social Revo-lution, 1900–1960.* Valley Forge, NY: Judson Press.

Broderick, Francis, and August Meier, eds. 1965. *Negro Protest Thought in the Twentieth Century.* New York: Bobbs-Merrill.

Campbell, James T. 1995. *Songs of Zion: The African Methodist Episcopal Church in the United States and South Africa.* New York: Oxford University Press.

Carmichael, Stokely, and Charles Hamilton. 1967. *Black Power.* New York: Random House.

Carson, Clayborne. 1981. *In Struggle: SNCC and the Black Awakening of the 1960s.* Cambridge, MA: Harvard University Press.

Carson, Clayborne, et al., eds. 1991. *The Eyes on the Prize Civil Rights Reader: Documents, Speeches, and Firsthand Accounts from the Black Freedom Struggle, 1954–1990.* New York: Penguin Books.

Clarke, John Henrik, ed., with the assistance of Amy Jacques-Garvey. 1974. *Marcus Garvey and the Vision of Africa.* New York: Vintage.

Clegg, Claude, III. 1998. *An Original Man: The Life and Times of Elijah Muham-mad.* New York: St. Martin's Press.

Coleman, Johnnie. 2000. *Open Your Mind and Be Healed.* New York: DeVorss.

Cronon, E. David. 1955. *Black Moses: Marcus Garvey and the United Negro Im-provement Association.* Madison: University of Wisconsin Press.

Cruse, Harold. 1967. *The Crisis of the Negro Intellectual from Its Origins to the Present.* New York: William Morrow.

Dahl, Robert. 1961. *Who Governs?* New Haven, CT: Yale University Press.

Dickerson, Dennis. 1998. *Militant Negotiator: Whitney M. Young, Jr.* Lexington: University Press of Kentucky.

Dittmer, John. 1994. *Local People: The Struggle for Civil Rights in Mississippi.* Urbana: University Press of Illinois.

Dodds, Elreta. 1997. *The Trouble with Farrakhan and the Nation of Islam: An-other Message to the Black Man in America.* Detroit: Press Toward the Mark Publications.

Dollar, Creflo A., Jr. 1999. *Total Life Prosperity: Fourteen Practical Steps to Re-ceiving God's Full Blessing.* New York: Thomas Nelson.

Dyson, Michael Eric. 1996. *Race Rules: Navigating the Color Line.* Reading, MA: Addison-Wesley.

Estell, Kenneth. 1994. *Reference Library of Black America.* Vol. 2. Detroit: Gale.

Fairclough, Adam. 1987. *To Redeem the Soul of America: The Southern Christian Leadership Conference and Martin Luther King, Jr.* Athens: University of Georgia Press.

Foster, William. 1974. "The Garvey Movement: A Marxist View." In John Henrik Clarke, ed., *Marcus Garvey and the Vision of Africa*, 415–427. New York: Vintage.

Franklin, John Hope, and Alfred Moss Jr. 1994. *From Slavery to Freedom.* New York: McGraw-Hill.

Frazier, E. Franklin. 1974. *The Negro Church in America.* New York: Schocken Books.

Garrow, David J. 1978. *Protest at Selma: Martin Luther King Jr. and the Voting Rights Act of 1965.* New Haven, CT: Yale University Press.

———. 1981. *The FBI and Martin Luther King Jr.* New York: W. W. Norton.

———. 1986. *Bearing the Cross: Martin Luther King, Jr., and the Southern Christian Leadership Conference.* New York: William Morrow.

George, Carol V. R. 1973. *Segregated Sabbaths: Richard Allen and the Emergence of Independent Black Churches, 1760–1840.* New York: Oxford University Press.

Grant, Joanne. 1998. *Ella Baker: Freedom Bound.* New York: Wiley.

Hanks, Lawrence J. 1987. *The Struggle for Black Political Empowerment in Three Georgia Counties.* Knoxville: University of Tennessee Press.

Holt, Thomas. 1982. "The Lonely Warrior: Ida B. Wells-Barnett and the Struggle for Black Leadership." In John Hope Franklin and August Meier, eds., *Black Leaders of the Twentieth Century.* Urbana: University Press of Illinois.

Hutchinson, Earl Ofari. 1972. *Let Your Motto Be Resistance: The Life and Thought of Henry Highland Garnet.* Boston: Beacon Press.

Jacques-Garvey, Amy. 1969. *Philosophy and Opinions of Marcus Garvey.* New York: Atheneum Press.

Jakes, T. D. 1999. *Maximize the Moment: God's Action Plan for Your Life.* New York: Putnam.

King, Barbara. 1995. *Transform Your Life.* New York: Perigee.

Klein, Michael. 1991. *The Man Behind the Sound Bite: The Real Story of Reverend Al Sharpton.* New York: Castillo International.

Levy, Peter B. 1998. *The Civil Rights Movement.* Westport, CT: Greenwood.

Lewis, John, with Michael D'Orso. 1998. *Walking with the Wind: A Memoir of the Movement.* New York: Simon and Schuster.

Lewis, Rupert. 1988. *Marcus Garvey: Anti-colonial Champion.* Trenton, NJ: Africa World Press.

Lincoln, C. Eric. 1994. *The Black Muslims in America.* 3d ed. Trenton, NJ: Africa World Press.

Lincoln, C. Eric, and Lawrence H. Mamiya. 1990. *The Black Church in the African American Experience.* Durham, NC: Duke University Press.

Logan, Rayford. 1972. *The Betrayal of the Negro.* New York: Collier.

Logan, Rayford, and Michael Winston, eds. 1982. *Dictionary of Negro Biography.* New York: W. W. Norton.

Loury, Glenn. 1995. *One By One From the Inside Out.* New York: The Free Press.

Lynch, Hollis Ralph. 1967. *Edward Wilmot Blyden: Pan-Negro Patriot, 1832–1912.* New York: Oxford University Press.

Lyons, Thomas T. 1971. *Black Leadership in American History.* Menlo Park, CA: Addison-Wesley.

Marinelli, Lawrence. 1964. *The New Liberia.* London: Pall Mall.

McKinney, George C., et al., eds. 1997. *The African American Devotional Bible.* Grand Rapids, MI: Zondervan.

McWhorter, John. 2000. *Losing the Race: Self-Sabotage in Black America.* New York: HarperCollins.

Million Man March Organizing Committee. 1995. *The Million Man March: Day of Absence Mission Statement.* Chicago: Third World Press.

Moore, Jesse Thomas, Jr. 1981. *A Search for Equality: The National Urban League, 1910–1961.* University Park: Pennsylvania State University Press.

Moore, Richard. 1974. "The Critics and Opponents of Marcus Garvey." In John Henrik Clarke, ed., *Marcus Garvey and the Vision of Africa,* 210–255. New York: Vintage.

Morris, Aldon. 1984. *The Origins of the Civil Rights Movement: Black Communities Organizing for Change.* New York: The Free Press.

Myrdal, Gunnar. 1944. *An American Dilemma.* New York: Harper and Row.

Oppenheimer, Martin. 1989. *The Sit-In Movement of 1960.* New York: Carlson.

O'Reilly, Kenneth. 1989. *Racial Matters: The FBI's Secret File on Black America, 1960–1972.* New York: The Free Press.

Payne, Charles M. 1996. *I've Got the Light of Freedom: The Organizing Tradition and the Mississippi Freedom Struggle.* Berkeley: University of California Press.

Peake, Thomas R. 1987. *Keeping the Dream Alive: A History of the Southern Christian Leadership Conference from King to the Nineteen-Eighties.* New York: Peter Lang.

Price, Frederick K. C. 1999. *Race, Religion, and Racism: Perverting the Gospel to Subjugate a People.* New York: Faith One.

Raboteau, Albert. 1980. *Slave Religion: The Invisible Institution in the Antebellum South.* New York: Oxford University Press.

Redkey, Edwin S. 1969. *Black Exodus: Black Nationalist and Back-to-Africa Movements, 1890–1910.* New Haven, CT: Yale University Press.

Reed, Adolph, Jr. 1986. *The Jesse Jackson Phenomenon.* New Haven, CT: Yale University Press.

Rivers, Eugene. 2001. "Faith in Politics: Beyond the Civil Rights Industry." *Boston Review* (April/May): 5–7.

Robinson, Randall. 2000. *The Debt.* New York: Penguin Books.

Scruggs, Otey. 1977. "We the Children of Africa in This Land: Alexander Crummell." In Lorraine Williams, ed., *Africa and Afro-American Experience: Eight Essays,* 77–95. Washington, DC: Howard University Press.

Sellers, Cleveland, and Robert Terrell. 1973. *The River of No Return: The Autobiography of a Black Militant and the Life and Death of SNCC.* New York: William Morrow.

Seraile, William. 1998. *Fire in His Heart: Bishop Benjamin Tucker Tanner and the A.M.E. Church.* Knoxville: University of Tennessee Press.

Shick, Tom W. 1980. *Behold the Promised Land: A History of Afro-American Settler Society in Nineteenth-Century Liberia*. Baltimore: Johns Hopkins University Press.

Smith, Charles Spencer. 1922 [reprint 1968]. *A History of the African Methodist Episcopal Church*. New York: Johnson Reprints.

Smith, Robert C. 1996. *We Have No Leaders: African Americans in the Post–Civil Rights Era*. Albany: State University of New York Press.

Smith-Irvin, Jeannette. 1989. *Marcus Garvey's Foot Soldiers of the Universal Negro Improvement Association (Their Own Words)*. Trenton, NJ: Africa World Press.

Spady, James G. 1985. *Marcus Garvey, Africa, and the Universal Negro Improvement Association: A UMUM Perspective on Concentric Activity in the Pan African World*. New York: Marcus Garvey Memorial Foundation.

Steele, Shelby. 1991. *The Content of Our Character: A New Vision of Race in America*. New York: HarperCollins.

Strickland, Arvarh. 1996. *History of the Chicago Urban League*. Urbana: University Press of Illinois.

Stuckey, Sterling. 1972. *The Ideological Origins of Black Nationalism*. Boston: Beacon Press.

Truman, David. 1951. *The Governmental Process*. New York: Knopf.

Walker, Jack L., Jr. 1991. *Mobilizing Interest Groups in America*. Ann Arbor: University of Michigan Press.

Walton, Hanes, Jr. 1972. *Black Politics*. Philadelphia: J. P. Lippincott.

Walton, Hanes, Jr., and Robert Smith. 2000. *American Politics and the African American Quest for Universal Freedom*. New York: Longman.

Washington, James E. 1968. *The Essential Writings and Speeches of Martin Luther King, Jr.* San Francisco: HarperCollins.

Watson, Denton. 1990. *Lion in the Lobby: Clarence Mitchell's Struggle to Pass Civil Rights Laws*. New York: William Morrow.

Weiss, Nancy. 1974. *The National Urban League*. New York: Oxford University Press.

West, Cornel. 1994. *Race Matters*. New York: Vintage Books.

Williams, Armstrong. 1995. *Beyond Blame: How We Can Succeed by Breaking the Dependency Barrier*. New York: The Free Press.

Wilson, Graham. 1990. *Interest Groups*. Cambridge: Blackwell.

Wynn, Daniel W. 1974. *The Black Protest Movement*. New York: Philosophical Library.

Young, Andrew. 1998. *An Easy Burden: The Civil Rights Movement and the Transformation of America*. New York: HarperCollins.

4

Participation in Electoral Politics

Byron D'Andra Orey and Reginald Vance

One of the axioms of empirical political science is that electoral participation is more prevalent among those who are better off and more educated. Consequent to this axiom is the belief that those who participate more also gain more benefits from the system. Hence it is hardly a surprise when Rosenstone and Hansen (1993, 10) argue that people participate in politics when the benefits of participating outweigh the costs. Under this assumption, we would expect that the overrepresentation of African Americans in the lower socioeconomic stratum would be accompanied by low levels of political participation. The literature on electoral behavior, however, has revealed that when socioeconomic factors and group consciousness are controlled for, poor African Americans tend to participate in politics at levels higher than those of their white counterparts (Shingles 1981; Verba and Nie 1972).

A second factor that helps us to determine what participation means is public opinion data—that is, aggregate information that citizens provide about their reasons for voting for or supporting political candidates. In democratic society there is little else as important as expressions about citizen preferences. A number of important assumptions inspire our confidence in the importance of public opinion data for clarifying participation. Among these are that information is important to good citizenship; amid other entities, organized political groups and leaders provide much of that information; and active citizens consume available information and use it to make rational decisions about their political preferences. Since in U.S. racialized history African Americans have been indelibly marked and have variously experienced widespread exclusion or status ambivalence, the group has consistently striven to alter those conditions. In the singularity of the group's political interest in securing universal inclusion, African American political opinion and consequent political preferences have been easy to characterize. The group's political opinion is by and large liberal and social-change oriented—expressing a preference for political leaders who promise to work toward altering conditions of racial exclusion and its concomitant barriers to socioeconomic advancement.

This chapter traces the evolution of African American electoral participation and characterizes the political behavior that it has generated for this racialized community. First, the chapter examines this community's behavior relative to the various political parties, the standard vehicles through which electoral participation is executed. It then examines the voting behavior of African Americans. This is followed by case studies examining Black third-party efforts, political behavior during Reconstruction, and Jesse Jackson's bid for the presidency.

Some Determinants of Political Behavior

Political Socialization

People develop opinions about political issues through a process called political socialization. Sources of such information include the church, family, school, peer groups, and protest demonstrations (Walton, Jones, and Ford 1997). These sources are referred to as agents of political socialization. Among African Americans, the church has been one of the most important such agents. Cone argues that the "black church was born in protest" (Cone 1997, 94). Even during the pre–Civil War period, churches encouraged liberation (Childs 1980). Katherine Tate (1991), in a study of Black participation in the 1984 and 1988 presidential elections, finds that African Americans who belonged to political churches were more likely to participate in politics. Aldon Morris reports that mass church involvement in the civil rights movement was inevitable, because the ministers of the movement were trained by those who "stressed human dignity" (Morris 1984, 8). Additionally, he and his colleagues note that "the movement itself was a tool of political socialization."

Walton and Smith describe nontraditional agents of political socialization, such as "cultural events and projects." The authors refer to a content analysis of African American popular music conducted by Robert Walker (1976), who found that there was an increase in "message songs" starting in the late 1950s. Walker also found that the apex of such "message music" occurred at the same time that the civil rights movement reached its peak, between 1966 and 1969 (Walton and Smith 2000, 54).

Similarly Walton and Smith (2000) argue that a significant amount of socialization has occurred through the presence of African American candidates standing for electoral office since 1960. A particularly important socializing effect has occurred when Blacks have sought the seemingly improbable prize of the American presidency. They then discuss how Representative Shirley Chisholm set this tone when she became the first African American within the two-party structure to pursue the presidency in 1972. The most successful socializing effect generated by a candidate occurred with Jesse Jackson's bid for the presidency in 1984 and 1988. Also notable is Alan Keyes's 1996 run as the first African American in the Republican Party presidential primary, although he reached fewer African Americans voters than Jackson had.

Socioeconomic Factors and Participation

In addition to the socialization process, socioeconomic factors play a major role in political participation among African Americans. Education is a major contributing variable, for example. Wolfinger and Rosenstone (1980, 18) note that because "schooling increases one's capacity for understanding and working with complex, abstract, and intangible subjects, that is, subjects like politics," education increases the likelihood that one will vote. Similarly, income has been found to have an impact on participation. Tate (1993) notes that poor people probably have less time and energy for the "nonessentials" in life, including political participation. Despite this, the data indicate that poor Blacks who are conscious of their economic subjugation are more likely to participate in politics, compared with whites.

Political Participation and Group Consciousness

Because African Americans have most often been treated as a racialized group in the society, some political scientists have reasoned that such a group distinction might also affect political participation. Verba and Nie (1972) were among the first to analyze political participation as it relates to group consciousness. In their explanation of African Americans, the authors find that those who are conscious of being members of an oppressed group are most likely to participate in campaigns and cooperative activities. Shingles (1981) confirmed this correlation and also found that when socioeconomic variables are controlled for, African Americans participate at higher levels than members of other groups. This finding led him to extend the group consciousness thesis by including an analysis of the African American poor. He found "black consciousness" to be a powerful explanatory tool for the participation of the African American poor. For Shingles, poor African Americans who are conscious of group oppression are more inclined to have a cynical perception of government. That cynicism, however, is converted into various types of political efficacy, or empowerment. This "counter" empowerment in turn induces greater political participation.

The findings of Shingles and others are inconsistent with the conventional wisdom about general determinants of political participation. However, the data are persuasive and suggest that there is something unique about political participation among Blacks as compared with other racial groups. Michael Dawson offers a solution to this conundrum. He argues that African Americans believe they have a "linked fate." That is, "a significant number of African Americans believe that what happens to the group as a whole affects their own lives" (Dawson 1994, 76). This group linkage is directly related to the historical struggles of African Americans in the United States. The struggles have played out in such a way that members of the group perceive that neither their life chances nor their ability to influence the allocation of political goods is determined by their individual standing. Hence, their history of economic subjugation and political disfranchisement yields a sense of common fate. The singularity of this expression of linked fate trumps even socioeconomic characteristics that one might expect would predict variations in behavior (Dawson 1994; Tate 1993).

African American Public Opinion and Partisan Identification

A Liberal Bias in Black Opinion

This notion of linked fate also serves as the basis for the fairly consistent strivings for inclusion and socioeconomic development in African American public opinion. Following Dawson's reasoning, we should expect that African American opinion is likely to deviate considerably from that of whites. And that is the case—African Americans and whites define their political interests in divergent ways and perceive different relationships to public authorities and institutions.

Table 4.1 compares opinion among Blacks and whites on various issues. A variety of issues have been selected, some of which relate to the key concern of Blacks, namely, racial inclusion. Others relate to issues that may be thought of as reflecting a liberal-conservative continuum. Between 1986 and 1992 the greatest differences between the two races appeared on the issue that was of most concern to Blacks—racial policy. Blacks, as one of the groups most vulnerable to downward shifts in the economy, were almost twice as likely as whites to favor a government guarantee of employment opportunity. There was an even greater divergence on a role for government in guaranteeing school desegregation (almost 83 percent of Blacks, compared with about 36 percent of whites). The differences grew wider and wider as the issue of preferential treatment for underrepresentation was introduced. And as the issues became further removed from a direct racial public policy, the gap between the races lessened but remained significant on most measures.

However, opinions diverge considerably between the races when information about alienation from public institutions and feelings of efficacy are taken into account. The different socialization experiences of Blacks vis-à-vis public authorities produce distinct opinions. They are quite skeptical of the government and believe that they have far less ability to influence what it does. This cast of opinion forms a good deal of the basis for the behaviors we observe among African American participants in political affairs.

TABLE 4.1   Public Opinion among Blacks and Whites, 1986–1992 (Percent)

	Whites	Blacks
Race Policy		
Government should ensure equal employment opportunity	46.2	89.8
Government should see to school desegregation	35.6	82.9
Increase spending on programs that assist Blacks	17.6	74.6
Government should make special efforts to help Blacks	11.9	39.9
Preferential hiring	15.4	67.7
College quotas	29.7	79.7
Implicit Racial Issues		
Increase support for food stamps	18.0	50.9
Sanctions against South Africa	26.5	45.8
More assistance for welfare	14.7	32.3
Solve underlying problems that give rise to urban unrest	48.3	71.7
Oppose capital punishment	14.4	36.9
Social Spending		
Expand government services	41.5	72.0
Increase Social Security	60.2	82.0
Federal support for education	61.0	81.0
Increase support for Medicare	83.2	93.9
Government assistance to the poor	50.5	81.0
Alienation from Government		
People like me have no say	13.3	28.3
Public officials don't care	15.3	29.0
Distrust government	56.1	74.4
Government run by big interests	66.0	73.3

SOURCE: Adapted from Kinder and Sanders 1996, 30. Reprinted with permission from the University of Chicago Press.

African American Partisan Identification

The sources of participation and the opinions of African Americans translate into certain general characteristics in partisan identification. Since the United States has one of the strongest two-party political systems in the world, political scientists have fairly easily determined how most citizens identify themselves politically—most of the time the population is fairly evenly divided between identifiers with the Democratic and Republican parties. Even when the division is not fairly even, rarely does one party or the other enjoy a long-

TABLE 4.2   Partisan Identification, by Race, 1952–1996 (Percent)

	Democrats		Republicans	
	Blacks	Whites	Blacks	Whites
1952	62	56	17	35
1956	59	56	22	34
1960	58	55	22	34
1964	82	58	08	32
1968	92	53	03	37
1972	75	49	11	36
1976	84	47	05	37
1980	81	49	08	37
1984	77	44	07	44
1988	81	40	11	46
1992	78	45	08	42
1996	81	48	09	44

SOURCE: Adapted from Barker et al. 1999, 216. Reprinted with permission from Prentice-Hall.

term monopoly of partisan supporters in the various local, state, and federal election contests. Between 1952 and 1996, for example, in only three elections (1952, 1956, and 1964) did the white voting partisans give more than 55 percent of their support to one party. African Americans, however, deviate from that general pattern. They tend to identify with one party at a time. Historically, they have given well over 60 percent of their support to just one party for long periods. Table 4.2 compares the two racial groups' party identification between 1952 and 1996. During this 54-year period, selected African Americans identified strongly with the Democratic Party. But that was not always the case. The analysis below shows that this pattern characterized African American partisan identification with the Republican Party at an earlier point in history.

Racially Polarized Voting: An Outcome of Racial Exclusion and In-Group Processes

The racial segmentation of African Americans in public life has often produced racial bloc voting. This is a situation in which large numbers of a racial or ethnic group vote for a particular candidate, or in which such a group uses its separate social base to form coalitions with other groups. Much objective evidence shows that Black partisan identification and voting occurs in a bloc. But it is equally true that the presence of Black candidates in elections often produces bloc voting on the part of whites against those candidates (Reeves 1997). Both outcomes seem to be consistent with the different realities that the races perceive in public life.

Racially polarized voting, on the other hand, occurs when at least two racial groups vote as a bloc for a set of different candidates. One can think of polarization as occurring when, given a head-to-head contest featuring an African American and a white candidate, the whites vote for other whites and the African Americans vote for other African Americans. In this scenario, Blacks gain most when they control more than a majority of the votes, a condition that obtains for most of the electoral seats held by them. But for Blacks there is a distinct other side to bloc voting. They have often used their votes in a bloc to advance their agenda of racial inclusion. They do this by bundling their votes for the party that seems most amenable to their agenda, hoping to serve as a counterweight in the two-way contest. The group is especially advantaged in this scenario when the competition is especially keen between the two parties. This analysis will show how the latter has been a feature of African American behavior, especially in national contests (Walters 1988).

There are other aspects to racialized voting that lead to especially deleterious effects in the electoral process. Polarized voting can become problematic when it leads to vote dilution. Davidson (1984) states that vote dilution occurs when one group voting as a cohesive bloc, either singly or when combined into districts via election laws, diminishes the opportunity of another group to elect the candidate of their choice. Lani Guinier (1994) invokes James Madison's warning about this phenomenon at the founding of the republic: "if a majority be united by a common interest, the rights of the minority will be insecure." According to Madison, "the accumulation of all powers, legislative, executive, and judiciary, in the same hands, whether of one, of few, or many," is defined as tyranny. Guinier goes on to show that such a "tyranny of the majority" characterizes the status of African Americans in the political process, making them permanent losers in the majority-rule system (Guinier 1994, 3–20).

A classic case of racially polarized voting and probably one of the most extreme cases occurred with Jesse Jackson's candidacies in the 1984 and 1988 Democratic primaries. According to the CBS News and the *New York Times* exit polls, in 1984 Jesse Jackson received 77 percent of the African American vote and only 5 percent of the white vote. In 1998 he received 93 percent of the African American vote and roughly 13 percent of the white vote (Plissner and Mitofsky 1988). In this case, even when Jackson sought to portray himself as a candidate with an all-inclusive platform of broad appeal—his "Rainbow Coalition" of diverse interests—he was unable to attract support from the substantial number of whites whose "interests" seemed consistent with the "rainbow." Moreover, he continued to appeal to all sectors of African Americans, even when the Rainbow platform appeared to disadvantage them.

The racially polarizing effect often occurs in two-party contests, even when there is no Black candidate. Walton and Smith (2000) have called this the "one-party" dominant effect among Blacks, who have historically cast the overwhelming majority of their votes for one or the other of the major two parties. During the Reconstruction era, they cast their votes overwhelmingly for the Republican Party, which had been Lincoln's party. Since the presidency of Franklin D. Roosevelt, however, Blacks have tended toward the Democratic Party. The 2000 election is an illustration. In one of the most controversial elections since the 1876 Hayes-Tilden contest, the polarization of the African American vote was visible. Hardly anywhere was the polarization more visible than in the state on which the outcome of the contest hinged—Florida. An aggregate-level analysis (using ecological regression) of registration data and Florida election returns, by county, provides strong evidence of racially polarized voting. These results show that African Americans overwhelmingly supported Al Gore, with 96 percent of their vote, compared with only 4 percent who supported Bush. Approximately 56 percent of whites, on the other hand, supported George Bush, while roughly 44 percent supported Gore.

Political Behavior in
the Colonial and Slavery Periods

To be sure, African Americans have been disfranchised from the political process for most of their time in America. However, since the passage of the Voting Rights Act of 1965 they have made considerable advances. In the words of the southern Baptist preacher, "We ain't where we want to be, we ain't where we ought to be, but thank

God we ain't where we was!" Election rates of African Americans still lag far behind their percentage of the population. African Americans constitute roughly 12 percent of the population but account for only 7 percent of the members of Congress (Davidson and Oleszek 2002, 127). Nevertheless, the past several decades have seen minority enfranchisement translated into the election of significant numbers of minority representatives at the local, state, and national levels. An overview of the evolution of African American political participation is provided below.

Petitions and Protests

African American political behavior began in colonial America, when the population was small, and before there were clear organized political factions. Political expression came from free Blacks located mostly in the New England states, where slavery was less prevalent. In some of these states a small number of Blacks were granted the franchise well before the Civil War. For example, in 1783 a Massachusetts court ruled that Blacks who paid taxes were entitled to the franchise (Aptheker 1951). By 1840 African Americans were granted the right to vote in only a few northeastern states—Maine, Vermont, New Hampshire, and Massachusetts; they could also vote in Rhode Island and New York, but with property qualifications (Wesley 1944). In the state of New York, for example, Blacks were granted suffrage if they owned "at least two-hundred fifty dollars' worth of property" (Walton 1972b, 21).

In the early history of the fledgling colonies, it is not easy to identify political behavior in the classical sense among African Americans, given their small numbers. What we do know is that those who had the franchise sought to exercise it in their perceived interest and that they did so by aligning with other organized interests insofar as these existed. Others who were free but disfranchised also sought to act on the system to attain or restore the right of formal participation. But what is perhaps most remarkable is that the overwhelming tenor of early African American political behavior was defined by the fact that the majority of Blacks were in slavery. That meant that African American political expression was overwhelmingly directed toward the attainment of universal freedom. Hence what was seen in the way of political behavior, even in this early period, was often in the form of protest.

Both slaves and free persons, with or without franchise, first expressed themselves in the form of petitions protesting slavery and demanding racial freedom. Later, those who were free or franchised associated themselves with the inchoate faction that seemed most agreeable to the inclusion of African Americans in the political community. No slave's voice matched that of the poet Phillis Wheatley, who desired liberty despite apparent good treatment by the Boston family that owned her. In 1773 she addressed a poem to the king's secretary of state in the colonies expressing a desire that no one should experience tyranny, not even she, a slave (Fishel and Quarles 1967, 37):

> Should you, my lord, while you peruse my song,
> Wonder from whence my love of Freedom sprung,
> Whence flow these wishes for the common good,
> By feelings heart best understood,
> I, young in life, by seeming cruel fate
> Was snatch'd from Afric's happy seat
> What pangs excruciating must molest,
> What sorrows labour in my parent's breast?

Many other slaves who petitioned for freedom joined Wheatley's pliant call. Among them was a group in Boston in 1773 that petitioned the Massachusetts legislature for freedom using the rhetoric of the colonists who declared their own intent to fight against the tyranny (which the petitioners dubbed the equivalent of slavery) of England. The petition by the Blacks was issued on behalf of "our fellow slaves in this province, and by order of their Committee" (Fishel and Quarles 1967, 45). (The entire text of this petition is reprinted in chapter 2.)

Early Federalist Partisan Leanings

Meanwhile, Blacks who had the franchise and voted sought out organized groups and allies that were opposed to slavery. Such groups varied from state to state, but those with whom Blacks were aligned were located in the Northeast and tended to be members of the business classes—merchants and such whose incomes were not derived from a plantation economy. They were the forerunners of the Republican Party with which Blacks aligned after emancipation. In the early days of partisan factions in the state of New York, for example, free voting Blacks aligned with the Federalists, largely a group of wealthy men who were thought to be opposed to slavery. That group would go through several different names before settling on the National Republicans (distinguished from the Jeffersonian Republicans, who favored maintenance of slavery).

Elsewhere in the Northeast were similar factions, and Blacks gravitated to those that took a position favoring the abolition of slavery. But this was not the only issue that animated Blacks in the colonial period. They were also interested specifically in issues related to the franchise. Recall that the franchise was limited not only for Blacks but also for Americans in general who did not own substantial property. Thus the expansion of the franchise was a major issue on which most of the emerging partisan groups took a position. Blacks tended to associate themselves with those who supported the expansion of the vote. Their reasoning was simple—they could gain additional rights only by supporting the broadening of the electorate for all. To this end, Hanes Walton shows that Blacks supported the Whigs in New Jersey, "anti-masonry, Whigs, and liberals" in Pennsylvania, and the lingering remnants of the Federalists in New York and New England (Walton 1972b, 26–27).

Black Third-Party Efforts: A Case Study

As we have seen, long before African Americans gained the franchise, they sought to influence the fortunes of the race through political action. Since the barriers of slavery militated against routine participation, Blacks often sought alternative routes. One of these was action through a third political party. They sought third-party leverage both through coalitions with whites who organized outside the major parties and through independent Black political parties. The linkages with others remained available at first, because before the Civil War some interests continued to challenge the emerging Democratic and Republican dominance. Sometimes these third parties were especially appealing because they opposed slavery. Such an option was especially attractive if neither of the emerging two dominant parties addressed the race-inclusion agenda. Just as often, independent Black political parties were utilized for the same purpose—when Blacks felt locked out of the routine vehicles for political expression, they sometimes developed their own race-exclusive alternatives. In all cases, the efforts were designed as leverage in a political environment where there were often outright barriers to full community membership, or societal ambivalence about the exercise of this membership. The third-party option formed an important and enduring race inclusion strategy because of its potential to disrupt or exact benefits from the two major parties. This strategy has been most visible and evident in presidential politics (Walters 1988), but, as shown below, it has also had a significant influence on local politics when other avenues were closed.

One of the early efforts of Blacks to choose a third party came in 1840, when some among them were first attracted to the Liberty Party, an organization that was almost exclusively dedicated to the abolition of slavery (Walton 1972b, 81). They were on one side of a split antislavery movement that sought to use the churches for relentless efforts to abolish slavery. The party, like several other antislavery organizations, had little success at the national level. However, the Liberty Party actually had several national conventions and fielded a presidential candidate in the 1840 and 1844 elections (Franklin and Moss 1994, 176). Blacks participated as delegates and were generally supportive of this essentially antislavery party.

Many Blacks sought to form their own parties during the abolitionist campaign and after the Hayes Compromise of 1876. The first major effort that referred to itself as a movement rather than as a party occurred in the 1840s—the Negro Convention Movement (see chapter 2). This represented the first effort to organize Blacks on a national scale. The movement conducted conventions, where statements of purpose and the equivalent of racial "platforms" were issued. They constituted virtually all of the important African American spokesmen of the time, whose energies were dedicated to putting a racial agenda before the public. Because of the difficulties of organization even for free Blacks during the period of continuing slavery, the national project proved very difficult to advance. Therefore, the movement dispersed a good deal of power and action to state-based units of the parent body. Inevitably this meant a weakening of the national program, because varying conditions in the states hindered concerted action. In the face of the harsh realities of plantation enslavement for most Blacks and because of discrimination and ambivalence elsewhere, this early effort fell into disuse as the Civil War approached and the nation was plunged into war.

With both the Republican and Democratic parties moving toward all-white membership, African Americans had no choice but to seek alternative parties. In 1890, national organizations such as the National Afro-American League (NAAL), later reorganized as the National Afro-American Council, encouraged Blacks to participate in third-party activities. Although neither of these organizations was technically a political party in the sense of office seeking, they sometimes mimicked one. For example, the NAAL organized several national conventions and issued "platforms." However, like so many Black organizations, it was focused first and foremost on the fundamental acquisition and protection of equal rights, and it was fairly decentralized in organization. The league had an interest in influencing politicians, to be sure, but possession of rights was a prior condition (Walton 1972a, 49). These efforts appeared to be futile, however, as racially polarized voting defeated Black third-party candidates at every turn. For example, the local Ohio state-organized Negro Protective Party unsuccessfully ran a candidate for governor in the 1897 election (Walton 1972a, 51). The party was unable to win the office or to have much influence on the platforms of other major contenders.

Political Participation during Reconstruction

The end of the Civil War brought about a series of laws, acts, and executive orders aimed at bridging the equality gap between whites and former slaves. After passage of the Fifteenth Amendment in 1870, African American men were granted the right to vote for a brief period during Reconstruction. The greatest impact was felt in the South, where over 90 percent of the Black population resided. Between 1869 and 1976, two Blacks were elected to the U.S. Senate and fourteen to the House (see chapter 5).

Although Blacks did not dominate politics throughout the South, white southerners saw them as a threat to their political and economic hegemony. As a result, white southerners began to employ various intimidation methods aimed at discouraging Blacks from participating in the political process. Such methods ranged from mob violence and lynching to economic sanctions. These methods, both violent and nonviolent, were tolerated by the North because both the public and political leaders lost interest in the fate of the freed Blacks or simply grew weary of the struggle.

In 1876 an election compromise abruptly ended Reconstruction. During the presidential election of 1876, white Democrats in the South bolted from their party in support of the Republican candidate, Rutherford B. Hayes. In exchange for the southern white vote,

Hayes agreed to remove northern troops from the South. With the removal of northern troops came the end of Black political participation and political representation in the South. Through intimidation and Jim Crow laws, African Americans in the South were denied the vote for another century. It was only in 1965 that the Voting Rights Act eliminated the blatant disfranchisement of African Americans.

The Republican Party Identification: The Legacy of Lincoln

According to Dianne Pinderhughes (1987, 113), African Americans tend to support the political party that is "most supportive of racial reform." In 1840, Blacks were faced with the dilemma of supporting a third party or one of the major parties. The Liberty Party was an uncompromising party of abolitionists and their supporters. The two major parties were the Whigs and the Democrats. The philosophy of supporting one of the major parties was that, although they would be supporting "the lesser of two evils . . . [it would] . . . prevent a greater evil." In other words, Blacks could become the "balance of power" between the two major parties, thus gaining respect in politics. Those adopting this philosophy supported the Whigs over the Democrats (Walters 1988).

The conflict over slavery brought a new party alignment. Abolitionists and proslavery factions split the Whig Party. By 1860 the Whigs disappeared and a new party, the Republicans, emerged. The new party came to have the abolition of slavery as a major feature of its platform. African Americans quickly identified with this project and gave strong support to this party, an affiliation that lasted far beyond Reconstruction.

Similarly, the emergence of Abraham Lincoln as the party's standard-bearer gave him a large following among Blacks. After Lincoln issued the Emancipation Proclamation, African Americans barely separated the man from the party, dubbing the organization "the Party of Lincoln." This continued support was well justified, because the party also led the way in Congress by supporting the passage of the Civil Rights Act of 1866 and the "Civil War Amendments"—the Thirteenth, Fourteenth, and Fifteenth Amendments. In an 1872 speech to a group of Black voters during a convention in New Orleans, the abolitionist orator and Republican appointee Frederick Douglass summed up this partisan affiliation as follows: "The Republican party is the deck, all else is the sea." Walton and Smith (2000) interpret Douglass's remarks to mean that only that party was willing to address the issues that confronted the African American community.

African American Electoral Behavior in Presidential Elections, 1868–1876

African American political behavior at the time thus could be characterized as solidly identified with the Party of Lincoln. Then, as now, the two-party variant in the general population did not fit the alignment of African Americans, who tended to find only one party amenable to their human and welfare rights agenda—universal freedom (Walton and Smith 2000). This early African American behavior can be sketched by looking at voting returns for presidents in the southern states during the Reconstruction years (1868–1876).

Table 4.3 summarizes the popular vote in presidential elections by party in this period, when African Americans first gained the franchise in large numbers in the areas where their population was concentrated. These determinations are based on the success of the Republicans in these states because of the heavy identification of the new Black voters with that party. The overwhelming sentiment in the other southern states was for two third parties, the Southern Democrats and the Constitutional Union. This illustrates the special character of the region vis-à-vis the rest of the nation, which was largely divided between Democrats and Republicans. In 1864 none of these eleven states participated in the election, having seceded from the Union.

By 1868, when seven of these states had returned to the Union, the presence of African American and other Republicans completely shifted the partisan affiliation of the region. These seven states were Alabama, Arkansas, Georgia, Louisiana, North and South Carolina, and Tennessee. Only Georgia and Louisiana did not vote for the Republican candidate, Ulysses Grant. Between 1868 and 1880, only Georgia and Texas never supported a Republican candidate for president. Thus in this small window of opportunity, Black voters had a major role in determining the presidential winners for at least two

TABLE 4.3   Partisan Popular Votes for President in Southern States, 1868–1880 (Percent)

		1868	1872	1876	1880
Alabama	Republican	51	53	40	37
	Democratic	49	47	60	60
	Greenback				3
Arkansas	Republican	54	52	40	39
	Democratic	46	49	60	56
	Greenback				4
Florida	Republican		54	51	46
	Democratic		46	49	54
Georgia	Republican	36	45	28	35
	Democratic	64	55	72	65
Louisiana	Republican	29	56	52	37
	Democratic	71	44	48	62
Mississippi	Republican		64	32	30
	Democratic		36	68	62
North Carolina	Republican	53	57	47	48
	Democratic	47	43	53	51
	Greenback				1
South Carolina	Republican	58	76	50	34
	Democratic	42	24	49	66
Tennessee	Republican	68	48	40	44
	Democratic	32	52	60	53
	Greenback				3
Texas	Republican		41	30	24
	Democratic		59	70	65
	Greenback				11
Virginia	Republican		51	40	40
	Democratic		49	60	60

SOURCE: *Congressional Quarterly's Guide to U.S. Elections,* 4th ed., 2001, 655–658. Reprinted with permission.

campaigns, those of 1868 and 1872. Their influence was short lived, as disfranchisement efforts were under way throughout the region as result of the resolution of the 1876 presidential election. Already, however, that year only Florida, Louisiana, and South Carolina remained under Republican control (see Table 4.3).

State-Level Electoral Behavior during Reconstruction

However, voting in local elections was an equally important indicator of the behavior of African Americans. This new class of citizens, only recently slaves and many exercising the franchise for the first time, voted in massive numbers. During Reconstruction, African Americans were especially successful in electing their candidates of choice throughout the South—usually Blacks. During this era these African American voters, almost always from districts where they held the majority, elected not just African American officials but always Republicans. Ultimately Blacks controlled approximately 15 percent of all elected seats in the South.

In the states where the African American proportion was the largest, the Black voters exercised a greater influence. South Carolina, with its majority-Black electorate, sent six representatives to Congress, Alabama sent three, and Florida, Georgia, Louisiana, Mississippi, and North Carolina each sent one representative during Reconstruction. Mississippi alone elected senators, sending two to Washington.

African Americans continued to strive to send their own to office even as the white Democratic Party regained its hegemony. For example, Mississippi's lone Black congressman, John R. Lynch, ran repeatedly after his term ended in 1877, with his vote totals declining in each successive contest against the white Democratic candidate. The historical evidence indicates that the decline in support for Lynch can be directly linked to the growing coercion and intimidation of his Black constituents. In 1868, Black constituents had a far higher voter registration rate than whites (97 percent for Blacks and 81 percent for whites). By 1892, registration rates had diminished dramatically, especially for Blacks, to the extent that the Black vote was of no consequence to election outcomes. Although whites were registered at a rate of 56 percent, less than 6 percent of Blacks remained registered (McMillen 1990, 36).

Reconstruction in South Carolina:
Black over White—A Case Study

During Reconstruction, South Carolina potentially represented the best of all possible worlds for African Americans—it was a majority-Black state that, with the obliteration of slavery, could become Black ruled. The level of African American participation in electing Blacks to office there exceeded that in all other states. However, it cannot be said that South Carolina, or any other state during Reconstruction, constituted Black rule. South Carolina did nevertheless exhibit a vast array of participation that gives an excellent view of what racial group sentiments were regarding public policy having to do with African American advancement and integration into the larger society.

The pattern of political action on the part of the Black citizenry was organized very early in response to the as yet unimplemented emancipation. Although local whites were seeking to undermine the Union success in the war, Blacks were organizing a race-exclusive political organization, a virtual parallel of the white Democratic Party. In 1865 they organized a statewide convention and appealed to the former Confederates for inclusion in political affairs. Alone they were unsuccessful, requiring the assistance of the Freedmen's Bureau and the Union military to implement the emancipation. However, their strategy provided a modal example of the African American struggle for political inclusion. Since they could not extract inclusion from their white counterparts in reasoned discussion, they resorted to the mobilization of the race for political action. They did not do so in order to structure a racialized regime, but rather as the means for getting what they deemed their share of benefits from the political system. In their particular context they had significant bargaining chips. When the Union forces upheld the emancipation directive, Black participants went on to significantly influence the direction of the Reconstruction—helping to rewrite the Constitution and electing their own to office.

The role of Black allies in the form of the Union army and the Freedmen's Bureau was considerable. In February 1865, General William Tecumseh Sherman and the Union forces burned about a third of the city of Columbia, South Carolina. Charleston was abandoned on the same day and was taken over by northern troops. Shortly afterward, the U.S. flag was again seen flying over Fort Sumter. This marked the beginning of the Reconstruction era in South Carolina.

In a case study of Edgefield County, South Carolina, Vernon Burton (1978) states that the Freedmen's Bureau, backed by federal troops, was instrumental in providing protection for Blacks during Reconstruction. In other words, whites were no longer allowed to commit crimes against Blacks without being punished. Burton reports that by 1867, 4,367 Blacks and 2,507 whites were registered to vote in Edgefield County. As a minority, whites felt that their political and economic hegemony was threatened and would diminish. Indeed, Burton quotes a Democratic leader, George Tillman, as stating, "Once [you] grant a negro political privileges . . . you instantly advance his social status."

At the outset of Reconstruction, Unionist Benjamin F. Perry served as governor of South Carolina and sought to write a new state constitution. The primary purpose of this new constitution was to repeal that written by ex-Confederate leaders, which included the infamous Black Codes, laws that were passed to relegate Blacks to second-class citizenship. A referendum was held on whether to have a convention to rewrite the state's constitution. Among the 128,056 persons registered to vote, approximately 60 percent were Black (Holt 1977). With roughly 85 percent of Blacks turning out to vote, they were instrumental in voting for a convention (Walton 1972a). Among the 124 delegates elected to rewrite the constitution, seventy-six were Black (Walton 1972a).

The delegates wrote a constitution that eliminated barriers to suffrage for Black men and quickly led to Black political representation. From 1868 to 1876, 255 Blacks were elected to state and federal offices. In the lower house of the state legislature they were able to elect eighty-seven Blacks compared with only forty whites. In 1872 they were able to elect a Black speaker, and by 1874, Blacks also enjoyed a majority in the state senate (Foner 1990).

The actual political behavior of Blacks in this majority-Black state was determined by a variety of factors other than their sheer majority. Their population majority was significantly leavened by the range of allies they developed in the routine processes of politics. South Carolina, like many of the other southern states, had a sizable group of migrants from the North who entered politics. Many of them were Republican businessmen who became a part of the ruling class. They became allied with the Black politicians elected from the Black-dominated constituencies in the southern part of the state ("low-country"). In the working relationship that developed, given the lack of Black interest in a racialized regime and a lack of economic resources, business interests often formulated more of the public policy agenda. And this was not without some cause. The state of South Carolina, like many of the other states disrupted by the war, was enveloped in a significant economic crisis. This was only deepened by the necessity of accommodating a Black class of virtual state wards. Despite the deployment of the Black vote to elect its own candidates whose views were consistent with the racial inclusion agenda, this was not sufficient to overcome economic crisis, efforts of the former Confederates to undermine the new social order, and the ambivalence from the federal government allies. The early Black success was therefore short-lived, and the election of Rutherford B. Hayes as president in 1876 sealed its fate. A stunning turnabout in fortunes occurred after 1875, when only two new Blacks were elected to Congress from South Carolina. After one Black candidate was elected in 1893, it would be another century before another was. In 1895 South Carolina joined other deep South states in rewriting their constitution for the purpose of disfranchising Black voters.

The Collapse of Reconstruction and Continued Republican Identification

African Americans remained on the Republican "deck" even after the collapse of Reconstruction with the Hayes Compromise of 1876. Already their political success could be attributed almost entirely to federal intervention. But once the terms of the compromise were in place, Republicans began to move away from policies favorable to Blacks. In fact, the party leadership moved the organization toward a "Lily-White" party with no interest in maintaining its stable of African American supporters in the South. The William McKinley administration (1900) is thought to reflect the moment of complete abandonment of this party's southern constituents, then almost entirely Blacks. McKinley ignored racial issues despite the increase in lynchings and race riots in the region. He also failed to address the issue of disfranchisement. Hence, as Valelly (1993, 31) writes, "the South became a 'sea' of disenfranchisement." Theodore Roosevelt and William Taft followed the lead of Hayes by also adhering to a hands-off policy. With the Republican hands-off policy in effect, many southern states rewrote their constitutions in a successful effort to disfranchise African American voters. Hence, after about 1878 there was little in the way of formal political expression for most African Americans who resided in the now "unreconstructed" South.

The Nadir of Black Participation and the Black and Tan Party Alternative

There was nevertheless political expression by African Americans in this lowest period, or nadir, of systematic political exclusion. Black

Republicans in the South maintained their loyalty to the party by establishing a race-exclusive satellite organization, the Black and Tan Party. Since Blacks were in effect barred from membership in local southern organizations, a trend developed whereby the party split into two groups, the Black and Tans and the Lily-Whites. The phrase "Black and Tans" was first used by Louisiana newspapers to describe Black members of the Republican Party (Walton 1975). The phrase was also used to refer to the "wide range of skin colors and hues that existed with the Black groupings" (Walton 1975, 46). Despite the popularity of reference to the organization among newspapers and the public, the party regulars never officially recognized it. Nevertheless, it was the means Blacks used for their continuing relationship with the national party hierarchy. The dual relationship remained in place until well into the 1920s.

The Designated "Race Leader" as Conduit for African American Expression

Meanwhile, national African American leadership (race spokesmen) also served as a significant indicator of the political behavior of the racialized community. During this low period of actual voting, the race spokesmen became the most important vehicles for expression about public life. Initially they were the old-line abolitionists, all Republicans, who had the ear of presidents and the Republican Party hierarchy. For a time Frederick Douglass, by then a diplomat and high-level bureaucrat, was the most significant among them. His entrée to the centers of power gave him a powerful voice of protest against the disfranchisement in the South, even as he exacted benefits from a system weighted against his constituency. He played this role supporting and consorting with Republican presidents from the time of Lincoln until his death in 1895.

Douglass was both a striking figure and a powerful spokesman for race interests. Even as a government official he never ceased to be assertive in his outspoken views on the racial condition, denouncing "such developments as the suppression of the Negro vote in the South, the leasing out of convicts as laborers, the crop-lien system, and the prevalence of lynching. He railed against the [anti–civil rights] rulings of the Supreme Court." As an example of how important he was to presidents was the role he played in the 1888 campaign that led to the election of Benjamin Harrison. Douglass was appointed the equivalent of a regional campaign manager, being "assigned four key states [where] he took the stump night and day despite his seventy years" (Logan and Winston 1982, 185–186).

An Accommodationist Interlude: Booker T. Washington

Douglass was followed by perhaps the single most important race spokesperson in African American history—Booker T. Washington. Although Washington, regarded as a political conservative, did not reflect Douglass's perspective, the two performed essentially the same function. Washington, while arguing that he eschewed formal politics, nevertheless advised every president in his time and virtually controlled the allocation of public benefits to the African American community. His publicly articulated view that African Americans should eschew politics, accept less than full equality with whites, and focus on sustaining their niche of economic southern agricultural economy appealed to many whites. It held out the possibility that there could be peace while a measured program of racial uplift was followed for Blacks. Washington's influence was so important because it served to make a safe world for the southern pursuit of complete political disfranchisement. Even the standard voices of protest (e.g., W.E.B. DuBois and the inchoate NAACP) were stymied by Washington's presence until well beyond World War I (Harlan 1972).

African American Migration and the Emergence of the New Deal Democratic Coalition

Although the Black and Tans continued, they represented little of the true political behavior of African Americans. The southern region, where the party's constituents remained, was completely off limits for active or even informal political participation by Blacks. African Americans could not vote for Republicans even if any campaigned in the solidly Democratic white South. And protest was met with the draconian state repression or terror. The death knell for the Black and Tan Party came with the election of Herbert Hoover in 1928. During his campaign Hoover had worked diligently to secure the support of the Black and Tans. Immediately after his inauguration, however, he launched a strategy to gain the support of southern whites. In fact, he initiated investigations to remove African American party leaders, and he pledged full support for the Lily-White Republicans (Walton 1975).

In short, the Lily-White strategy employed by Hoover precipitated a significant enough shift in partisan African American identity to make the national Democratic Party competitive with the GOP. The modest overtures from the national Democratic Party hierarchy that accompanied the reelection of President Franklin D. Roosevelt in 1936 brought a sense of hope to the Black community. Among other things the New Deal provided some jobs for poor Blacks and eventually lay the foundation for their new partisan identification and expression.

African Americans also evinced another kind of political expression in response to the disfranchisement in the South. They voted with their feet starting after 1890, beginning a long-term migration from the South to the urban North. They concentrated in racially segregated residential areas in central cities of the industrial North. Moreover, many of these southern migrants became enrolled as voters on arrival in the cities. It was not long before they constituted majority African American districts with the ability to control both local and national electoral offices. The earliest identification they exhibited was with the Party of Lincoln, and their electoral behavior reflected that in the election of their own who were also members of the Republican Party.

Chicago was among the first cities where the political behavior of African Americans became important. It was in this machine-controlled city where the Blacks elected some of their first representatives and exercised considerable influence on some aspects of city politics. In tracking mayoral elections from 1915 to 1939, Pinderhughes (1987, 73) has shown that the partisan alignment of Blacks in Chicago was solidly Republican before 1930. In only one mayoral contest, that of 1923, did the Democrats draw a majority of the community's support. Otherwise the support for the Republicans was overwhelming among these constituents, averaging about 70 percent. The immigrants settled in what was then the city's second ward and elected their first alderman in 1915, the Republican Oscar DePriest. It was "very likely that the Negro voters constituted a majority of the second ward" even then, since they were 70 percent of it by 1920 (Gosnell 1935, 74). They used their votes in a bloc to become the first area to end the absence of Blacks in national elected positions. In 1929 this racially compact area sent Oscar DePriest to Congress as a Republican, a seat continuously held by a Black ever since.

A shift in Black partisan identification became discernible in the 1935 Chicago election, and later became a stampede. DePriest was to be the last Black Republican member of Congress for more than fifty years when he was defeated by the Black Democrat Arthur Mitchell that year. (Massachusetts elected Senator Edward Brooke in 1967, and Connecticut elected Congressman Gary Franks in 1991, but neither was from a Black constituency.) Despite the remarkable shift in partisan identification, however, the segregated residential enclave in Chicago continued to select Black candidates for a variety of elective posts, which eventually resulted in multiple Black congressmen in Washington. The community was rapidly evolving from a one-party Republican identity to a one-party Democratic identity.

African American political behavior in Chicago presaged what was to happen in other northern cities with similar population concentrations. Hence a racially compact district in Harlem, New York, elected Adam Clayton Powell in 1945. It is safe to say that by that time the revolution in Black partisan identification had already occurred in local politics in the urban North. The majority partisan sentiment among these urban voters was in favor of the Democrats. Thus when Charles Diggs won a congressional seat in Detroit, Michigan, in 1955, it was a foregone conclusion that he was a Democrat.

As we shall see, the concomitant transformation in presidential politics evolved a bit more slowly, but it was equally certain; here too, the racial community by and large hewed to a single party in the two-party system. It constituted the most substantial change since the era of Republican Party dominance initiated by Lincoln. The shift to Democratic Party identification represented the evolving political preference that Blacks maintain to the present.

The Democratic Party: Post–New Deal Coalition

To be sure, early traces of the African American movement into the Democratic Party can be found in the North during Reconstruction. However, strong inroads into the party were not created until the New Deal era of Franklin D. Roosevelt. The decrease in support for the Republicans owed to what Blacks portrayed as the party's abandonment of its core support for the race against the traditional southern plantation power hierarchy. This abandonment can be traced to 1876, when the Republicans acquiesced in the restoration of citizen rights for the white planter class. Gradually Blacks calculated that the Republican support of states rights for the resolution of such issues as voting, lynching, segregation, and the white primary were fundamentally inconsistent with core Black interests. Increasingly the Democrats looked like a more favorable option in their support of some of these same core issues. Franklin D. Roosevelt was the first president to become fairly astute in nurturing this favorable disposition among Blacks (Hamilton 1973, 291–296).

Roosevelt's "Black Cabinet"

Roosevelt was able to lure African American voters with his social programs, the creation of the Fair Employment Practices Commission, and his appointment of a "Black Cabinet." Roosevelt's Black Cabinet consisted of a group of Black civic leaders who were unofficially appointed as advisers to the president. He appointed such notable Black leaders as Mary McLeod Bethune, Robert Weaver, William Hastie, Eugene Kinckle Jones, John P. Davis, and Walter White as informal advisers to his administration (Perry and Parent 1995). This marked the first time that a U.S. president openly recognized the influence and legitimacy of Blacks on the group level.

These Black leaders were instrumental in beginning the dialogue that would lead to fairer governmental practices along all race lines, specifically where Blacks were concerned. Although recognized as prominent citizens, they held no official power that would permit them to directly affect policy-making decisions. However, they were able to speak in one voice for the rights of other Blacks. Krislov (1967) mentions that the Black Cabinet was often met with criticism, and some of the criticism came from fellow African Americans. Despite this criticism, Blacks continued to support the Democratic Party. Indeed, in 1936 roughly 85 percent of the Black vote went to Roosevelt (see chapter 5).

The Utility of the Black Vote in Two-Party National Competition

The growth in the fortunes of the Democratic Party can be observed by looking at patterns of voting among urban African Americans. The second Roosevelt election became the critical contest in starting this trajectory. By 1936 the visible appointments of Blacks as bureaucrats and as part of an informal cabinet was hardly lost on northern

TABLE 4.4   Percentage of Votes Cast for Roosevelt in Selected Majority-Black City Wards in the Presidential Elections of 1932–1940

	Detroit		Pittsburgh		Baltimore		Chicago	
Ward	5	7	5	3	14	17	2	3
1932	50	54	53	46	49	43	25	21
1936	75	79	77	64	55	47	48	50
1940	79	80	77	72	61	50	51	54

SOURCE: Adapted from Walters 1988, 18. Reprinted with permission from the State University of New York Press.

Black voters, segregated in their residential enclaves in the inner cities. Moreover, participation levels among these mostly straight-ticket voters were often quite high, giving the Democrats some assurance that the affiliation of local partisans could be translated into broader support.

This broader support was especially sought after in presidential contests because of the stability of the Black vote. It could make the difference when the rest of the electorate was fairly evenly split between the two parties (Glantz 1967, 339). The balancing factor became more critical because the migration of Blacks to central cities greatly accelerated between 1910 and 1930. For example, "the Black population in Michigan went from 17,115 to 169,453; Illinois from 109,049 to 328,927; Indiana from 60,320 to 111,982; and Ohio from 111,452 to 309,304" (Walters 1988, 17).

Partisan support by Blacks for the Democrats in the first three elections involving Roosevelt shows how this kind of balance was evolving. The data in Table 4.4 compare Black majority voting wards—that is, wards in which 50 percent or more of the population is African American—in four cities in the 1932, 1936, and 1940 presidential elections. What one observes is that in Detroit and Pittsburgh a majority of the wards were already voting for Roosevelt by 1932. Even so, the increase from 1932 to 1936 was dramatic—more than 20 percent for each election. In the machine-dominated cities of Chicago and Baltimore, none of the wards cast more than 50 percent of the votes for Roosevelt in 1932, although the two wards in Baltimore came close. Chicago was less Democratic. By 1936, clearly both of these cities had moved considerably toward the Democrats. All of these wards, in all four cities, were solidly Democrat by 1940.

The African American Democratic Bloc in National Politics

The Democrats now appeared to be the party of "racial reform." This trend continued with the Truman administration. Following the lead of Franklin D. Roosevelt, Harry S. Truman appealed to the compassion of Congress to enact laws that would level the playing field for African Americans in the workforce. In 1946 President Truman created the Civil Rights Committee as an attempt to address the growing civil unrest of African Americans. Although none of the recommendations became law during the Truman administration, the committee did make several recommendations to curtail racial discrimination. The recommendations included enactment of a civil rights bill; strengthening the civil rights section of the Department of Justice; and special training for police officers in handling civil rights–related disputes. The proposals also sought to end Jim Crow laws and to withhold federal grants-in-aid from public and private agencies that practiced discrimination and segregation (Perry and Parent 1995).

When Congress failed to pass substantive civil rights legislation, Truman was highly successful in his use of executive orders. In 1948 he laid the cornerstone for policy that would eventually lead to the permanent desegregation of the U.S. armed services. Executive Order 9981 mandated equal treatment and opportunity for all persons in the armed services without regard to race, color, religion, or national origin. This executive order came at the end of World War II, a conflict in which Black military service had generated additional support from some legislators as well as the general citizenry. Truman's efforts solidified Black support of the Democratic Party and empowered the group to make further demands for civil justice.

Again, the voting behavior of Blacks in central cities foretold the trend in growing support for Democratic candidates. The strength of these voters was clearly helping to sustain the national majority for the Democratic Party. The increased Black population was tipping the balance in the urban industrial states, where there was intense two-party competition, even as the "Solid South" started to drift (sometimes supporting favorite sons such as Strom Thurmond in 1948). Table 4.5 lists the proportion Democratic in four key midwestern cities between 1948 and 1956 where the impact of the Black vote was strongest in influencing the total presidential vote for the Democratic Party. Chicago, Detroit, and Cleveland consistently exhibit less competitiveness vis-à-vis the general population and clearly influence the outcome of con-

TABLE 4.5   Percentage of Democratic Voters in Presidential Elections in Selected Midwestern Cities, 1948–1956 (Percent)

City	All Democratic Voters			Black Democratic Voters		
	1948	*1952*	*1946*	*1946*	*1952*	*1956*
Chicago	58	54	48	70	75	63
Cleveland	65	60	55	61	79	63
Detroit	59	60	62	84	90	84
St. Louis	64	62	61	68	80	75

SOURCE: Adapted from Glantz 1967, 350. Reprinted with permission from Charles Merrill.

tests where the level of competition in the general population is highest—Chicago and Cleveland. But everywhere the greater African American loyalty to the Democratic Party is striking.

In 1956, however, there was a temporary national shift in African American support from the Democratic Party, as these voters aligned themselves with Eisenhower. This shift owed to a number of difficulties within the fragile Democratic coalition after the *Brown v. Board of Education* Supreme Court case. Once the Court declared the "separate but equal" policy dead, the reaction from white segregationist southerners who wanted to sustain the system was dramatic. Because many of them remained ensconced in the Democratic Party, the former racial moderate candidate Adlai Stevenson had to deal with their wrath. He sought to do so by trying to placate and accommodate this vital party base. What he achieved in the end was massive desertion on the part of northern Blacks, who had also become a vital part of the party's base. Enough Black voters shifted their allegiance to also temporarily interrupt the party's long-running control of the presidency. Figure 4.1 clearly illustrates the increase in Black support for Eisenhower in 1956. Indeed, Black leaders such as Adam Clayton Powell endorsed his candidacy.

The African American Presidential Vote, 1952–2000

A case can be made that Black partisan realignment occurred as early as 1936, but it was certain by 1964. (Ordinarily political scientists argue that realignment is precipitated by one or more critical elections that polarize voters on the issues [Campbell 1966; Key 1955]). As Figure 4.1 shows, Black support for the Democratic presidential candi-

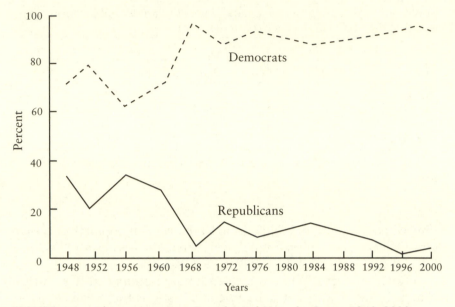

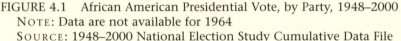

FIGURE 4.1   African American Presidential Vote, by Party, 1948–2000
NOTE: Data are not available for 1964
SOURCE: 1948–2000 National Election Study Cumulative Data File

dates greatly increased between 1960 and 1968. The 1964 election perhaps best illustrates the point. Barry Goldwater's position on civil rights and his states' rights platform clearly moved African Americans away from the Republican Party. After the election campaigns of Goldwater and Lyndon Johnson, the distinction between the two parties on racial issues was stark. The Democrats became more racially liberal, while the Republicans, with the support of southern Democrats, became more racially conservative (Scher 1997). Since 1964, Black support for Democratic presidential candidates has not fallen below 80 percent in a single election.

The Republican Party Surge in Presidential Contests

The 1968 election revealed the other side of realignment, the counter to the ascendancy of Blacks in the Democratic Party. What was white dissonance within the Democratic Party in 1964 became a virtual desertion by 1968. Indeed, the shift had inspired Richard Nixon, the Republican standard-bearer, to devise a "southern strategy" to attract white voters away from the Democratic Party. He did not actually succeed, because of the presence of independent candidate George Wallace (33 percent). However, even with Wallace's strong showing, the Republicans took the South (36 percent), outpolling the Democrats (31 percent) (Stanley and Niemi 2000, 118). The realignment improved the fortunes of the Republicans in presidential elections considerably. They have won six of the nine contests between 1968 and 2000.

Nixon's conservative platform on busing and education as well as his judicial appointments during his early administration ensured that African Americans would continue to identify strongly with the Democrats. According to Ambeau, Perry, and McBride (1995), the Nixon administration represented a retreat from the civil rights advances of the Johnson administration. Two distinct policy actions by Nixon were clear appendages of his cavalier handling of civil rights issues and tend to support the argument that Nixon's administration represented a step backward in the struggle for equality. First, Nixon ordered the Justice Department to step in and slow down school desegregation. This marked the first time that a U.S. president had ordered the Justice Department to intervene in such a capacity since the *Brown* decision. Historically, the Justice Department worked with the proponents of civil rights. Second, Nixon opposed the 1970 extension of the Voting Rights Act of 1965, which was due to expire. Although his efforts were unsuccessful, Nixon was perspicacious in his assessment of the benefits the Republican Party would have obtained by weakening the protection of Black voting rights (Perry and Parent 1995). On the other hand, despite his less than favorable civil rights record, Nixon did appoint Blacks to subcabinet positions in his administration, with the highest-ranking position being that of an assistant secretary (Warshaw 1996).

The next administration was marred by the Watergate scandal that unseated Nixon and ushered Vice President Gerald Ford into office. Ford also inherited a general public mood that included some mistrust of the Republican Party. If the general public was suspicious about the politics of the controlling party, Blacks in America had even deeper concerns. The Voting Rights Act, which was a major component of the migration of African Americans into the democratic processes in the United States, was less than ten years old and facing extinction when Ford took office. Like Nixon's, Ford's civil rights record was less than favorable among Blacks and other civil rights advocates. Following in the footsteps of his predecessor, in 1975 Ford initially opposed the extension of the Voting Rights Act.

Jimmy Carter: Leveraging the Black Vote in Intense Partisan Competition

With Ford tainted by the Nixon White House scandal, Jimmy Carter was able to prevail in the 1976 election, restoring the Democrats to power after an eight-year hiatus. The return of the Democrats owed a great deal to the strong African American support for Carter in key areas of the country, a fact that perhaps enabled Blacks as a group to determine the partisan victor. This view is consistent with a general theory of how the Black vote can be used as a balancing agent when competition between the two parties is intense. Ronald Walters has calculated how the concentration of Black voters in competitive urban areas and in the South translated into control of electoral votes for Democrats in the 1976 election. According to his analysis, Black voters provided the critical balance of votes for Carter in major northern, border, and southern states (Walters 1988, 36ff). (See Table 4.6.) Indeed, during the campaign Carter made significant alliances with African American politicians and sought the Black vote by evincing a strong interest in some of the core issues associated with that community. The general assessment is that the Carter administration "sustained its commitment to civil rights throughout its duration, unlike the Nixon and Ford administrations, which lapsed into dormancy in civil rights enforcement" (Perry, Ambeau, and McBride 1995, 117).

Party Realignment in Presidential Elections: The Reagan-Bush Victories

Carter's term was to be a mere interlude for the Democrats. The Republicans returned to power in 1980 and remained in the White House for three terms. Clearly, the New Deal coalition that had been heavily oriented to African American core interests had dissolved, with the Republican Party becoming much more successful in presidential contests. In this instance they were able to put together a winning coalition by using something akin to Nixon's southern strategy. They relied on increased support for the GOP among southern whites, to the disadvantage of the strong single-party orientation of African American voters (Kinder and Sanders 1996). It did illustrate, however, that under these conditions, when the intensity of competition decreased, Blacks were less likely to determine the outcome of national contests. Reagan carried the South in both 1980 and 1984,

TABLE 4.6   Presidential Electoral Votes in Selected States, 1976

	Electoral Vote	Black Voting-Age Population (%)
North		
New York	41	12.6
Pennsylvania	27	08.2
Illinoisa	26	12.4
Michigan[a]	21	11.3
New Jersey[a]	17	10.8
Ohio	25	08.9
Region Total	**157**	
South		
Alabama	9	22.0
Arkansas	6	14.4
Georgia	12	23.7
Louisiana	10	26.4
Mississippi	7	30.5
North Carolina	13	18.8
South Carolina	8	26.1
Texas	26	11.6
Tennessee	10	13.8
Florida	17	10.6
Region Total	**118**	
Border		
Maryland	10	18.3
Missouri	12	09.3
Region Total	**22**	
Nationwide		
Total Democratic	**297**	
Total Republican	**240**	

[a] States carried by the Republican Party.
SOURCE: Adapted from Walters 1988, 36–37. Reprinted with permission from the State University of New York Press.

winning by a landslide 26 percentage points in the latter. Bush also prevailed in the South in 1988, by 20 percentage points (see Table 4.7).

During these Republican administrations, African Americans perceived that their core agenda issues were placed on the back burner. Ronald Reagan captured the public wave of disenchantment with aggressive government intervention in the social sector of domestic affairs, at the same time that he faced an economic recession. Mean-

TABLE 4.7 Presidential Electoral Votes, Southern Region, 1964–2000

	Democrats	*Republicans*	*Independents*[a]
1964	52	48	
1968	31	36	33
1972	29	71	
1976	54	45	
1980	44	52	
1984	37	63	
1988	40	60	
1992	38	45	17
1996	44	46	10
2000	43	55	

a Independent candidates were Wallace in 1968 and Perot in 1992 and 1996.

SOURCES: Data from Stanley and Niemi 2000, 118–119; Walton and Smith 2002, 161.

while, the conservative wing of the Republican Party that Reagan represented also captured control of the party hierarchy. The president thus oversaw the implementation of a conservative agenda that aggressively attacked welfare and civil rights issues associated with African Americans. Needless to say, the partisan identification of Blacks with the Democratic Party only hardened. The Bush administration that succeeded Reagan's was perceived by Blacks to have made little change in the policy trajectory. Indeed, Bush's appointment of the conservative judge, Clarence Thomas, to the Supreme Court (replacing the stalwart liberal Thurgood Marshall), was widely seen as an especially egregious reflection of this policy shift (Barker et al. 1999, 117).

Trading Places: From Clinton to Bush

The White House once again returned to the Democrats in 1992, for two terms. And once again, the African American vote proved to be of strategic importance as a balance in the South, where about 50 percent of this population lived. Bill Clinton received overwhelming support from African American voters everywhere, but their support was especially important in the South. This region was the most intensely competitive of his two campaigns. And while Clinton did not carry the South in either 1992 or 1996, it was his overwhelming support among Blacks there that counterbalanced whites who remained in the Republican fold. The competition, however, intensified between the two parties (see Table 4.7).

A part of what propelled Blacks to mobilize so intensely for Clinton in 1992 was his promise and the experience of twelve years of Republican rule. With the help of many African American leaders, Bill Clinton campaigned on a promise of diversity and economic reform in a way that appeared to reflect the core issues important to Blacks. This was fortuitous because even the Blacks who achieved middle-class status after the civil rights movement found themselves unable to influence the Republican policymakers. Motivated by three terms of perceived exclusionary Republican policies, approximately one million more African Americans voted in 1992 than in 1988, and Clinton received 82 percent of the Black vote (Perry and Parent 1995). He increased that margin slightly in 1996. Clinton reclaimed the White House for the Democrats and announced that he would build a White House administration that "looks like America" (Warshaw 1996).

Black skepticism of the Republican Party in the 2000 election rose to its highest level since the 1964 election of Lyndon Johnson. In large measure it was driven by the same considerations about reflection of core African American issues in the Republican platform. There was little in the Bush platform that attracted large numbers of Blacks. Meanwhile, measuring Bush against the track record of the Clinton-Gore administration left African Americans little choice but to go with what was deemed a "known" quantity. In this controversial election the African American electorate gave 90 percent of its vote to the Democrats. Ironically, the election outcome hinged on the resolution of disputes in Florida about ballot improprieties in heavily African American and other Democratic districts. But just as important was the level of partisan competition in the balance of the South. This region was less competitive than it had been since the 1988 Bush-Dukakis election (see Table 4.7).

Post–Civil Rights Local Political Behavior

African American Behavior in State and Local Politics

Although national trends are the best indicators of aggregate behavior on the part of African Americans in the post–New Deal era, local behavior clearly remains the base from which it all springs. The power of the local arena in defining how this population behaves politically remains bound up in the racialized social order. It is of profound consequence that African Americans have more often than not been racially isolated in the political arena. They often live and vote in segregated racial districts, and have most often been formally empowered by electing one of their own to represent them. Most importantly, the continuity of racial discrimination and ambivalence about their citizenship status have led them to align with a single party that espouses support for improving these circumstances. All the consequences of these preconditions for political expression are writ large in the local arena, and hence one finds that, contrary to the conventional wisdom, African American political expression is most intense at the local level.

As noted earlier, when the shift to the Democratic Party began in the Roosevelt era, it first became visible in the local wards and precincts in central cities. When Blacks were able to elect their own at these levels, the shift to the Democratic Party soon reverberated upward to presidential contests. In this sense it is not odd that these voters seemed most animated by the availability of the likes of DePriest, Diggs, Powell, and others in congressional districts. They could combine their votes in these central cities and be assured of a representative whose central mission was to regularize the status of Blacks in American society. Once these representatives were elected, their congressional seats became some of the safest in the nation. This pattern of behavior spread across the country as the disfranchisement in the South ended with the civil rights movement.

African American Voter Registration in the Post–Civil Rights South

What is the evidence regarding the aggregate patterns of behavior for Blacks in state and local politics? Since we already have some sense of the pattern in the North after the Great Migration, the task is to explain how the South completed the picture. In order to do this, we have to expand our focus, as the constituent base in the South was as much rural as urban. The first important point to be made about political behavior among African Americans in the South is that as soon as restrictions were removed, they prepared in great numbers to exercise the franchise. And they had a good deal of ground to make up. After all, in 1940, estimates were that no more than 5 percent of the Black voting-age population in the region was registered to vote.

About the time of the Montgomery bus boycott, barely 25 percent were registered. Despite the intensive mobilization that spread through the region in 1960, there were still spectacular levels of disfranchisement in some states. Mississippi was the worst in this regard, with only 6 percent of eligible Black voters registered. The figure for Alabama was twice that, with only 13 percent registered.

The civil rights mobilization and concomitant federal legislation had a dramatic effect in increasing opportunities for African American participation. The increase in the voter registration numbers was the first indication. Registration in the South rose precipitously on the eve of passage of the Civil Rights Act (1964) and the Voting Rights Act (1965). In 1964, for example, only Mississippi did not show dramatic progress; the proportion of eligible Blacks registered was still barely over 6 percent. In Alabama the proportion neared 25 percent, and in most of the other former Confederate states it was well above 30 percent. Tennessee and Florida had already topped the 60 percent mark.

The 1965 Voting Rights Act altered the registration rates almost immediately. One of its provisions allowed the placement of federal registrars in states where barriers to registration had not been immediately removed. A mere two years after passage of the act, no southern state had African American registration rates below 50 percent. The evidence is incontrovertible that the federal registrars played a major role in increasing registration rates in the most egregious cases of intimidation and refusal to follow the law. In Mississippi, 61 percent of the new registrants were enrolled by federal registrars, and in Alabama and Louisiana, 48 percent were. In any case, the Black population was eager in its pursuit of voter registration.

African American Turnout in the Mobilized South

The real challenge in evaluating political behavior lies in determining actual participation. Did the southern Blacks vote, and what patterns can be discerned from analysis of voting participation? Once again the conventional wisdom that Blacks, with a low socioeconomic status, will participate less, does not hold. Enfranchised southern Blacks had some of the highest participation levels in the region. A study of rural Black voters in Mississippi discovered that post-1965 voting was exceedingly high across all socioeconomic levels and that such participation seemed much more related to political mobilization in majority-Black districts (Morrison 1987, 174). There is similar

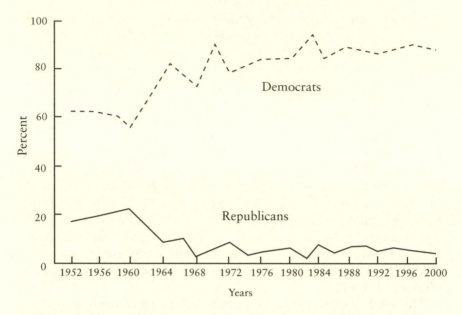

FIGURE 4.2   Party Identification among African Americans, 1952–2000
SOURCE: 1948–2000 National Election Study Cumulative Data File

evidence comparing relative racial turnout in presidential elections between 1952 and 1972—contests just before and just after the height of the mobilization movement in southern cities. Figure 4.2 shows the dramatic upsurge in turnout of Blacks between 1956 and 1968. Once Blacks got the franchise back, they turned out to vote in presidential elections at rates almost double those for whites.

As described earlier, the character of this participation can be seen in the increased election of African Americans for local, state, and national offices and in the support of presidential candidates deemed to be supportive of an agenda of racial inclusion. African Americans who began to identify with the Democratic Party in the late 1930s had turned almost exclusively to that organization by the 1960s. They did so because, in a reversal of roles between the two major parties, the Democratic Party, which had always had a more diverse membership, became more supportive of civil liberties, human rights, and racial inclusion. In the process, African Americans became one of the Democratic Party's fundamental constituent groups.

The foundation of this national support for Democrats, however, rested in the development of local organizations that sponsored

Black candidates in mostly majority-Black districts. The availability of Black candidates became a major by-product of the intense political mobilization in the South. The participation in the South soon matched and then exceeded that achieved by Blacks in the North. Just as the Black migrants to northern cities elected their own to local and congressional posts around World War II, the same pattern characterized the South from about 1967.

Electing Their Own: Black Representatives for Black Districts

The early pattern of political behavior among Blacks showed them putting significant energy into electing Black candidates when their numbers assured victory. Since voter registration levels were so low, a first order of business was mobilization for registration and subsequent political action. Much of this process was carried out by grassroots community organizers. The Student Nonviolent Coordinating Committee in Mississippi is a prime example. In 1973 a massive contingent of civil rights workers descended on the state with the express purpose of increasing Black registration. Among their number were hundreds of students, who not only ran registration campaigns and freedom schools but also made remarkable use of the national media to expand the cause to the general population. Perhaps the best signal of what the effort was aiming for was the controversial concept of "Black Power." Although the term was widely interpreted by the media to mean some kind of Black separatism, chief exponent Stokely Carmichael defined it as Blacks using their voting power to win allocations from the system. It was conceptually more related to the group theory of politics, which suggested that political success could be realized only by organizing into a group for the pursuit of interests. In the nature of the racialized circumstances, Carmichael argued that Blacks were relegated to functioning as a racial interest group vis-à-vis other similarly organized interests (Carmichael and Hamilton 1967), and it was essentially this model that Blacks followed.

The result was that the South hewed to a pattern very much like that in the North. Living in racially segregated political districts, they organized largely by race and selected candidates by race at the local level. Coalitions, if they presented themselves, were also used. After all, these new citizens, as noted, maintained a high level of action in the interest of their preferred presidential and statewide candidates.

But the intense action was at the local level. In Atlanta in 1962 Black voters sent Leroy Johnson to the state senate, and a few years later several southern states had elected Black legislators, mayors, city council representatives, and school board members. After 1967 the local Black electorates had been especially successful in seating Black mayors in small towns. Even a cursory review of the extent of Black elected officials (see chapter 5) reveals that the strategy of their constituents was successful—Black people were electing Black officials to represent them all over the South.

With the help of the Supreme Court, malapportionment in legislative districts was undermined in the *Reynolds v. Sims* (1965) and *Wesberry v. Sanders* (1964) cases. With the destruction of gerrymandering and all manner of racial voter dilution schemes, soon southern legislatures and congressional districts saw Black representatives. Black majority congressional districts in Texas (Houston) and Georgia (Atlanta) sent the first Blacks to Congress in almost 100 years. The strategy has successfully been employed in all but the state of Arkansas in the South.

National Black Turnout

Considering these outcomes along with Black electoral participation nationwide, there has been remarkable change and success. Blacks are participating at high levels, especially where they have the opportunity to win with a candidate of their own or a candidate supportive of an agenda for racial inclusion. Nationally, Black voter registration has remained around 60 percent, achieving its highest rate of 66 percent in 1984 when Jesse Jackson was first a candidate. As Table 4.8 shows, in the 1968 election, the Black proportion of the voting electorate was 8 percent. In 1996, the proportion was close to 11 percent—for a group estimated to constitute about 12 percent of the general population (Barker et al. 1999, 235). This growth in Black voter registration levels has resulted in the highest number of Black elected officials and the greatest influence on electoral districts where their numbers give them a balance in or control of the electorate. From 1970 to 1997 the number of African American elected officials, most from majority Black constituencies, increased from 1,400 to nearly 9,000.

Elected African Americans represent districts all over the nation and at all levels. At the national level this influence has been exercised largely within the confines of the Democratic Party in the

TABLE 4.8   Black Voter Registration and Turnout in Presidential Election Years, 1968–1996 (Percent)

	Registration Rate (%)	Turnout (% of Total Population)
1968	66.2	8.0
1972	65.5	8.2
1976	58.5	8.4
1980	60.0	8.9
1984	66.3	10.1
1988	64.0	10.0
1992	63.9	10.0
1996	63.5	10.8

SOURCE: Data from Barker et al. 1999, 235.

House of Representatives. As Table 4.9 shows, African American candidates are able to win elections in congressional districts almost exclusively where the majority of their constituents are African American. This success is seen in all areas of the country. Meanwhile, they win more than 50 percent of the time when African Americans are the predominant minority group in the district. In 1998, Black majority or combined Black and other minority districts (sixty-three) elected Blacks to more than half (thirty-two) of the seats. Majority-Black electorates controlled twenty-three of those seats. All but Texas and Arkansas of the former Confederate states had at least one congressional representative from a majority-Black district. In Texas the lone Black representative represented a Houston district that had recently slipped below a Black majority.

The Black Political Party Revisited

In the long history of the American republic, third-party movements have consistently failed to prevail in national contests, and they have rarely succeeded when organized at the regional level. Efforts to form Black political parties have shared the same fate. However, in the almost unique racial isolation of African Americans from routine influence on the two-party structure, there have been repeated efforts to form third parties. Perhaps the most visible effort at the national level was the Black Political Party Convention in Gary, Indiana, in 1972. The prime movers behind this event were the Black mayor of Gary, Richard Hatcher, Congressman Charles Diggs of Michigan, and

TABLE 4.9   Predominantly Minority Congressional Districts and Black Seats, 1998

Description of District	Number of Districts	Percent of Seats Held by Blacks
Predominantly Minority	63	52
Black Majority	23	96
Predominantly Minority (South)	22	55
Black Majority (South)	10	100

Source: Data from Stanley and Niemi 2000, 95.

the writer Amiri Baraka. Although the meetings over several days drew some 5,000 delegates and observers, the effort did not succeed in fielding candidates for election or in developing much of a secretariat (Marable 2000, 635–640). However, regionally based African American parties have also continued and have been relatively more successful in changing the agenda and sometimes the structure of one of the two major parties. The examples below include such parties in South Carolina and Mississippi.

The South Carolina Progressive Democratic Party

The most popular third-party efforts came in the form of what Walton (1972a) calls "satellite parties." These were largely state-level organizations that sought to parallel local branches of the two regular but segregated major parties. In most instances the stated aims of these organizations or movements were to break down the solidly Democratic southern parties, from whose primaries Blacks were barred. The South Carolina Progressive Democratic Party (SCPDP) was one of the first such organizations to pose a meaningful challenge to a regular state political party. It was founded in 1944, the same year that the Supreme Court ruled "white primaries" unconstitutional. Also in that year, the SCPDP sent twenty-one citizens to the National Democratic Convention in Chicago to challenge the seating of the regular Democrats representing South Carolina (Walton 1972a, 72). To their dismay, they were not allowed to participate at the convention and were turned away. Undaunted, the SCPDP returned to South Carolina and unsuccessfully ran one of its own members for the U.S. Senate.

Faltering at electoral success, the party changed strategies. During the next two years the SCPDP focused its attention on voter registration drives. They were able to increase the number of registered voters from a dismal 3,500 in 1944 to a respectable 50,000 by 1947. During its annual convention in 1946, the SCPDP decided to end its status as a formal party and to function instead as a caucus concerned with uplifting the Black community. Not surprisingly, it was pressure from the colossal strength of the two regular parties that caused the South Carolina effort to falter. As Blacks were shifting alignment to the national Democratic Party, such local efforts were seen as a distraction. Hence the decision to dissolve was made primarily at the request of such prominent leaders as Thurgood Marshall and the Reverend James Hinton (head of the statewide conference of the NAACP). They felt that the organization did not possess enough resources to unseat the party regulars (Walton 1972a, 72–75).

United Citizens Party of South Carolina

In 1969 Blacks in South Carolina formed still another organization—the United Citizens Party (UCP). The primary objective of the UCP was to get Black candidates elected. In 1970 and 1972 the party ran a slate of candidates at the local, state, and national levels. They also entered the governor's race in 1970 with a write-in campaign for their candidate. This time, with African Americans almost completely identified with the Democratic Party and with disfranchisement in the South reversed, this Black party had a significant influence both in electing candidates and in changing the structure of the state Democratic Party. The UCP remained a force in electing its candidates in 1970, siphoning off votes from the segregated state organization. The pressure applied by the UCP forced the state Democratic Party organization to appoint an African American as assistant director. Subsequently four UCP candidates for the South Carolina House of Representatives won endorsement by the regular state party. Three of these candidates won in the 1970 general election. Having achieved at least the partial goal of acceptance by the regulars, the UCP disbanded shortly after that election (Legette 2000).

The Mississippi Freedom Democratic Party

The Mississippi Freedom Democratic Party (MFDP) was organized in the early 1960s in the midst of an intense social movement in the state where racial exclusion at all levels was most prevalent. White resistance to social change was also perhaps more prevalent and violent there too. The MFDP developed from the combined work of all the major civil rights organizations in the state—the NAACP, the Congress of Racial Equality (CORE), and the Student Nonviolent Coordinating Committee (SNCC). The principal target that developed over time was the racial exclusion of African Americans from the state Democratic Party. In light of the abject conditions of Blacks in Mississippi, the organizations formed a confederation, centralizing its attack on the status quo.

Although CORE and the NAACP remained very active, it was SNCC that led a grassroots campaign for local community leadership development in tandem with voter registration (Carson 1981). Given the African American majority voting-age populations in many parts of rural Mississippi, increasing voter registration was deemed the key to overturning the system. However, as long as Blacks were locked out of the Democratic Party, which was the normal vehicle for exercising political rights, voter registration alone was useless.

The MFDP was originally settled on as an organizing tool to demonstrate the potential of the rural vote to Blacks. But it was also used to dramatize the plight of these potential voters to the nation. In 1963 and 1964, a summer was dedicated to voter registration and a mock election was held that fielded candidates for state and congressional offices that Blacks could not contest through the regular Democratic Party. After succeeding in their efforts at precinct and county organization, the MFDP made its boldest move by challenging the seating of the regular state party at the 1964 National Democratic Convention. The regular party made little pretense of being open to Black participation, resolving in its July 1964 convention that "we believe the Southern white man is the truest friend the Negro ever had; we believe in separation of the races in all phases of life" (Southern Exposure 2000, 517).

A week later, 300 people from all over Mississippi attended the Mississippi Freedom Democratic Party's state convention in Jackson. Unlike the regular state party, the MFDP pledged their support to the national party, and because of their loyalty, they were convinced they would be allowed to represent Mississippi at the Democratic National convention. They elected 38 delegates and alternates from their number to travel to Atlantic City, with Aaron Henry as chairperson of the delegation and Fannie Lou Hamer as vice-chairperson.

The strength of the MFDP created conflicts for [President] Lyndon Johnson, who virtually controlled the convention but feared a walkout by the entire South if the Freedom Delegation was seated. He assigned Hubert Humphrey, a leader of the liberal wing of the Democratic Party, the job of defeating the Freedom Delegation.

Besides putting intense pressure on the members of the Credentials Committee to reject the MFDP cause, the president offered a compromise: the MFDP could have two at-large seats, with the delegates selected by the president, and a pledge from the National Democratic Party never to seat a lily-white delegation again, beginning in 1968. The regular Mississippi delegation would be seated after taking a [party] loyalty oath. (Southern Exposure 2000, 518–519)

The challenge was not won, despite a hearing that brought favorable notices from the national audience. The impassioned speech of grassroots leader Fannie Lou Hamer, whose limp betrayed the racial violence perpetrated against her in rural Mississippi, captivated the nation. Her signal rejection of the compromise, however, indicated the decision of the MFDP to reject the Johnson compromise. She expressed the sentiment of many of the delegates in saying that her burdens in racist Mississippi were worth more than two seats (Lee 1999; Mills 1993) and the offer of a partial victory, which it rejected.

However, in another four years the MFDP succeeded in unseating the regular delegation at the 1968 convention (Dittmer 1994). Thereafter the remnants of the MFDP, then dubbed the Loyal Democrats, effectively supplanted the regular state party and the racially integrated organization elected an African American as party chairman— Aaron Henry. Although the MFDP passed from the scene, this movement-cum-political-party was one of the most successful in the history of grassroots political participation. Its aim was the destruction of the segregated party system and the integration of African Americans into the political process, which it accomplished in a mere eight years in the most avowedly racialized political structure in the states. Aaron Henry and a liberal, integrated leadership fully reformed the old party, whose agenda was subsequently heavily influenced by the large and highly mobilized African American electorate. The new Democratic Party oversaw the transformation of the face of political leadership in Mississippi. The state has gone from twenty-eight African American elected officials in 1968 to 803 in 1997, the largest number in the country.

Democratic Party Conventions:
Black Delegates and Black Presidential Candidates

A major shift in the influence of African Americans within the Democratic Party was indicated in their increased selection as delegates to the national conventions. Such delegates inspired the candidacies of both Shirley Chisholm and Jesse Jackson. The first dramatic increase in their involvement as party delegates happened between presidential campaigns of John Kennedy and Lyndon Johnson. In 1960 there were a mere forty-six Black delegates, but four years later there were 209. By 1972 they constituted 15 percent of the delegates, and their proportion has rarely dropped below that level since. When Jesse Jackson ran the second time in 1988, they were 23 percent of the convention delegates (see Table 4.10). Moreover, these single-party-allegiant Democratic voters have played prominent roles in the outcomes of several presidential elections since 1964, where competition in the South was especially high—those of Johnson, Carter, and Clinton. (See chapter 5.)

Jesse Jackson and the Presidential Primaries

The civil rights movement of the 1950s and 1960s generated the most significant wave of African American social activism and political participation since the Reconstruction. Perhaps the zenith of that activism and participation was reached when Jesse Jackson became a serious contender for the American presidency, first in 1984 and again in 1988. Jackson rode the crest of the most successful social movement since the abolition of slavery. As we saw in chapter 2, the movement grew from contentious interactions between grassroots citizens and the racially exclusively state systems throughout the South. Blacks demanded public inclusion and social integration, while the white power structure resisted it. The Black resistance, however, escalated to a comprehensive challenge to the status quo. In the process, the challenge was sustained by significant organized resources, especially college students and decentralized, largely Baptist, church organizations. Leaders emerged within the enormous organized networks of students, ministers, and civil rights groups that then provided the glue for political mobilization. The most successful of these leaders all had an agenda for the elimination of racial exclusion and discrimination. It was from this network that Jesse Jackson sprang as a lieutenant of Martin Luther King Jr. Jackson came to ma-

TABLE 4.10   African American Democratic Party Delegates, 1972–1996

	Number	Percent
1972	452	15
1976	323	11
1980	481	14
1984	697	18
1988	962	23
1992	771	18
1996	908	21

SOURCE: Data from Walton and Smith 2000, 147.

turity only after the death of King, but at a moment when the movement was already shifting to another phase.

The new challenge was focused on translating the benefits of social mobilization into political gains. Enormous gains had been made in the passage of statutes restoring the franchise to Blacks in the South, and there seemed to be a national consensus that a public policy agenda that included racial inclusion was desirable. Indeed, the first signs of the successful campaign for Black Power could be discerned as early as 1965, when newly enrolled Black voters elected several of their own to local posts in the South. Around the same time, roughly in 1967, a new wave of political successes of the African American migrants to the cities began. Several large industrial cities elected Black mayors. In almost all cases in the South and the North, these political successes came on the heels of voter registration and mobilization efforts specifically designed to elect Black candidates.

The end result was that by 1984 there was a highly mobilized national Black electorate. Its size and relatively focused agenda spawned Jackson's efforts to seek the presidency using that Black base. By 1988 he had succeeded in organizing the majority of this racial bloc to support his presidential bid in the presidential primaries. Although he did not win the Democratic Party nomination, he probably generated the highest level of mobilization of Blacks for primary participation in U.S. history. Clearly most Blacks saw his candidacy as a sign of political achievement.

The majority of African Americans saw Jesse Jackson's 1984 bid for the presidency as a sign of hope. It occurred in a political environment in which racial progress had slowed, even within their chosen party. Many had taken an economic hit during the Reagan recession, at the same time witnessing an increase in economic disparities between themselves and whites. Reagan's 1982 budget cuts included reductions in a variety of social welfare policies—job training, health services, food stamps, and guaranteed student loan programs (Tate 1993). With about one-third of African Americans living below poverty level, these cuts potentially had a disproportionate negative impact for them. Although the momentum was still high from the Chicago election of Harold Washington in 1983, many African Americans remained disappointed at the lack of national Democratic support for Washington in that highly visible campaign. Indeed, two potential presidential candidates, Edward Kennedy and Vice President Walter Mondale, endorsed other candidates—Mayor Jayne Byrne and Richard Daley Jr., respectively. Jackson would exploit that voter unhappiness.

Although the climate appeared to be right for an African American bid for the presidency, there were some strong reservations and opposition to Jackson's candidacy. Among Blacks, some high-profile leaders, such as Coretta Scott King, Martin Luther King Sr., and Andrew Young, endorsed Vice President Mondale. They accepted the view that Jackson was unable to win and was thus a distraction. In addition, they, like many white party cadre, feared that Jackson's candidacy would propel more white voters toward the Republican Party. Many African American leaders also questioned Jackson's lack of political experience compared with other potential Black candidates. They felt that a more attractive candidate was needed to challenge a strong Republican incumbent.

Jackson's efforts were further weakened when an African American reporter of the *Washington Post* leaked information to a colleague claiming that Jackson had referred to Jewish Americans as "Hymies" and referred to New York City as "Hymietown." After initially denying the report, Jackson was forced to apologize to the Jewish community for his comments. This and the other combination of elements led Democratic leaders, both Black and white, to support Walter Mondale for the party's nomination.

Notwithstanding the damage done to his reputation with the Jewish community, Jackson was able to capitalize on his charismatic personality by "making news" (Walters 1988, 170). He operated on a budget roughly a third of those of other Democratic candidates (Tate 1993), yet he made headlines. One such event occurred when he helped in the repatriation of a Black Navy flier, Lt. Robert Goodman Jr., who had been captured and imprisoned by the Syrian government. Later Jackson received favorable coverage of a proposal for a humanitarian immigration policy while in Mexico and in asking the

USSR not to boycott the Los Angeles summer Olympic Games during a visit with the Soviet ambassador to the United States, Anatoly Dobrynin (Walters 1988). These high-profile acts showed him not only to be capable of making the grand gesture but also of having keen negotiating skills and a command of broad national issues.

Given that there was some clear opposition to Jackson's bid for the presidency, he had to first legitimize his efforts. He began this effort by forming an exploratory committee headed by Mayor Richard Hatcher, whose earlier election to the mayoralty of Gary, Indiana, made him a powerful symbol of the promise of racial mobilization. In doing so, Jackson attempted to convey the message that he or some other Black candidate would compete for the Democratic nomination (Walters 1988). His aims seemed to be endorsed by the grassroots African American population, if not by the Black hierarchy in the Democratic Party. The nation's most popular Black magazine, *Ebony*, reported that 67.1 percent of its subscribers granted approval to the idea of a Black running for president, and that 61.6 percent approved of Jackson's candidacy (Walters 1988). Other nationwide polls indicated that Jackson also was popular among white voters (Walters 1988), but clearly the driving force of his candidacy was that he could mobilize his African American base. Meanwhile, voter registration levels among Blacks during the 1984 election season were the highest they had been since the 1968 presidential contest, which succeeded the 1965 Voting Rights Act (Walton and Smith 2000, 168).

With the stage set for Jackson to compete for the party's nomination, the next step was to mobilize financial support. Like so many other Black politicians before him, Jackson turned to the Black church. As a Baptist minister and consort of Martin Luther King, Jackson had immediate entrée to that vast network of powerful clergymen and their congregations. He received an important endorsement from the Reverend T. J. Jemison, then president of the National Baptist Convention U.S.A., Inc., which possessed a congregation of some 6.8 million members (Walters 1988). But even more critical was Jemison's formidable organizing skills, which he had first demonstrated in the successful execution of the bus boycott in Baton Rouge, Louisiana, in 1953. He deployed those skills in the interest of Jackson's campaign, mobilizing Baptist clergy all over the country. Other denominations followed suit. Jemison was able to garner the support of the Reverend J. O. Patterson, primate of the Church of God in Christ, a fast-growing sect of Pentecostal churches. Patterson served as the representative of almost 4 million Black churchgoers, for example.

One of the most notable strategies Jackson adopted in the 1984 campaign was his effort to establish the Rainbow Coalition. Pinderhughes (1988) states that the Rainbow idea was first implemented by Mel King in his campaign for mayor of Boston. According to Walters, "care was taken to assure that the coalition was comprised of three categories of representatives: male and female, ethnic/racial, and issue representation" (1988, 166). Indeed, special efforts were made to include Blacks, Hispanics, and Native Americans. Although this type of strategy was probably necessary for a presidential campaign, it did have its downside. According to Pinderhughes (1988), it forced Jackson to deal with a broader set of issues, which made the campaign a much more complex process.

Just how effective was Jackson in generating African American participation for his candidacy in 1984? Although he was a favorite among Black voters, he was unable to garner unanimous support. Among Blacks voting in their state's caucus or primary, approximately 55 percent voted for Jackson (Tate 1993, 138). And even though Jackson campaigned on a "bottom-up" theme, poor people and less-educated Blacks were less likely to support his candidacy. Tate (1993) argues that poor Blacks may have been so hard hit economically during the Reagan administration that they felt compelled to support a candidate who had the potential to win the general election.

Once the dust cleared, Jackson finished third behind Walter Mondale and Gary Hart. However, as the data in Table 4.11 reveals, Jackson make an exceptional showing in a campaign where Mondale, one of the strongest party insiders, was the presumptive nominee. Mondale had been a prime prospect for the presidency for many years, first achieving notice as a senator from Minnesota. He had also been elected as Jimmy Carter's vice president in 1976 and had been selected again for that slot in the failed 1980 contest. Senator Gary Hart, too, was a formidable candidate, actually remaining the front-runner for almost half of the primary season. Yet Jackson carried more than 20 percent of the vote in every primary state in which Blacks constituted more than 20 percent of the population and states that had major cities with substantial Black populations. These were largely southern states and highly urbanized industrial northern states. Under the most competitive circumstance, in which a sitting vice president and an equally attractive candidate from the Senate were seeking the party's nomination, Jesse Jackson was able to significantly mobilize African American voters, placing first in Louisiana and the District of Columbia. He placed second in the highly competitive state of Maryland, where the primary was conducted in May, late in the season.

TABLE 4.11   Jesse Jackson Votes by State in the 1984 Presidential Primaries[a]

State[b]	Votes	Percent	Position	Black Percentage of State Population, 1980
New Hampshire	5,311	5.3	4	0.47
Vermont	5,761	7.8	3	0.23
Alabama	83,787	19.6	4	25.50
Florida	144,263	12.2	3	13.78
Georgia	143,730	21.0	3	26.81
Massachusetts	31,824	5.0	5	3.85
Rhode Island	3,875	8.7	3	2.89
Illinois	348,843	21.0	3	14.65
Connecticut	26,395	12.0	3	6.97
New York	355,541	25.6	3	13.70
Wisconsin	62,524	9.8	3	3.89
Pennsylvania	264,463	16.0	3	8.79
District of Columbia	69,106	67.3	1	70.24
Tennessee	81,418	25.3	3	15.79
Louisiana	136,707	42.9	1	29.45
Indiana	98,190	13.7	3	7.55
Maryland	129,387	25.5	2	22.70
North Carolina	243,945	25.4	3	22.43
Ohio	237,133	16.4	3	9.97
Nebraska	13,495	9.1	3	0.22
Oregon	37,106	9.3	3	1.42
Idaho	3,104	5.7	3	0.29
California	546,693	18.4	3	7.68
Montana	388	1.1	3[c]	0.22
New Jersey	159,788	23.6	3	12.56
New Mexico	22,168	11.8	3	1.77
South Dakota	2,738	5.2	3	0.31
West Virginia	24,697	6.7	3	3.34
Total	**3,282,431**	**18.2**	**3**	**11.70**

[a] Other serious contenders for more than half of the primary season (February through June) were Walter Mondale (38 percent), Gary Hart (35 percent), and George McGovern (2 percent).

[b] States are listed in order of the dates the primaries were held.

[c] Write-ins, where 83 percent of voters expressed no preference.

SOURCES: Data from *Congressional Quarterly Guide to U.S. Elections,* 4th ed., 1994, 372–377; Salzman et al., *Encyclopedia of African American Culture and History,* vol. 5, 1996, 3032.

Although Jackson finished third in the 1984 primary, his bid in 1988 appeared to have more favorable circumstances. With improved name recognition and a more issue-oriented campaign, he set his eyes on the Democratic nomination. Jackson's candidacy was aided when one of the potential front-runners, Gary Hart, dropped out of the race. Moreover, the presumptive favorite for the nomination was not a party insider, as Mondale had been in 1984. At the same time, more primaries were being held. The number of states holding Democratic primaries increased from twenty-eight in 1984 to thirty-five in 1988.

Jackson finished second in 1988 behind front-runner Michael Dukakis. Compared with his 1984 campaign, he more than doubled his votes and nearly tripled the number of delegates he received at the national convention. This increase in delegate support may have been a function of the decrease in the threshold necessary to win delegates from 20 percent to 15 percent (Smith 1990, 221). His supporters were very similar to those who supported him in 1984. His strongest consisted of middle-aged and college-educated Blacks, while those without a high school diploma and older Blacks were less inclined to support him.

The data in Table 4.12 illustrate the spectacular increase in the mobilization and participation levels of African Americans between the 1984 and 1988 campaigns. They also indicate a certain degree of success of the Rainbow Coalition concept. In 1988 Jackson carried five southern states and the District of Columbia, all with substantial African American constituents. Even more remarkable was that he held second place in twenty-four states, including all of the major population centers across the country. Again, registration among African Americans was about equal to that of 1984 and 1968. Their turnout on election day was higher still, enabling African Americans to influence outcomes far beyond their numbers. At the same time, Jackson's Rainbow Coalition had clearly gelled. He placed second in twelve states where the African American population was well under 10 percent, meaning that he was obviously attracting others to his platform for racial inclusion and broader social change. Tate (1993, 15) argues that he succeeded in mobilizing new Black voters and interest for presidential contests.

Conclusion

This chapter has traced the behavior African Americans have exhibited since the end of slavery. The path dictating their behavior has

TABLE 4.12   Jesse Jackson Votes[a] by State in the 1988 Presidential Primaries

State[b]	Votes	Percent	Position	Black Percentage of State Population, 1980
New Hampshire	9,615	7.8	4	0.47
South Dakota	3,867	5.4	6	0.31
Vermont	13,044	5.7	2	0.23
Alabama	176,764	43.6	1	25.50
Arkansas	85,003	17.1	3	16.31
Florida	254,912	20.0	2	13.78
Georgia	247,831	39.8	1	26.81
Kentucky	49,667	15.6	3	9.81
Louisiana	221,532	35.5	1	29.45
Maryland	152,642	28.7	2	22.70
Massachusetts	133,141	18.7	2	3.85
Mississippi	160,651	44.7	1	35.19
Missouri	106,386	20.2	2	10.44
North Carolina	224,177	33.0	2	22.43
Oklahoma	52,417	13.3	4	6.77
Rhode Island	7,445	15.2	2	2.89
Tennessee	119,248	20.7	2	15.79
Texas	433,335	24.5	2	11.98
Virginia	164,709	45.1	1	18.86
Illinois	484,233	32.2	2	14.65
Connecticut	68,372	28.3	2	6.97
Wisconsin	285,995	28.2	2	3.89
New York	585,076	37.1	2	13.70
Pennsylvania	411,260	27.3	2	8.79
District of Columbia	68,840	80.0	1	70.24
Indiana	145,021	22.5	2	7.55
Ohio[c]	378,866	27.4	2	9.97
Nebraska	43,380	25.7	2	0.22
West Virginia	45,788	13.5	2	3.34
Oregon	148,207	38.1	2	1.42
Idaho	8,066	15.7	2	0.29
California	1,102,093	35.1	2	7.68
Montana	26,908	22.1	2	0.22
New Jersey	213,705	32.7	2	12.56
New Mexico	52,988	28.1	2	1.77
Total	**6,685,699**	**29.1**	**2**	**11.70**

[a] Other serious contenders for more than half of the primary season (February through June) were Michael Dukakis (43 percent), Al Gore (14 percent), Richard Gephardt (6 percent), Paul Simon (4 percent), and Gary Hart (2 percent).

[b] States are listed in order of the date the primaries were held.

[c] Jackson slate.

SOURCES: Data from *Congressional Quarterly Guide to U.S. Elections,* 4th ed., 1994, 378–385; Salzman et al., *Encyclopedia of African American Culture and History,* vol. 5, 1996, 3032.

been one of continuing struggle in a racialized environment. This path has sometimes featured resistance to or ambivalence about the inclusion of Blacks in the political process and broader American society, including discriminatory practices toward their exercise of the franchise. However, through struggle and in collaboration with significant allies throughout America, African Americans have achieved the formal legal mechanisms for universal freedom. In practice they have used these mechanisms and a variety of social-change strategies, such as mobilization, to participate in the political system. As the analysis showed, they began to do this with regularity during the colonial period, when they aligned with those who supported inclusion in a relentlessly racialized environment.

That early platform for racial inclusion has constituted the primary political agenda guiding African American political behavior ever since. Its primary effect is that African Americans act mostly as a bloc in electoral politics and consistently select partisan allies for their position on the question of racial inclusion. In the two-party system that has been in place for much of the nation's history, only rarely have both parties been regarded as having optimal positions on racial inclusion. Even long before the Civil War, it has been one or the other, forcing Blacks into a kind of one-party affiliation in an otherwise two-party system.

First Blacks associated with the northern business classes, the partisan forerunners of the Republican Party, because they opposed slavery. At the time of the Civil War they supported the Party of Lincoln, the Republicans, regarded as the architects of the emancipation. Residual support for the Republicans outlasted the party's affirmative efforts for racial inclusion, a relatively short-lived period after the war. That was followed by a long period of virtually complete political exclusion resulting from the breach of the franchise in the South, where most Blacks lived.

With the Great Depression and shifting alignments within the two parties, the Democrats became the party of choice for Blacks. Franklin Roosevelt's New Deal and a party platform espousing racial inclusion were signal events to the shift. Meanwhile, a major migration that eventually brought nearly half of the African American population to urban centers in the North began to produce political results. Cities such as Chicago, Detroit, and New York used mobilization strategies in majority-Black electoral districts to elect their own to offices at the congressional and municipal levels. By 1940 most of these officials were wearing the Democratic Party label, a sentiment that continues apace to the present. This political success in the

North was matched in the South after an intense social movement for inclusion through the 1950s and 1960s. It began to bear fruit in the late 1960s, when the first Blacks were elected to local office in small towns and villages in majority-Black southern towns. By the 1970s Blacks were sending their first congressional representative to Washington in 100 years.

Overall, this mobilization produced what may be called a national Black electoral constituency, which Jesse Jackson brought to its highest level of mobilization during his campaigns for the presidency. Voting registration levels among Blacks averaged well over 60 percent, and in some local and congressional districts where they were a voting majority, levels reached or exceeded 80 percent. The proof that this potential was being converted to actual voting lay in the extraordinary increase in the number of elected officials whose election was completely controlled by the turnout of Black voters. Clearly, they largely determined the fortunes of Jesse Jackson in his remarkable presidential primary successes.

Moreover, the bloc voting of Blacks for the Democratic Party has on occasion influenced the outcome of presidential contests since the Voting Rights Act of 1965, notably those of Jimmy Carter and Bill Clinton. The influence of African American political participation remains greatest in those districts and communities where they are able to pool their votes for the selection of one of their own. It is in these instances that their foremost agenda item, racial inclusion, is most consistently manifested. In the general partisan arena, it remains the case that the broader bases of the two parties make racial agenda items more difficult to support. And in any case, historically African Americans have perceived that only one of the parties at a time warranted the group's affiliation.

References

Aptheker, Herbert. 1951. *A Documentary History of the Negro People in the United States*. New York: Citadel Press.

Barker, Lucius, et al. 1999. *African Americans and the American Political System*. Saddle River, NJ: Prentice-Hall.

Burton, Vernon. 1978. "Race and Reconstruction: Edgefield County, South Carolina." *Journal of Social History* 12: 31–56.

Campbell, Angus. 1966. "A Classification of the Presidential Elections." In Angus Campbell et al., eds., *Elections and the Political Order*. New York: Wiley.

Carmichael, Stokely, and Charles Hamilton. 1967. *Black Power*. New York: Random House.

Carson, Clayborne. 1981. *In Struggle: SNCC and the Black Awakening of the 1960s*. Cambridge, MA: Harvard University Press.

Childs, John Brown. 1980. *The Political Black Minister: A Study in Afro-American Politics and Religion*. Boston: G. K. Hall.

Cone, James H. 1997. *Black Theology and Black Power*. Maryknoll, NY: Orbis.

Davidson, Chandler. 1984. *Minority Vote Dilution*. Washington, DC: Howard University Press.

Davidson, Roger H., and Walter J. Oleszek. 2002. *Congress and Its Members*. 8th ed. Washington, DC: Congressional Quarterly Press.

Dawson, Michael. 1994. *Behind the Mule*. Princeton, NJ: Princeton University Press.

Dittmer, John. 1994. *Local People: The Struggle for Civil Rights in Mississippi*. Urbana: University Press of Illinois.

Fishel, Leslie, Jr., and Benjamin Quarles. 1967. *The Negro American: A Documentary History*. Glenview, IL: Scott, Foresman.

Foner, Eric. 1990. *A Short History of Reconstruction*. New York: Harper and Row.

Franklin, John Hope, and Alfred Moss. 1994. *From Slavery to Freedom*. 7th ed. New York: McGraw-Hill.

Frazier, E. Franklin. 1974. *The Negro Church in America*. New York: Schocken Books.

Glantz, Oscar. 1967. "The Negro Voter in Northern Industrial Cities." In Harry Bailey Jr., ed., *Negro Politics in America*, 338–352. Columbus, OH: Charles Merrill.

Gosnell, Harold. 1935. *Negro Politicians: The Rise of Negro Politics in Chicago*. Chicago: University of Chicago Press.

Guinier, Lani. 1994. *The Tyranny of the Majority*. New York: The Free Press.

Hamilton, Charles, ed. 1973. *The Black Experience in American Politics*. New York: Capricorn.

Hamilton, Charles V. 1991. *Adam Clayton Powell, Jr.: The Political Biography of an American Dilemma*. New York: Atheneum Press.

Harlan, Louis. 1972. *Booker T. Washington: The Making of a Black Leader, 1856–1901*. New York: Oxford University Press.

Holt, Thomas. 1977. *Black Over White*. Urbana: University Press of Illinois.

Key, V. O., Jr. 1955. "A Theory of Critical Elections." *Journal of Politics* 17: 3–18.

Kinder, Donald, and Lynn Sanders. 1996. *Divided by Color: Racial Politics and Democratic Ideals*. Chicago: University of Chicago Press.

Krislov, Samuel. 1967. *The Negro in Federal Employment: The Quest for Equal Opportunity*. Minneapolis: University of Minnesota Press.

Lee, Chana. 1999. *For Freedom's Sake: The Life of Fannie Lou Hamer*. Urbana: University Press of Illinois.

Legette, Willie M. 2000. "The South Carolina Legislative Black Caucus, 1970 to 1988." *Journal of Black Studies* 30: 839–858.

Logan, Rayford, and Michael Winston, eds. 1982. *Dictionary of Negro Biography*. New York: W. W. Norton.

Marable, Manning. 2000. "The Gary Black Political Convention of 1972." In Jonathan Birnbaum and Clarence Taylor, eds., *Civil Rights Since 1787: A Reader on the Black Struggle,* 635–640. New York: New York University Press.

McMillen, Neil. 1990. *Dark Journey: Black Mississippians in the Age of Jim Crow.* Urbana: University Press of Illinois.

Mills, Kay. 1993. *This Little Light of Mine: The Life of Fannie Lou Hamer.* New York: Dutton.

Morris, Aldon. 1984. *The Origins of the Civil Rights Movement.* New York: The Free Press.

Morrison, Minion K. C. 1987. *Black Political Mobilization.* Albany: State University of New York Press.

Perry, Huey L., and Wayne Parent, eds. 1995. *Blacks and the American Political System.* Gainesville: University of Florida Press.

Perry, Huey, Tracey Ambeau, and Frederick McBride. 1995. "Blacks and the Executive Branch." In Huey Perry and Wayne Parent, eds., *Blacks and the American Political System.* Gainesville: University Press of Florida, 105–129.

Pinderhughes, Dianne. 1987. *Race and Ethnicity in Chicago Politics.* Urbana: University Press of Illinois.

———. 1988. "The Articulation of Black Interests by Black Civil Rights, Professional, and Religious Organizations." In Lorenzo Morris, ed., *The Social and Political Implications of the 1984 Jesse Jackson Presidential Campaign,* 126–134. New York: Praeger.

Plissner, Martin, and Warren Mitofsky. 1988. "The Changing Jackson Voter." *Public Opinion* 11(2): 56–57.

Reeves, Keith. 1997. *Voting Hopes and Fears: White Voters, Black Candidates, and Racial Politics in America.* New York: Oxford University Press.

Rosenstone, Steven J., and John M. Hansen. 1993. *Mobilization, Participation, and Democracy in America.* New York: Macmillan.

Scher, Robert. 1997. *Politics in the New South: Republicanism, Race, and Leadership in the Twentieth Century.* 2d ed. Armonk, NY: M. E. Sharpe.

Shingles, Richard. 1981. "Black Consciousness and Political Participation: The Missing Link." *American Political Science Review* 75: 76–90.

Smith, Robert. 1990. "From Insurgency Toward Inclusion: The Jackson Campaigns of 1984 and 1988." In Lorenzo Morris, ed., *The Social and Political Implications of the 1984 Jesse Jackson Presidential Campaign,* 215–230. New York: Praeger.

Southern Exposure. 2000. "The Mississippi Freedom Democratic Party." In Jonathan Birnbaum and Clarence Taylor, eds., *Civil Rights Since 1787: A Reader on the Black Struggle,* 517–520. New York: New York University Press.

Stanley, Harold, and Richard Niemi, eds. 2000. *Vital Statistics on American Politics, 1999–2000.* Washington, DC: Congressional Quarterly Press.

Tate, Katherine. 1991. "Black Political Participation in the 1984 and 1988 Presidential Elections." *American Political Science Review* 85: 1159–1176.

———. 1993. *From Protest to Politics.* Cambridge, MA: Harvard University Press.

Valelly, Richard M. 1993. "The Puzzle of Disfranchisement: Party Struggle and African American Suffrage in the South, 1867–1894." Paper prepared for the Workshop on Race, Ethnicity, Representation, and Governance. Center for American Political Studies, Harvard University, January 21–22, 1993.

Verba, Sidney, and Norman H. Nie. 1972. *Participation in America.* Cambridge, MA: Harvard University Press.

Walker, Robert. 1976. "Society and Soul." Ph.D. dissertation, Department of Sociology, Stanford University.

Walters, Ronald. 1988. *Black Presidential Politics in America: A Strategic Approach.* Albany: State University of New York Press.

Walton, Hanes, Jr. 1972a. *Black Political Parties.* New York: The Free Press.

———. 1972b. *Black Politics: A Theoretical and Structural Analysis.* Philadelphia: Lippincott.

———. 1975. *Black Republicans: The Politics of the Black and Tans.* Metuchen, NJ: Scarecrow Press.

Walton, Hanes Jr., and Robert Smith. 2002. *American Politics and the African American Quest for Universal Freedom.* New York: Longman.

Walton, Hanes, Jr., Oliver Jones Jr., and Pearl K. Ford. 1997. "African American Political Socialization: The Protest Resignations of Councilpersons Jerome Woddy and Renee Baker." In Hanes Walton Jr., ed., *African American Power and Politics: The Political Context Variable,* 113–128. New York: Columbia University Press.

Warshaw, Shirley A. 1996. *Powersharing: White House–Cabinet Relations in the Modern Presidency.* Albany: State University of New York Press.

Wesley, Charles. 1944. "The Participation of Negroes in Anti-slavery Political Parties." *Journal of Negro History* 29: 32–74.

Wolfinger, Raymond E., and Steven J. Rosenstone. 1980. *Who Votes?* New Haven, CT: Yale University Press.

5

African Americans in Office

Minion K. C. Morrison and Richard Middleton, IV

The story of African American political office holding is in many ways indicative of the ambiguous status of the community since its enslavement in the United States. There have been extensive periods of either formal or de facto denial of participation in the electoral political arena. In these periods African Americans had little or no formal venues for participation. At other times, however, in the ebb and flow of legal although often ambivalent participation (Higginbotham 1980), they have held a wide range of political offices. They began to hold offices in relatively substantial numbers only during Reconstruction, when participation for the majority of Blacks received state sanction for the first time (Bennett 1967). This period, which lasted from 1865 to about 1880, represented the first of two important waves of participation by African Americans (Franklin and Moss 1994). The second great wave started roughly 100 years later, in about 1960, and continues today (Joint Center for Political Studies [JCPS] 1976; Jones 1976).

This chapter documents the formal participation of African Americans in offices, elective or otherwise, since the arrival of the community in the Americas. It begins with the types of formal participation that occurred in the era of slavery, most of which occurred among freed Blacks outside of the southern United States. This discussion considers activity from the beginning of the republic through the end of the Civil War. Then it addresses the first wave of substantive formal office holding that occurred during Reconstruction, documenting the electoral positions secured largely in the former Confederacy in the South. The chapter then turns to the long period of disfranchisement (from around 1880 to the 1930s) and documents the extent to which residuum offices of Reconstruction continued for a small number of African Americans.

This is followed by a discussion of the reemergence of formal office holding by Blacks after the Great Migration (1890–1960), when a substantial proportion of the African American population moved from the South to the North. They began to have an impact in northern urban electoral constituencies around the turn of the century, and that trend has continued to the present. From there, the chapter documents participation in the second great wave for African Americans, the civil rights movement and beyond. A discussion is included of the civil rights movement and several important pieces of legislation that reestablished the franchise for African Americans in the South, the most significant among them being the Civil Rights Acts of 1960 and 1964 and the Voting Rights Act of 1965. Then the analysis tracks the first electoral positions in urban northern cities and in rural southern communities and accounts for a number of significant formal office holders who held appointive positions in this period. The chapter ends with a consideration of the significant departure in representation reflected by the emergence of Jesse Jackson as a national contender for the presidency.

The Meanings of Formal Office Holding

Procedural Representation

Formal participation for African Americans has always been affected by the previous slave status of most of this population. However, in the context of this discussion, formal participation refers to service in a public position that is official. Such positions include those filled by an authorized person or those that are authorized by statute. Authorized persons are generally those who have appointive power by virtue of occupying a statutory position such as an executive official—the president, a governor, or a member of Congress, for example. This chapter covers such formal positions occupied by African Americans and the restriction of such office holding by slavery and its subsequent residual effects. The bulk of such office holding occurred just after the Civil War, but it has ebbed and flowed overall against the backdrop of continued disfranchisement and other practices of racial exclusion. The best records of formal participation, therefore, have occurred in two great periods—the Reconstruction period that began in 1865 and lasted about ten years, and the political mobilization period of the civil rights movement, roughly from 1967 to 1980.

These records also provide a census of African American participation—the number of people who served in various positions, and a demographic description of them. This can include such information as the frequency of service in a particular political universe, where it was performed, and by whom. It also refers to the exercise of procedural powers that are assigned to the positions (Pitkin 1967). In this sense one considers what authority is attendant to the particular positions that African Americans have held over time—are these powers executive, legislative, or judicial, and what degrees of power are invested in them? These aspects are included in the analysis because they can reveal a great deal of information about the scope of participation and the relative power attached to them. This can be an especially useful approach in this field of study, where good data on African American historical participation are not readily available. This chapter surveys and documents this record, pulling together some data rarely presented in this form.

Substantive Representation

Then there is the question of participation to what end. The point of formal participation in government is to influence the allocation of public resources among competing interests or community members. In this context, one asks how well political office holders allocate given resources to those whom they are designated to serve. Historically the assumptions inherent in racial division in the United States have predisposed Black office holders to represent other Blacks. The universal enfranchisement of African Americans succeeded their widespread enslavement, which left them largely in isolated racial enclaves. These race-exclusive enclaves became the constituent bases for most of the formal positions, elective or appointive, subsequently held by Blacks. Only in recent times have major representative positions been held by African Americans with allocative authority for broader constituent bases. Hence a large part of the story to be told is how racial segregation has structured and limited office holding among African Americans. At the same time, the chapter assesses the extent to which the racial divide has been crossed.

This fact of segregation and isolation brings another aspect of participation to the forefront—substantive incorporation (Browning et al. 1990). In this context the question is whether office holders are anchored in the system with sufficient power and authority to meet the demands of their constituents. In other words, how substantive are the allocations that the representative can make to an already racialized community burdened with the residuals of enslavement (Held 1996)? Over time, it has often been the case that elected and appointed officials designated to serve the African American community have themselves been isolated from the main centers of power. The analysis to follow documents this racialization of leadership and assesses its impact on the exercise of power for African American interests.

Foundations of Constant Struggle for Equality: Slavery and Ambivalence in Application of the Law

The United States has always been a country of laws. However, some groups were originally excluded from citizenship and thus defined as outside the law (Native Americans and Black slaves), while others were systematically denied the franchise (women) (Shklar 1991). At the same time, some of those who were subsequently awarded citizenship have had the consequent laws unequally applied. This has been an enduring feature for the participation of African Americans as office holders. As previous chapters have shown, the denial of citizenship or its operation in the breach has placed inordinate limits on the exercise of power for African Americans. It is worth reiterating, too, that the scope and character of African American office holding have been strongly affected by the barriers to such participa-

tion, including complete bars to it and ambivalence toward uphold-
ing the laws protecting it.

Ambivalence about the membership of African Americans in the
general political community has been expressed both in the application of the law (Higginbotham 1980) and in a hegemonic white leadership aggressively asserting a vision of racial exclusion (Jones 1972).
The position of African Americans has often been determined by evasion or misapplication of the law. In such cases, whatever representation African American constituents received was not bound to deliver
the political benefits demanded or expected by the group. The unwillingness or inability of the representatives to apply the law led to
a gross underrepresentation of the group's interests in the political
arena.

Similarly, because the power structure in the United States has essentially been dominated by a white elite (Dolbeare and Edelman
1979; Parenti 1978), it has left the representation of African Americans dependent on the goodwill of white power holders or any
social-change-oriented visions that might emanate from them. Thus
it can be argued that office holding and incorporation for African
Americans have been dependent on the willingness of whites to
make concessions of power to the group. African Americans as a
group have rarely had an independent ability to exercise control over
their fate or to garner arenas of power for their independent use. This
has been a general problem, although there have been many variations in the outcomes for formal participation by Blacks.

One variant of limitations has been those placed on free Blacks.
There was always a free Black population in the United States that
was able more or less to participate before the Civil War. Nevertheless, free Blacks often were limited in their participation because of
the presumptions of their racial inferiority. In some states they were
treated little different from their enslaved kinsmen. This was particularly evident in some southern states where the overwhelming majority of other Blacks were enslaved.

Later, when the emancipation and the Thirteenth, Fourteenth,
and Fifteenth Amendments ostensibly provided universal freedom, a
major struggle ensued to maintain the status quo, especially in the
South. A mere ten years after Reconstruction began, less in some
places, there was a barely masked campaign to disfranchise the recently freed population. In most southern states, everyday state-
sanctioned actions effectively overturned the legal citizenship status
of African Americans. Often these actions were backed up and sus-

tained by force and terror. Virtually all the southern states rewrote their Reconstruction constitutions to legally disfranchise Blacks, and in 1896 they received federal sanction to do so with the Supreme Court's "separate but equal" decision in *Plessy v. Ferguson.* These developments presaged a long period of sharply constrained formal participation for African Americans that began to shift significantly only with the migration of segments of the Black population from the South to the North. Blacks in northern urban centers were able to win some legislative offices in the 1940s, and those remaining in the South complemented this development with a widespread civil rights mobilization in the 1950s.

African Americans have met these circumstances with a constancy of struggle against both the color bar and the misapplication or neglect of the law. They have been consistent in their demand for a more equitable share of political power. These demands can be seen in the continuity of resistance during slavery and after emancipation. African Americans never accepted either the conditions of servitude or the subsequent conditions of isolation and discrimination. In large measure, therefore, their ability to acquire political offices has been a product of demands expressed in intracommunal mobilization (Morris 1984). This approach is consistent with Frederick Douglass's dictum that power is conceded only as a product of demand (Douglass 1962). However, because the group has always been a numerical minority, it has used its mobilization in concert with a variety of allies. Even so, more often than not, this political bidding has been in oppositional ways vis-à-vis the established political authorities (Barnett 1976).

Although resistance has been highly prominent in African American political behavior (Bracey et al. 1970), it has occurred fairly consistently within the framework of the American philosophical tradition of equality and universal freedom (Harding 1983). African Americans have mobilized, by and large, to attain the benefits of the American Revolution, as incorporated in the Declaration of Independence, the Constitution, and its amended Bill of Rights. Although African Americans have used a wide range of tactics in mobilization, the most consistent one has been that which accepts the precepts of the American revolutionary ideals of democracy defined as equality and universal freedom. Other conceptualizations, too, have been evoked that were based on a radical departure from the American democratic ideology, more often identifying the accompanying capitalist market system as the chief problem (Dawson 2001).

Formal Participation during Reconstruction

The foundations for the formal participation of African Americans rest in the Civil War emancipation from slavery in the southern states and the subsequent passage of constitutional amendments and legislation effectuating their citizenship rights. The question of slavery was a fundamental issue in the war campaign when President Abraham Lincoln indicated that ending it was one requirement for saving the Union. Subsequently his Emancipation Proclamation in January 1863 (Fishel and Quarles 1967) freed all slaves in the Confederate states. During the next few years, a trilogy of constitutional amendments passed by Congress followed—the Thirteenth (1865), Fourteenth (1868), and Fifteenth (1870) Amendments, altered the status of all Blacks by abolishing their enslavement and authorizing their citizenship and voting rights.

At the same time, a broad spectrum of statutory law was passed specifically to protect the civil rights of African Americans. The first of these, passed in 1866 over a presidential veto, was designed to protect Blacks from practices of racial discrimination in everyday life. Two other acts followed within the next year—one barring kidnapping people of color for purposes of servitude (1866), the other protecting them from being the subject of peonage in the country (1867). In 1870 and 1871, two statutes were passed criminalizing acts against Blacks who were exercising their freedoms: the Enforcement Act barred interference with Blacks exercising the franchise; and the Ku Klux Act provided sanctions against anyone who violated the equal protection clause of the Fourteenth Amendment (Blaustein and Zangrando 1968). Together these constituted a formidable body of law, which if fully implemented, could have completely reversed the fortunes of the African American population. As we will see, they were never fully implemented, but they nevertheless did provide a basis for the first formal office holding among Blacks.

It took little time for Blacks to begin to exercise the freedoms they acquired in the Civil War and the subsequent Reconstruction. In short order they were engaged in changing the political leadership in the places where their numbers were sufficient for them to bid against white power holders. These places were largely in the former Confederate states: Alabama, Arkansas, Florida, Georgia, Louisiana, Mississippi, North Carolina, South Carolina, Tennessee, Texas, and Virginia.

The African American population and their mobilization in these states reveals the importance of the franchise for their potential influence on the outcome of elections. As Table 5.1 shows, Blacks constituted a major portion of the population of the Confederate states. They were a majority in several of these states, and if sufficiently enrolled to vote, they could serve as a balance of power where the white electorate was divided. "In 1870 [Blacks] comprised nearly 60 percent of the population of South Carolina; over half in Mississippi and Louisiana; between 40 and 50 percent in Alabama, Florida, Georgia, and Virginia; over one-third in North Carolina; and between one-quarter and one-third in Arkansas, Tennessee, and Texas" (Foner 1996, xiii). At the same time, Black mobilization was very high. In 1867, "1,363,000 American citizens had registered in the old states of the Confederacy, and of that number 700,000 were black. Because of the disfranchisement of some Confederate officers and the passive resistance of some whites, black voters constituted a majority in . . . Alabama, Florida, Louisiana, Mississippi, and South Carolina" (Bennett 1967, 74).

The Reconstruction Constitutional Conventions

The first order of political business during Reconstruction was to change the legal armature of government to sanction Black citizenship—the state constitutions. Under the Reconstruction Act of 1867,

> the ex-Confederates states except Tennessee, whose Reconstruction was moving satisfactorily, were divided into five military districts in which martial law was to prevail. On the basis of universal male suffrage a convention in each state was to draw up a new constitution acceptable to Congress. No state was to be admitted until it ratified the Fourteenth Amendment. Former rebels who could not take the ironclad oath were of course disfranchised. (Franklin and Moss 1994, 226)

More than 250 African American representatives attended these Reconstruction conventions, representing each of these states (see Table 5.2) (Foner 1996, xvi). South Carolina actually had a majority, 72 of 124 elected delegates (58 percent), which was almost exactly proportionate to their representation in the population (Holt 1979, 35).

TABLE 5.1   African American Population in the Former Confederacy, 1870–1880

State	1870		1880	
	Total Population	Black Population (%)	Total Population	Black Population (%)
Alabama	996,992	475,510 (48)	1,262,505	600,103 (48)
Arkansas	484,471	122,169 (25)	802,525	210,666 (26)
Florida	187,748	91,689 (49)	269,493	126,690 (47)
Georgia	1,184,109	545,162 (46)	1,542,180	725,133 (47)
Louisiana	726,915	364,210 (50)	939,946	483,655 (51)
Mississippi	827,922	444,201 (54)	1,131,597	650,291 (57)
North Carolina	1,071,361	391,650 (37)	1,339,750	531,277 (38)
South Carolina	705,606	415,814 (59)	995,577	604,332 (61)
Tennessee	1,258,520	322,321 (26)	1,542,359	403,151 (26)
Texas	818,579	253,475 (31)	1,591,749	393,384 (25)
Virginia	1,225,163	512,841 (42)	1,512,565	631,616 (42)

SOURCE: Data from U.S. Census.

TABLE 5.2   Representation in State Reconstruction Constitutional Conventions

State	Total Delegates	Black Delegates
South Carolina	124	72
Louisiana	99	49
Georgia	166	33
Virginia	105	25
Florida	46	17
Alabama	100	17
Mississippi	100	17
North Carolina	120	13
Texas	90	9
Arkansas	68	7

SOURCES: Data from Foner 1996; Smith and Horton 1995.

Convention Delegates: A Demographic and Political Profile

Who were these representatives and what was the political import of their service? They were an interesting lot, hardly fitting the stereotypical portrayal of illiteracy and irresponsibility. Many of them could read and write, and some were well trained. Many were free men who had won their freedom or had been born free. Among the free men in almost every state were some migrants from the northern states. Forty-four percent of those in South Carolina were literate, including ten with some higher education. "Most appear to have been tradesmen, merchants, teachers, ministers, and small farmers" (Holt 1979, 37). Mississippi's smaller delegation had a similar profile. At least five had considerable education, and at least eight of them were Protestant ministers (Wharton 1947).

Their contribution to the development of a new political order was significant throughout the entire former Confederacy. The speed with which a cadre of leaders assumed these important legislative roles was remarkable. Some were among the most learned and distinguished Americans of their day. Many were clergymen whose growing independent churches foretold the later singular importance of these organizations in the social and political development of the community. These conventions of ordinary people, a cross section of the country, have been called the "first democratic assemblies in the South, and, in some respects, the first democratic assemblies in America" (Bennett 1967, 81).

But these first leaders did not exist in a vacuum. They rapidly linked to an emerging cadre of leaders outside the conventions, some of whose activism preceded the rewriting of the constitutions. Among these were free migrants from the North who were involved in many aspects of Black community life—schools, churches, and political organizations.

Coalition Politics for Progressive Legislation during Reconstruction

The Black delegates were also significant for the business they undertook. The charge for all of the constitutional conventions was to uphold the principles of universal freedom for the integration of Blacks into the political community. Theirs was a task to both dismantle and create. And again, this too was executed with remarkable speed. Since Blacks rarely dominated these constitutional processes, however, they were required to develop coalitions. More often than not, they made alliances with whites from both the North and South in this dynamic environment. In the end, all of these conventions, with the backdrop of a military presence, codified principles of universal freedom in the new constitutions. They "were the most progressive the South had ever known. Most of them abolished property qualifications for voting and holding office; some of them abolished imprisonment for debt. All of them abolished slavery, and several sought to eliminate race distinctions in the possession or inheritance of property" (Franklin and Moss 1994, 298). They also laid the foundation for the election of the first African Americans in the history of the former Confederacy.

Blacks in the Federal Congress and Impact of the Compromise of 1876

The most visible positions occupied by the first Black office holders were the congressional seats. Eight of the eleven states had Black congressmen or senators during Reconstruction. Only Mississippi elected Black senators—Hiram Revels in 1870 and Blanche Bruce in 1875. The watershed of the electoral success occurred early, between 1870 and 1875, when there were sixteen Black representatives in Congress.

After this spurt of success, the controversial presidential election of 1876 brought a precipitous decline in African American participation. In order to prevail in the disputed election, presidential candidate Rutherford B. Hayes made a compromise with white southerners by which the military occupation of the region would end. The number of Blacks in official offices dropped rapidly. Only three of those who won federal legislative seats in the early period served beyond 1880, and thereafter the critical mass was much reduced. In 1880 and 1881, Congress had only one Black representative—Senator Bruce of Mississippi; in 1882 and 1883, two Black representatives served—Smalls of South Carolina and Lynch of Mississippi; and between 1883 and 1887, two Blacks served—Smalls, and O'Hara of North Carolina. A few others won seats through 1897, but during that time there were never more than two Black representatives serving at the same time. After Bruce left the Senate in 1881, all succeeding Black representatives in the period served in the House. The data in Table 5.3 show the extent of the representation from the Reconstruction period through the end of the century.

The Policy Influence of the Black Lawmakers

The impact of Black federal legislators was greatly affected by two factors—their numerical minority status and the widespread belief that they were genetically inferior. Although the African American population was significant in many of the former Confederate states, the group never had anywhere near proportionate representation in public office at the federal level. Nor did it ever achieve the critical mass of elected officials required to allow the group any significant influence in Congress. Hence African Americans were unable to structure an independent "Black agenda" and bargain for its consideration. This minority status was further complicated by a competing national agenda for rapid industrial development that largely excluded the southern region. The priority of this industrial economic project, for example, seriously undermined the remedial efforts of the Freedmen's Bureau (DuBois 1962, 228).

Moreover, despite emancipation and the trilogy of amendments, the status of African Americans remained contested at the federal level, which severely limited the modest power of Black congressional leaders. The notion that Africans and their descendants were genetically inferior was widespread, and a good deal of so-called scientific evidence was marshaled to prove it. Even more prevalent but no less invidious was the assumption that African Americans were not equal to their white counterparts. Scientists and physicians set

TABLE 5.3   African American Members of Congress during Reconstruction

State	Name	Service Dates
Senate and House of Representatives		
Alabama	Benjamin Turner	1871–1873
	James Rapier	1873–1875
	Jeremiah Haralson	1875–1877
Florida	Josiah Walls	1871–1876
Georgia	Jefferson Long	1870–1871
Louisiana	Charles Nash	1875–1877
Mississippi	Hiram Revels (Senate)	1870–1871
	John Lynch	1873–1877
	Blanche Bruce (Senate)	1875–1881
North Carolina	John Hyman	1875–1877
South Carolina	Joseph Rainey	1870–1879
	Robert Elliott	1871–1874
	Robert De Large	1871–1873
	Richard Cain	1873–1875
		1877–1879
	Alonzo Ransier	1873–1875
	Robert Smalls	1875–1879
Post-1880 House of Representatives		
Mississippi	John Lynch	1882–1883
North Carolina	James O'Hara	1883–1887
	Henry Cheatham	1889–1893
	George White	1897–1901
South Carolina	Robert Smalls	1882–1883
		1884–1887
	Thomas Miller	1890–1891
	George Murray	1893–1895
		1896–1897
Virginia	John Langston	1890–1891

SOURCES: Data from Barker et al. 1999; Bennett 1967; Foner 1996.

out to prove that whites had superior natural intellectual capacity. First the two races were seen as separate species, with whites being superior. Another approach was to use measurements of human brains to argue the superiority of whites. Such ideas had all manner of social, psychological, and political consequences. One of the most important was the support they gave to the perceived superior lifestyle choices and social progress of whites. The research work of these "scientists," which was often underwritten by government, became a fundamental underpinning of public policy (Jones 1973; Nobles 2000). Even among whites who did not accept the genetic arguments, some, including principal African American allies, remained skeptical about the equality of the races. Among these were Lincoln and some of the Christian abolitionists. Their ambivalence about racial equality or laissez-faire neglect resulted all too often in the maintenance of the status quo.

Most of the Black legislators worked consistently to reflect the interests deemed important to the newly freed, often with white allies. The foremost issue for them was civil rights. In a content analysis of a selection of the speeches they gave in Congress (McFarlin 1976), civil rights was found to be far and away the issue to which they spoke the most. They sought the full implementation and enforcement of the postwar civil rights statutes and the three amendments. This concern was driven by the fact that even early on, a disjuncture developed between the law and its implementation. It remained an enduring challenge because many white southerners sought to maintain the status quo and employed a variety of tactics to undermine the new laws.

It is perhaps surprising that a large number of public expressions by the legislators concerned the stabilization of the political order in the South. This led a number of them to take the apparently conservative position of enabling the former Confederates to move forward as quickly as possible. What most of them were seeking was the return of stability to the region so that Blacks could begin to reap the benefits of their emancipation in an orderly manner. They recognized that little stability could occur when about half of the electorate remained disfranchised.

Education, not surprisingly, was the third most often mentioned issue in a context where the majority of the African American population was illiterate. Since educational achievement had already emerged as a critical factor to advancement in this "egalitarian" society, these leaders reasoned that it was also key to African American progress. They all supported public education, a position consistent with the relative deprivation of their illiterate and economically dependent constituents.

Generally, however, the Black legislators spoke on a wide range of issues. They, like their white counterparts, used the platform of office to speak about general issues regarding the developing republic, such as tariffs and railroad subsidies. At the same time, they spoke on a number of issues in their districts that principally affected their white constituents, such as levees.

In the passage of legislation, however, the Black representatives enjoyed little success. Many of them were active sponsors of legislative proposals, usually related to priority issues such as civil rights. However, skepticism about the appropriateness of Blacks as legislators left them bereft of supporters for the bills they offered in Congress. Indeed, this skepticism was so widespread that two of the first Blacks to win congressional races in Louisiana were denied their seats. The lack of support, however, did not silence the voices of the legislators or completely efface their effectiveness. Most of them were quite capable men, with considerable political experience by the time they arrived in Washington. Not a few of them had been members of their state constitutional conventions or served as state legislators or in other state and local positions. They used this experience as best they could to advance their proposals, and for a time they found allies among the Radical Republicans. Thus while the scope of their influence was limited by a number of factors in a racialized environment, they had a major influence in redefining the social order for the short duration of Reconstruction.

Blacks in the Federal Executive

Black elected officials had their counterparts in the executive branch of the federal government, although their presence and influence shared some of the same limits. Although Blacks were now allowed membership in the ruling Republican Party and were providing services for which the payoff was usually high-level patronage jobs, they were the least likely to receive such positions. Indeed, the range of opportunities was so circumscribed that the positions assumed by Blacks became known as "Negro jobs"—a few ambassadorships and a variety of federal managerial bureaucratic posts.

Before the Compromise of 1876, the highest formal executive appointments African Americans received were in the diplomatic corps—two served the equivalent of ambassadorships to Haiti and Liberia. These positions had been assigned because the missions were in Black-run nations, apparently the only posts available to nonwhites (Morrison 2002). Otherwise, the overwhelming majority of appointive federal positions held by African Americans were lower-level bureaucratic positions in various cabinet offices. As Table 5.4 shows, the largest number of these were in the postal system, a few as postmasters. Next were positions as customs officers, and smaller numbers occupied positions as census officers, clerks, and tax asses-

TABLE 5.4   African American Federal Appointees, 1865–1876

Office	Number
Postal Service	57
Customs Service	40
Census Bureau	20
Assessor	10
Clerk	12
U.S. Marshal	11
Other U.S. Agents	10
Ambassador	2

SOURCE: Adapted from Foner 1996, xv.

sors. Although these were not high-level positions, they were often very visible. These appointments were seen to represent progress in a racialized social order where all too often such jobs were completely off limits to Blacks. The value of the posts was also raised by the fact that some very high-profile Black leaders occupied them, especially after 1876. Frederick Douglass, for example, served in various of these positions in Washington, as did several former members of Congress whose political careers were truncated with the end of Reconstruction.

The involvement of African Americans as executive appointees and informal advisers began toward the end of the Civil War and continued beyond the end of Reconstruction. A number of advisers at the executive level began to have some influence even during the Civil War. Some were prominent abolitionists who had an active part in making it possible for African American soldiers to serve in the Union campaign. Others had attained influence by their service in the war effort. Among the abolitionists Frederick Douglass, a "fugitive slave," was perhaps the most prominent. He had become an outstanding orator, publicist, and Republican Party adviser through his speeches and writings on the moral and political evils of slavery. He was also a strong supporter of deputizing Blacks for service in the war, where ultimately more than 200,000 of them did serve (DuBois 1962). Douglass was a trusted adviser to President Lincoln and became a cadre member of the Republican Party. He was tapped for a number of positions prior to his ministerial appointment to Haiti in 1889. He served President Hayes as U.S. Marshal for the District of Columbia (1877), and served President James Garfield as Recorder of Deeds, also in Washington (1881). After playing an active role in the Republican Party campaign of 1888, the candidate he helped elect,

Benjamin Harrison, appointed Douglass to his last federal post as ambassador to Haiti and Head of Mission in Santo Domingo (Logan and Winston 1982).

Other prominent Republican Party cadre, elected officials, educators, and activists also served in these appointive positions. Two ambassadors preceded Douglass, serving in the designated spots in Haiti and Liberia before 1876. The first was Ebenezer Bassett, a man most known for his educational achievements. He did not appear to be as active in Republican politics as many others, but he was a distinguished educator in Philadelphia who had studied at Yale. Bassett was appointed to Haiti by President Ulysses Grant in 1869 and served through 1877, the longest serving diplomat between Reconstruction and 1900 (Logan and Winston 1982; Miller 1978).

Others, however, were far more likely to be activists in the Republican Party and to have been active in political movements such as abolition prior to the Civil War. Many had also held formal political positions in state and local politics. In other words, they were seasoned politicians and community leaders with significant experience. J. Milton Turner, the second ambassador and the first Black appointed to Liberia (1871), was deeply engaged with Republican politics and helped mobilize the Black vote (Morrison 2002). President Lincoln first appointed Henry McNeal Turner, a clergyman and educator, as a military chaplain. He later served as an official in the Freedmen's Bureau and exerted himself in Republican politics as a proponent of the colonization movement to repatriate African Americans to Africa (Logan and Winston 1982). Another clergyman and a man of extensive international experience, Henry Highland Garnet, served as a diplomat in Liberia. John Langston, of Virginia, was a distinguished educator and lawyer who served in the Freedmen's Bureau and later as ambassador to Haiti. Some widely known members of Congress and former Confederate state-level politicians were tapped for federal service when their local careers were terminated by the end of Reconstruction. Blanche Bruce and John Lynch, from Mississippi, and P. B. S. Pinchback, the flamboyant governor and lieutenant governor of Louisiana, received federal patronage appointments after 1876 (Logan 1976).

Blacks in State-Level Offices

The largest number of African American office holders, electoral and appointive, served at the state level. Here again, however, their numbers were hardly proportional to the size of the African American population, and their postwar service was brief. The great majority of the representation by Blacks, as at the federal level, occurred early and in the legislative realm. As noted earlier, more than 250 delegates served on the conventions that produced new constitutions in the entire former Confederacy. However, the state legislatures offered a larger number of opportunities and the largest number of Black elected officials held such positions—which were among the highest state offices available. In the combined upper and lower houses, they held a total of 795 posts.

In the executive offices Blacks also occupied a fair number of positions but never gained long-term control of the most important executive office of governor (see Table 5.5). The closest they came to controlling the executive office was the slightly more than a month-long interval when Louisiana Lieutenant Governor P. B. S. Pinchback seized control of the governorship. Five other African Americans also served as lieutenant governors. Among the cabinet bureaus in the states, Blacks held several significant posts. They were most successful in capturing the position of secretary of state, with nine Black incumbents, an office that among other things conducted elections and administered some state lands. Four Blacks held the post of superintendent of education, a position of strategic importance in structuring a system of public schools, and two held the office of state treasurer. Because of the early role of the military in Reconstruction, a sizable number of African Americans (sixty) were service officers. The smattering of judicial offices held was minuscule and largely insignificant, except for a lone supreme court justice in South Carolina. Louisiana's four state-level executive officers occupied the highest positions, while Mississippi and South Carolina had the greatest scope of Black leadership in the various executive, cabinet, and legislative positions. (Both Mississippi and South Carolina had two Black Speakers of the House.)

Less is known about positions at the county, municipal, and town levels. There was significant representation here as well, but rarely at the level of domination in local and municipal governments seen in the post–civil rights mobilization period in the 1970s. However, as in the later period many of the electoral positions were at the level of city and county councillors, educational posts, various commissioners, magistrates, clerks and registrars, and law enforcers. Table 5.5 includes a selection of the most frequently occupied positions at these levels. The largest numbers of local offices won by Blacks were city council and county commissioner posts (259), followed closely by

TABLE 5.5   Selected State and Local Political Offices Held by Blacks during Reconstruction in the South

Position	Number
State Level	
Legislative	1,063
Constitutional Convention	268
Senate	112
House of Representatives	683
Military	60
Executive	25
Governor	1
Lieutenant Governor	4
Secretary of State	9
State Commissioner	5
Superintendent of Education	4
Treasurer	2
Judiciary	1
Local Level	
Local Total	828
City/County Commissioner	259
Judicial	244
Law Enforcement	159
Education	93
Clerk	68
Mayor	5

SOURCE: Adapted from Foner 1996.

low-level justices of the peace (244 magistrates). Another 159 were in law enforcement, and 93 were in the highly sought education positions. Only five Blacks are known to have served as municipal or town mayors, which suggests that the ability of elected officials to influence small-town, grassroots government was severely circumscribed.

Political Participation from Post-Reconstruction to the Great Migration

The combination of forces that congealed to end the Reconstruction of the South effectively short-circuited the march toward universal freedom on which African Americans had embarked after the Civil

War. The forces were national in scope and represented the same degree of commitment that had "saved the Union" from slavery. The
ruling coalition of the Republican Party remained for the most part
intact, but it yielded to the pressures from southern allies to remove
the federal militia. At the same time, nationwide skepticism and ambivalence about the actual implementation of full citizenship rights
for Blacks militated against affirmative protection for these new citizens. As a result, a broad program of informal and formal disfranchisement was set in motion across the region. The election of
African Americans to office was greatly curtailed as their voting constituencies shrank, and their patronage positions dropped almost to
nil. The decline already noted in the number of Black congressional
representatives after 1876 was merely symptomatic of what was occurring at the local levels.

Among the measures that developed to virtually disfranchise
African Americans were political realignments, a laissez-faire attitude
toward white southern violations of law, judicial reinterpretation of
civil rights laws, the use of violence and terror against Blacks, and ultimately the overturn of the Reconstruction constitutions. The new
political realignment saw Republican presidents lose their partisan
base in the South with the rehabilitation of the Confederate leadership. The region became the "Solid South" as the Democratic Party
forced out Republican partisans.

Fusion Politics and Supreme Court Complicity in
Southern Resurgence

One of their tactics was "fusion" politics, whereby many Blacks previously identified with the Republican Party were forced into alliances with the Democrats to preserve their modest positions. Some
of the congressmen who remained in Washington or in the state delegations after 1876 reflected the residuum of participation that remained. But often the alliances were sustained with the perpetration
of extreme duress and violence; other times threats of violence and
intimidation were used for a still largely economically dependent
population. Racialized codes of conduct, buttressed with the most extreme social segregation the region had ever experienced, came to be
the order of the day. In spite of this, successive presidents and national leaders maintained a hands-off attitude. In some quarters it
was designed to curry favor with white southerners, but as often it re-

flected a skepticism about the equality of African Americans, despite acceptance of their membership in the republic.

The Supreme Court became an early partner in the disfranchisement when it declared several important civil rights enforcement statutes unconstitutional. At the same time, the Court began to interpret the broadest of the three Reconstruction amendments, the Fourteenth, as applicable only at the federal and not the state level. This gave the southern states full license to rewrite their constitutions to legally remove African American rights. By 1890 this process of revision was well under way, and these efforts, too, were legally sanctioned when the Supreme Court agreed in *Plessy v Ferguson* that state restrictions segregating Blacks were constitutionally permissible so long as the segregated facilities were equal to those for whites. It mattered little that actual equality in institutions was nowhere present or that in the absence of separate institutions Blacks often had no access at all.

The Emergence of the Race Spokesperson as "Informal" Leader

The impact these developments had on formal office holding was dramatic. After 1876 the number of Black congressional representatives in Washington dropped by half, and after 1890 it dropped by three-fourths. Only two congressmen served after the *Plessy* decision in 1896; the last one finished service in 1901. In executive positions, although some Blacks received appointments, most were removed from their patronage jobs in the South. Indeed, partisan affiliation with the Republican Party in the South was virtually barred, forcing Blacks to carry on partisan activity in a new but segregated party, the Black and Tans (Walton 1972).

These reductions in the numbers of African American office holders had the effect of placing a premium on the informal spokesman as leader in the Black community, which remained a fact of life until the mass mobilization that succeeded the next major realignment of the political parties in the 1930s. Since Blacks were barred from seeking office and from voting, it was left to the selection of prominent figures whose ideas or visibility received attention from white political leaders and served as the conduit for whatever allocations were made to this "subcommunity." As the partisan leadership of Blacks attached to the Republican Party during Reconstruction left the scene, the most prominent informal leader to fill this vacuum was Booker T. Washington.

The Role of Booker T. Washington

The stock in trade of the informal leader was the ability to acquire influence on the strength of relationships with those who had power. Since formal leadership posts were now barred to Blacks, the successful African American notable had to strike an acceptable balance with would-be patrons in the power hierarchy. When this balance was struck, the notable could become a race spokesman and the conduit for whatever benefits were dispensed to African American citizens. Booker T. Washington mastered this new social order with consummate skill. He appeared to accept the disfranchisement of African Americans on the grounds that they were not ready to assume full equality and that they should accept a service role in vocational and agricultural production, from which economic self-sufficiency would develop. After verbalizing this approach in a widely disseminated 1895 speech (Washington 1967), he gained great favor with white political and philanthropic leaders. Washington became the primary race spokesman, and his views were sought and his racial projects received support until his death in 1915.

Booker T. Washington's leadership stretched across the full spectrum of African American life. He was born into slavery in 1856 but successfully worked his way through college after emancipation. He began his public career with leadership of the Tuskegee Institute, a vocational and industrial institution that became a laboratory for the implementation of Washington's vocational ideas for Blacks. Tuskegee subsequently became the model of accommodation and generated a broad range of contacts and financial support for the institution and beyond. The college became well endowed when philanthropists answered Washington's call for financial support. Its prominence was further strengthened when President McKinley visited the campus. In the process, Washington was also currying favor in his local environment. Harlan quotes him as follows: "'Any movement for the elevation of the southern Negro, in order to be successful, must have to a certain extent the cooperation of the southern whites.' After all, they controlled the government and the property, and 'whatever benefits the black man benefits the white man'" (Harlan 1972, 160).

Soon Washington, the nonelected race spokesman, was advising presidents, corporate leaders, and practically all other significant wielders of power in the country. His influence with presidents far exceeded that of any previous African American leader, formal or informal; he advised Cleveland, McKinley, Roosevelt, and Taft. The tremendous power he enjoyed also provided him vast control over the opportunities for many local African American spokesmen. They often emulated him in their local initiatives and sought his intervention in their solicitations to government and philanthropists. In effect he became their conduit, dispensing such benefits as were available in an environment where accommodation was a necessity. Until the turn of the century, by which time the new social order was fully institutionalized, Washington had few competitors in his ability to influence national race policy, despite widespread objections among African Americans to his accommodationist approach. Still, Washington had very little influence on the ever-escalating scope of the political disfranchisement of Blacks, especially in the South, where most of them continued to live.

W.E.B. DuBois's Alternative Model: NAACP Protest Leadership

Although Washington was a dominant figure until his death, a dormant alternative model began to reassert itself just after the turn of the century. When W.E.B. DuBois and a coalition of social activists met to form the Niagara Movement (Lewis 1993), they represented a long tradition of opposition to the racialized order. Theirs was a movement based on an interpretation of the American liberal tradition as espousing equality among the races. They opposed segregation and the accompanying political disfranchisement, and they directly opposed Booker T. Washington, whom they saw as their chief nemesis. Eventually the Niagara Movement evolved into the National Association for the Advancement of Colored People (NAACP), which became the principal organized opposition to the status quo.

The NAACP immediately identified its fundamental purposes as the political enfranchisement of African Americans and the destruction of legalized segregation. From the outset it was an interracial coalition that attracted a collection of African American and white activists—scholars, religious faithful, philanthropists, and some socialists. While organizing chapters across the country, the movement quickly developed lobbying and legalism as strategies for challenging disfranchisement and segregation (McNeil 1983).

These efforts came to supplant the leader-spokesman whose success depended on attachment to white patrons. The oppositional stance of this movement in effect obviated any role for accommodation. As such it was not an acceptable channel for the delivery of benefits to the African American subcommunity. Its course of action invariably involved creating pressure on political leaders to the end of support for integration, or filing legal challenges. As early as 1915, the organization began to chip away at the armor of segregation when it assisted in overturning the infamous "grandfather clause" (*Guinn v. United States* 1915) that restricted the franchise. These tactics proceeded slowly, sometimes succeeding, until additional opportunities were created with the realignment of the ruling coalition in the late 1930s.

The NAACP's lobbying and legal challenges also created an environment in which other voices, some oppositional, could be heard. Perhaps the earliest of these voices were from the urban, central cities of the North, to which a Black migration had been under way since about 1890. As segregation and terror rose in the South and industrialization expanded in the North, Blacks moved northward. By 1929 they had already congregated in sufficient numbers in central Chicago to elect the first northern Black congressman in history. As they remained largely aligned with the Republican Party, Oscar DePriest was elected from that party. However, he was to be the last for many years after he was defeated by Arthur Mitchell, an African American Democrat, in 1935 (Cayton 1964). By the time Detroit elected its first African American to Congress in 1955, the shift to the Democratic Party was virtually complete.

But these partisan politicians also shared the stage with several oppositional spokesmen who made radical critiques of the American racial situation. Marcus Garvey, a Jamaican who moved to New York, organized a nationalist campaign that resurrected the idea of repatriation to Africa. Garvey argued that salvation for Blacks lay in their developing a solid foundation in the African homeland, based on cultural affinities (Cronon 1955). In his opposition to the racial status quo, he, too, acquired a significant voice as a spokesman for the race in this period of widespread disfranchisement. A. Philip Randolph was another oppositional voice whose radical critique of the social order was in many ways consistent with a socialist thesis (Quarles 1982). He was a labor organizer and leader who focused on the need for redistribution of resources and power, thereby also rejecting the racial status quo. His efforts, like Garvey's, were devoted to mobilizing a mass movement, although unlike Garvey, his focus was on the United States. He proposed the first mass march on Washington, a threat that generated the first direct civil rights action from a sitting president since Reconstruction. President Franklin Roosevelt issued an executive order creating the Federal Employment Practices Commission (FEPC) guaranteeing Blacks access to federal employment (Kryder 2000).

The Great Migration and Party Realignment

African Americans began to move from the South after the formal institutionalization of disfranchisement that the *Plessy* decision endorsed. It was not long before a realignment of political forces in the country allowed new opportunities for this population on the move. The movement began just after 1890 and had become quite visible by 1910. In that year, for the first time, less than 90 percent of the Black population lived in the South. By 1920, Blacks were departing the South in large numbers. Their numbers continued to decline in the South, from some 85 percent in 1920 to the lowest point of 53 percent in 1970. Their destination was the North, with its promise of a less harsh system of segregation and greater opportunities for social, economic, and political participation. There they concentrated in central cities—ironically, in light of the promise, in quite rigidly segregated residential enclaves (Taeuber and Taeuber 1969). These enclaves, later essentially ghettoes, nevertheless became the foundations for political participation in this region where the franchise was not restricted. They were able to capture space in the national political party realignment in the early 1930s, when the Democratic Party was in the ascendancy.

With the nation in an economic depression and with a major international conflict looming, African Americans who had been anchored in the Republican Party began to find appeal in the "new" Democratic Party of the Roosevelt administration. The greatest opportunities for their political involvement, however, were largely limited to the North—where a formally franchised black constituency was now developing. As early as 1936 it seems a majority of these voters were casting ballots for the Democratic Party. For example, all of the following cities voted Republican in the 1932 presidential election but had shifted to the Democratic column by 1936: Detroit (75 percent), Baltimore (55 percent), and Chicago (49 percent). By 1948,

56 percent of Black voters nationally identified with the Democratic Party (Walton and Smith 2000, 138).

The Democratic Party organization created some incentives to attract this new constituency. Aside from the modest efforts in the New Deal, Roosevelt yielded to pressure from an urban-based mobilization movement led by the Black union organizer A. Philip Randolph, leading to the establishment of the FEPC to monitor the desegregation of the federal employment sector (Kryder 2000). This was soon followed by similar and more far-reaching executive orders by President Harry Truman in the interest of civil rights defined in terms of desegregation in the federal and military services.

The combination of an increasingly mobilized and important African American constituency led the Democratic Party in 1948 to put its first civil rights plank into a convention platform. This move, engineered by Hubert Humphrey, of Minnesota, significantly alienated the party's remaining southern white membership. They walked out of the convention and started an effort to establish a third party, the Dixiecrats. However, by the 1960 election, Black voting strength in the Democratic Party was sufficient to determine much of the direction of a civil rights agenda. The migration coupled with this political realignment lay the foundation that ultimately generated a complete reversal of the political fortunes of African Americans in both the North and the South. The changes evolved slowly over the next thirty years to provide a second great flowering of formal African American participation.

Pre–Civil Rights African American Officeholders

The opportunities presented by this urban, northern context reversed the long drought of Black office holders and appointees. The renewal, however, was limited to the northern central cities, where the migrant population congregated, and the early success occurred principally at the local levels. The southern migrants, in their racially segregated enclaves, wasted little time in registering to vote, and they gained considerable experience in various local positions before gaining success at the national level. Between 1910 and 1915 they sought offices in local wards and at the state level. The states of Illinois, Michigan, New York, and Pennsylvania were among the first where "Black" wards and districts elected Black aldermen, city councilmen, various county board representatives, and state legislators.

An early comprehensive study of Chicago is illustrative of how African Americans fared in winning offices and other public positions. Blacks had held at least a single seat in the Illinois legislative House since 1876. Only in 1914 with the increased migrant population did they achieve a second seat. Four years later, in 1918, they had three seats, and six years after that, in 1924, four seats in the House and one in the Senate. Legislative representation by Blacks never again fell below that number. Black candidates were also enjoying success at the city council level. Meanwhile, a relatively significant, if not representative, number of them were serving in bureaucratic positions. Among them 16 percent had jobs in the postal service, 3 percent were in low-level public safety positions as sheriffs or marshals, and a similar proportion were lawyers, judges, or magistrates (Gosnell 1935, 375).

Some of the other major cities saw a similar, if less extensive, development of Black leadership. As in Chicago, those who were first elected to these positions became the strongest leaders of the community, organizing their wards and earning favor for sponsorship in, first, the Republican Party and, later, the Democratic Party. Indeed, as elaborated below, all of them soon aspired to and attained election to national offices, usually Congress.

Urban Black Voters Send Their Own to Congress

The earliest and most successful political activity occurred in Chicago. The growth in the migrant population there, as in other northern cities, started slowly. Blacks constituted just over 1 percent of the Chicago population in 1880, and this figure had changed little by 1890. But by 1900 the proportion had almost doubled, and by 1930 it had leaped to almost 7 percent. The importance of this relatively small proportion of the population was magnified by its concentration in a small, machine-dominated, ward-based city (Pinderhughes 1987). By 1910 African Americans were a quarter of the population in two wards (wards 2 and 3), providing them significant potential leverage in electoral politics. They elected their first alderman, Oscar DePriest, in 1915 (Gosnell 1935, 75). In just ten years, Blacks were a majority in ward 2 (70 percent), and in another ten years they claimed an almost equally large majority of ward 3 (Pinderhughes 1987, 82).

It was on the strength of this politically active and highly concentrated migrant population that the drought of electoral representation for Blacks in Congress ended. Oscar DePriest, by now an experienced local politician, won the First District seat to Congress from Chicago. He did so on the Republican ticket, reflecting the continuing affiliation of the African American population with the Party of Lincoln.

Black Political Realignment: Democratic Party Identification

The northern urban electorates were effectively leading a transformation of the Democratic Party in the North. As the concentration of African American voters in these cities grew, it could easily be discerned that their support for the Democrats would form a critical part of the partisan coalition needed to assure victory against the Republicans in the North. By the 1948 election, the edge that Black partisan Democrats brought was evident in key cities. Blacks were rapidly developing into a one-party Democratic faction in their concentrated urban enclaves. In Detroit, Chicago, New York City, and St. Louis, African Americans gave over 70 percent of their votes to the Democratic Party that year. Black votes for the party increased in the 1952 election, but dropped slightly in 1956. In short, well before the mobilization in the South effectively brought Black voters in that region into the Democratic fold, their urban counterparts in the North had already overwhelmingly made the shift (Glantz 1967, 350).

The realignment of the two major parties that harnessed the shift in African American partisan identification is most readily seen in Chicago politics, which elected a Black congressman, Oscar DePriest, in 1929. That district elected only Black candidates to Congress from then on, but the partisan affiliation of the representatives changed from Republican to Democratic after DePriest was defeated by Arthur Mitchell in 1935. DePriest was the last Black Republican to serve in Congress until 1967, when Edward Brooke, of Massachusetts, was elected to the Senate. No other Black Republican served in the House until 1995, when J. C. Watts was elected from Oklahoma. Meanwhile, Blacks in Chicago have successively elected congressmen from this district ever since, and they have all been Democrats since 1935.

The same pattern of migration and residential concentration had a similar outcome in other major cities in the Midwest and the Northeast starting in the mid-1940s. The New York City urban enclave of Harlem elected Adam Clayton Powell Jr. in 1945. He joined Chicago's representative at the time, William Dawson, marking the first time since 1891 that multiple Blacks served in Congress. Charles Diggs, from Detroit, and Robert Nix, from Philadelphia, joined them in 1955 and 1958, respectively (Wilson 1960). These were all cities where the African American migrants congregated, electing one of their own as soon as their numbers were sufficient to control the majority of votes in a congressional district. And after DePriest left Congress in 1935, all of these representatives were members of the Democratic Party. Many had acquired considerable experience in local and state political offices and in routine work within the local Democratic Party organizations.

Adam Clayton Powell Jr. was an exception to this pattern of partisan affiliation. In the more complex political landscape of New York City, he took advantage of the broad range of options beyond the standard two parties elsewhere in the country. Indeed, he appeared intent on not affiliating with one of the two main parties. He was elected to the city council in 1941 and was regarded as an adherent of both the Fusion Party and the American Labor Party. Despite his more eclectic partisan path to national politics when he arrived in Congress in 1945, he too did so as a Democrat (Hamilton 1991).

The Civil Rights Movement, the New Democratic Coalition, and Judicial Activism

The success of African American politicians in the North was soon followed by a combination of forces that challenged the continued disfranchisement of Blacks in the South. The stirrings unleashed by A. Philip Randolph's march on Washington movement, the solid African American partisan affiliation with the Democratic Party, and increased NAACP successes before the Supreme Court led to a mass mobilization of Blacks in the South. The greatest symbol of the mobilization was Martin Luther King Jr., who through the SCLC helped coalesce a broad range of political interest groups and coordinate protest demonstrations, boycotts, and other actions. His leadership of the Montgomery bus boycott was merely the prelude to a much broader protest campaign that had spread to virtually every southern state by the time of his death in 1968 (Lewis 1970).

King and his foot soldiers were often pushing limits that had been opened up with successful NAACP challenges to disfranchisement and segregation. Perhaps the most notable political shifts in this regard resulted from two Supreme Court decisions: *Smith v. Allwright* (1944) and *Brown v. Board of Education of Topeka, Kansas* (1954).

The *Allwright* decision overturned the infamous "white primary" that barred Blacks who could vote from doing so in the Democratic primary election, the only one that mattered in the one-party South (Hine 1979). This restoration of the franchise to Blacks was further strengthened two decades later by the Court's reiteration of voter equality in *Baker v. Carr* (1962). In this decision the Court reaffirmed the requirement of decennial legislative reapportionment, undermining the rural domination of state legislatures. The decision's effect was to distribute legislative districts more equally to urban areas, where by now most Blacks lived. The Court went even further in *Wesberry v. Sanders* and *Reynolds v. Sims* (1965) and established the "one man, one vote" principle for legislative apportionment that significantly reduced racial gerrymandering, especially in the South. This paved the way for the Court, in *White v. Regester* (1973), to disqualify a variety of tactics used by the states to dilute the vote of residentially segregated racial and ethnic community groups. This trajectory of Supreme Court support for racially compact districts that guaranteed the election of Black and other minority candidates remained in force until 1980. Then the direction shifted significantly in *City of Mobile, Alabama v. Bolden* (1980), when the Court set a higher standard for discrimination in legislative apportionment. This new direction was strengthened in several succeeding cases, such as *Thornburg v. Gingles* (1986) and *Shaw v. Reno* (1993).

The Supreme Court Demolishes Separate but Equal

The *Brown v. Board of Education* decision similarly dealt a death blow to segregation when the system was declared inherently unequal. Over the three decades that followed, the Court continued to refine this decision as it worked out means for the full desegregation of public schools in the South. Although it got off to a slow start, the Court eventually decided a number of related school cases and virtually oversaw the implementation of those decisions. As schools districts resorted to a number of stalling tactics to prevent desegregation, the Court appointed its own "masters" to devise the strategies for implementation. Perhaps one of the most interventionist Court-mandated policies was that requiring the busing of students to achieve racial balance in the school population (*Swann v. Charlotte-Mecklenburg Board of Education* 1971). This path remained solid until the 1990s. In *Board of Oklahoma City v. Dowell* (1991), the Supreme Court revised its activist role in favor of citizen control over public school desegregation policy.

Meanwhile, by 1960 the Democratic Party coalition was fundamentally reconstituted. Not only did the party claim the overwhelming majority of Black voters, it also presented a platform that directly articulated a civil rights program. This development led to the passage of landmark legislation, especially the Civil Rights Act of 1964 and the Voting Rights Act of 1965, which transformed the formal political status of African Americans in the South, where the majority of the population still resided. Paralleling the *Brown* and *Allwright* decisions of the Supreme Court, the Civil Rights Act of 1964 tackled segregation of public accommodations, and the Voting Rights Act tackled disfranchisement.

The Restoration of the African American Franchise in the South

This African American civil rights insurgency (McAdam 1982), and the acquisition of institutional political capital led to swift national changes. The Civil Rights Act of 1964 and the Voting Rights Act of 1965 were the most significant legislation in the restoration of the franchise to African Americans, restoring their opportunities for formal representation in government. The 1964 statute generally authorized the U.S. attorney general to use the power of law to do away with many of the Jim Crow barriers to the free exercise of basic African American civil rights. The Voting Rights Act specifically targeted the franchise. It required the states to enroll Black citizens or to be subjected to the use of federal registrars to do so. The state of South Carolina challenged the constitutionality of the act on the grounds that it was an unwarranted exercise of Section 2 of the Fifteenth Amendment, which granted Congress the power to enforce the amendment. The Supreme Court, however, found the act to be "a valid means for carrying out the commands of the Fifteenth Amendment" (*South Carolina v. Katzenbach* 1966). Subsequently many of the states in which continuing barriers to Black registration were found were forced to accept federal registrars, whose work helped to completely alter the southern political landscape.

Despite the negative reaction toward the passage of the Voting Rights Act of 1965, its positive effect on African American participation in politics was dramatic. For example, in 1940, only 140,000 Blacks were registered to vote in the South, a mere 3 percent of those eligible in the region. By 1960 the figure had risen to almost 1.5 million (28 percent), and a year after the passage of the Voting Rights

Act, the figure had taken the dramatic leap to almost 3 million (58 percent of eligible voters) (Jaynes and Williams 1989, 233). In the first year after the passage of the act, the proportion of registered Black voters in Mississippi, perhaps the most egregious case of disfranchisement, increased from nearly 7 percent to almost 60 percent (see chapter 4). In addition, overall Black voter participation dramatically increased nationally, with almost half of the new participants being southerners. Whereas less than 4 million Blacks voted in 1964, more than 10 million did so in 1984 (Scheb and Stephens 1998).

Post–Voting Rights Act Office Holding: A Census

Since the Voting Rights Act of 1965, the numbers of Blacks elected to political offices have risen at a phenomenal rate, even though they remain disproportionate to the size of the population. Yet these numbers have far exceeded those of the Reconstruction era. In the entire Reconstruction period, there were just over 1,500 elected officers. The Joint Center for Political and Economic Studies (1976) reports that in 1970, five years after the Voting Rights Act of 1965, the total number of Black elected officials serving that year was 1,469. The states with the most elected Black officials in that year were California (105), Michigan (110), and Ohio (89). At the same time, the participation of women in 1970, which was minuscule during Reconstruction, accounted for 160 of these offices (10.9 percent).

Several southern states also had a significant number of Black elected officials in 1970, although the region had not yet become dominant. At this time, Alabama led all southern states with 86 Black elected officials; Mississippi had 81, Louisiana had 64, and North Carolina had 62. But the rates of Blacks being elected in this region were growing so rapidly that it was only a matter of time before the South would produce the greatest number of Black elected officials of any region. Indeed, by 1988 the region claimed more than 65 percent of Black elected officials.

As detailed in Table 5.6, the total number of Black elected officials has increased notably every year since 1970. In 1975, for example, ten years after the passage of the Voting Rights Act, there were 3,503—an increase of 139 percent over the number for 1970. By 2000, the total number had reached 9,040, a sixfold increase since 1970.

Meanwhile the success of Black women in winning elections has been equally dramatic. Since 1970 their representation in elective offices has risen in every year except 1972 (6.8 percent). Moreover,

TABLE 5.6   Number of Black Elected Officials, by Gender, 1970–2000

Year	Total	Male	Female Number	Female Percent of Total
1970	1,469	1,309	160	10.9
1971	1,860	163	225	12.1
1972	2,264	2,111	153	6.8
1973	2,621	2,276	345	13.2
1974	2,991	2,575	416	13.9
1975	3,503	2,973	530	15.1
1976	3,979	3,295	684	17.2
1977	4,311	3,529	782	18.1
1978	4,503	3,660	843	18.7
1979	4,607	3,725	882	19.1
1980	4,912	3,936	976	19.9
1981	5,038	4,017	1,021	20.3
1982	5,160	4,079	1,081	20.9
1983	5,605	4,383	1,223	21.8
1984	5,700	4,441	1,259	22.1
1985	6,056	4,697	1,359	22.4
1986	6,424	4,942	1,482	23.1
1987	6,681	5,117	1,564	23.4
1988	6,829	5,204	1,625	23.8
1989	7,226	5,412	1,814	25.1
1990	7,370	5,420	1,950	26.5
1991	7,480	5,427	2,053	27.4
1992	7,552	5,431	2,121	28.1
1993	8,015	5,683	2,332	29.1
1994	8,162	5,694	2,468	30.2
1995	8,419	5,782	2,637	31.3
1996	8,579	5,830	2,749	32.0
1997	8,656	5,847	2,809	32.5
1998	8,868	5,944	2,924	33.0
1999	8,936	5,939	2,997	33.5
2000	9,040	5,921	3,119	34.5

SOURCE: Joint Center for Political and Economic Studies 2000 (www.jointcenter.org). Reprinted with permission.

their proportion has exceeded the 10 percent figure in 1970 in all years but one since then. After ten years it reached 20 percent, and currently women occupy just over a third of all elective offices. Despite these growth rates for women, men continue to hold a disproportionate number of the offices.

Varieties of Electoral Positions Held

The range of offices that African Americans hold is broad. By 1997, with the exception of president, they had held virtually every executive, judicial, and legislative position at all levels in the federal system (see Table 5.7). Moreover, by 1984, African Americans had twice stood for the office of president—Shirley Chisholm in 1972 and Jesse Jackson in 1984. By 1993 two African Americans had served as senators—Brooke in 1967 and Moseley-Braun in 1993; and in 1989 Douglas Wilder, of Virginia, became the first African American elected governor to fill a complete term.

Congressional Representation after 1965

Just before passage of the Voting Rights Act of 1965, there was a small contingent of African American congressmen, all from the North: Representatives Arthur W. Mitchell, William L. Dawson, Adam Clayton Powell Jr., Charles C. Diggs Jr., Robert N. C. Nix, and Augustus F. Hawkins. The presence of these six congressmen at the same time reflected the greatest flowering of African American representation at this level since Reconstruction. They constituted a preface to the mobilization that would greatly increase the number of Black representatives largely as a result of passage of the Voting Rights Act. Although soon the first representatives from the South would increase their numbers, the greatest wave for a time remained from the urban enclaves where the migrant population was concentrated in the North. In 1971, the House of Representatives had thirteen Black members from seven northern and two border states. Three of the first states to have Black representatives since Reconstruction now each had more than one. Illinois had three, William Dawson, George Collins, and Ralph Metcalf; Michigan had two, Charles Diggs and John Conyers Jr.; and New York had two, Shirley Chisholm and Charles Rangel. The long-serving Robert Nix, from Pennsylvania, remained in office. California now joined this group of early states, with two Black representatives, Ronald Dellums and Augustus Hawkins. Ohio elected Louis Stokes, Maryland elected Parren Mitchell, and Missouri elected William Clay Sr. In addition, Walter Fauntroy served as the nonvoting delegate from the District of Columbia.

TABLE 5.7   African American Elected Officials, by Position, 1997

Position	Number
Federal	40
State	586
Substate/Regional	18[a]
County	937
Municipal	4115
Judicial	996
Education	1962

[a] Most of these are in the U.S. Virgin Islands.
SOURCE: Adapted from Bositis 1998. Reprinted with permission from the Joint Center for Political and Economic Studies.

The Congressional Black Caucus

This group represented something of a critical mass that allowed the delegation of African Americans in the House to organize. The Black representatives had first come together in 1968 to form an informal organization that evolved into the Democratic Select Committee. Charles Diggs, as the most senior member present, assumed leadership of the group (Barnett 1982). On February 2, 1971, the group formally organized a caucus. At the suggestion of Rangel, it became known as the Congressional Black Caucus. Diggs was selected as its first chairman. The group sought to make a positive impact on the political processes affecting African Americans, and to work for equality of persons of African heritage in the domestic and foreign policy sectors (Clay 1992). In short, the congressmen designed the Congressional Black Caucus for the advancement of agendas to protect the civil and welfare rights of people of color, and specifically those of their African American constituents. They anticipated correctly that their numbers would only increase with the now enfranchised and highly mobilized Black voting population in the South.

The First Southern African American Congressmembers since Reconstruction

The impact of the Voting Rights Act on the enfranchisement of southern Blacks was soon sufficient to elect the first representatives from this region since Reconstruction. They, like their northern counterparts, won election first from populous urban centers with concentrated Black populations. Andrew Young was elected from Atlanta and Barbara Jordan from Houston in 1973. Other southern states soon followed: Tennessee in 1975, Virginia in 1979, Mississippi in 1987, Louisiana in 1991, and Florida, North Carolina, South Carolina, and Alabama in 1993. Among the deep South states, only Arkansas has not had a Black representative in this period.

Since the passage of the Voting Rights Act of 1965, eighty-three African Americans have been elected as members and delegates to Congress—eighty-one in the House of Representatives and two in the Senate (see Table 5.8). Of these, only five, all in the House, held office before passage of the 1965 act. One other House member was elected in 1965. Since 1965 the number in the House has risen significantly. In 2001, the number of Black members of Congress stood at thirty-nine, with one serving as a delegate from the District of Columbia and two from the Virgin Islands. Of these, only thirteen were elected from districts that did not have a majority-Black voting-age population. This raises the question of whether it is necessary for Blacks to constitute a majority of a district before a Black can win (Barker et al. 1999). Perhaps the difficulty in winning places in the Senate helps to answer the question. In the post–Voting Rights Act era, only two Black senators have served thus far.

Black Municipal Leaders

Urban areas in the United States have become the single most important venue for the development of local Black leadership. Opportunities for leadership at the local levels was also enhanced by the passage of the Voting Rights Act of 1965, which led to an increase in Black voter registration not just in the South but all across the country (Barker et al. 1999). The early success in winning the top municipal post as mayor occurred in both the North and the South about the same time. In 1967 Carl Stokes of Cleveland became the first African American mayor of a major American city (its 1960 population was about 900,000). On the same day, the industrial city of Gary, Indiana, elected Richard Hatcher mayor (1960 population, 175,000). Both of these cities had taken in large numbers of Black migrants from the South. These migrants had over time aligned themselves almost exclusively with the Democratic Party, which became the base for launching Black candidates (Nelson and Meranto 1977). And as the civil rights mobilization led to political mobilization, the racially

TABLE 5.8   African American Membership in Congress after Enactment of the Voting Rights Act of 1965

Name (Party Affiliation and State)	Dates of Service
Senate	
Edward W. Brooke (R–MA)	1967–79
Carol Moseley-Braun (D–IL)	1993–98
House of Representatives	
William L. Dawson (Independent–IL)	1943–70
Adam Clayton Powell Jr. (D–NY)	1945–67, 1969–71
Charles C. Diggs Jr. (D–MI)	1955–80
Robert N. C. Nix (D–PA)	1958–78
Augustus F. Hawkins (D–CA)	1963–90
John Conyers Jr. (D–MI)	1965–present
William L. Clay Sr. (D–MO)	1969–2000
Louis Stokes (D–OH)	1969–98
Shirley Chisholm (D–NY)	1969–82
George W. Collins (D–IL)	1970–72
Ronald V. Dellums (D–CA)	1971–98
William Jefferson (D–LA)	1991–present
Ralph H. Metcalfe (D–IL)	1971–78
Parren H. Mitchell (D–MD)	1971–86
Charles B. Rangel (D–NY)	1971–present
Walter E. Fauntroy (Delegate) (D–DC)	1971–90
Yvonne Brathwaite Burke (D–CA)	1973–79
Cardiss Collins (D–IL)	1973–96
Barbara Jordan (D–TX)	1973–78
Andrew Young (D–GA)	1973–77
Harold E. Ford (D–TN)	1975–96
Julian C. Dixon (D–CA)	1979–2000
William H. Gray III (D–PA)	1979–91
Mickey Leland (D–TX)	1979–89
Melvin Evans (Delegate) (R–VI)	1979–80
Bennett McVey Steward (D–IL)	1979–80
George W. Crockett (D–MI)	1980–90
Mervyn M. Dymally (D–CA)	1981–92
Gus Savage (D–IL)	1981–92
Harold Washington (D–IL)	1981–83
Katie Hall (D–IN)	1982–84
Major Owens (D–NY)	1983–present
Edolphus Towns (D–NY)	1983–present
Alan Wheat (D–MO)	1983–94
Charles Hayes (D–IL)	1983–92
Alton R. Waldon Jr. (D–NY)	1986–87
Mike Espy (D–MS)	1987–93
Floyd Flake (D–NY)	1987–97

(continues)

TABLE 5.8   *(continued)*

Name (Party Affiliation and State)	Dates of Service
John Lewis (D–GA)	1987–present
Kweisi Mfume (D–MD)	1987–95
Donald Payne (D–NJ)	1989–present
Craig A. Washington (D–TX)	1989–94
Barbara-Rose Collins (D–MI)	1991–96
Gary Franks (R–CT)	1991–96
Eleanor Holmes Norton (Delegate) (D–DC)	1991–present
William Jefferson (D–LA)	1991–present
Maxine Waters (D–CA)	1991–present
Lucien Blackwell (D–PA)	1991–94
Eva Clayton (D–NC)	1992–present
Sanford Bishop (D–GA)	1993–present
Corrine Brown (D–FL)	1993–present
Jim Clyburn (D–SC)	1993–present
Cleo Fields (D–LA)	1993–96
Alcee Hastings (D–FL)	1993–present
Earl Hilliard (D–AL)	1993–present
Eddie Bernice Johnson (D–TX)	1993–present
Cynthia McKinney (D–GA)	1993–present
Mel Reynolds (D–IL)	1993–95
Bobby Rush (D–IL)	1993–present
Bobby Scott (D–VA)	1993–present
Walter Tucker (D–CA)	1993–95
Mel Watt (D–NC)	1993–present
Albert Wynn (D–MD)	1993–present
Bennie Thompson (D–MS)	1993–present
Chaka Fattah (D–PA)	1995–present
Victor O. Frazer (Delegate) (D–VI)	1995–96
Sheila Jackson Lee (D–TX)	1995–present
Julius Caesar Watts (R–OK)	1995–present
Jesse Jackson Jr. (D–IL)	1995–present
Juanita Millender-McDonald (D–CA)	1996–present
Elijah Cummings (D–MD)	1996–present
Julia Carson (D–IN)	1997–present
Donna Christian-Christensen (Delegate) (D–VI)	1997–present
Danny K. Davis (D–IL)	1997–present
Harold Ford Jr. (D–TN)	1997–present
Carolyn Cheeks Kilpatrick (D–MI)	1997–present
Gregory Meeks (D–NY)	1998–present
Barbara Lee (D–CA)	1998–present
Stephanie Tubbs Jones (D–OH)	1999–present
William Clay Jr. (D–MO)	2001–present
Diane E. Watson (D–CA)	2001–present

SOURCE: Congressional Black Caucus.

segregated enclaves of Blacks began to elect their own. This started a trend in the North whereby majority or near-majority Black voting-age populations gained control of the mayoralty in central cities.

Meanwhile, two years later Charles Evers, of Mississippi, the brother of the slain NAACP field secretary, became mayor of the small town of Fayette (Morrison and Huang 1972). This ushered in a trend in the South that eventually outpaced what was occurring among Blacks in the North.

Unita Blackwell Incorporates and Administers Rural Mayersville, Mississippi

Mayersville is ... a dusty spot at the edge of a great river. It is typical of so many exceedingly small places in rural Mississippi, where scale and isolation combine to give an idyllic picture of calm parochialism. With its many weather worn houses and trails of dust across so many miles of cotton and soybean acres, Mayersville very much looks its part.

Contradictions abound.... The mid-town square is actually the seat of county government, with a courthouse and offices.... Mayersville is the largest town in the county (albeit an unincorporated one until 1976), with barely 500 inhabitants and a mere two stores.... [T]his idyllic setting was transformed in 1977. A black woman, Unita Blackwell, succeeded in getting the town incorporated, became its mayor, and subsequently became an international figure....

The mobilization in this town, ... related to the strategies of Martin Luther King, Jr. and the early student movement. It is in this context that the theory of heroic invention [applies to Unita Blackwell]. The isolation of the Mayersville black community (marked by apathy, fear, and complete disfranchisement) created a static situation that was more easily activated by a catalyzing symbol. Unita Blackwell used a creative, individual approach in cultivating and building on local organizations and unpublicized but generalized sentiments for change. She melded this with traditional American values as espoused by King and others. In seeking to mobilize her racially mobilized community, she could be creative, even daring because the community was in another sense inchoate—ripe, open, malleable.

For a long time, Mayersville appeared to languish. A black child could only look forward to a future on the farm that paralleled that of the parents. Mayor Unita Blackwell explained that her own life had been made up of cycles of hoeing and picking cotton. One either lived as a tenant, or hired oneself out on a daily basis to white plantation owners.

(continues)

(continued)

Mrs. Blackwell was born to poor, farming parents in Coahoma County, Mississippi. This delta country north of Issaquena is also on the Mississippi River, and has a similar history. Mrs. Blackwell and her sister (the only sibling) grew up in a home of integrity. Her mother, anxious for them to continue their school year uninterrupted by plantation chores, regularly sent them across the river to an aunt in Arkansas. Her father demonstrated equally strong if not uncommon convictions.... (He was said to reject the efforts of "white men to tell him what to do with his family.") ... The outcome was quite familiar—her father was required to leave by night because "they wanted to kill him."

[After much effort voter] registration was achieved. But not without frustration and not before Mrs. Blackwell was radicalized to invest all of her time in the effort for local mobilization. The experience ... catapulted her into a formal position as a SNCC worker and as a perpetual thorn in the side of Mississippi officials.... [As a result she] became unemployable at the only outlet for making a living—the cotton farms. Quite suddenly she had undertaken a level of commitment not unlike that for her [SNCC] student counterparts.

By associating herself with the only forces of change available [students], she dared to engage in activities unacceptable to the white power structure. (Most of those around her feared intimidation and violence from whites, though they agreed that social conditions were inadequate.) She accepted these challenges at a very early time in the movement when personal risks were greatest. When COFO [the Council of Federated Organizations] inaugurated its concentrated 1964 summer campaign, Mrs. Blackwell was thoroughly involved, locally and elsewhere.... In Mayersville she continued to move from house to house as a SNCC worker ... to convince blacks to register.

Little symbolizes or illustrates the heroic and inventive acts of Unita Blackwell in the Mayersville mobilization as the achievement of town incorporation. She achieved this ... in late 1976, and was thereupon appointed its first mayor. Before, Mrs. Blackwell says, Mayersville was just a "village" ... without a "personality," or any independent development or vision for the future. Nurturance of the town was not a concern of those who lived within its boundaries; indeed it had no boundaries.

[P]rior to the civil rights movement, County politicians saw little or no need to change this status. Their livelihood was based on farm ownership. Their decreased agricultural production was in fact encouraged [with] their economic shortfalls sustained by federal subsidies. Many of these farmers also did not live in the "village" proper; they lived in plantation houses in the outlying farms or in adjacent counties. Incorporation was [therefore] of no immediate concern to them, but would be of prime benefit to their former black laborers who did live in the village....

[She set about to attain incorporation, when others feared.]

The initial phases of the work required Mrs. Blackwell to talk with state officials and lawyers about the requirements for incorporation.... In short order she discovered that the process could only be set in motion on the basis of a formal referendum....

The trick was to politically educate the constituents so that the importance of the measure would be understood, and then to get them to a central meeting place for the vote. To do this "first I used the style I know best—this is to organize people [by] call[ing] a meeting. I called a meeting in the church ... [to which] everybody that showed up was black." At this meeting the virtues of achieving new status were explained and a consensus to go forward was reached. From this group she selected a team of eight people to do a house-to-house survey to verify the broader commitment of all citizens in Mayersville.

The house-to-house survey was organized around a "survey instrument" that Mrs. Blackwell and the group had prepared. It asked simply whether one wanted the town to be incorporated. This detailed work was required in order to guarantee the participation of at least two-thirds of those registered in the upcoming vote. The process ... was completed in two days, to the amazement of the lawyers who advised her.... It appears that all of this went rather smoothly, including the final vote. Indeed, it was a lone white [man] ... who refused to sign. His reasoning was that "he didn't know what he was signing and ... wasn't going to fool with it."...

[The campaign for incorporation was on, holding out the promise that] there would be a water system, sewers, and all the usual service items.

Mrs. Blackwell also had to spend considerable time demarcating boundaries and thinking about resource capabilities.... She enjoyed the services of black attorneys in nearby Greenville.... There were meetings with local farmers whose land within the new corporate limits would be taxed.... Afterward [she had] engineers and airplane surveyors [who] completed their task of setting boundaries.

In short order, the last meting to vote on the final decree was scheduled. It was here that all present, except one, signed the document after appointing an interim government. The crowning achievement for Mrs. Blackwell's leadership was her unanimous selection by the body to hold the office of mayor. Thus she became Mississippi's first black woman mayor that we can identify in history, and the first black mayor ever in Issaquena County. (Morrison 1987, 95–122)

TABLE 5.9   African American Mayors, by City Size and Region, 1976

City Size	Total Number	Total in South
100,000 +	8	2
50,000–99,000	8	2
25,000–49,000	11	3
15,000–24,999	8	4
5,000–14,999	19	10
Under 5,000	98	74
Total	**152**	**95**

SOURCE: Adapted from Joint Center for Political and Economic Studies, 1976, xxxv. Reprinted with permission.

The growth in success among African Americans at municipal leadership was rapid everywhere. By 1973 there were thirty-eight Black mayors in southern states, most in small towns with majority-Black populations (Voter Education Project 1973). By 1976, not quite ten years after Carl Stokes won the mayoralty in Cleveland, there were 152 African American mayors, some in the most populous and most prominent of cities. The most populous of these cities remained in the North, and most had majority or near-majority African American populations. The most populous at this time was Los Angeles, a city that in fact did not have a sizable African American population. Other cities with population over 100,000 that had a Black municipal head in 1976 included Detroit, Washington, D.C., Atlanta, Newark, Dayton, Gary, and Berkeley, California. Among these, only Atlanta and Washington could be considered southern. However, the vast majority of the mayors (117 or 77 percent) were located in cities and towns of less than 15,000 people, and 71 percent of those were located in the South (JCPS 1976), where the Voting Rights Act was having a huge impact (see Table 5.9).

The number of Blacks elected to the position of mayor has risen steadily since the late 1960s. Only three years after Gary and Cleveland elected Black mayors, forty-eight other municipalities had Black mayors. By 1973 the number had already more than tripled to 153. In the next seven years the pace slowed a bit, with 182 in 1980. However, by 1990 there were nearly seven times as many Black mayors as in 1970—313, and in 2000 there were 451 (Joint Center for Political Studies 2000).

It has already been observed that a majority of these municipalities are southern and that they have fairly small populations. Hence the fact remains that the most substantial number of Black people who are served by a Black mayor are in central cities, now in both the North and the South. Among cities of more than 50,000 where Blacks have won office, after Cleveland, Gary, and Washington, D.C. (Lyndon Johnson appointed Walter Washington the first mayor of the District), others followed: Kenneth Gibson of Newark was elected in 1970; Tom Bradley of Los Angeles, Maynard Jackson of Atlanta, and Coleman Young of Detroit were all elected in 1973; Ernest Morial of New Orleans was elected in 1977; and Richard Arrington of Birmingham in 1979. The pattern continued in the 1980s until virtually every major American city was or had been represented by an African American mayor: Harold Washington, Chicago (1983), W. Wilson Goode, Philadelphia (1983), Kurt Schmoke, Baltimore (1987), and David Dinkins, New York (1989). By 1998, there were forty Black mayors of cities with a population of 50,000 or more. Although most cities had substantial African American population enclaves, a few reflected circumstances where the mayors owed their election to support from largely white constituents, such as San Francisco, Denver, and Minneapolis (Bositis 1998). (See Table 5.10.)

African American Political and Bureaucratic Leadership

The post-Depression success of African American elected officials and the prominence of their constituents in the new Democratic Party coalition did not result in appointment to a comparable number of high-level patronage jobs. These limits related to the unwillingness of the general public or presidential advisers to support such appointments. There were two basic reasons for this view. First, too strong an association with African Americans was thought to diminish party prospects in future elections. And second, inveterate beliefs in the racial inferiority of Africans Americans caused many white leaders to see them as unsuitable for the exercise of public authority.

It is remarkable how few African Americans served in official capacities based on their party membership and competence from the Civil War until the mid-1960s. The practice of selecting a few Blacks started with Abraham Lincoln. And practically every president since then has had informal Black advisers and has appointed Blacks to a smattering of ambassadorships and certain designated federal bureaucratic positions. Nevertheless, the first significant increases came when President Roosevelt appointed a number of Blacks in informal

TABLE 5.10   African American Mayors in Cities with Populations of 50,000 or More, 1998

City	Population	Percent Black
Houston, Tex.	1,630,553	28
Detroit, Mich.	1,027,994	75
Dallas, Tex.	1,006,877	29
Baltimore, Md.	736,014	59
San Francisco, Calif.	723,959	11
Memphis, Tenn.	610,337	55
Washington, D.C.	606,900	67
Cleveland, Ohio	505,616	47
New Orleans, La.	496,938	62
Denver, Colo.	467,610	13
Kansas City, Mo.	435,146	30
St. Louis, Mo.	396,685	48
Atlanta, Ga.	396,017	67
Oakland, Calif.	372,242	44
Minneapolis, Minn.	368,383	13
Newark, N.J.	275,221	59
Birmingham, Ala.	265,968	63
Arlington, Tex.	261,717	8
Rochester, N.Y.	231,636	32
Jackson, Miss.	196,637	56
Des Moines, Iowa	193,187	7
Portsmouth, Va.	160,728	36
Chesapeake, Va.	151,982	27
Paterson, N.J.	140,891	36
Flint, Mich.	140,761	48
Rockford, Ill.	139,426	15
Savannah, Ga.	137,560	51
Pasadena, Calif.	131,591	19
Inglewood, Calif.	109,602	52
Compton, Calif.	90,454	55
Trenton, N.J.	88,675	49
East Orange, N.J.	73,552	90
Evanston, Ill.	73,233	30
Wilmington, Del.	71,529	52
Pontiac, Mich.	71,166	42
Saginaw, Mich.	68,512	40
Mt. Vernon, N.Y.	67,153	55
Irvington, N.J.	59,774	70
Monroe, La.	54,909	56
Victorville, Ga.	50,103	10

Source: Adapted from Bositis, 1998, 13. Reprinted with permission from the Joint Center for Political and Economic Studies.

Harold Washington Elected Mayor of Chicago (1983)

The Harold Washington Primary Campaign

Harold Washington was born into the regular Democratic Party. His father Roy was one of the first precinct captains of the old Dawson organization, having previously worked for Oscar DePriest. A Baptist minister and lawyer, his father never held public office. Washington attended public schools, graduating from DuSable High School in 1940. He spent four years at Roosevelt University and was elected president of the student body his senior year....

After earning his law degree at Northwestern University in 1952, Washington worked with the Illinois Industrial Commission (1960–64) and was Assistant State's Attorney in Chicago from 1954 to 1958. It was not until 1964 that Washington won his first elective position as a member of the Illinois General Assembly for the 26th District.

In the Assembly from 1965 to 1976 and as state senator from 1976 to 1980, Washington served on numerous committees and commissions. He drafted liberal legislation in the areas of consumer credit, witness protection, small business and minority set-asides (affirmative action programs), fair employment practices, and the Human Rights Act of 1979; he was also the prime sponsor of the Illinois Martin Luther King, Jr., Holiday Act of 1973. From 1965 to 1975 he voted generally with the Cook County Democratic Caucus in the Assembly. After 1976, and while in the state Senate, he consistently voted his conscience and that of his constituency, which often put him into opposition to the Cook County machine.

Washington Campaign Strategy: An Overview

Harold Washington emerged victorious in the Democratic primary [for mayor], riding the crest of an unprecedented mobilization of the city's Black community, which includes nearly 1.2 million people, or 40% of the total Chicago population. Underpinning this campaign victory and augmenting the tremendous Black community mobilization was the significant coalition built among Latinos, white liberals from middle-class backgrounds, and poor whites from working-class origins.

Mobilization

The most important factor explaining the election of Black mayors (at the macro level of analysis) is the percentage of Black people in the population of the political jurisdiction. The larger the proportion of the Black population, the greater the chances for election—especially since absolute population increase is typically accompanied by a

(continues)

(continued)

greater quantity of resources (money, skills, talent pools) needed by Black candidates. This population of Blacks must be mobilized and they must cast their votes for the successful Black candidate.

In the case of Chicago, the most significant factors in Harold Washington's victory were the increases in voter registration, voter turnout, and bloc voting of the Black electorate. We examined the patterns of the electorate in the 18 most homogeneous wards in Chicago: 11 are 90% or more Black (wards 2, 3, 6, 8, 16, 17, 20, 21, 24, 28, 34) and 7 are 90% or more white (wards 13, 23, 26, 38, 41, 45, 50). In the 11 Black wards, net new voter registrations increased by 78,919 between the 1979 and 1983 mayoral primaries. By contrast, in the 7 white wards there was an average increase of only 600 net new voters. The registration drive in these 18 most homogeneous Black wards showed an average increase in registrations of over 4,000 per ward! Thus the addition of 180,000 new voters to the rolls was a key tactic that led to Washington's success.

In the same 11 Black wards, the average voter turnout was 73.7%, compared to 79.1% in the 7 white wards. Although the turnout rate among whites was higher, this was offset by a big increase in the number of Black voters between 1979 and 1983. The Black voter turnout in 1983 increased by 21.5 percentage points from the 1979 level of 52.2%. In the 7 white wards, the percentage increase over 1979 was only 13.9%, up from 65.2% that year. In 1983 the election was defined by the role of the new Black electorate, made up of many voters who had previously been alienated from electoral participation.

Racial bloc voting was the principal characteristic of the primary returns. The white community split 88% of its vote between two white candidates, Byrne and Daley, while Washington got less than 8% of their votes. Overall in the primary election, more than 1,200,000 people turned out. Over 500,000 Blacks voted—or some 77.7% of an estimated 600,000 Black voters. It is estimated that Washington received over 80% of the Black vote; at the ward level, the higher the percentage of Black voters, the higher the percentage vote Washington received in that ward....

Significantly, the voting capacity of the Black electorate nearly doubled, from 34.5% in 1979 to 64.2% in the 1983 primary, while during that time, white voters only increased their voting capacity by 14.0%. This would lead to the conclusion that the Black electorate, while numerically smaller relative to the white electorate, exercised a higher vote capacity and was more highly mobilized than the white electorate—a prime factor in accounting for the Washington primary success....

Washington's support among whites and Latinos was critical to his plurality of 32,573 votes. Overall, Washington received about 8% of the white ballots cast, but in some wards his share was higher. In the 48th ward, with a 16% Black population, he won 21% of the vote. In three other wards Washington won 5% of the vote, although the Black population was less than 1%. Taken together, the Washington vote in these wards totaled 8,520, nearly 25% of his margin of victory. In six wards ranging from 46.3 to 75.6% Latino (and only 8% Black), Washington won 13.4% of the vote. These 12,775 votes contributed 40% of his margin of victory. Thus, while the Washington support base was not as broad as many would have hoped, it was broader than his campaign expected, and it sealed the primary victory.

Viability

The fact that Harold Washington was eminently the most "qualified" candidate became obvious to many people: the son of a machine precinct captain and an activist in the machine since his youth, a member of the state Legislature for 16 years, and a member of the United States Congress since 1981. Clearly he was viewed as the most viable Black candidate by a broad cross section of the Black community.

In addition to these credentials, Washington had three major traits that enhanced his viability. First, he had a gift for combining polysyllabic words with a sharp wit and culturally symbolic references that appealed to the predominantly Black audiences wherever he spoke. Second, he had a tremendous oratorical presence and appearance of command of the subject that captivated white audiences as well as Blacks. Third, Washington's apparent frugality and indifference to contemporary fashion matched his ability to engage in straight, nononsense dialogue with the "masses" and the "elites," qualities deeply appreciated within Afro-American culture.

The Outcome

On February 23 at 2:00 A.M., Harold Washington accepted the resounding mandate by 79 percent of the voting electorate in the Black community: the Democratic Party nomination for mayor. At the McCormick Inn, a throng of 30,000 to 35,000 people anxiously waited for him to say: "It's our turn!" The Washington campaign had opened with "Harold" promising to take his campaign into every community, into every ward, and to every sector of the Black community.

SOURCE: Alkaliment and Gills 1984. Reprinted with permission of Synthesis Publications.

advisory capacities. The authority of his appointees was limited, however. They rarely acquired executive-level appointments with broad authority over policy or personnel. Still later, despite a sustained civil rights mobilization and Black partisan support, appointments moved slowly. There was a single Black federal Appeals Court justice and no Black cabinet members before the 1960s.

However, changes ensued when the Democratic coalition gained the presidency in 1960. After the Eisenhower interlude of Republican rule, when little happened, significant improvements began. African Americans acquired significant appointments to a wide range of judicial, executive, and bureaucratic positions. This reflected the now generally recognized importance of this constituency to the new Democratic coalition.

The New Deal offered by Franklin Roosevelt is regarded as the first fundamental shift in African American representation since Reconstruction. Roosevelt was the first president to have a coterie of Black advisers. As a result of the increased pressure from the new constituents about jobs and military service, very prominent issues as a result of the Depression and World War II, Roosevelt sought to shore up his standing with Blacks. He sought their advice and made a number of bureaucratic appointments, usually for "Negro affairs."

Perhaps the most prominent individual among this class of advisers was Mary McLeod Bethune, first and foremost an educator, who in 1904 founded the eponymous Bethune-Cookman College in Daytona Beach, Florida. She was well ensconced as a primary race spokesperson, being at the peak of her powers during the Roosevelt administration. She formally held the position of director of Negro affairs in the National Youth Administration from 1936 to 1943.

But more important, she was a central figure in President Roosevelt's "Black Cabinet," a group of advisers who occupied advisory positions in various bureaucratic offices in the administration (see Table 5.11). In the war effort William Hastie, dean of Howard University Law School, was appointed as aide for Negro affairs in the War Department, and Benjamin O. Davis became the first Black brigadier general (Kryder 2000, 35). Robert Weaver, who occupied a number of positions in the administration, eventually headed up a "Negro affairs" position in the Labor division. Frank Horne had responsibilities for housing. One who, like Weaver and Hastie, played a much more important role later was Ralph Bunche. He served at both the Library of Congress and the State Department (Franklin and Moss 1994, 392). It was this group that had the greatest access, sharing the limited authorities assigned to Blacks at the time.

TABLE 5.11   New Deal Federal Council of Negro Advisers

Bureau	Number of Advisers
Youth Administration	7
Housing Authority	5
Defense	4
Social Security	4
War	3
Agriculture	3
Justice	3
Commerce	2
Works Progress Administration	2
Treasury	1
Farm Credit Administration	1
Selective Service	1
Public Works	1
Education	1
Children's Bureau	1
Conservation	1
Post Office	1
District of Columbia	1

SOURCE: Data from Kryder 2000, 38–39.

The offices in which African Americans served as bureaucratic as-sistants give some indication of the policy areas to which the admin-istration was responsive. A review of the members of the Federal Council of Negro Advisers shows the various functional areas of re-sponsibility (see Table 5.11). They were found in the following de-partments: Commerce, War, Agriculture, Justice, Treasury, Farm Credit Administration, Selective Service, Defense, Public Works, Housing, Works Progress Administration, Social Security, Education, Youth, Conservation. In all instances, however, these officers were as-signed roles that had to do specifically with service to other Blacks. In ways their role assignments replicated the racialized character of the society—the essentially segregated status of life all over the country for Blacks. And during the war, military role assignments were equally segregated (Kryder 2000).

Both the Roosevelt and especially the Truman administrations re-inforced the importance of an activist executive to create a climate for increased African American participation. In the utilization of Blacks in new roles, although in a manner consistent with the segre-gated society, Roosevelt significantly improved opportunities for the inchoate mobilization that was occurring among Blacks in the post-

Depression period. And although the FEPC he established by executive order may have been flawed, it made the welfare and employment rights of African Americans an agenda item.

Similarly, when Truman succeeded Roosevelt in 1945, the environment was considerably improved for him to act. He continued much of what Roosevelt had started but significantly improved on it. In 1946 Truman issued an executive order establishing a Committee on Civil Rights, the report from which formed the basis for his unprecedented civil rights speech to Congress in 1948. This was all the more remarkable for its coming after Truman prevailed in a highly contested presidential election in 1947. The speech was followed by two other executive orders, one targeting employment discrimination and the other segregation in the military. The latter provided the basis for significantly increased integration of the military services, a practice that began to be enforced with more success during the Korean conflict.

In all of these instances Truman made significant use of African American assistants and experts in integrated work environments (Fishel and Quarles 1967, 478). The appointment of Blacks to traditional ambassadorial roles continued, and a few more roles were added. Roosevelt appointed a Black ambassador to Liberia, and Truman appointed two. Roosevelt appointed William Hastie the first Black federal district judge in the Virgin Islands in 1937 and Truman advanced him to a circuit judgeship in 1949, also a first. It was these slow and halting beginnings that attained momentum in the 1960s and propelled African American formal representation in public positions to new heights.

The greatest increase in appointments of Blacks to positions of public authority followed the election of John Kennedy in 1960 and continued through the 2000 election, with the best records provided by Democratic presidents. The short-lived Kennedy administration earned a great deal of attention for its appointments and for its overtures to African American leaders in the civil rights establishment. He appointed Thurgood Marshall to a U.S. Court of Appeals and Wade McCree, James Parsons, Marjorie Lawson, Joseph Waddy, and Spottswood Robinson to District Courts (Franklin and Moss 1994, 499). Kennedy was also the first president to expand Black ambassadorial posts beyond African countries. In addition to his appointment of an ambassador to Niger, he also sent Blacks to Finland and Norway (Miller 1978). He gave voice to some of the core concerns expressed by Blacks and evinced an unusual willingness to seek advice from race spokespeople. He was most widely praised for his high-profile public intervention on the side of the jailed Martin Luther

King and in the integration of the University of Mississippi (O'Reilly 1995, 189–237).

President Lyndon Johnson had the greatest impact on shifting the public authority exercised by Blacks. Johnson was the first president to appoint a Black cabinet head, Robert Weaver, at the Housing and Urban Development (HUD). He elevated a Black to the Supreme Court and initiated the broadest inclusion of African Americans as heads of managerial bureaus and regulatory boards in history. At the same time, he significantly increased the number of Blacks as ambassadors by naming them to the newly independent African countries and several European countries. Many of these positions were invested with significant authority, especially the cabinet bureau and some of the boards. Meanwhile, the pattern of appointments was accompanied by the most expansive and sustained public policy program focused on African American issues in history, which is widely seen as the program that had the most significance for political participation. With passage of the Voting Rights Act in 1965, the type of electoral successes already described escalated all over the country.

Republican Richard Nixon, who followed Johnson, certainly had less impact on the appointment of Blacks, as have the three other Republicans who served since Nixon—Gerald Ford, Ronald Reagan, and George H. W. Bush. Nixon appointed some Black judges and Ford appointed several judges and a cabinet secretary in the Department of Transportation. The appointment of Blacks declined significantly during the Reagan administration at all levels in concert with a major departure from the civil rights issues deemed important to African Americans. Reagan did have one Black cabinet secretary, Samuel Pierce, at HUD. Bush appointed more Black judges than any of his Republican counterparts, including a Supreme Court justice (Clarence Thomas). He also had a Black cabinet secretary in Health and Human Services (Louis Sullivan) and a Black chairman of the Joint Chiefs of Staff (Colin Powell). Perhaps the most interesting departure is that Bush used his appointees to fulfill a set of roles with little relationship to the traditional interest areas of African Americans (Smith 1996). In short, there appeared to be little sustained responsiveness to the African American electorate, which had overwhelmingly shifted its alignment to the Democratic Party by 1960.

The pattern established by Johnson was followed by his Democratic successors to date—Carter and Clinton. Carter was the first to have a multiple number of African Americans in cabinet-level posts. Patricia Harris, formerly an ambassador under Johnson, served as secretary both of HUD and of Health, Education, and Welfare (HEW),

TABLE 5.12 Proportion of African American Political Appointees, 1960–2000 (Percent)

Administration	Proportion
Kennedy/Johnson	2
Nixon/Ford	4
Carter	12
Reagan	5
Bush	6
Clinton	13

SOURCE: Adapted from Walton and Smith 2000, 247. Reprinted with permission from Longman.

and Andrew Young and Donald McHenry served at the United Nations. Carter also appointed a range of senior-level assistants in bureaus, judges, and personal assistants at the White House. At the time, his appointments were the most widespread and extensive to that date (some 12 percent).

However, Bill Clinton went even further in the appointment of Blacks. They occupied four cabinet posts, none of which were normally associated with a civil rights agenda—the Departments of Commerce, Energy, Veterans Affairs, and Agriculture. Clinton appointed an extensive number of senior-level executives, including those at the White House. Although the number of high-level appointments was not proportionate to the African American population, during the Clinton administration Blacks were at their most influential level in history on general and civil rights public policy in American government. (See Table 5.12.)

The Republicans returned to power in 2000 in the controversial election of George W. Bush, a race in which African Americans gave their strongest support since 1964 to the Democratic candidate. This did not bode well for sentiment for core African American interests from the new president. The early list of presidential appointments has included few African Americans, and almost none of the appointees are responsible for policy development in areas of core interest to African Americans.

Yet the administration has appointed high-profile African Americans to significant policy positions within the administration. Colin Powell, who previously served the elder President Bush, was appointed secretary of state, and Condoleezza Rice, also an appointee of the elder Bush, became national security adviser. Neither of these positions, two of the highest in the administration, is in any direct way associated with the promotion of African American interests. Nor are the occupants regarded as part of the traditional Black leadership class, having no significant advocacy experience with core African American interests. They reflect the administration's view that "race interests" or "racial representation" are not reflective of the "color-blind" society it wishes to promote. The appointment of two Blacks as high executives purely on the basis of their "merit" signals that the administration itself harbors no residual taint of past practices of racial discrimination. This perspective leaves unresolved how the administration will treat the significant remaining differentials in society that appear to be directly linked to the racialization of African Americans.

African Americans in the Federal Judiciary

The importance of the federal judiciary on Black political participation cannot be underemphasized. The courts as an institution have both restricted and forged positive changes for the social, political, and economic development of African Americans throughout history. The road from *Plessy v. Ferguson* (1896) to *Brown v. Board of Education* (1954), for example, was a long and arduous one, from restriction to positive change. It was not until the courts began to increasingly accept the claims of Black plaintiffs, represented largely by the NAACP, that unprecedented victories were claimed in the push for civil rights. The role of Thurgood Marshall as a legal advocate was far reaching. It was his litigation with the NAACP Legal Defense and Educational Fund that led to most of the important civil rights victories that changed African American representation (Barker et al. 1999, 160ff). The pinnacle of achievement for Black representation in the judiciary was his appointment to the Supreme Court in 1967 by President Johnson. Before that time there was little Black presence in the courts.

African American representation in the federal judiciary has generally been at the U.S. District Court level. There have not been a large number of Blacks to rise to the level of the U.S. Courts of Appeal, and only two have reached the U.S. Supreme Court. The most progress for their representation in the federal judiciary, not surprisingly, has come under the administration of Democratic presidents. Presidents Johnson, Carter, and Clinton were most instrumental in increasing Black representation in the federal judiciary.

Since the Johnson administration, the number of Blacks in the federal judiciary increased dramatically. Between 1964 and 1967, Johnson made eight key appointments to federal courts—including the appointment of Constance Baker Motley to the District Court for the Southern District of New York in 1966. With her appointment, Baker Motley became the first African American woman to serve in the federal judiciary. Johnson also elevated two Blacks to U.S. District Court judgeships and appointed Thurgood Marshall to the Supreme Court. It would not be until the Carter administration, however, that Blacks would once again make such expansive strides in the federal judiciary.

During the Nixon and Ford administrations, Blacks made only marginal gains in federal judgeships. Nixon appointed six Blacks to serve as federal judges, including David W. Williams—the first district judge west of the Mississippi, and Robert M. Duncan, the first in Ohio. Ford appointed three African American District Court judges—among them Cecil F. Poole, the first Black District Court judge for the Northern District of California. During these Republican administrations, appointments of Blacks to the federal judiciary were all at the District Court level. This pattern did not end until 1977, when President Jimmy Carter elevated Judge A. Leon Higginbotham from the District Court for the Eastern District of Pennsylvania to the Court of Appeals for the Third Circuit ("Just the Beginning Foundation, A History").

During the Carter administration more Blacks were appointed or elevated to federal judgeships than during all previous administrations combined. Carter appointed or elevated nine Blacks to the Court of Appeals—including the first Black judges for the Eighth (Theodore McMillan), Ninth (J. Jerome Farris), and Eleventh Circuits (Joseph W. Hatchett). Amalya L. Kearse would become the first Black female judge on the Court of Appeals (Second Circuit) under the Carter administration. In addition, twenty-eight African Americans became District Court judges—many as the first Black judges appointed in their respective states. Blacks made significant strides in representation in the federal judiciary under the Carter administration.

In the 1990s Blacks would make more strides in gaining representation in the judiciary. The elder President Bush made thirteen appointments or elevations of Blacks—including appointing Clarence Thomas to the Court of Appeals for the D.C. Circuit in 1990. The following year, Bush elevated Thomas to the Supreme Court, replacing Thurgood Marshall. Bush also appointed Timothy Lewis in 1992 as the first Black to the District Court for the Western District of Pennsylvania. Three other judges became the first in their districts under President Bush: Fernando Gaitan in the Western District of Missouri, Joe B. McDade in the Central District of Illinois, and Garland E. Burrell Jr. in the Eastern District of California. Also during the Bush administration, two women became the first Black female

Thurgood Marshall Goes
to the Supreme Court

Few Americans have affected our nation's legal, political, and social lives as significantly as Thurgood Marshall. His contributions mark him as one of history's truly great jurisprudential leaders. While Marshall's work and reputation are best known in connection with the struggle to secure the civil rights of African Americans, his influence is felt in other areas of the law as well. His efforts—first as lawyer, then as judge, later as Solicitor General, and finally as Supreme Court Justice—have pushed the law to be more fair, more inclusive, more sensitive, and more responsive. His life's service challenges all Americans to join the battle for equal opportunity and justice.

Throughout his long career, Marshall directed his challenge with particular urgency to the practitioners and interpreters of the law. Behind his elegant legal arguments and incisive dissents is a philosophy of social fairness that required changing the dominant paradigm of power and privilege that exists throughout the political-social-economic order. And as far as Marshall was concerned, courts had a central role to play in that effort, consistent with their constitutional role and legal competence. Marshall keenly understood that judicial opinions, resulting from their interplay of judges, lawyers, procedures and principles, could never escape the shadow of politics....

Born in 1908 into a world permeated by formal distinctions based on race, Marshall attended the segregated public schools of Baltimore, Maryland. It was in these schools that Marshall developed an interest in the federal Constitution. At Douglas High, the Negro high school in Baltimore, a favorite form of disciplinary actions was sending student offenders to the school's basement with "instructions to read and memorize sections of the Constitution." "I went to the basement so often," recalls Marshall, "that I knew the whole thing by heart before I reached my senior year."

Upon graduating from Douglas, Marshall entered Lincoln University with plans to study dentistry, but his interest in the area waned after he won a place on Lincoln's debating team.... In the fall of 1930, Marshall entered Howard University Law School in Washington, D.C.

Shortly before Marshall's arrival, Howard University appointed a new dean of its law school, a young, black graduate of Harvard Law School named Charles H. Houston. For Houston, Howard could not just be another law school; rather it had to be an institution devoted to social change. Keenly aware of both the need for black lawyers and the role that such lawyers could play in American society, Houston em-

(continues)

(continued)

barked on a crusade to train and develop legal minds who would devote their careers to improving the legal status and lives of African Americans. Marshall, excited by Houston's challenge, quickly fell under the dean's influence.

Three years after graduating from Howard, Marshall served as Houston's assistant at the NAACP, succeeding his mentor as NAACP special counsel when Houston resigned in 1938 due to ill health. When the separate NAACP Legal Defense Fund [LDF] was established in 1940, Marshall became the first director-counsel. Marshall's efforts at the NAACP-LDF resulted in a number of court victories that bolstered the civil rights movement. His greatest victory came when the Supreme Court handed down its path-breaking decision, *Brown v. Board of Education*, in which the Court declared racial segregation in public schools unconstitutional. *Brown* was the culmination of a careful legal strategy developed by Marshall to lead the Court to repudiate the doctrine of "separate but equal" established in *Plessy v. Ferguson*.

The Jurisprudence of Social Change: Viewing the Courts in Systematic Perspective

Part of Marshall's genius as a litigator was his willingness to view the federal judiciary in systematic perspective: as a branch of government not insulated from the whims and vagaries of the political process (as one might contend) but actively engaged in the day-to-day business of governance. Such a perspective recognizes that ours is a system in which various political and legal actors work interdependently, responding to one another within the constraints of various constitutional roles. Thus Supreme Court Justices, like other governmental actors, are an integral part of the policy-making process. This even includes Justices who ostensibly refrain from judicial activism.

SOURCE: Barker 1992, 1237–1247. Reprinted with permission from the *Stanford Law Review*.

judges in their districts: Saundra B. Armstrong in the Northern District of California and Carol Jackson in the Eastern District of Missouri.

With the election of Bill Clinton in 1992, Black appointments to the federal judiciary accelerated. Clinton made forty-six judicial appointments of Blacks to federal judgeships. Among his appointments were Judith W. Rogers, the second African American female judge appointed to the U.S. Court of Appeals and the first to the D.C. Circuit.

Clinton also appointed more black female judges than any previous president.

Electoral Leadership and the African American Agenda

For much of African American history race leaders or spokespeople who were not formally elected or appointed to official positions have exercised a large part of leadership. The African American adviser was of significance in part because the racialized political order militated against otherwise formal positions of equality. This circumstance privileged the emergence of some of the most outstanding African American leaders, those generated from both within and outside the community (White 1990). Among them have been such leaders as Frederick Douglass, Booker T. Washington, W.E.B. DuBois, Ida B. Wells-Barnett, and Marcus Garvey in the post-Reconstruction period. After the Depression it generated the likes of educational leader Mary McLeod Bethune, labor leader A. Philip Randolph, NAACP leaders Roy Wilkins and Ella Baker, Urban League director Whitney Young, and SNCC leaders Robert Parris Moses, Fannie Lou Hamer, Stokely Carmichael, and Diane Nash. Still others included Malcolm X, originally of the Nation of Islam, and Huey Newton, of the Black Panther Party. The most outstanding characteristic of all of these leaders was that not a single one was elected. After 1965 that trend fundamentally changed.

Perhaps the single most significant change in office holding in this second period of successful formal leadership is the aspiration to national executive office. The expansion of the franchise after 1965 that created a fully enfranchised Black population for the first time since Reconstruction also significantly expanded the leader options available. The examples of the expansion of options began first in Northern congressional districts and soon followed in urban municipalities and in a vast array of state and local offices across the South. Then finally in 1972 Shirley Chisholm's candidacy for the presidency indicated that the scope and partisan mobilization of this national African American electorate was deemed sufficient to bargain for the highest political office. Although Chisholm did not command a significant portion of the vote in that outing, her candidacy revealed the ascendancy of the national African American elected official vis-à-vis the formerly exhalted status of the informal adviser.

Jesse Jackson: A Democratic Party Contender for President

The growth in the participation of Blacks as Democratic Party convention delegates was one of the measures of this newfound status. They constituted a mere 5 percent of the delegates to the Democratic convention in 1968, the first real test of the expansion of the franchise. However, by 1972 the proportion of Black delegates grew to 15 percent of the convention (see chapter 4). They lost a bit of ground in 1976 (11 percent) but were at the height of their powers through the 1980s, reaching 23 percent in 1988 (Stanley and Niemi 2000). This ushered in the remarkable role of Jesse Jackson as a presidential contender. He was also the first national-level Black leader who attained this status on the strength of a following in the electorate. And the African American constituency was fundamental to his success.

Jesse Jackson was born in 1941 in Greenville, South Carolina, in the heart of the former Confederacy. He entered college not at one of the nearby Black colleges but at the University of Illinois on an athletic scholarship. He thus began on a path that an increasing number of African Americans would follow out of the segregated South. This venture was not to succeed for him, however, and he returned to the South to attend North Carolina A&T College in Greensboro. He became a star football player and president of the student body. Here he was recognized by William Thomas, a member of the Congress of Racial Equality (CORE), as a person with the personality needed for leading protests. Jackson was recruited to participate in marches in downtown Greensboro and soon became identified as a sit-in leader. Once when he was jailed, leaflets were distributed with a headline that read "Your great leader has been arrested" (White 1990).

This signaled something of the ambitions of the young Jackson as his prominence rose in a period when African American students were avowedly challenging the status quo in the South. During his time at A&T he was on the cutting edge of a movement mobilization that eventually enveloped and shattered the system of disfranchisement. Like a number of his student cohorts, he was poised for a greater role as opportunities for action expanded.

Jesse Jackson earned a reputation as a great organizer after he joined the SCLC in 1963. Behind the direction of Martin Luther King, Jackson joined the SCLC campaign in Selma, and in 1966 he facilitated the union of the Chicago Coordinating Council of Community

Organizations and SCLC into the Chicago Freedom Movement. Later King appointed him to head the SCLC's Operation Breadbasket, where Jackson led protests demanding nondiscriminatory practices in hiring in Chicago (White 1990).

Not long after King's death, Jackson fell out of favor with the SCLC, and in 1971 he organized Operation PUSH—People United to Save (later Serve) Humanity (Faw and Skelton 1986). The seeds were sown here for his emergence as a national leader. Over time Jackson gained substantial national notice for his charisma and daring; he seemed to tap a chord with both the disaffected urban youth and the southern church-based mobilized Black constituency. In the vacuum left by the loss of other prominent African American spokespeople, Jackson had spectacular appeal.

Operation PUSH grew to over 80,000 members and helped Blacks make significant economic strides—including the signing of an agreement with the Coca-Cola Company and other major vendors to spend millions of dollars with minority vendors and increase minority management. This was accompanied with a strategy of developing a network of supporters who would enhance the influence of the African American electorate within the Democratic Party, in which Blacks were already the most loyal support base.

In the summer of 1983, Jackson began his campaign for the Democratic nomination for the presidency. Jackson's candidacy was propelled by his reading of the national Black electoral base and by the national implications of local Chicago politics. All indicators showed that African Americans voters could be mobilized to support a Black candidate for president. Meanwhile, in the local campaign for mayor, Harold Washington was making a strong run (which he subsequently won). However, during the local campaign Washington was spurned by a number of presidential contenders, who were nevertheless hoping to capture the Black vote in the campaign for the White House. This combination of factors led Jackson to declare his own intentions for a White House bid. He sought most to mobilize Blacks, but he also pitched for the development of a "Rainbow Coalition" of social-change-oriented voters. The long-standing ambivalence about Jackson on the part of some traditional Black leaders led many of them to distance themselves from this effort, while the national party hierarchy sought to diminish its impact. Despite this skepticism, Jackson nevertheless became the first serious African American presidential contender whose campaign was based on direct appeals to constituents on the traditional terms of delegate commitments and state primary elections.

His broad appeal to liberals and minorities was evident early on in the campaign, but so was the intraparty disagreement the Jackson candidacy generated. The campaign attained a high level of visibility because of its uniqueness, thus broadening Jackson's public recognition. However, the campaign demonstrated many things about Jackson as a presidential prospect, the party process, and those who were willing to support him. In the widespread media coverage he had to face the wrath of Jewish voters after the use of an ethnic slur, a fact that also sullied his reputation among potential allies. He fought unsuccessfully to alter the party's policy on delegate selection and primary run-off rules. But he showed remarkable savvy and success on some fronts (Tate 1993, 12). In the New York State primary election, Jackson captured 34 percent of the Puerto Rican vote and was the only Democratic candidate to address the National Congress of American Indians. Jackson's foreign policy and diplomacy skills delighted many and displeased others. Jackson promoted such policies as the removal of cruise missiles from Europe, normalized relations with Cuba, and an end to U.S. intervention in Central America (White 1990). He was also successful in persuading Syrian President Hafez al-Assad to release a young Black navigator whose plane had been shot down. Although some heralded Jackson's ability to have the pilot freed, others were upset with his intervention into foreign affairs—some of these were mainstream Democratic supporters who were also upset that Jackson met Yasir Arafat (White 1990).

The failure to win the nomination masked Jackson's phenomenal rise as a national leader. At the Democratic National Convention in 1984 he garnered 384 delegates. He received over 3 million votes in primaries, whereas Shirley Chisholm had received only slightly more than 400,000 in 1972. The strength he demonstrated in the primaries was remarkable for its scope and for the proportion of the vote won in some primaries. He carried the District of Columbia with 67 percent of the vote. He garnered 43 percent in Louisiana and carried 20 percent or more in eight other states—Alabama, Georgia, Maryland, North Carolina, Tennessee, Illinois, New York, and New Jersey (Walton and Smith 2000, 145). Clearly, he was successful in primary states with a sizable African American population in the South. He made his point in Illinois by mobilizing the Black wards in Chicago, and the Rainbow Coalition enjoyed success in New York and New Jersey. Meanwhile, the party front-runner, Walter Mondale, won the nomination and gained 200 Black delegates in the process.

Jackson's fervor was not dampened, however, and he again sought the Democratic nomination in 1988. Again he did not win, but he was much more successful than in his 1984 outing. He captured the imagination of many more voters, gained more delegate strength, and had a genuine influence on tilting the party agenda toward some of his issues. He succeeded in more carefully cultivating a Rainbow Coalition by positioning himself as a more centrist option for a greater cross section of voters. The intraparty ambivalence about Jackson was not as evident in the 1988 campaign, as he did not seek to put the party hierarchy on the defensive. Thus he received much more solid support from African American party leaders and sustained a negotiating stance with other competitors for the nomination. In a general sense, by 1988 he had become the first national African American leader whose standing was based on aspiration to an elective office. This was a distinction of profound importance. Jesse Jackson had become a national leader with command of a solidly recognized portion of the electorate, as a member of one of the two major parties in government.

How did the results confirm this conclusion? First, he thoroughly controlled his electoral base of African American voters. It is estimated that he carried over 90 percent of their votes in the primaries. And he significantly expanded his support all over the country. He went from winning 18 percent of the delegates in 1984 to 29 percent in 1988—a total of 1,218 delegates. He did better in caucus states (36 percent) than in primary states (28 percent) (Stanley and Niemi 2000), and he improved his fortunes in a number of states. He carried more than 20 percent of the vote in twenty-six states. Again his greatest share of the votes was in Washington, D.C., where he gained 80 percent. He had above 40 percent in four states, above 30 percent in seven, and over 20 percent in fourteen (Walton and Smith 2000, 145).

In short, Jackson had a degree of support in virtually every sector of the Democratic Party, in a true cross section of the states. Michael Dukakis, ultimately the party's standard-bearer, had to negotiate with Jackson about the platform that the organization continued into its fall campaign. This was a long way from the time when African Americans served only as advisory leaders because a national constituency could not countenance the possibility of complete racial equality. It had taken more than 200 years of struggle and opposition before such an opening to formal leadership in American politics became available. Although there remains limits on this kind of racial mobilization at the national level, Jackson has demonstrated that it is possible to organize from a base of African American supporters and develop alliances with a variety of interests to bid as a national leader in the political process. He may well have also significantly altered the perception that African Americans cannot function in a more general context as national leaders. Alan Keyes, a Black Republican, for example, was fielded as a presidential candidate for the 1996 and 2000 elections. He reflected an agenda not significantly related to core issues supported by African Americans.

Conclusion

The African American experience in formal positions in U.S. politics, as in all other aspects of public life, has been defined by the struggle for inclusion. This chapter has shown that this struggle began in the colonial period with the efforts of Blacks to secure an equal place. Although they were technically free people or indentured servants, their status vis-à-vis similarly situated peoples was always lower, and they were subject to harsher treatment from the authorities. These conditions led African Americans to engage in persistent protests against this differential treatment.

The end of the colonial period saw the institutionalization of slavery, in which Blacks could be reduced to the status of property and denied all rights to participate in public affairs. However, the African American community never accepted these conditions. From the outset, they objected in innumerable public and private ways. Because the system effectively barred their leaders from any formal positions of authority, the first individuals to emerge were notables in the independent Black churches and those whose stances of resistance somehow gained public notice. Some of the most notable resisters who attained public personas were people like Nat Turner, who organized armed rebellions. Others were escapees from the system of servitude, such as Frederick Douglass and Harriet Tubman, who became national spokespeople for abolition. They carried out their activities with great personal risk because practically all authorities had the legal means and force to take sanctions against African Americans who resisted.

Despite official barriers during slavery, a full-blown abolition movement eventually developed that had great influence on the destruction of the system. The formal role that Blacks played in this campaign was significant indeed. Primary examples include Harriet

Tubman, organizer of the Underground Railroad after her own escape to freedom, and Frederick Douglass, who movingly told his own story of resistance as slave and of his eventual escape to freedom in the North. They were prominent and public symbols of a sizable class of individuals who simply ran away from the plantations. Runaways were so numerous that fugitive slave laws were passed guaranteeing plantation owners the right to "repossess their property" if the slaves were found. What happened instead was that former slaves became the most powerful speakers on behalf of the destruction of the system. The few who became prominent achieved a degree of power and influence that easily matched those of formally recognized public officials.

The first period of formally permitted participation for Blacks came after the Civil War in the Reconstruction. This chapter has documented how rapidly the Black population rose to the task of leadership and electoral participation. Everywhere across the former Confederate states they participated first in the conventions organized to rewrite state constitutions to acknowledge the citizenship status of the newly freed Blacks. Concurrently their residentially segregated communities organized to contest elections. The result was that Blacks acquired their first representatives in state, local, and national offices. This period of open and full participation for Blacks did not last long—about five years in most places—but the scope of elected offices won in such a short period was remarkable.

It was also in this period that Blacks first received appointments to public positions in the federal government. Some of the active abolitionists (Douglass among them), clergy, and educated Blacks became advisers to presidents or held a few carefully selected and circumscribed bureaucratic and executive positions, and several diplomatic positions were reserved for Blacks (Liberia and Haiti).

As white resistance and often violence blunted the effects of Reconstruction, the position of race spokesman or adviser became all the more exalted. However, after Reconstruction was truncated and the traditional ruling class in the South regained power with the Compromise of 1876, the premium was on an adviser who could accommodate the new dispensation of restricted African American participation and rights. Booker T. Washington was willing to accept such a role, and he became the most important Black spokesman and adviser in the period from the 1880s until about 1915. He appeared to advocate acceptance of the diminished status that the betrayal of Reconstruction wrought for Blacks, arguing that they should focus on agricultural pursuits and not the acquisition of political power.

His tremendous power resulted from his widespread acceptance by whites as the arbiter of core racial issues.

Washington was not unchallenged. The emergence of W.E.B. DuBois and the NAACP just after 1900 brought back the focus on protest and struggle to acquire full rights and equality. They reframed the public debate on protest in light of what was the lowest level of African American participation since 1786. The focus on protest presaged the greatest social movement among Blacks for equality in the history of the republic. It also came at the time of the first large wave of Black migration from the South to the urban North.

Those who migrated immediately became politically engaged. They sent African Americans to national elective offices for the first time since the reemergence of the "Old South." These formal office holders quickly gravitated from local and state offices to seats in the House of Representatives. They evinced the first signs that there was also a partisan realignment occurring among Blacks. Previously solidly behind the Republican Party, they now began to affiliate with the Democratic Party in the North. The diverse membership of this party seemed more amenable to representing Black interests, which the Republicans had long since abandoned. Thus elected Blacks, formerly all Republicans, soon were solidly Democratic. The election of Franklin Roosevelt and his New Deal coalition seemed to seal the realignment.

Meanwhile, in the South the movement that DuBois and his fledgling NAACP initiated in the early 1900s had caught fire by the early 1940s. Although segregation and legal barriers to Black participation remained in the region, challenges were mounting. The movement for change had many milestones, but none was more important than the Montgomery bus boycott in 1955. A year-long event, it catalyzed communities elsewhere in the former Confederacy to challenge public accommodations and to seek voting rights. The movement rapidly expanded—mobilizing students and churches and then expanding to allies in the North. It eventually spawned the second great period of African American participation, resulting in many Black elected officials and appointees to public positions.

The partisan realignment of Blacks with the Democratic Party was complete by the 1948 election, and by the 1964 election, Blacks were also one of the most highly mobilized groups in the country. In several elections they clearly provided a sufficient portion of the votes to determine the outcome. In 1984 Jesse Jackson, as a Democrat, launched the first major campaign for the presidential nomination by a Black candidate. In a second attempt in 1988, he placed second in the national primary contests. That year's elections also brought a substantial leap in the number of Black office holders all over the country, including in the South, which soon exceeded the North in this regard.

The number of appointments that Blacks received to executive, bureaucratic, and advisory positions also increased over time, and so did the authority exercised in such positions. Franklin Roosevelt started this trend with the appointment of informal advisers. Truman took it further with the appointment of Blacks to formal positions and with the development of an executive-level civil rights strategy. After the Eisenhower administration, in which little advancement was made, Kennedy was unapologetic in espousing core issues associated with Blacks. When Johnson stepped in after Kennedy's assassination, he became the first to appoint a Black cabinet member, a Black Supreme Court justice, and a number of lower federal court judges. No president since has failed to appoint an African American to the cabinet, and Democratic presidents have appointed multiple Blacks to the cabinet.

Hence even as full equality remains an enduring challenge, African Americans have moved progressively toward greater realization of the goal of universal freedom. Few of the elected officials, appointive officials, or community activists argue that the core issues for Blacks are fully resolved. Representation by Blacks remains disproportionately small relative to the population, and there are still active and institutionalized pockets of resistance to full participation. These are some of the elements that cause many African American leaders to argue that their commitment to core issues of equality remain fundamental.

References

Alkalimat, Abdul (Gerald McWorter), and Doug Gills. 1984. "Black Power vs. Racism: Harold Washington Becomes Mayor." In Rod Bush, ed., *The New Black Vote: Politics and Power in Four American Cities*, 53–152. San Francisco: Synthesis.

Barker, Lucius, et al. 1999. *African Americans and the American Political System*. Saddle River, NJ: Prentice-Hall.

Barnett, Marguerite Ross. 1976. "Introduction." In Marguerite Ross Barnett and James Hefner, eds., *Public Policy for the Black Community*, 1–54. New York: Alfred.

———. 1982. "The Congressional Black Caucus: Illusions and Realities of Power." In Michael Preston et al., *The New Black Politics: The Search for Power.* New York: Longman.

Bennett, Lerone Jr. 1967. *Black Power U.S.A.: The Human Side of Reconstruction, 1867–1877.* Chicago: Johnson.

Blaustein, Albert P., and Robert L. Zangrando, eds. 1968. *Civil Rights and the American Negro: A Documentary History.* New York: Clarion.

Bositis, David. 1994. *The Congressional Black Caucus in the 103rd Congress.* Lanham, MD: University Press of America.

———. 1998. *Black Elected Officials: A Statistical Summary, 1993–1997.* Washington, DC: Joint Center for Political and Economic Studies.

Bracey, John, Jr., et al., eds. 1970. *Black Nationalism in America.* Indianapolis, IN: Bobbs-Merrill.

Browning, Rufus, et al. 1990. *Racial Politics in American Cities.* 2d ed. New York: Longman.

Cayton, Edward. 1964. *The Negro Politician: His Success and Failure.* Chicago: Johnson.

Clay, William. 1992. *Just Permanent Interests: Black Americans in Congress, 1870–1991.* New York: Amistad Press.

Cronon, E. David. 1955. *Black Moses: The Story of Marcus Garvey.* Madison: University of Wisconsin Press.

Dawson, Michael. 2001. *Black Visions.* Chicago: University of Chicago Press.

Dolbeare, Kenneth, and Murray Edelman. 1979. *American Politics.* 3d ed. Lexington, MA: D. C. Heath.

Douglass, Frederick. [1892] 1962. *Life and Times of Frederick Douglass, Written by Himself.* New York: Macmillan.

DuBois, W.E.B. [1935] 1962. *Black Reconstruction in America, 1860–1880.* New York: Meridian.

Faw, Bob, and Nancy Skelton. 1986. *Thunder in America.* Austin: Texas Monthly Press.

Fishel, Leslie, Jr., and Benjamin Quarles. 1967. *The Black American: A Documentary History.* Glenview, IL: Scott, Foresman.

Foner, Eric. 1996. *Freedom's Lawmakers: A Directory of Black Officeholders During Reconstruction.* Baton Rouge: Louisiana University Press.

Franklin, John Hope, and Alfred Moss. 1994. *From Slavery to Freedom.* 7th ed. New York: McGraw-Hill.

Glantz, Oscar. 1967. "The Negro Voter in Northern Industrial Cities." In Harry A. Bailey Jr., ed., *Negro Politics in America,* 338–352. Columbus, OH: C. E. Merrill Books.

Gosnell, Harold. 1935. *Negro Politicians: The Rise of Negro Politics in Chicago.* Chicago: University of Chicago Press.

Hamilton, Charles. 1972. *The Black Preacher in America.* New York: William Morrow.

Hamilton, Charles V. 1991. *Adam Clayton Powell, Jr.: The Political Biography of an American Dilemma.* New York: Atheneum Press.

Harding, Vincent. 1983. *There Is a River.* New York: Vintage.

Harlan, Louis. 1972. *Booker T. Washington: The Making of a Black Leader, 1856–1901.* New York: Oxford University Press.

Held, David. 1996. *Models of Democracy.* 2d ed. Palo Alto, CA: Stanford University Press.

Higginbotham, Leon. 1980. *In the Matter of Color.* New York: Oxford University Press.

Hine, Darlene Clark. 1979. *Black Victory.* Millwood, NY: KTO Press.

Holt, Thomas. 1979. *Black Over White: Negro Leadership in South Carolina During Reconstruction.* Urbana: University Press of Illinois.

Jaynes, Gerald, and Robin Williams Jr., eds. 1989. *Common Destiny: Blacks and American Society.* Washington, DC: National Academy Press.

Joint Center for Political Studies. 1976. *National Roster of Black Elected Officials.* Washington, DC: Joint Center for Political Studies.

Jones, Mack. 1972. "A Frame of Reference for Black Politics." In Lenneal Henderson Jr., ed., *Black Political Life in the United States,* 7–20. San Francisco: Chandler.

———. 1976. "Black Political Officeholding and Political Development in the Rural South." *Review of Black Political Economy* 6(4) (Summer): 375–407.

Jones, Rhett. 1973. "Proving Blacks Inferior: The Sociology of Knowledge." In Joyce Ladner, ed., *The Death of White Sociology,* 114–135. New York: Vintage.

Kryder, Daniel. 2000. *Divided Arsenal: Race and the American State During World War II.* New York: Cambridge University Press.

Lewis, David L. 1970. *King: A Biography.* Urbana: University Press of Illinois.

———. 1993. *W.E.B. DuBois: Biography of a Race, 1868–1919.* New York: Henry Holt.

Logan, Rayford. [1954] 1976. *The Betrayal of the Negro: From Rutherford B. Hayes to Woodrow Wilson.* New York: Collier.

Logan, Rayford, and Michael Winston, eds. 1982. *Dictionary of Negro Biography.* New York: W. W. Norton.

McAdam, Doug. 1982. *Political Process and the Development of Black Insurgency.* Chicago: University of Chicago Press.

McFarlin, Annjennette. 1976. *Black Congressional Reconstruction Orators and Their Orations, 1869–1879.* Metuchen, NJ: Scarecrow Press.

McNeil, Genna Rae. 1983. *Groundwork: Charles Hamilton Houston and the Struggle for Civil Rights.* Philadelphia: University of Pennsylvania Press.

Miller, Jake. 1978. *The Black Presence in American Foreign Policy.* Lanham, MD: University Press of America.

Morris, Aldon. 1984. *The Origins of the Civil Rights Movement.* New York: The Free Press.

Morrison, Minion K. C. 1987. *Black Political Mobilization.* Albany: State University of New York Press.

———. 2002. "Prologue: Who Is J. Milton Turner and Why Is His Story Important?" In Hanes Walton Jr. et al., eds., *Liberian Politics: The Portrait by African American Diplomat J. Milton Turner.* Lanham, MD: Lexington Books.

Morrison, Minion K. C., and Joe Huang. 1972. "The Transfer of Political Power in a Bi-racial Mississippi Town." *Growth and Change* 4(2): 25–29.

Nelson, William, Jr., and Philip Meranto. 1977. *Electing Black Mayors: Political Action in the Black Community.* Columbus: Ohio State University Press.

Nobles, Melissa. 2000. *Shades of Citizenship: Race and the Census in Modern Politics.* Palo Alto, CA: Stanford University Press.

O'Reilly, Kenneth. 1995. *Nixon's Piano: Presidents and Racial Politics from Washington to Clinton.* New York: The Free Press.

Parenti, Michael. 1978. *Power and the Powerless.* New York: St. Martin's Press.

Pinderhughes, Dianne. 1987. *Race and Ethnicity in Chicago Politics.* Urbana: University Press of Illinois.

Pitkin, Hanna. 1967. *The Concept of Representation.* Berkeley: University of California Press.

Quarles, Benjamin. 1982. "A. Philip Randolph: Labor Leader At-Large." In John Hope Franklin and August Meier, eds., *Black Leaders of the Twentieth Century.* Urbana: University Press of Illinois.

Scheb, John M., Jr., and Otis H. Stephens. 1998. *American Civil Liberties.* Belmont, CA: Wadsworth.

Sklar, Judith. 1991. *American Citizenship: The Quest for Inclusion.* Cambridge, MA: Harvard University Press.

Smith, Jessie, and Carrell Horton. 1995. *Historical Statistics of Black America.* Detroit: Gale.

Smith, Robert. 1996. *We Have No Leaders: African Americans in the Post–Civil Rights Era.* Albany: State University of New York Press.

Stanley, Harold, and Richard Niemi, eds. 2000. *Vital Statistics on American Politics, 1999–2000.* Washington, DC: Congressional Quarterly Press.

Taeuber, Karl E., and Alma F. Taeuber. 1969. *Negroes in Cities: Residential Segregation and Neighborhood Change.* New York: Atheneum Press.

Tate, Katherine. 1993. *From Protest to Politics: The New Black Voters in American Elections,* enlarged ed. Cambridge, MA: Harvard University Press.

Voter Education Project. 1973. *Black Elected Officials in the South, 1973.* Atlanta: Voter Education Project.

Walton, Hanes, Jr. 1972. *Black Political Parties.* New York: The Free Press.

Walton, Hanes, Jr., and Robert Smith. 2000. *American Politics and the African American Quest for Universal Freedom.* New York: Longman.

Washington, Booker T. 1967. "Atlanta Exposition Address, 1865." In Leslie Fishel Jr. and Benjamin Quarles, eds., *The Black American: A Documentary History,* 342–345. Glenview, IL: Scott, Foresman.

Wharton, Vernon. 1947. *The Negro in Mississippi, 1865–1890.* Chapel Hill: University of North Carolina Press.

White, John. 1990. *Black Leadership in America: From Booker T. Washington to Jesse Jackson (Studies in Modern History).* Reading, MA: Addison-Wesley.

Wilson, James. 1960. *Negro Politics.* New York: The Free Press.

6

Conclusion: A Limited Democracy for Blacks

Minion K. C. Morrison

The path of participation for African Americans has deviated considerably from that of the general white population. For the latter, participation has steadily expanded with the trajectory toward full realization of the principle of one person, one vote, or optimal influence on the allocation of public resources. Both the scope and quality of that participation is lauded around the world. It is a great irony therefore that African American participation was severely limited even before the colonies attained independence. Then those minuscule rights were revoked in favor of enslavement in the South, and an ambivalent status for "free" Blacks elsewhere. Indeed, Reconstruction was the first interval of near-inclusive formal Black participation. That lasted for five to ten years. Thereafter, while technically free, most Blacks were barred from political participation, a status legal in the South until the early 1960s. Even today, most African Americans perceive that full participation is yet to be achieved.

This condition has spawned continual resistance from Blacks, with support from significant allies. The resistance has largely been framed around the liberal democratic principles in the Constitution. Together with their allies Blacks have sometimes made inroads that expanded their participation in the ebb and flow of shifting values and alliances in U.S. politics. This continuing struggle for "universal freedom" is the story this volume has revealed.

The initial part of this analysis consisted of a demographic description of the African American population and an overview of its political history. The analysis showed that African Americans have a different reality from the dominant population, and that it is rarely captured by political science theory. In the first place they are a minority group in a majoritarian system, and are unable to control most political outcomes. But they are also a racialized minority, whose status is determined by negative assessments of the racial group. The political consequence is that Blacks are ranked lower in the allocation of political resources, including the very right to participate. Our demographic survey included the factors of housing, education, economics, criminal justice, and health. On all of these measures the assessments show African Americans in a negative position compared to whites. Moreover, this web of lower socioeconomic conditions reinforce each other and seem stable over time among Blacks.

This socioeconomic profile provided the foundation for the balance of the analysis—a survey of African Americans in politics in seven major periods: colonialism, enslavement, Reconstruction, post-Reconstruction and migration, partisan realignment, the civil rights movement, and the use of electoral politics. The periods were assessed via four themes—protest, organizations, political behavior, and office holding.

During the colonial period there was some formal, legitimate participation by "free" Blacks. However, everywhere their freedom was limited by the general opinion that the race was inferior. They were not invisible, however. Despite the cloud of suspicion about their equality, they bargained for political recognition by protesting discrimination, especially as taxpayers. They acquired allies among some wealthy white patrons and religious organizations. So vital and common were these early patterns of political action that they became a formula for the struggle through U.S. political history.

The long period of enslavement followed in the South. It lasted just past the Civil War, which was partially fought over this issue. The aim of this chattel system was to obtain free labor by treating Blacks as property. It sought to destroy any spirit and desire for freedom and equality on the part of the Africans. Despite its brutality as a total barrier to formal participation, the system was rent with op-position, resistance, and the fear of revolts. Many Africans found spaces for individual and spontaneous acts of resistance (self-defense, sabotage, escape, revolt, etc.) requiring tremendous use of force for maintenance of enslavement.

The first elaborate period of formal African American participation occurred during Reconstruction (about 1866–1877). It included a full complement of constitutional provisions—the Thirteenth, Four-teenth, and Fifteenth Amendments and statutory laws—that together were designed to guarantee universal freedom. The process, albeit flawed, achieved rapid engagement by the Black population in the South. First, Blacks helped rewrite regional constitutions, and many of them rapidly won elective offices, exclusively as Republicans. Among them were representatives in Congress, presidential advisors, federal appointees, and diplomats.

Yet this relative bonanza of participation was also accompanied by continual protest. In the South the resistance was particularly heavy because the former Confederates returned to citizenship in the Com-promise that resolved the 1876 presidential contest. The former Con-federates soon attained political dominance, and revoked the voting rights extended to Blacks. The reversal was first sustained by nonac-tion on the part of the federal government, and then sanctioned by the Supreme Court in 1896 with the "separate but equal" doctrine in *Plessy v. Ferguson*. This decision remained the law for seventy-five years.

An informally annointed race-leadership class filled the rights vac-uum. A singular individual, Booker T. Washington, dominated this period from roughly 1885 to 1915. He rejected political action in fa-vor of a secondary status for Blacks that was deemed suitable for this perpetual "laboring class." Nevertheless, he became an arbiter and a conduit for resource allocations to Blacks.

It was not to last. At the turn of the twentieth century, the NAACP renewed a protest strategy in combination with legal challenges to the Jim Crow system. W.E.B. DuBois was a major figure in this devel-opment, even as Blacks in large numbers deserted the harsh reality of virtual peonage in the South. As the interracial NAACP developed its legal and protest challenges in the South, Black migrants to the North elected their first representative to Congress from Chicago. Slowly, but with deft certainty, the NAACP began to chip away at the elements of segregation and disfranchisement in the South. The Supreme Court outlawed the "White Primary," in which Blacks were barred from voting in 1944. However, the right to vote remained largely proscribed for another twenty years because of poll taxes and other forms of discrimination. Meanwhile the culmination of the legal strategy was the Supreme Court rejection of the separate but equal doctrine in *Brown v. Board of Education* in 1954.

Opportunities for a civil rights movement began about this time when a party realignment saw Franklin Roosevelt elected president. Soon his administration, in response to economic crisis, developed a "New Deal," which greatly expanded the breadth of the Democratic Party, including Blacks. African Americans deserted the Republican Party in droves. Early in the 1940s, A. Philip Randolph advanced the civil rights framework with a threat to march on Washington, which precipitated a major policy shift on Black employment in the federal sector. The momentum in 1956 continued with a citizen-inspired boycott in Montgomery, Alabama, catalyzed by Rosa Parks and Martin Luther King Jr.

The success of the movement was perhaps best signaled in the Democratic coalitions that won two successive presidential contests in the early 1960s, each avowedly espousing civil rights programs. John Kennedy's proposed Civil Rights Act would have been the first substantive legislation of its kind since the so-called Civil War statutes. He did not live to see its promulgation, but his successor, Lyndon Johnson, shepherded the bill through in 1964. He also gave unparalleled support the following year to the most significant legislation for Black enfranchisement since the passage of the Fifteenth Amendment (1870), the Voting Rights Act of 1965.

These successes ushered in the final period—electoral politics as a principal avenue of political participation. Like their northern counterparts, when Blacks regained the franchise in the South, they began to elect their own to office. First they won local offices on town councils and as mayors. Soon state legislators followed, and in 1973 the first southern Black representatives in nearly a century returned to Congress. As in the North, they represented racially compact districts in cities—Houston and Atlanta. Their electoral success has been spectacular, though Black constituents do not yet control elective positions proportionate to their numbers in the population.

Meanwhile, the appointement of Blacks to government positions has exceeded that for any other period in U.S. history. Since Lyndon Johnson assumed the presidency in 1963 and appointed Robert Weaver to a cabinet position, it has become *sine qua non* for every president since. However, Blacks have enjoyed their greatest range of power in executive and judicial appointments under Democratic presidents. They have all appointed multiple Black cabinet secretaries, some with portfolios far beyond those associated with core African American interests, and have recruited a significant number of them as executive deputies throughout the federal government.

Perhaps the most telling illustration of the power of the first completely franchised Black electorate since Reconstruction was the presidential candidacy of Jesse Jackson. In 1984 and again in 1988, for the first time, an African American was a major party contender for this office. Jesse Jackson demonstrated that with a highly mobilized Black constituent base and sufficient allies (members of the Rainbow Coalition), it is entirely possible to become a serious contender within a major party organization. Although he clearly could not wholly devote his candidacy to core African American issues, he demonstrated that these interests could successfully be woven together with a range of other similar interests. The scope of Jackson's influence in the primary process was especially broad in 1988, when he exacted major concessions for his agenda from the nominee. His achievement perhaps represents the pinnacle of the power of the highly mobilized African American constituency in the electoral process to date. Yet, even with his assimilation within the party system, he operated from a stance of protest. Jackson demonstrates the continuing vitality of the formula of protest resistance against intractable pockets of discrimination. The revitalization of organizations such as the NAACP raising their voices against retrenchments on such policies as affirmative action also illustrate the continuing vitality of this proven formula for a common struggle for universal inclusion.

Key People, Laws, and Terms

Ralph Abernathy (1926–1990): Prominent African American minister in Alabama and second in command to Martin Luther King Jr. in the Southern Christian Leadership Conference.

Abolition movement: The organized fight to end slavery in the United States. This movement was led by Frederick Douglass and William Lloyd Garrison, among others.

Abolitionists: Advocates of slavery's abolition in the United States. Their efforts culminated in Abraham Lincoln's Emancipation Proclamation on September 22, 1862, and in the post–Civil War amendments (Thirteenth, Fourteenth, and Fifteenth) to the U.S. Constitution.

Abyssinian Baptist Church: Harlem home church of Adam Clayton Powell and Adam Clayton Powell Jr. It was from this base that Powell Jr. became a nationally known civil rights voice and later a longtime congressional representative from Harlem.

Affirmative action: The policy of actively seeking to recruit minorities and women to overcome the effects of previous discrimination.

African Methodist Episcopal Church: The first organized African American religious group in America. Founded by Richard Allen and currently serving the United States, Africa, Canada, and the Caribbean.

Richard Allen (1760–1831): A formerly enslaved clergyman, founder and first bishop of the African Methodist Episcopal Church.

Amendment: An alteration or addition to a motion, bill, or constitution.

American Colonization Society: A group organized in 1816 to raise money and publicize the effort to send free African Americans back to Africa.

Americo-Liberians: Formerly enslaved African Americans who resettled in Liberia and became a ruling elite. They and their descendants controlled this West African country from the 1830s until 1980.

Amicus curiae: Latin phrase meaning "friend of the court"; a person or group that is not a party to a case but is permitted to file a brief (written argument) in the court supporting a particular view of the case.

Amistad **mutiny:** Revolt by captured Africans aboard the ship *Amistad*. The mutineers succeeded in killing a number of whites before being subdued. They were eventually awarded their freedom by the Supreme Court in 1841.

Apportionment: The process by which legislatures establish the representation of legislative districts according to population.

Atlanta Exposition speech: An 1895 address by Booker T. Washington in which he argued for the economic uplift of African Americans and accepted the "separate but equal" doctrine in all social aspects of American life.

Ella Baker (1903–1986): Civil rights organizer who worked with Martin Luther King Jr. and the Southern Christian Leadership Conference before moving on to help found the Student Nonviolent Coordinating Committee (SNCC).

Balance of power: A condition and maintenance of an equilibrium in which the ambitions of individual nations or alliances are held in check by the lack of a dominating strength capable of imposing its will on the others.

Daisy Bates (1914–1999): The head of the Arkansas NAACP in 1957 who helped nine African American students integrate Little Rock Central High School.

Mary McLeod Bethune (1875–1955): Educator and political leader who became an adviser to Franklin D. Roosevelt (in his "Black Cabinet") and to the president's wife; founder of Bethune-Cookman College in Florida.

Bill: A proposal for a law to be considered by a legislative body.

Black and Tans: The Reconstruction-era Republican Party in the South, largely controlled by African Americans. It became the vehicle for their political participation after Reconstruction failed.

Black Congressional Caucus: The organization of African Americans currently serving in the U.S. Congress. They meet to discuss legislation important to the African American community.

Black Nationalism: In the black liberation movement, any of several strategies that emphasize the need for Black communities to stay together geographically and to win control of and upgrade their local institutions.

Black Panther Party: Founded by Bobby Seale and Huey Newton in Oakland, California, in 1966. The party fought for African American self-defense and community improvement with health, education, and antibrutality programs through the promulgation of a nationalist program.

Black Power movement: A political movement based on the ideal of African American political, social, and economic uplift through internal community development.

Black Star Line: The corporation created by Marcus Garvey to buy ships and help African Americans begin the process of emigration to Africa.

Unita Blackwell (1933–): A civil rights activist and later one of the first African American mayors in the state of Mississippi (Mayersville).

Julian Bond (1940–): A civil rights activist and former member of the Georgia legislature, who currently serves as chairman of the board of the NAACP.

Edward Brooke (1919–): The first African American elected to the U.S. Senate since Reconstruction. He was elected in 1966 as a Republican from Massachusetts.

Brotherhood of Sleeping Car Porters: An African American labor union led by A. Philip Randolph. It helped to organize for the first planned march on Washington in 1941, although the march was never held.

John Brown (1800–1859): A strong abolitionist who led fugitives from slavery and free African Americans on a raid of Harpers Ferry in 1859.

Ron(ald) Brown (1941–1996): The first African American to head one of the major political parties (the Democratic Party); he later served as secretary of commerce in the Bill Clinton administration.

Blanche K. Bruce (1841–1898): A former tax collector, sheriff, and superintendent of schools who became one of the Reconstruction-era African American senators from Mississippi. He was elected in 1874 and was the only African American to serve a full six-year term during Reconstruction.

Ralph Bunche (1904–1971): The first African American winner of the Nobel Peace Prize. He served as a CIA officer, a diplomat, and undersecretary of the United Nations.

Cadre: The nucleus of activists within a political party.

Stokely Carmichael (1941–1998): A leader of the Student Nonviolent Coordinating Committee. After changing his name to Kwame Toure, he became a prominent proponent of Black Nationalism and Pan-Africanism.

Caucus: A meeting of a group of legislators (usually members of the same party) to decide a position on electing leadership, on a bill, and the like.

Shirley Chisholm (1924–): African American congressional representative from New York, who also became the first Black woman to seek the nomination for president of the United States.

Civil liberties: A series of prohibitions against government interference in the lives of citizens, such as freedom of speech, press, assembly, and others.

Civil rights: Regulations permitting government intervention to guarantee the rights of full political participation to groups unfairly excluded from participation.

Civil Rights Act of 1964: The first comprehensive civil rights legislation since Reconstruction. It had a strong public accommodations section that undermined social segregation.

Civil rights movement: The era from 1954 to 1968 in which African American protest in the streets and in the halls of government culminated in a social movement that overturned legalized segregation in America.

Kenneth Clark (1914–2000): African American psychologist who researched the impact of segregation on African American children. His "doll test" results were used to help win the 1954 *Brown v. Board of Education* case.

Septima Clark (1898–1987): A schoolteacher and civil rights activist who led citizenship schools at the Highlander Folk School and later in Mississippi and Alabama.

Eldridge Cleaver (1935–1998): Propaganda leader of the Black Panther Party who at one time advocated alliances with sympathetic whites. He fled the country after a shooting incident and returned years later as a conservative Republican.

Coalition: The joint forces of two or more persons or organizations who share complementary goals.

Compromise of 1876: In exchange for the votes from southern Democrats that would allow Republican candidate Rutherford B. Hayes to win the contested 1876 presidential election, Hayes agreed to remove federal troops from the region, which ended Reconstruction.

The Congress of Racial Equality (CORE): A civil rights group that initiated the Freedom Rides in the deep South in the 1960s, challenging segregation in interstate transportation.

Conservatism: Generally a trend in democratic ideology that emphasizes the importance of national traditions, social stability, and the responsibility of each individual for his or her success or failure in the world.

Constituency: A body of citizens entitled to elect a representative to a legislative or other public body.

Co-optation: The practice of controlling or attempting to control a protest movement by offering its leaders elite status and privileges and by making symbolic concessions to the members of the movement.

***Crisis* magazine:** The official magazine of the NAACP, founded by W.E.B. DuBois. It publishes news articles and opinion pieces as well as literary essays and poems.

Alexander Crummell (1819–1898): African American intellectual and proponent of emigration to Liberia, where he subsequently took up residence.

Paul Cuffee (1759–1817): A wealthy African American captain and shipbuilder who organized and led thirty-eight African Americans to Sierra Leone in 1815. He saw repatriation to Africa as a desirable goal for African Americans.

Angela Davis (1944–): A professor and activist who embraced radical politics by joining the Communist Party. She was the subject of a high-profile legal case involving a kidnapping and the death of a judge that involved a gun registered to her; she was acquitted and resumed her academic career.

De facto segregation: Racial segregation that actually exists but has not come about as a result of laws or acts officially performed or legally permitted.

De jure segregation: Racial segregation brought about by official acts and specific laws. Such acts and laws are now unconstitutional.

Decentralization: In city government, the policy of transferring power away from the central administration and bringing it down to the neighborhood level, often by establishing channels for community participation.

Martin Delaney (1812–1885): African American minister and father of Black Nationalism. He argued for African American emigration and independence.

Democracy: Rule by the people.

Oscar DePriest (1871–1951): One of the first African American members of Congress after Reconstruction. He was elected in 1928 and served three terms as a Democrat from Chicago.

Dominant party system: A political system in which a single powerful party wins every election, year after year, yet in which opposition parties are allowed to function freely.

Frederick Douglass (1817–1895): A former slave who became one of the most powerful abolitionist voices in the country. After the Civil War he served as a diplomat and presidential adviser.

***Dred Scott* decision:** The 1857 Supreme Court decision in which Justice Roger B. Taney declared that Black slaves could not sue for freedom because they were property and had "no rights that a white man was bound to respect."

W.E.B. DuBois (1868–1963): Author, educator, activist, and cofounder of the NAACP. The first African American to receive a Ph.D. at Harvard. He authored numerous works of history and sociology, including *The Souls of Black Folks* and *Black Reconstruction*.

Due process: A course of legal proceedings carried out in accordance with established principles and rules.

Electoral College: An institution created by the Federal Convention of 1887 to select the president. Each state has a number of votes equal to the number of its seats in the U.S. House of Representatives plus its two senators.

Elite: A small group of people or a social class within a larger group that makes decisions (or controls others who do) as to "who gets what, when, and how."

Elite theory: The theory that power is held and shared by a small group of people who dominate the major institutions.

Elitism: Any of several social or political theories that assert the dominance of single or plural elites in society's decision-making processes.

Emancipation Proclamation: The document signed by President Lincoln in 1862 that freed all slaves in the states that rebelled against the Union during the Civil War.

Equal Employment Opportunity Commission (EEOC): A government agency designated with the responsibility of enforcing antidiscrimination laws in the workplace.

Medgar Evers (1925–1963): The head of the Mississippi NAACP during the 1950s and 1960s. He was assassinated and became a martyr of the civil rights movement. His killer, Byron De La Beckwith was tried twice, before being convicted more than thirty years later in a third trial.

Fair Employment Practices Committee: A committee created in 1941 by executive order of President Franklin Roosevelt to oversee desegregation of employment in the defense industries.

Louis Farrakhan (1933–): The current spiritual leader of the Nation of Islam, a Black nationalist, and organizer of the 1995 Million Man March.

Federal court system: In the United States, the basic federal courts, which include the Supreme Court, eleven Circuit Courts of Appeals, and ninety-three federal District Courts.

Federalist: Supporters of a strong national government who favored ratification of the document produced by the Constitutional Convention of 1787.

Fifteenth Amendment: The post–Civil War amendment that granted the right to vote to African American men.

James Forman (1928–): A civil rights activist and leader of CORE who helped organize Freedom Rides in the South during the civil rights movement.

Fourteenth Amendment: The post–Civil War amendment that guaranteed equal protection and due process of the law to all citizens.

Franchise: The right to vote.

Freedmen's Bureau: A government agency created after the Civil War to help former slaves begin the process of becoming independent citizens.

Freedom Rides: A set of challenges by civil rights activists to segregation in interstate transportation. Groups of African Americans and whites rode buses together and attempted to eat and use segregated facilities in bus stations across the South.

Lloyd Gaines (1911–): The African American student who successfully sued the University of Missouri for admission to its segregated law school in 1938. He disappeared after the court victory and never enrolled at the school.

Henry Highland Garnet (1815–1882): A militant abolitionist and African American nationalist who founded the African Civilization Society, which attempted to carry Western influence to Africa.

William Lloyd Garrison (1805–1879): A militant abolitionist who once burned a copy of the U.S. Constitution; he founded and edited the antislavery newspaper *The Liberator*.

Marcus Garvey (1887–1940): One of the most prominent proponents of Black Nationalism, who led a Back to Africa Movement and founded the largest mass racial organization in American history, the Universal Negro Improvement Association.

General election: A final or definitive election in which candidates representing their respective parties run for office.

Gerrymandering: In legislatures, the practice of redrawing boundaries in order to give special advantage to the candidates of the majority party, faction, or coalition.

Ghetto: An area within a city in which a minority group is forced to live because of de facto racial and economic segregation.

Grandfather clause: A provision instituted in the South after the Civil War that assigned the franchise only to those who could prove that their grandfather voted, thus disqualifying all Blacks.

Grass roots: At the local level—that is, at a distance from the centers of social and political power.

Great Society: A set of large-scale programs initiated by President Lyndon Johnson in the 1960s for dealing with social, economic, and political problems that was meant to wipe out poverty.

Alex Haley (1921–1992): Noted author of two central works of African American history, *The Autobiography of Malcolm X* and *Roots*. He was the first African American known to directly trace his African ancestry back to continental Africa.

Fannie Lou Hamer (1917–1977): Mississippi sharecropper and member of the Mississippi Freedom Democratic Party. Her passionate speech at the 1964 Democratic Convention shed light on the plight of African American voters in the state of Mississippi.

Harlem Renaissance: An era of the early twentieth century (principally in the 1920s) in which African American art, literature, and music flourished in the racial residential enclave of Harlem in New York City.

Patricia Roberts Harris (1925–1985): The first African American woman to serve in the cabinet of a U.S. president. She served as Secretary of Housing and Urban Development and later of Health and Human Services under President Jimmy Carter. She also served as an ambassador in the Lyndon Johnson administration.

William Hastie (1904–1976): A dean of the Howard University Law School who became the first African American federal District Court judge. He later became a federal appeals court judge, serving more than two decades.

Hegemony: Special influence or power exercised by one group or nation over another.

Aaron Henry (1922–1997): The head of the Mississippi NAACP and the Council of Federated Organizations who was a candidate for governor of Mississippi on the Mississippi Freedom Democratic Party ticket; later he served as head of the state Democratic Party and as a legislator.

Highlander Folk School: A Tennessee workshop of the Social Gospel variety founded by Myles Horton, which helped to train civil rights workers and citizens in aspects of citizenship and nonviolent political protest.

Charles Hamilton Houston (1895–1950): The first counsel for the NAACP, developing its legal strategy for civil rights. He later founded the NAACP Legal Defense Fund, which litigated and won a number of landmark civil rights cases.

Ideology: A system of abstract beliefs providing the basis of action for a political party, government, or mass movement.

Incumbent: The current holder of an office.

Injunction: A court order enjoining a party—an individual or a group—from doing something that it has not yet done.

Integration: In the Black liberation movement, the traditional strategy of achieving equality through dispersing the Black minority within the white community.

Interest groups: Organized groups whose members have common views about certain policies or actions and so undertake activities to influence government officials and policies.

Interstate Commerce Commission (ICC): First independent regulatory commission, established in 1887, to develop, implement, and adjudicate fair and reasonable freight rates.

Jesse Jackson (1941–): Clergyman, civil rights activist, and Democratic Party presidential candidate in 1984 and 1988; founder of Operation PUSH (People United to Serve Humanity) and the Rainbow Coalition.

Jim Crow laws: Laws passed after Reconstruction to legally separate the races; these laws prevented African Americans from sharing trains, schools, and other public facilities around the nation.

Lyndon B. Johnson (1908–1973): President of the United States from 1963 to 1969 who fought for and signed the 1964 Civil Rights Act and the 1965 Voting Rights Act, which were the legislative culmination of the civil rights movement; initiated the Great Society programs and the War on Poverty.

John F. Kennedy (1917–1963): President of the United States from 1960 to 1963 who reached out to the African American community during the 1960 presidential election, and later as president by using federal troops to integrate the University of Mississippi. He sent to Congress what would become the Civil Rights Act of 1964.

Martin Luther King Jr. (1929–1968): The best-known civil rights activist in American history. His nonviolent philosophy dominated the protest movement of the civil rights movement. He was president of the Southern Christian Leadership Conference and is best known for his "I Have a Dream" speech, given during the March on Washington in 1963. This Nobel Peace Prize–winner was assassinated in 1968.

Ku Klux Klan: A group founded after the Civil War that enforced white supremacy through violence (including lynching) and terror (such as cross burnings).

Left-right continuum: The conventional scale, or spectrum, of parties and ideologies by which radicals and revolutionaries are placed on the left, moderates in the center, and conservatives and reactionaries on the right.

Legal Defense and Education Fund: This is the legal arm of the NAACP, which engages in civil rights litigation and has won landmark cases such as *Brown v. Board of Education* in 1954.

Liberalism: Generally a trend within democratic ideology that emphasizes the importance of civil liberties and of vigorous governmental action to guarantee the economic and social welfare of the individual.

Liberia: The West African destination set by the American Colonization Society. Before the Civil War it was continually viewed as a place where African Americans could escape slavery and racism and establish a Christian outpost of hope.

Abraham Lincoln (1809–1865): President of the United States from 1861 to 1865 who led the nation during the Civil War and who issued the Emancipation Proclamation freeing the slaves in the Confederacy.

Lobbying: The practice of trying to influence legislators in favor of some special interest, by personal persuasion, public testimony, or the dissemination of published materials.

Lobbyist: A representative of a group or organization seeking the passage or the defeat of certain legislative measures.

Malcolm X (1925–1965): A noted African American Muslim minister and Black nationalist who rose to prominence in the Nation of Islam. He later broke away from the group to embrace a Pan-Africanist philosophy. He was assassinated in 1965.

March on Washington, 1963: The major civil rights protest of the era. Over 250,000 people were involved in the march, which was capped off with the famous Martin Luther King Jr. speech "I Have a Dream."

March on Washington movement: Movement led by A. Philip Randolph to protest discrimination in society during World War II. The proposed 1941 march was called off after President Roosevelt issued an executive order banning employment discrimination in defense industries.

Thurgood Marshall (1908–1993): The first African American to serve on the Supreme Court of the United States. Earlier, as the director-counsel of the NAACP Legal Defense Fund, he won a number of landmark Supreme Court cases, including *Brown v. Board of Education.*

James Meredith (1933–): The first African American to attend the University of Mississippi, in 1962. He attended under federal escort because Governor Ross Barnett attempted to have him prevented from entering the campus to enroll. The arrival of troops caused a riot on campus.

Minority group: A district group—especially an ethnic, religious, or racial group—within a group, nation, or community that is dominated by a larger group.

Mississippi Freedom Democratic Party (MFDP): Created to demonstrate the racial exclusion of the Democratic Party of Mississippi. It offered the opportunity for African Americans to learn about the political process as the party nominated candidates for numerous offices in Mississippi, including for the governorship.

Missouri ex rel. Gaines v. Canada: The Supreme Court case that forced the University of Missouri to admit Lloyd Gaines as the first African American student at the law school. The provision of a separate law school at Lincoln University was ruled to not be enough since it was clearly not equal to the one at the University of Missouri.

Clarence Mitchell (1911–1984): The long time Washington lobbyist for the NAACP. His work on behalf of civil rights helped earn him the nickname "The Fifty-first Senator."

Montgomery bus boycott: A mass protest of segregation in public transportation, sparked by the arrest of seamstress Rosa Parks for not giving up her seat to a white man on a bus. The boycott, led by Martin Luther King Jr., became the model for many other mass protests during the civil rights era.

Robert Moses (1888–1981): A Harlem schoolteacher who became a prominent civil rights activist with SNCC (the Student Nonviolent Coordinating Committee) in Mississippi. He later created the Algebra Project to encourage math literacy for children in the Mississippi delta region and elsewhere.

Elijah Muhammad (1897–1975): The spiritual founder and leader of the Nation of Islam in America. He helped craft the ideology of nationalism and racial separatism that came to characterize the group.

Nation of Islam: A large African American religious organization with a nationalist perspective and a separatist agenda originally under the leadership of Elijah Muhammad. The group produced Malcolm X, a charismatic speaker and leader who drew attention to the Nation of Islam during the civil rights era, and Louis Farrakhan, who convened the 1995 Million Man March. The group has moved closer to orthodox Islam over the years.

National Advisory Commission on Civil Disorders: This body, also known as the "Kerner Commission," issued a report on the causes of urban unrest during the decade of the 1960s. Its findings referred to "two nations (black and white)," that were separate, hostile, and unequal.

National Association for the Advancement of Colored People (NAACP): The NAACP is the preeminent civil rights organization in the United States. It was founded in 1909 by an interracial coalition of intellectuals and activists. The group has focused on lobbying and legal challenges in order to bring about social change.

National Urban League: A moderate African American organization founded in 1910 to assist African Americans in social reform and business opportunities in urban areas. In its early decades it catered to southern Black migrants in northern cities.

Nationalism: The love of one's homeland, national culture, and historical heritage and a strong devotion to the political independence of one's nation.

Negro Convention Movement: The first national organization of African Americans dedicated to political action. It was a quasi-political party developed in the 1840s and had membership affiliates in many states, mostly in the North.

New Deal: A series of programs initiated by President Franklin D. Roosevelt during the Great Depression of the 1930s calling for greater governmental intervention in the economy.

New Left: An amorphous radical movement in the United States that developed during the 1960s consisting mainly of young people who rejected the style and dogmas of all political establishments and favored moral protest, small group initiatives, and "participatory democracy."

Huey Newton (1942–1989): Cofounder of the Black Panther Party in Oakland, California, in 1966. He helped organize community efforts against police brutality, for health care, and for political dissent. Newton was imprisoned for shooting a policeman and subsequently was released after an intense legal effort.

Niagara Movement: The Canadian gathering of intellectuals that presaged the founding of the NAACP. The group, founded in 1905 by W.E.B. DuBois and William Trotter, sought solutions to the dominant leadership of Booker T. Washington.

Nomination: The process by which political parties and the general electorate choose whom to put on the ballot as party candidates.

Office of Economic Opportunity: The organizational base for the War on Poverty launched by President Lyndon Johnson. This government agency attempted to address the problems of poverty through job skills and business development programs.

Off-year elections: In the United States, any election held during a non-presidential election year.

One-party system: A political system in which a single party controls every level of government and is the only party legally allowed.

Operation PUSH: People United to Serve Humanity. An organization founded by Jesse Jackson in 1971 to serve the needs of the community in Chicago.

Rosa Parks (1913–): A Montgomery, Alabama, seamstress who was arrested in 1954 for refusing to give up her seat on a segregated city bus to a white man. Her arrest sparked the Montgomery bus boycott, which is considered the event that triggered the era of mass protest.

Party identification: A sense of loyalty to a particular political party and a tendency to vote for its candidates.

Picketing: The practice of maintaining a line or procession of protestors, usually with placards, outside the establishment that is the object of the discontent in an attempt to express demands or grievances and, in the case of a strike or boycott, to discourage entry by nonstriking workers or customers.

P. B. S. Pinchback (1837–1921): One of the most powerful African American politicians of the Reconstruction era. He served as lieutenant governor of Louisiana and also served as governor for forty-three days in 1873.

Platform: A declaration of the principles and positions held by a candidate for office.

Plessy v. Ferguson: An 1896 Supreme Court decision that sanctioned Jim Crow laws across the nation. The doctrine of "separate but equal" in public facilities was formalized with this decision.

Plural elitism: The theory that America is ruled by a number of specialized, competing elites whose membership varies with the times and with the issues.

Pluralist system: A system in which power is shared among a number of different groups, none strong enough to dominate but each able to protect its own interest with help from others.

Policymaking: The process whereby goals are set and alternative approaches to solving identified problems are outlined, adopted, and pursued.

Political alienation: A state of mind in which people feel that the social and political system in which they live threatens them or that it no longer protects them or fulfills their needs. This estrangement may progress through several stages, from withdrawal or isolation to verbal protest to possible violent protest.

Political machine: A well-entrenched organization of leaders and followers with considerable power in determining nominations and elections.

Political party: An organization that supports particular candidates in elections.

Political socialization: The process by which people acquire certain political values, beliefs, and orientations toward the political system.

Political violence: Any extralegal act or threat of injury to persons, damage to property, or disruption whose purpose is to protest or influence the policies of government.

Poll tax: A fee paid when an individual registers to vote. The poll tax was declared illegal by the Twenty-fourth Amendment.

Populism: In the United States, a trend within democratic ideology that stresses the government's role as the defender of small business and the common man against large concentrations of wealth.

Adam Clayton Powell Jr. (1908–1972): A clergyman, civil rights leader, and controversial member of Congress representing Harlem in New York City. He was first elected in 1944, serving as the first African American congressman from Harlem until 1970. His consistent advocacy (before and after his election to Congress) earned him the nickname "Mr. Civil Rights."

Colin Powell (1937–): A U.S. Army general who became the first African American to serve as chairman of the Joint Chiefs of Staff and, later, the first to serve as secretary of state.

Primary: A preliminary election in which voters select candidates to stand under their party labels in a later and definitive general election.

Proportional representation: The allocation of seats in the legislature so that each political party receives a percentage of the seats that accurately reflect the percentage of the vote received in the election.

Public opinion: The set of ideas and opinions concerning candidates, policies, parties, and political ideologies held collectively by the people.

Public policy: The general goals and actions outlined by government officials in their efforts to resolve problems of public concerns.

A. Philip Randolph (1879–1979): A civil rights activist and journalist who published (along with Chandler Owen) the socialist newspaper *The Messenger*. He later led the Brotherhood of Sleeping Car Porters, a Black labor union. He also organized the march on Washington movement in the 1940s.

Reconstruction: The era after the Civil War in which African Americans acquired their first formal political power in the United States. The era brought new amendments to the Constitution outlawing slavery and guaranteeing equal protection under the law for all men. It was truncated, lasting perhaps five to ten years.

Resource mobilization model: The resource mobilization model suggests that since social strain is always present, the key to the success or failure of a movement is the type and quality of resources that the aroused group can apply in the pursuit of their rights.

Hiram Revels (1822–1901): One of two African American U.S. senators during the Reconstruction era. He represented the state of Mississippi for one year in 1870 and 1871.

Condoleezza Rice (1954–): A former provost at Stanford University, the first African American appointed national security adviser in the White House.

Franklin Delano Roosevelt (1882–1945): President of the United States from 1933 to 1945. His administration implemented the New Deal in response to the Great Depression. President Roosevelt issued an executive order desegregating defense industries during World War II and appointed multiple Black advisers, contributing enormously to an African American partisan realignment.

Bobby Seale (1936–): Cofounder of the Black Panther Party in 1966.

Segregation: The separation or isolation of a racial or other group by setting up barriers to regular interaction. De jure segregation is grounded in law, whereas de facto segregation is grounded in custom or practice.

Separatism: In the Black liberation movement, a nationalist strategy that urges a separate Afro-American state, either somewhere within the United States or in Africa.

Smith v. Allwright: The 1944 Supreme Court decision that outlawed the white primary, which barred Blacks from the Democratic Party in the South.

Social movement: A collective enterprise to change the way society is organized and operates in order to produce changes in the way opportunities and rewards are distributed.

Socialism: An economic system in which the government, rather than private individuals, owns and operates the major means of production and distribution of goods and services.

Southern Christian Leadership Conference (SCLC): The SCLC was founded and led by Martin Luther King Jr. in the wake of the Montgomery bus boycott. The SCLC was the organizational base for the mass protests led by King throughout the country.

States' rights: All rights not granted to the federal government by the Constitution nor forbidden by it to the separate states. A number of groups, including segregationists in southern states, have used the term to define their opposition to federal laws that supersede local laws.

Statutory law: The body of laws established by legislative acts or statutes.

Strike: A cessation of work by employees, whose aim is to cut off the profits of their employer in order to force him to concede to such demands as higher wages and improved working conditions.

Student Nonviolent Coordinating Committee (SNCC): SNCC began as the student unit of the Southern Christian Leadership Conference. It later served as the vanguard for the sit-ins and protest marches before evolving ideologically toward a more nationalist stance. It also focused on local community organization.

Supreme Court: The high court or court of last resort in the U.S. judicial system.

Thirteenth Amendment: The amendment to the Constitution that outlawed slavery in the United States.

Clarence Thomas (1948–): After serving as head of the Equal Employment Opportunity Commission under President Reagan, he became a justice of the U.S. Supreme Court in 1991, after his nomination by President George H. W. Bush initiated a difficult confirmation process in the U.S. Senate, in which he survived challenges to his ideology as well as a former coworker's charges of sexual harassment.

Harry S. Truman (1884–1972): President of the United States from 1945 to 1952. He won a tough reelection fight in 1948 while maintaining a civil rights plank in his platform. After winning the election, he issued orders desegregating the U.S. military.

Sojourner Truth (1797–1883): A former slave who became an abolitionist and orator. She also served as a spy for the Union army during the Civil War, and later she fought for free land to be awarded to former slaves.

Harriet Tubman (1823–1913): A slave who escaped slavery in the South and became a prominent abolitionist. She founded and ran the Underground Railroad, which helped Blacks escape to freedom. She served as a nurse and a scout for the Union during the Civil War.

Henry McNeal Turner (1834–1915): A noted Black Nationalist and AME Church bishop who pushed for emigration from the United States to escape the oppression of racism.

Nat Turner (1800–1831): A Virginia slave who escaped in 1831 and led one of the most violent slave revolts in U.S. history against white plantation owners. After killing fifty whites, he and his army were captured and put to death.

Two-party system: A political system in which two major parties vie for power, while other parties have only minor political strength.

Underground Railroad: The network used to help Blacks escape slavery in the southern states. Harriet Tubman and Josiah Henson made numerous trips to the South, and with the help of sympathetic whites led escapees to freedom in the North.

Universal Negro Improvement Association: The organization created by Marcus Garvey to articulate and carry out his Black Nationalist goals. It was used to raise money for the Black Star Line, a corporation whose ships would carry African Americans back to Africa.

Voter registration: The process by which members of the voting-age population register to establish their right to cast a ballot on election day.

Voter turnout: That portion of the voting-age population that actually votes on election day.

Voting-age population: Total population over the age of eighteen.

Voting bloc: Any group of people with similar political interests who are likely to vote in the same way.

Voting Rights Act of 1965: The legislative act that banned poll taxes, literacy tests, and other tactics used to prevent African Americans from voting. The law provided for federal registrars to assist in enrolling Blacks in districts, mostly in former Confederate states, where progress was slowed by recalcitrance.

David Walker (1785–1830): A passionate African American abolitionist who in 1829 published *Walker's Appeal to the Coloured Citizens of the World,* an aggressive and militant tract calling for active resistance against slavery.

Warren Court (1953–1969): A term used to describe the U.S. Supreme Court under Chief Justice Earl Warren, which dealt with many important issues concerning civil and criminal rights and legislative reapportionment.

Booker T. Washington (1856–1915): A former slave who became an educator and political leader. He was educated at Hampton Institute and went on to found Tuskegee Institute in Alabama. He emphasized vocational education at the school and pushed for economic uplift before political equality.

Harold Washington (1922–1987): The first African American elected mayor of Chicago. He served as a local city politician, a state senator, and a congressional representative before becoming mayor in 1983. He was re-elected in 1987 but died the same year.

Robert Weaver (1907–): One of the first African Americans to serve in high-level government positions. He served as an adviser in the Department of the Interior under President Roosevelt, and later, in 1966, he became the first African American cabinet member when President Johnson named him to head the Department of Housing and Urban Development.

Ida B. Wells-Barnett (1864–1931): Well known antilynching and civil rights activist during the late nineteenth and early twentieth centuries. She also worked with the emerging National Association for the Advancement of Colored People (NAACP).

Phillis Wheatley (1753–1784): A former slave who became one of the first poets to receive wide public recognition for her work.

L. Douglas Wilder (1931–): The first African American to be elected governor of a state in the United States. He was elected governor of Virginia in 1989 after serving as the first elected lieutenant governor of that state in 1985.

Roy Wilkins (1901–1981): A journalist who became executive secretary of the NAACP during the civil rights movement of the 1950s and 1960s. In his role as executive secretary, Wilkins emphasized legal challenges and lobbying to bring about social change.

Carter Woodson (1875–1950): A scholar considered the "father of African American history." He founded the Association for the Study of Negro Life and History and also created Negro History Week (later Black History Month).

Andrew Young (1932–): One of the most prominent civil rights activists and aides to Martin Luther King Jr. He later served in public office as mayor of Atlanta and as ambassador to the United Nations under President Jimmy Carter.

Whitney Young (1922–1971): The head of the Urban League during the civil rights era who helped build a strong coalition with the NAACP and the SCLC.

References

Cord, Robert L., et al. (1974). *Political Science: An Introduction.* New York: Appleton-Century-Crofts.

Hamilton, Charles V. (1982). *American Government.* Glenview, Ill.: Scott, Foresman, and Company.

Jillson, Cal (1999). *American Government: Political Change and Institutional Development.* New York: Harcourt Brace.

Resources

Political Organizations

A. Philip Randolph Institute
260 Park Avenue South, 6th Floor
New York, NY 10010

APRI's mission has been to fight for racial equality and economic justice. Its role is unique; members work with black trade unionists, the people best suited to serve as a bridge between labor and the black community.

AFL-CIO
Department of Civil Rights
815 16th Street, N.W.
Washington, DC 20006
http://www.aflcio.org

The mission of the AFL-CIO is to improve the lives of working families—to bring economic justice to the workplace and social justice to our nation. To accomplish this mission we will *build* and *change* the American labor movement.

African American Institute
Chanin Building
380 Lexington Avenue
New York, NY 10168-4298
http://www.interaction.org.org/mb/aai.html

For over five decades AAI has worked to engage Africans and Americans through training programs and dialogue. AAI's programs aim to encourage greater understanding of Africa among a wide spectrum of Americans and to bring American and African policymakers together to focus on issues of mutual concern.

American Association for Affirmative Action
11 East Hubbard Street, Suite 200
Chicago, IL 60611

Founded in 1974, the American Association for Affirmative Action (AAAA) is dedicated to the advancement of affirmative action, equal opportunity, and the elimination of discrimination on the basis of race, gender, ethnic background, or any other criterion that deprives people of opportunities to live and work. The organization's dedication is realized in its many activities designed to help Equal Employment Opportunity/Affirmative Action (EEO/AA) professionals be more successful and productive in their careers.

Association for the Study of Afro-American Life and History
1407 14th Street, N.W.
Washington, DC 20005

The mission of the Association for the Study of Afro-American Life and History is to promote, research, preserve, interpret, and disseminate information about Black life, history, and culture to the global community.

Black Women's Roundtable on Voter Participation
1629 K Street, N.W., Suite 801
Washington, DC 20006
http://www.telecity.org/concernedwomen

The Black Women's Roundtable (BWR): A project of the National Coalition comprised of black women's organizations and individuals who are committed to social justice and economic equality through increased participation in the political process.
　　Initiated in 1983, BWR focuses on three major goals:

* to sponsor projects that will emphasize the importance of women's votes;
* to develop the leadership potential of black women, encourage them to become familiar with the political process, and prepare them to run for public offices; and
* to ensure the involvement of black women in policy discussions about the importance of the women's vote as it influences elections and other issues relevant to gender. Over the years BWR has provided information on issues important to women such as health care, child care, and literacy.

Blacks in Government
1820 11th Street, N.W.
Washington, DC 20001-5015
http://www.bignet.org

Blacks in Government was organized in 1975 and incorporated as a non-profit organization under the District of Columbia jurisdiction in 1976. BIG has been a national response to the need for African Americans in public service to organize around issues of mutual concern and use their collective strength to confront workplace and community issues. BIG's goals are to promote Equity in all aspects of American life, Excellence in public service, and Opportunity for all Americans.

Congress of National Black Churches
2000 L Street, N.W., Suite 225
Washington, DC 20036-4962
http://www.cnbc.org

CNBC's mission is to foster Christian unity, charity, and fellowship and to collaborate in ministries that promote justice, wholeness, fulfillment, and affirm the moral and spiritual values of our faith. CNBC stands in the tradition of the old Fraternal Council of Negro Churches—the last ecumenical mechanism supported by Black churches. As part of that tradition, CNBC invites denominations with national constituencies to join its membership to create an effective instrument for Black church ministry in the world today.

Congress of Racial Equality (CORE)
817 Broadway, 3rd Floor
New York, NY 10003
http://www.core-online.org

Founded in 1942, CORE is the third oldest and one of the "Big Four" civil rights groups in the United States. From the protests against "Jim Crow" laws of the 1940s to the "Sit-ins" of the 1950s and the "Freedom Rides" of the 1960s, through the cries for "Self-Determination" in the 1970s and "Equal Opportunity" in the 1980s to the struggle for community development in the 1990s, CORE has championed true equality for all people. As the "shock troops" and pioneers of the civil rights movement, CORE has paved the way for the nation to follow. As we enter the twenty-first century, CORE has turned its focus to preparing minorities for the technical and skills demands of the new millennium.

Under the banner of "Truth! Logic! and Courage!," CORE will continue to promote harmony and healing in all aspects of society; calling the shots straight—even when it hurts—and combating the haters, race baiters, and racial racketeers bent on keeping us apart.

Congressional Black Caucus
319 Cannon HOB
Washington, DC 20515
http://drum.ncsc.org/-carter/CBC.html

The CBC was born in 1971. The thirteen founding members were: Representatives Shirley Chisholm, William Clay, George Collins, John Conyers, Ronald Dellums, Charles Diggs, Augustus Hawkins, Ralph Metcalfe, Parren Mitchell, Robert Nix, Charles Rangel, Louis Stokes, and the Washington, D.C., Delegate Walter Fauntroy. Their goals were to positively influence the course of events pertinent to African Americans and others of similar experience and situation and to achieve greater equality for persons of African descent in the design and content of domestic and international programs and services. Although the CBC has been primarily focused on the concerns of African Americans, the caucus has also been at the forefront of legislative campaigns for human and civil rights for all citizens.

Joint Center for Political and Economic Studies
1090 Vermont Avenue, N.W., Suite 1100
Washington, DC 20005-4961
http://www.joinctr.org

The Joint Center for Political and Economic Studies informs and illuminates the nation's major public policy debates through research, analysis, and information dissemination in order to: improve the socioeconomic status of black Americans and other minorities; expand their effective participation in the political and public policy arenas; and promote communications and relationships across racial and ethnic lines to strengthen the nation's pluralistic society.

Lawyers' Committee for Civil Rights under Law
1401 New York Avenue, N.W., Suite 400
Washington, DC 20005

The Lawyers' Committee for Civil Rights under Law, a nonpartisan, nonprofit organization, was formed in 1963 at the request of President John F. Kennedy to involve the private bar in providing legal services to address racial discrimination. The principal mission of the Lawyers' Committee is to secure, through the rule of law, equal justice under law.

The committee's major objective is to use the skills and resources of the bar to obtain equal opportunity for minorities by addressing factors that contribute to racial justice and economic opportunity. Given our nation's history of racial discrimination, de jure segregation, and the de facto inequities that persist, the Lawyers' Committee's primary focus is to represent the interest of African Americans in particular, other racial and ethnic minorities, and other victims of discrimination, where doing so can help to secure justice for all racial and ethnic minorities.

The Lawyers' Committee implements its mission and objectives by marshaling the pro bono resources of the bar for litigation, public policy advocacy, and other forms of service by lawyers to the cause of civil rights.

Leadership Conference on Civil Rights
1629 K Street, N.W., Suite 1010
Washington, DC 20006
http://www.lccr.org11ccr.htm

The Leadership Conference on Civil Rights (LCCR) was founded in 1950 by three giants of the civil rights movement—A. Philip Randolph, founder of the Brotherhood of Sleeping Car Porters; Roy Wilkins, executive secretary of the NAACP; and Arnold Aronson, a leader of the National Jewish Community Relations Advisory Council. It is the nation's premier civil rights coalition, and has coordinated the national legislative campaign on behalf of every major civil rights law since 1957. LCCR consists of more than 180 national organizations, representing persons of color, women, children, labor unions, individuals with disabilities, older Americans, major religious groups, gays and lesbians, and civil liberties and human rights groups. Its mission: to promote the enactment and enforcement of effective civil rights legislation and policy.

As a 501(c)(4) organization that engages in legislative advocacy, LCCR receives most of its operating support from its member organizations, the annual Hubert H. Humphrey Civil Rights Award Dinner and foundation, corporate and individual contributions. LCCR is committed to a cost-effective, results-oriented central operation that unifies and furthers the efforts of its member organizations.

A recently revised strategic framework and enhancement of the organization's core functions promises to increase LCCR's strong record of legislative achievement. What remains unchanged is the mission to which the Leadership Conference on Civil Rights remains steadfast: uniting all Americans as one nation true to its promise of equal justice, equal opportunity, and mutual respect.

NAACP Legal Defense and Educational Fund
99 Hudson Street, 16th Floor
New York, NY 10013
http://www.naacp.org

The NAACP Legal Defense and Educational Fund, Inc. (LDF) was founded in 1940 under the leadership of Thurgood Marshall. Although LDF's primary purpose was to provide legal assistance to poor African Americans, its work over the years has brought greater justice to all Americans.

LDF has been involved in more cases before the U.S. Supreme Court than any organization except the U.S. Department of Justice. It has more than 100 cases on its docket, one of the largest legal loads of any public service organization. Its main program areas are education, civic participation, economic access, affirmative action, and criminal justice. Although LDF works primarily through the courts, its strategies include advocacy, educational outreach, legislation monitoring, coalition building, and policy research. Additionally, it provides scholarships for exceptional African American students.

By sharing its legal and functional expertise, LDF has been instrumental in the formation of similar organizations serving other minority constituencies in the United States. It also has been involved in the global campaign for human rights by assisting in the creation of public interest legal organizations in South Africa, Canada, and Brazil.

National Association of Blacks in Criminal Justice
North Carolina Central University
Criminal Justice Building, Room 106
P.O. Box 19788
Durham, NC 27707
http://www.nabcj.org

The mission of this organization is to act upon the needs, concerns, and contributions of African Americans and other people of color as they relate to the administration of equal justice.

The National Association of Blacks in Criminal Justice is a multiethnic, nonpartisan, nonprofit association of criminal justice professionals and community leaders dedicated to improving the administration of justice. The association was founded as a vehicle by which criminal justice practitioners could initiate positive change from within, while increasing opportunities for the average citizen to better understand the nature and the operation of our local, state, and federal criminal justice processes. Membership and participation in the activities of the association are open to all, irrespective of race, creed, or country of national origin.

For NABCJ members, criminal justice is more than just a career; it is a commitment to a fundamental aspect of our democracy—justice.

The National Association of Blacks in Criminal Justice seeks to focus attention on relevant legislation, law enforcement, prosecution, and defense-related needs and practices, with emphasis on the courts, corrections, and the prevention of crime. Among its chief concerns is the general welfare and increased influence of African Americans and people of color as it relates to the administration of justice.

NABCJ is designed to serve the needs of African Americans and people of color at all levels, including nonprofessionals, paraprofessionals, and professionals. Anyone can become a member of the association. The National Association of Blacks in Criminal Justice encourages ex-offenders to join and contribute their perspectives to this unique and dynamic organization.

National Black Caucus of Local Elected Officials
1301 Pennsylvania Avenue, N.W. Suite 550
Washington, DC 20004

The National Black Caucus of Local Elected Officials (NBC-LEO) was created in 1970 to represent the interests of African American elected officials. NBC-LEO's objectives include increasing African American participation on the NBC's steering and policy committees to ensure that policy and program recommendations reflect African American concerns and benefit their communities. The organization also works independently with its members to inform them on issues affecting the African American community and helps to devise ways to achieve their community objectives through legislation and direct action. NBC-LEO conducts its annual meetings in conjunction with NBC's Congress of Cities and the Congressional City Conference.

National Black Caucus of State Legislators
Hall of States
444 North Capitol Street, N.W., Suite 622
Washington, DC 20001

The National Black Caucus of State Legislators' (NBCSL) primary mission is to develop, conduct, and promote educational, research, and training programs designed to enhance the effectiveness of its members, as they consider legislation and issues of public policy that impact, either directly or indirectly, upon "the general welfare" of African American constituents within their respective jurisdictions.

In support of its mission, NBCSL has adopted the following fundamental objectives:

1. To serve as a national network and clearinghouse for the discussion, dissemination, and exchange of ideas and information among African American state legislators and their staffs;
2. To provide research, training, and educational services to African American state legislators and their staffs;
3. To improve the effectiveness and quality of African American state legislators; and
4. To serve as a strong, united, and effective advocate for African American state legislators and their constituencies at the federal level.

National Black Leadership Roundtable
1424 Longworth House Building
Washington, DC 20515

The National Black Leadership Roundtable is the national network vehicle of the Congressional Black Caucus (CBC), the thirty-eight African Americans who serve today in the U.S. House of Representatives. The roundtable is composed of the heads of more than 200 national African American organizations who meet twice a year to develop and implement collective initiatives that support the public policy agenda of the CBC and that enhance the political, economic, and spiritual development of our people.

National Coalition on Black Voter Participation
1629 K Street, N.W., Suite 801
Washington, DC 20006
http://www.bigvote.org

The National Coalition strives to create an enlightened community by building institutional capacity at both the national and local levels that provides and develops African American leadership. By educating, organizing, and mobilizing citizens in our communities, the coalition seeks to encourage full participation in a barrier-free democratic process. Through educational programs and leadership training, the coalition works to expand, strengthen, and empower our communities to make voting and civic participation a cultural responsibility and tradition.

National Coalition of Blacks for Reparations in America
P.O. Box 62622
Washington, DC 20029-2622
http://www.ncobra.com

The National Coalition of Blacks for Reparations in America is a mass-based coalition organized for the sole purpose of obtaining reparations for African descendants in the United States. It was organized in late 1987 and early 1988 to broaden the base of support for the long-standing reparations movement. Organizational founders of NCOBRA include the New Afrikan Peoples Organization, the National Conference of Black Lawyers, and the Republic of New Afrika. It has individual members and organizational affiliates, a few of which include the National Association of Black Social Workers, Sigma Gamma Rho Sorority, National Black United Front, Black Reparations Commission, and the International Peoples' Democratic Uhuru Movement. NCOBRA has chapters throughout the U. S. and in Ghana and London. It is directed nationally by a board of directors. Its work is organized through nine national commissions: Economic Development, Human Resources, Legal Strategies, Legislation, Public Information and Education, Membership and Organizational Development, International Affairs, Youth, and Education.

Since its inception NCOBRA has embraced public education, mobilization, organization, and more recently, transformation, to obtain reparations. It has organized town hall meetings and rallies in cities throughout the United States, bringing long-time reparations advocates, the newly converted, and skeptics together to talk about the necessity of reparations to obtain racial justice. Its members and leaders have participated in conferences, radio and television programs, and people's tribunals discussing conditions that require reparations and strategies for moving forward. NCOBRA publishes an annual magazine, ENCOBRA, and a periodic newsletter and has a website: www.OfficialNCOBRA.org

NCOBRA supports legislative strategies and initiatives, such as H.R. 40, the Reparations Study Bill, introduced by Congressman John Conyers annually since 1989. It recognizes that the passage of this bill is important to obtaining reparations and remains committed to this process although Congress has not yet favorably acted upon it. NCOBRA puts this in context: it took twelve years for Congressman Conyers to obtain success in the Martin Luther King, Jr. Holiday Bill, a bill much less contentious than a reparations study bill for African descendants. NCOBRA has organized a number of legislative lobby days on Capitol Hill during which hundreds of people lobbied members of Congress to support H.R. 40. NCOBRA's Commission on Legislation has embarked on a project, A Year of Black Presence, inspired by "The Debt" by Randall Robinson. This project will enhance NCOBRA's presence on Capitol Hill, by bringing thousands of reparations supporters to lobby for passage of H.R. 40.

NCOBRA also supports state and municipal legislative initiatives. Its members have participated in the successful efforts in Michigan, Louisiana, the District of Columbia, California, Illinois, Ohio, and other places to obtain resolutions in support of reparations initiatives.

NCOBRA is developing lawsuits that will raise the issue of the legal right of African descendants to reparations based on the continuing vestiges of slavery. These lawsuits will focus on the many areas in which we as African people continue to suffer due to the legacy of slavery that include health, wealth/poverty, education, self-determination, and the imposition of criminal punishments.

NCOBRA engages in direct action to obtain reparations. Its leadership organized a highway slowdown on the Washington Metropolitan Area Beltway in the early 90s as well as demonstrations in front of federal buildings on what has become Reparations Awareness Day, February 25. The Economic Development Commission has begun an annual demonstration on April 4, on which day people are asked to boycott school or work and engage in reparations education and mobilization activities. NCOBRA also joins in direct action organized by other groups such as the Millions for Reparations Rally.

National Conference of Black Lawyers
2 West 125th Street
New York, NY 10027
http://www.geocities.com/capitolhill/loNariobby/9470

Its mission is to serve as the legal arm of the movement for Black liberation, to protect human rights, to achieve self-determination of Africa and African Communities in the diaspora, and to work in coalition to assist in ending oppression of all peoples.

National Conference of Black Mayors
1422 West Peachtree Street, N.W., Suite 800
Atlanta, GA 30309
http://www/votenet.com/members/b/l/a/blackmayors

A national organization of elected heads of municipal governments. In its periodic meetings it seeks to influence public policy on municipal governance and to organize support for voter participation.

National Conference of Black Political Scientists
c/o Kathie Stromila
Data Reseach and Cultural Institute
Mississippi Valley State University
Itta Bena, MS 38941-1400
http://www.poli.NCAT.edu/NCOBPS

The National Conference of Black Political Scientists (NCOBPS) is organized to study, enhance, and promote the political aspirations of people of African descent living in America. It is organized primarily as an intellectual vehicle and an educational instrument to resolve the multifaceted predicament that confronts people of African descent both in the United States and throughout the diaspora. The organization promotes research in, and critical investigation of those aspects of the discipline of political science and the larger sociopolitical and economic order that are directly and indirectly related to this multifaceted predicament. This organization is similarly concerned with the critical investigation of a wide range of mechanisms that must be considered as we move toward the resolution of this multifaceted predicament both at "home" and abroad.

National Forum for Black Public Administrators
777 North Capital Street, N.E., Suite 807
Washington, DC 20002

The mission of the NFBPA is embodied in the organization's commitment to strengthen the position of Blacks within the field of public administration; to increase the number of Blacks appointed to executive positions in public service organizations; and, to groom and prepare younger, aspiring administrators for senior public management posts in the years ahead. The NFBPA mission is realized through the pursuit of the following important goals:

* To serve the magnet organization for linking public, private, and academic institutions into an effective network to support interdisciplinary communications, management innovation, and professional development among Blacks choosing public service careers.
* To provide intensive and rigorous training in critical management areas in response to the specialized needs of Black public sector professionals.
* To identify and groom younger, emerging Black administrators and provide relevant exposure to the challenges and rewards of public service careers.
* To conduct research on selected social and economic issues endemic to Blacks.
* To sponsor and conduct national and regional forums that enable the discussion of timely issues and topical concerns of the Black community.
* To develop and maintain a national information bank on the nation's growing Black public administrative leadership.
* To promote, strengthen, and expand the roles of Blacks in all aspects of public administration.

National Organization of Black County Officials
440 First Street, N.W., Suite 1018
Washington, DC 20006
http://www.nobco.org

The National Organization of Black County Officials (NOBCO) is a 501 (c) 3 corporation, established in 1984, representing a coalition of Black elected and appointed officials within county government for all fifty states. The NOBCO corporation has its roots in the National Association of Black County Officials (NABCO), which was founded in 1975 as a membership association to bring focus on the nation's African American communities, their issues and their resolution, by providing direct assistance to Black county officials.

NOBCO provides services as an information clearinghouse for organizational concerns and provides a program and project structure to educate, train, and assist government officials and community members. NOBCO provides education and training to Black county officials, others in government, representatives from community-based organizations and agencies, and concerned citizens. Current program areas of focus include, but are not limited to, economic and community development and environmental justice issues. NOBCO serves more than 2,500 Black elected and appointed county officials in fifty states. Black county officials share responsibility for the promotion and maintenance of U.S. public and private forests. As local decisionmakers, the policies that Black county officials enact can either support or detract from a community's attempts to create a sustainable economy and sustainable environment.

NOBCO shares the common goals to conserve, protect, restore, and improve America's natural resources, provide products in the marketplace now and in the future, and eradicate barriers to equitable program delivery.

National Urban League
500 East 62nd Street
New York, NY 10021
http://www.nul.org

The Urban League is the nation's oldest and largest community-based movement devoted to empowering African Americans to enter the economic and social mainstream.

The Urban League movement was founded in 1910. The National Urban League, headquartered in New York City, spearheads its nonprofit, nonpartisan, community-based movement. The heart of the Urban League movement is its professionally staffed Urban League affiliates in more than 100 cities in thirty-four states and the District of Columbia.

The mission of the Urban League movement is to enable African Americans to secure economic self-reliance, parity and power, and civil rights.

Its three-pronged strategy for pursuing the mission is:

* Ensuring that children are well-educated and equipped for economic self-reliance in the twenty-first century;
* Helping adults attain economic self-sufficiency through good jobs, homeownership, entrepreneurship, and wealth accumulation; and
* Ensuring civil rights by eradicating all barriers to equal participation in the economic and social mainstream of America.

Urban League affiliates employ these three strategies, plus others tailored to local needs, in order to implement the mission of our movement.

Operation Big Vote
c/o National Coalition on Black Voter Participation
1629 K Street, N.W., Suite 801
Washington, DC 20006
http://www.bigvote.org

Operation Big Vote is one of the largest and most successful voter participation programs in the nation. The primary goals of Operation Big Vote (OBV) are to:

* Increase black registration and turnout,
* Educate black voters in ways that make their elected officials more responsive, and
* Promote empowerment of African Americans through full voter participation.

Operation PUSH (People United to Serve Humanity)
930 East 50th Street
Chicago, IL 60615

Operation PUSH is dedicated to achieving economic and political parity for blacks, other minorities, females, and poor people of all races. With fifty local chapters and thirty-eight affiliates across the country, PUSH promotes full employment, enactment of an "economic bill of rights" to assure the basic needs of black young people and the elderly, greater minority participation in the political system, and prison reform. The group also advocates improved health care, adequate housing, and educational facilities for all people; greater attention to the needs of veterans; and the enhancement of African/African American unity.

Southern Christian Leadership Conference (SCLC)
334 Auburn Avenue, N.E.
Atlanta, GA 30303

In the spirit of Martin Luther King Jr., the Southern Christian Leadership Conference is renewing its committment to bring about the promise of "one nation, under God, INDIVISIBLE" together with the commitment to activate the "strength to love" within the community of humankind.

Its goals are to promote spiritual principles within the membership and local communities; to educate youth and adults in the areas of personal responsibility, leadership potential, and community service; to ensure economic justice and civil rights in the areas of discrimination and affirmative action; and to eradicate environmental classism and racism wherever it exists.

Southern Poverty Law Center (SPLC)
1001 South Hull Street
Montgomery, AL 36104
http://www.splcenter.org

The Southern Poverty Law Center is a nonprofit organization that combats hate, intolerance, and discrimination through education and litigation. Its programs include the Intelligence Project, Teaching Tolerance, and Tolerance.org. The center also sponsors the Civil Rights Memorial, which celebrates the memory of those who died during the civil rights movement.

TransAfrica
1744 R Street, N.W.
Washington, DC 20009

The work of TransAfrica is summarized by the words from a section of the declaration of the fifth Pan-African Congress (1945), which reads in part: "We believe the success of Afro-Americans is bound up with the emancipation of all African peoples and also other dependent peoples and laboring classes everywhere." As such, the organization serves as a major research, educational, and organizing institution for the African American community offering constructive analyses of issues concerning U.S. policy as it affects Africa and the diaspora in the Caribbean and Latin America. A center for activism focusing on conditions in the African world, it sponsors seminars, conferences, community awareness projects, and training programs. These activities allow it to play a significant role in presenting to the general public alternative perspectives on the economic, political, and moral ramifications of U.S. foreign policy.

Internet Resources

African American Census Data
http://www.thuban.com/census/index.html

African American Internet Resources
http://http2.sils.umich.edu/HCHS/Afroam/Afroam_sources.html

African American Mosaic: Colonization
http://www.loc.gov/exhibits/african/acsbegin.html

African American Mosaic: A Library of Congress Resource Guide for the Study of Black History and Culture
http://www.loc.gov/exhibits/african/intro.html

African American Mosaic: Migrations
http://www.loc.gov/exhibits/african/migr.html

African American News Service
Gopher://gopher.igc.apc.org/11/race/aanews

African Americans in Politics and Government
http://www.usc.edu/Library/Ref/Ethnic/black_politics.html

Birmingham Civil Rights Institute: Birmingham, Alabama
http://www.the-matrix.com/bcri/bcri.html

Historical Notes on the African Methodist Episcopal Church
http://www.andersonchapel.org/history1.html

Martin Luther King Jr. Papers Project at Stanford University
http://www-leland.stanford.edu/group/king

Mary McLeod Bethune Council House National Historic Site
http://www.nps.gov/mamc/index.htm

Nation of Islam
http://www.noi.org/index.html

National Civil Rights Museum: Memphis, Tennessee
http://www.mecca.org/~crights/ncrm.html

Pan African Political and Organizational Information
http://www.panafrican.org/panafrican

Taking the Train to Freedom
http://www.nps.gov/undergroundrr/contents.htm

Timeline of the American Civil Rights Movement
http://www.wmich.edu/politics/mlk

References

Gregory, Vicki et al. 1999. *Multicultural Resources on the Internet: The United States and Canada*. Englewood, CO: Libraries Unlimited, 43–85.

Schultz, Jeffrey, et al. 2000. *Encyclopedia of Minorities in American Politics*, Vol. 1. New York: Oryx Press, 208–222.

Chronology

1492	A Black sailor accompanies Christopher Columbus to the Americas.
1501	The transport of Blacks to the Americas begins as enslavement commences in Spain.
1518	England enters the enslavement trade, licensing commercial ships for the purpose.
1581	The first enslaved Blacks arrive in what will become the United States, at St. Augustine, Florida.
1619	The first enslaved Blacks within the North American colonies arrive at Jamestown, Massachusetts.
1639	Blacks are prohibited from bearing arms in Virginia.
1641	Massachusetts becomes the first colony to legalize enslavement.
1663	The first documented rebellion by enslaved Blacks in North America occurs in Virginia.
1688	The Quakers begin what will become an enduring campaign for the abolition of enslavement.
1691	Virginia prohibits the manumission of enslaved persons and their residence in the colony.
1705	Massachusetts prohibits interracial marriage.
1712	South Carolina makes it illegal to punish whites who kill enslaved persons for resisting.
1770	The Quakers establish a school for Blacks in Philadelphia.
1776	An antislavery clause is deleted from the Declaration of Independence at the request of South Carolina and Georgia.
1787	The U.S. Constitution calls for the abolition of the enslavement trade in 1808, but Congress ratifies a compromise to count the enslaved as three-fifths of a person.
	Richard Allen and Absalom Jones establish the Free African Society.

1793	The first Fugitive Slave Act is passed.
1808	An act to prohibit the importation of enslaved persons becomes law.
1816	The African Methodist Episcopal Church is founded.
1819–1821	The Missouri Compromise is passed, which limits the expansion of enslavement states.
1822	Denmark Vesey conspires to organize a rebellion in North Carolina. The effort is betrayed.
1829	David Walker issues his provocative appeal to Blacks for rebellion.
	The National Negro Convention holds its first meeting.
1831	The Nat Turner rebellion occurs in Virginia, the largest of its kind for the violent overthrow of enslavement.
1849	Harriet Tubman escapes, later to lead the Underground Railroad that spirits hundreds of enslaved men and women to freedom in the northern United States and Canada.
1854	The Kansas-Nebraska Act is passed (repealing the Missouri Compromise), and permits continued expansion of the enslavement system.
1855	The first known Black official, John Langston, is elected town clerk in Lorain, Ohio.
	Massachusetts legalizes integrated schools.
1857	The Supreme Court issues the *Dred Scott* decision denying Blacks citizenship.
1859	John Brown's raid takes place at the Harpers Ferry ammunitions depot in Virginia.
1861	The Civil War begins.
1862	Blacks are allowed to enlist in the Union army.
1863	President Abraham Lincoln issues the Emancipation Proclamation.
1865	The Civil War ends.
	The Thirteenth Amendment passes outlawing enslavement.
	The Freedmen's Bureau is established.
	The Ku Klux Klan terrorist organization is founded.
1866	Fisk University is founded to educate Blacks.
1868	The Fourteenth Amendment passes giving Blacks citizenship.
1870	The Fifteenth Amendment passes giving Black males the right to vote.
1875	A Civil Rights Act passes granting equal access to public accommodations.
1876	President Rutherford Hayes withdraws Union troops from the South.
	Meharry Medical School, the first for Blacks, is founded in Nashville, Tennessee.
	Frederick Douglass receives a presidential appointment as Marshal of Washington, D.C.

1883	The Supreme Court declares the 1875 Civil Rights Act and associated statutes unconstitutional.
1892	Ida B. Wells-Barnett launches the antilynching campaign.
1895	Booker T. Washington gives his famous "Atlanta Compromise" speech calling for status quo ante in race relations.
	W.E.B. DuBois becomes the first Black to receive a Ph.D. from Harvard University.
1896	The Supreme Court issues the "separate but equal" doctrine in *Plessy v. Ferguson.*
1905	The Niagara Movement is formed, a forerunner to the National Association for the Advancement of Colored People (NAACP).
1909	The NAACP is founded in New York City.
1910	The National Urban League is founded.
1913	President Woodrow Wilson officially introduces segregation into the federal government.
1915	Carter Woodson, historian, founds the Association for the Study of Negro Life and History.
1916	Marcus Garvey, the Black nationalist thinker, arrives in the United States.
1917	In *Buchanan v. Warley,* the Supreme Court disqualifies residential racial zoning in housing districts.
	An NAACP campaign enables African Americans to be commissioned as officers in World War I.
1919	The "Red Summer" of racial riots and KKK terror takes place.
	W.E.B. DuBois leads the "first" Pan African Congress in Paris.
	Blacks are admitted to jury service.
1920	Marcus Garvey and the United Negro Improvement Association convene in New York City.
1922	The Harlem Renaissance, largely a literary movement, begins and continues through the decade.
1925	A. Philip Randolph organizes the Brotherhood of Sleeping Car Porters Union.
1930	The NAACP launches its first protest against Supreme Court nominee John Parker for support of discrimination.
1931	The Nation of Islam is founded.
1935	The NAACP wins the legal battle to admit a Black student to the University of Maryland.
	Mary McCleod Bethune founds the National Council of Negro Women.
1937	William Hastie, the first Black appointed to a federal district judgeship, is appointed by President Franklin Roosevelt.
1941	The NAACP leads the effort to ensure nondiscrimination in war-related industries and federal employment.

1942	The Congress of Racial Equality (CORE), a civil rights group dedicated to nonviolent direct action, is founded in Chicago.
1944	The United Negro College Fund is founded.
1947	Winston-Salem, North Carolina, elects the first Black since Reconstruction to the city council.
1948	President Harry Truman signs an executive order banning discrimination by the federal government.
1950	Ralph Bunche wins the Nobel Peace Prize.
1954	The *Brown v. Board of Education of Topeka, Kansas* decision overturns the "separate but equal" policy, declaring that separate schools are "inherently unequal."
1955	Rosa Parks is arrested for violating segregated bus seating policy in Montgomery, Alabama, leading to a year-long boycott and the emergence of Martin Luther King Jr.
1957	Emmett Till is lynched in Mississippi.
	President Dwight Eisenhower sends U.S. Army troops to Little Rock, Arkansas, to enforce the desegregation of schools. Congress passes the Civil Rights Act of 1957, the first such legislation in more than seventy-five years.
	The Southern Christian Leadership Conference (SCLC) is founded by Martin Luther King Jr. to coordinate the fight for civil rights.
1960	Greensboro, North Carolina, college students initiate sit-ins at segregated lunch counters.
	The Student Nonviolent Coordinating Committee (SNCC) is founded.
1961	The "Freedom Rides" begin in Washington, D.C. to desegregate public transportation facilities.
1962	James Meredith is admitted to the University of Mississippi under protection of federal troops, sparking a campus riot.
1963	The March on Washington of more than 200,000 people occurs, featuring Martin Luther King Jr.'s "I Have A Dream" speech.
	Medgar Evers, Mississippi NAACP leader, is assassinated in Jackson, Mississippi.
	A Birmingham, Alabama, church is bombed, killing four young girls at worship.
1964	Racial riots in Harlem and six other American cities occur.
	The poll tax is outlawed in the Twenty-fourth Amendment.
	The Civil Rights Act of 1964 is passed, barring discrimination in public accommodations.
	The MFDP challenges the seating of the white delegates at the National Democratic Party Convention.
	Martin Luther King Jr. is awarded the Nobel Peace Prize.

Three civil rights workers are murdered at Philadelphia, Mississippi, spawning national expression of rage at white violence against movement workers.

Malcolm X makes a pilgrimage to the Middle East and Africa.

1965 The Voting Rights Act is passed.

Malcolm X is assassinated.

A major riot occurs in Watts, an African American neighborhood of Los Angeles.

President Lyndon Johnson initiates the "War on Poverty," creating Headstart, VISTA, Job Corps, and the Office of Economic Opportunity, among other programs.

1966 The Black Panther Party is founded in Oakland, California.

Robert Weaver becomes the first Black appointed to a cabinet position, secretary of the U.S. Department of Housing and Urban Development.

Edward Brooke, a Republican, is the first Black elected to the U. S. Senate since Reconstruction.

1967 Racial riots and other civil disturbances occur in more than 100 cities.

Thurgood Marshall is appointed to the Supreme Court by President Lyndon Johnson.

Muhammad Ali, world boxing champion, is stripped of his title after being convicted for draft evasion.

Carl Stokes and Richard Hatcher become the first African American mayors of major cities in Cleveland, Ohio, and Gary, Indiana, respectively.

1968 Martin Luther King Jr. is assassinated in Memphis, Tennessee.

Shirley Chisholm of New York becomes the first Black woman elected to Congress.

The MFDP alternative delegation is seated at the National Democratic Party Convention.

Imari Obadele founds the Republic of New Africa, a nationalist organization seeking a separate Black nation in several southern states.

1970 The Philadelphia Plan, which becomes a template for future affirmative action programs, is adopted by executive order of President Richard Nixon. The plan establishes goals and timetables for remedying discrimination in the trade unions in Philadelphia.

1971 Jesse Jackson founds Operation People United to Serve Humanity (PUSH) in Chicago.

The Muhammad Ali conviction for draft evasion is overturned.

The Supreme Court sanctions busing to achieve racial integration in schools in *Swann v. Charlotte-Mecklenburg Board of Education.*

1972   The National Black Political Party Convention is held in Gary, Indiana.

The South elects its first Black congressional representatives since 1900—Barbara Jordan of Texas and Andrew Young of Georgia.

Shirley Chisholm seeks the Democratic Party presidential nomination.

1973   Los Angeles, Detroit, and Atlanta elect their first African American mayors in history.

The National Black Feminist Organization is founded.

Seven members of the nationalist Republic of New Africa are convicted for a shootout at their Jackson, Mississippi, headquarters in which an FBI agent is killed.

1974   Boston, Massachusetts, public schools are ordered to desegregate by a federal court.

Muhammad Ali regains his heavyweight boxing title.

1976   U.S. Representative Barbara Jordan makes the keynote address at the National Democratic Convention.

1977   Andrew Young is named United Nations Ambassador by President Jimmy Carter.

1978   The *Regents of California v. Allan Baake* Supreme Court decision states that race alone cannot be used by educational institutions to integrate professional schools. However, the ruling also says that race can be used in combination with other factors for such a remedy.

1980   Samuel Pierce is named secretary of the U.S. Department of Housing and Urban Development by President Ronald Reagan.

Riots occur in Liberty City, Florida, after the acquittal of police officers accused of beating an African American insurance executive in Tampa.

1981   The controversial conservative Clarence Pendleton is named chair of the U.S. Civil Rights Commission by President Ronald Reagan.

Harold Washington is elected first Black mayor of Chicago, Illinois.

President Ronald Reagan initiates a policy of "constructive engagement" to end the "isolation" of the apartheid government of South Africa.

1982   Clarence Thomas is named chair of the Equal Economic Opportunity Commission (EEOC) by President Ronald Reagan.

Andrew Young is elected mayor of Atlanta, Georgia.

Bryant Gumbel becomes the first African American to host a major network television morning news program.

1983   Guion Bluford becomes the first African American astronaut to go into space.

Jesse Jackson negotiates the release of U. S. Marine Lieutenant Robert Goodman, whose reconnaissance plane was shot down, from the government of Syria.

1984   Jesse Jackson runs as a Democratic candidate in the presidential primary election.

Randall Robinson, head of African American lobby organization TransAfrica, Mary Frances Berry of the U.S. Civil Rights Commission, Eleanor Holmes Norton of Georgetown Law School, and Walter Fauntroy, U.S. delegate from the District of Columbia, initiate a sit-in at the South African Embassy. This anti-apartheid protest continues for more than a year, and hundreds of people are arrested.

1985   Douglas Wilder is elected lieutenant governor of Virginia.

The Supreme Court affirms in *Thornburg v. Gingles* the use of minority electoral districts to prevent African American voter dilution.

The Congressional Black Caucus (CBC) leads a march against apartheid in South Africa.

1986   The Martin Luther King Jr. national holiday is established.

Congress overrides President Ronald Reagan's veto of legislation placing economic sanctions against South Africa.

The National Black Gay and Lesbian Conference is established to address HIV-AIDS in the African American community.

Ed Perkins, an African American career diplomat, is named U. S. ambassador to South Africa.

1988   The Supreme Court rules against affirmative action set-aside programs for minorities to win public contracts in *City of Richmond v. J. A. Crosson Company.*

Jesse Jackson runs as a Democratic candidate in the presidential primary elections.

1989   General Colin Powell is the first Black named as chair of the Joint Chiefs of Staff, by President George H. W. Bush.

Louis Sullivan is named secretary of the U.S. Department of Health and Human Services by President George H. W. Bush.

David Dinkins is elected mayor of New York City; Douglas Wilder is elected governor of Virginia—each the first Black elected to those positions.

Ron Brown is elected chair of the National Democratic Committee.

Imari Obadele and colleagues establish the National Coalition of Blacks for Reparations in America (NCOBRA).

1990   Nelson Mandela is released after twenty-eight years in prison in South Africa for opposing the policy of apartheid, and visits twelve U. S. cities.

1991   Clarence Thomas, amidst controversy because former subordinate Anita Hill charges him with sexual harassment, is named to the Supreme Court by President George H. W. Bush.

Earvin "Magic" Johnson, star of the National Basketball Association (NBA), announces his retirement due to HIV infection.

Arthur Ashe, prize-winning tennis pro, announces his AIDS infection due to a tainted blood transfusion during surgery.

Rodney King is beaten and was arrested by Los Angeles police, and the event is captured on videotape and publicly aired.

1992   Carol Moseley Braun is elected the first Black female in the U. S. Senate.

The police officers indicted for the Rodney King beating are acquitted in Los Angeles, precipitating a major riot in which nearly forty people are killed, thousands arrested, and property damage in the millions of dollars perpetrated.

1993   Toni Morrison is awarded the Nobel Prize for literature.

U.S. Representative John Conyers of Detroit introduces a bill in Congress seeking acknowledgment of the injustice of enslavement, creating a commission to examine the question of reparations.

Lani Guinier, civil rights attorney and professor of law, is nominated head of the Civil Rights Division of the Justice Department. The nomination is later withdrawn after a storm of controversy regarding her writings in support of affirmative action.

1994   Benjamin Chavis becomes the executive director of the NAACP.

1995   Louis Farrakhan leads the "Million Man March" in Washington, D.C.

O. J. Simpson, former professional football player and actor, is found not guilty of charges of murdering his ex-wife and her friend.

J. C. Watts is elected to the U.S. House of Representatives from Oklahoma, the first Black Republican from the South since Reconstruction.

President Bill Clinton names Christopher Edley, a Harvard law professor, as special counsel for the revision of affirmative action policies.

1995   Myrlie Evers Williams, widow of the assassinated Medgar Evers, is named chair of the board of the NAACP.

Alan Keyes, a conservative Black Republican, announces his candidacy for the U. S. presidency.

Military veterans and Black businesspeople launch a drive to nominate Colin Powell for the U. S. presidency.

The "Million Woman" March takes place in Washington, D.C.

1996   Kweisi Mfume, former U.S. representative from Maryland, is named executive director of the NAACP.

Colin Powell speaks to the Republican National Convention, and Jesse Jackson does so at the Democratic National Convention.

President Bill Clinton signs into law an act for welfare reform, making work a requirement for receiving public assistance, and giving states responsibility for these programs.

Commerce Secretary Ronald Brown is killed in an air crash.

In *Hopwood v. Texas*, the Supreme Court rules against the University of Texas Law School affirmative action program, saying that race is not permissible as a factor in admission to the school.

1997   Clifford Wharton is named deputy secretary of the U.S. State Department.

Vernon Jordan is named to head the transition team of president-elect Bill Clinton.

Abner Louima, a Black immigrant from Haiti, is tortured by New York City police, several of whom are indicted and convicted of associated charges. This situation sparks public demonstrations and calls for civilian review of police departments.

President Bill Clinton appoints historian John Hope Franklin to head a national advisory committee to start a "national conversation" on continuing racial division in U.S. society.

1998   President Bill Clinton names four African American cabinet secretaries: Ronald Brown, Commerce; Michael Espy, Agriculture; Hazel O'Leary, Energy; and Jesse Brown, Veterans Affairs.

President Bill Clinton also names Joycelyn Elders surgeon general and Drew Days solicitor general.

President Bill Clinton becomes the first U.S. president to make an official visit to Africa. He announces the Africa Growth and Opportunity Act, a program to stimulate market development.

1999	Amadou Diallo, a Black African immigrant from Guinea, West Africa, is shot by four New York City police officers in a hail of forty-one bullets, triggering weeks of protest demonstrations.
2000	Donna Brazile leads the 2000 presidential campaign of Vice President Al Gore, becoming the first African American in such a role.

Colin Powell is named secretary of state; Condolezza Rice is named national security adviser—both by President George W. Bush.

Randall Robinson of TransAfrica publishes the book *The Debt*, discussing the question of reparations for African American enslavement.

2003	The Supreme Court reaffirms the 1978 *Baake* decision that race can be a factor in college admissions as long as it does not take the form of a quota system.

References*:*

Asante, Molefi, and Mark Mattson. 1992. *Historical and Cultural Atlas of African Americans*. New York: Macmillan.

Davis, Townsend. 1998. *Weary Feet, Rested Souls: A Guided History of the Civil Rights Movement*. New York: Norton.

Hornsby, Alton, Jr. 1997. *Chronology of African American History*. Detroit: Gale. http://www.naacp.org.

Ploski, Harry A., and James Williams. 1989. *The Negro Almanac: A Reference Work on the African American*. 5th ed. Detroit, MI: Gale.

Annotated Bibliography

Alexander v. Holmes Board of Education. 392 U. S. 430 (1969).

    The Supreme Court ruled that continued operation of racially segregated schools under the standard of "all deliberate speed" is no longer constitutionally permissible. School districts must immediately terminate dual school systems based on race and operate only unitary school systems.

Alex-Assensoh, Yvette, and Lawrence J. Hanks (2000). *Black and Multiracial Politics in America.* New York: New York University Press.

    A collection of essays about interracial relations and the political behavior of minorities.

Altman, Susan (1997). *The Encyclopedia of African-American Heritage.* New York: Facts on File.

    An encyclopedic volume about Black history in America and the African heritage.

Amaker, Norman C. (1988). *Civil Rights and the Reagan Administration.* Washington, D.C.: Urban Institute Press.

    Analysis of civil rights for African Americans during the Reagan administration.

Appiah, Kwame Anthony, and Henry Louis Gates Jr. (1999). *Africana: The Encyclopedia of the African American Experience.* New York: Basic Civitas Books.

    A comprehensive record of the Pan-African diaspora. A reference work outlining the contributions of people of African descent around the world, but especially those in the Americas.

Aptheker, Herbert (1942). *American Negro Slave Revolts.* New York: International Press.

    A history of revolts by slaves in the United States. It details the major revolts of Prosser, Vesey, and Turner as well as smaller acts of resistance.

—— (1951). *A Documentary History of the Negro People in the United States.* New York: Citadel Press.

    A history of African Americans from the earliest time through documents.

—— (1971). "The Turner Cataclysm." In John Duff and Peter Mitchell, eds., *The Nat Turner Rebellion.* New York: Harper & Row.

    An essay analyzing the Nat Turner rebellion.

Asante, Molefi, and Mark Mattson (1992). *Historical and Cultural Atlas of African Americans*. New York: Macmillan.

A history of African Americans from African origins through the social and economic realities in the twentieth century.

Ashmore, Harry S. (1994). *Civil Rights and Wrongs: A Memoir of Race and Politics 1944–1994*. New York: Pantheon Books.

A former newspaper editor's reflections on the historical impact of race and its continuing influence on society, especially in the South.

Baker v. Carr. 369 U. S. 186 (1962).

The Supreme Court decision that authorized judicial intervention to remedy legislative malapportionment.

Balandier, Georges (1965). "The Colonial Situation." In Pierre van den Berghe, ed., *Africa: Social Problems in Conflict and Change*, 36–57. San Francisco: Chandler.

An essay analyzing European colonialism in Africa.

Baldwin, James (1955). *Notes of a Native Son*. New York: Beacon Press.

A collection of essays dealing with the politics of race on the cusp of the civil rights movement by the award-winning African American essayist and novelist.

Baldwin, Lewis V. (1983). *Invisible Strands in African Methodism: A History of the African Union Methodist Protestant and Union American Methodist Episcopal Churches, 1805–1980*. Metuchen, N.J.: Scarecrow Press.

A religious history of two African American Methodist sects in the United States.

Barker, Lucius, et al. (1999). *African Americans and the American Political System*. Saddle River, N.J.: Prentice-Hall.

Systematic analysis of the impact of American governmental institutions on African Americans. Examines African American participation, voting behavior, and influence in Congress.

Barnett, Marguerite Ross (1976). "Introduction." In Marguerite Ross Barnett and James Hefner, eds., *Public Policy for the Black Community*, 1–54. New York: Alfred Publishing.

A theoretical analysis of racial hierarchy and its effects on the policy process for African American interests.

———. (1982). "The Congressional Black Caucus: Illusions and Realities of Power." In Michael Preston et al., eds., *The New Black Politics: The Search for Power*. New York: Longman.

An examination of the operation and history of the Congressional Black Caucus (African Americans in Congress).

Bauer, Raymond, and Alice Bauer (1942). "Day to Day Resistance to Slavery." *Journal of Negro History*, vol. 27 (October): 388–449.

An essay analyzing the less well-known aspect of slavery—the day-to-day resistance of African Americans.

Beard, Charles (1913). *An Economic Interpretation of the American Constitution*. New York: Macmillan.

A critical analysis of the creation of the U.S. Constitution, arguing that the founders sought to protect their wealth as opposed to political democracy.

Bell, Derrick (1989). *And We Are Not Saved: The Elusive Quest for Racial Justice*. New York: Basic Books.

Analysis using allegory to elaborate the inherent features of racism in the American political and social environment.

———. (1992). *Faces at the Bottom of the Well: Permanence of Racism*. New York: Basic Books.

Dramatized accounts of the dilemma of race relations in America. Examines the role of violence, interracial relationships, and scapegoating, with stories and fables.

Bennett, Lerone (1977). *Black Power, U. S. A.* Chicago: Johnson Publishing.

A history of African Americans in the United States during the Reconstruction period—1867 to 1877.

———. (1985). *Before the Mayflower*. New York: Penguin Books.

A history of African Americans from the 1690s to the 1960s.

Berea College v. Kentucky. 211 U.S. 45 (1908).

The Supreme Court upheld a state law forbidding any institution, including private colleges and universities, to admit African Americans and whites to the same educational facilities.

Berry, Mary Frances, and John Blassingame (1982). *Long Memory: The Black Experience in America*. New York: Oxford University Press.

A survey of African American history, focusing on themes such as family and church, military service and the paradox of loyalty, and Black Nationalism.

Birmingham, David (1998). *Kwame Nkrumah: The Father of African Nationalism*. Athens: Ohio University Press.

A biography of Kwame Nkrumah, first postindependence president of the Republic of Ghana, who campaigned for Pan-African solidarity.

Blalock, Hubert, Jr. (1967). *Toward a Theory of Minority Group Relations*. New York: Wiley.

Essays that examine status, competition, and power relationships regarding prejudice.

Blassingame, John (1979). *The Slave Community*. New York: Oxford University Press.

Detailed history of Black community life on plantations during the antebellum era.

Blaustein, Albert, and Robert Zangrando, eds. (1970). *Civil Rights and the Black American: A Documentary History*. New York: Clarion.

A collection of public documents detailing the evolving status of African Americans in the fight for freedom.

Blyden, Edward (1971). "The Call of Providence to the Descendants of Africa in America." In Okon Edet Uya, ed., *Black Brotherhood: Afro-Americans and Africa*, 83–95. Lexington, Mass.: D. C. Heath.

An essay appealing to African Americans to raise the land of their forefathers from degradation and to establish an African nationality.

Board of Oklahoma City v. Dowell. 498 U.S. 237 (1991).

The Supreme Court authorized the termination of court supervision of school desegregation decrees when it could be shown that the purposes of the litigation were fully achieved.

Bositis, David (1994). *The Congressional Black Caucus in the 103rd Congress*. Lanham, Md.: University Press of America.

A detailed analysis of the recent changes in African American representation—both quantitative and qualitative—in the wake of the landmark 1992 elections.

———. (1998). *Black Elected Officials: A Statistical Summary, 1993–1997*. Washington, D.C.: Joint Center for Political and Economic Studies.

A statistical account of the trends and status of Black elected officials in the United States between 1993 and 1997.

Bracey, John, et al., eds. (1970). *Black Nationalism in America*. Indianapolis: Bobbs-Merrill.

A collection of documents devoted to Black nationalism, documenting its persistence and variety.

Branch, Taylor (1988). *Parting the Waters: America in the King Years, 1954–64*. New York: William Morrow.

A biography of Martin Luther King Jr. during the early phase of the civil rights movement. The author profiles key players and events that helped shape the American social landscape after World War II.

Brisbane, Robert H. (1976). *The Black Vanguard: Origins of the Negro Social Revolution, 1900–1960*. Valley Forge, N.Y.: Judson Press.

A history of African Americans leading up to the civil rights movement, from 1900 to 1960.

Broderick, Francis, and August Meier (1965). *Negro Protest Thought in the Twentieth Century*. Indianapolis: Bobbs-Merrill.

A collection of social and political writings by African Americans that illustrate the diverse ideological ideas and strategies among activists.

Brown v. Board of Education of Topeka, Kansas. 347 U.S. 483 (1954).

Supreme Court decision that required the desegregation of public schools, thus overturning the "separate but equal" principle that sustained segregation.

Browning, Rufus, et al. (1990). *Racial Politics in American Cities*, 2nd ed. New York: Longman.

A collection of original articles on racial city politics in U.S. cities.

Bullock, Henry A. (1967). *A History of Negro Education in the South*. Cambridge, Mass.: Harvard University Press.

The historical development of African American education in the South and the impetus for desegregation.

Burk, Robert (1985). *The Eisenhower Administration and Black Civil Rights*. Knoxville: University of Tennessee Press.

A detailed analysis of the Eisenhower administration programs and policies on civil rights.

Burner, Eric (1994). *And Gently He Shall Lead Them: Robert Parris Moses and Civil Rights in Mississippi*. New York: New York University Press.

An analytic biography of Robert Moses and the evolution of his moral and political philosophy in the Mississippi civil rights movement and the Student Nonviolent Coordinating Committee.

Burton, Vernon (1978). "Race and Reconstruction: Edgefield County, South Carolina." *Journal of Social History*, vol. 12: 31–56.

A paper examining the changing patterns of race relations in Edgefield County, South Carolina, during Reconstruction.

Button, James (1978). *Black Violence: The Political Impact of the 1960s Riots*. Princeton, N.J.: Princeton University Press.

This work examines how government and local communities responded to the urban riots in American cities in the 1960s.

Campbell, Angus (1966). "A Classification of the Presidential Elections." In Angus Campbell et al., eds., *Elections and the Political Order.* New York: Wiley.

An essay elucidating the theory of maintaining, deviating, and realigning elections, based on survey data.

Campbell, James T. (1995). *Songs of Zion: The African Methodist Episcopal Church in the United States and South Africa.* New York: Oxford University Press.

A history of the development of the African Methodist Episcopal Church in the United States and South Africa.

Carmichael, Stokely (1971). *Stokely Speaks: Black Power Back to Pan-Africanism.* New York: Vintage Books.

A collection of Carmichael's writings from the 1960s.

Carmichael, Stokely, and Charles Hamilton (1967). *Black Power: The Politics of Liberation.* New York: Vintage.

A work that examines the institutional nature of racism in America, proposing a new united group strategy for political emancipation for African Americans—Black Power.

Carson, Clayborne (1981). *In Struggle.* Cambridge, Mass.: Harvard University Press.

The ideological and organizational history of the Student Nonviolent Coordinating Committee.

———. (1986). "Civil Rights Reform and the Black Freedom Struggle." In Charles Eagles, ed., *The Civil Rights Movement in America.* Jackson: University Press of Mississippi.

This essay explores the political impact of civil rights reform on the ever-changing Black freedom struggle.

Carson, Clayborne, et al., eds. (1991). *The Eyes on the Prize Civil Rights Reader: Documents, Speeches, and Firsthand Accounts from the Black Freedom Struggle, 1954–1990.* New York: Viking Penguin Books.

An exhaustive collection of eyewitness accounts of the major events during the civil rights era.

Childs, John Brown (1980). *The Political Black Minister: A Study in Afro-American Politics and Religion.* Boston: G. K. Hall.

A study of African American religion and its political dimensions.

City of Mobile, Alabama v. Bolden. 446 U.S. 55 (1980).

The Supreme Court ruled that at-large electoral systems do not violate the rights of minority voters in contravention of the Fifteenth Amendment.

Civil Rights Commission (1967). *Political Participation.* Washington, D.C.: Government Printing Office.

An official report on African American electoral and political activities in ten southern states since the Civil Rights Act of 1964.

Clarke, John Henrik, ed., assisted by A. Peter Bailey and Earl Grant (1969). *Malcolm X: The Man and His Times.* Toronto: Collier Books.

A selection of essays by and about the life of Malcolm X from 1925 to 1965.

Clarke, John Henrik, ed., with the assistance of Amy Jacques-Garvey (1974). *Marcus Garvey and the Vision of Africa.* New York: Vintage.

A collection of essays detailing the life and work of Marcus Garvey.

Clay, William. (1992). *Just Permanent Interests: Black Americans in Congress, 1870–1991*. New York: Amistad Press.

The long-time U.S. representative from Missouri documents the presence of African Americans in Congress from Reconstruction to the present.

Clayton, Edward (1964). *The Negro Politician: His Success and Failure*. Chicago: Johnson Publishing.

An analysis of the political behavior of elected Black politicians, largely in the urban cities of the North.

Clegg, Claude, III (1998). *An Original Man: The Life and Times of Elijah Muhammad*. New York: St. Martin's Press.

The biography of Elijah Muhammad, leader of the Nation of Islam.

Colburn, David, and Jeffrey S. Adler (2001). *African American Mayors: Race, Politics, and the American City*. Urbana: University of Illinois Press.

An analytical history of Black mayors. Offering a diverse portrait of leadership, conflict, and obstacles, this volume assesses the political alliances that brought Black mayors to office, their accomplishments, and the challenges that marked their careers.

Coleman, Johnnie (2000). *Open Your Mind and Be Healed*. New York: DeVorss and Company.

A book focused on spiritual healing; discovering how to tap into the spiritual power latent within all mankind.

Cone, James H. (1997). *Black Theology and Black Power*. Maryknoll, N.Y.: Orbis.

A systematic presentation of Black liberation theology. It identifies liberation as the heart of the Christian gospel, and Blackness as the primary mode of God's presence.

Congressional Quarterly (2001). *Congressional Quarterly's Guide to U. S. Elections*, 4th ed. Washington, D.C.: Congressional Quarterly Press.

A comprehensive reference collection of election statistics and narrative explanations and interpretations of the context of elections.

Cronon, E. David (1955). *Black Moses: Marcus Garvey and the United Negro Improvement Association*. Madison: University of Wisconsin Press.

A political biography of Marcus Garvey.

Crowell, John (1971). "The Aftermath of Nat Turner's Insurrection." In John Duff and Peter Mitchell, eds., *The Nat Turner Rebellion*. New York: Harper & Row.

What was the impact of African enslavement? For the author, the brutality of the rebellion also illustrated the savagery of the system and marked the beginning of its end.

Crowley, Jocelyn, and Theda Skocpol (2001). "The Rush to Organize: Explaining Associational Formation in the United States, 1860s–1920s." *American Journal of Political Science*, vol. 45 (October): 813–829.

The essay analyzes factors influencing the historical development of voluntary membership associations in the United States, the impact of modernizing economic transformations, and the effects of the Civil War.

Crummell, Alexander (1971). "The Relations and Duties of Free Colored Men in America to Africa." In Okon Edet Uya, ed., *Black Brotherhood: Afro-Americans and Africa*, 63–70. Lexington, Mass.: D. C. Heath.

In the epistolary form, the author advocates emigration, encouraging free Blacks in America to return to Africa.

Cruse, Harold (1967). *The Crisis of the Negro Intellectual.* New York: William Morrow.
> A comprehensive critique of the ideologies, programs, African American social and political groups, and leaders in the period leading to the civil rights movement.

Curtin, Philip (1969). *The Atlantic Slave Trade.* Madison: University of Wisconsin Press.
> A detailed quantitative history of the scope of the Atlantic slave trade and the system of slavery, with estimates of the number of Africans removed from the African continent.

Dahl, Robert (1961). *Who Governs?* New Haven: Yale University Press.
> A pluralist study of local power, using New Haven, Connecticut, as a case.

———. (1971). *Polyarchy.* New Haven: Yale University Press.
> A theory of democratic pluralism.

Davidson, Roger H., and Walter J. Oleszek (2002). *Congress and Its Members,* 8th ed. Washington, D.C.: Congressional Quarterly Press.
> An encyclopedic text analyzing results of congressional elections.

Davis, Abraham, and Barbara Hill Graham (1995). *The Supreme Court, Race, and Civil Rights.* Thousand Oaks, Calif.: Sage.
> Constitutional law case book dealing with civil rights law throughout American history.

Davis, Angela (1981). *Women, Race, and Class.* New York: Vintage.
> This book examines the role of race and class among African American women in American society.

Dawson, Michael (1994). *Behind the Mule: Race and Class in African American Politics.* Princeton: Princeton University Press.
> An investigation of African American group identity, positing a linked-fate argument to explain continuing ideological cohesion among African Americans.

———. (2001). *Black Visions: The Roots of Contemporary African American Political Ideologies.* Chicago: University of Chicago Press.
> A comprehensive study of African American ideologies, using empirical tests to explore how they function in politics.

Dickerson, Dennis (1998). *Militant Negotiator: Whitney M. Young, Jr.* Lexington: University of Kentucky.
> A biography of Whitney M. Young.

Dittmer, John (1994). *Local People: The Struggle for Civil Rights in Mississippi.* Urbana: University of Illinois Press.
> A history of the civil rights movement in Mississippi.

Dodds, Elreta (1997). *The Trouble with Farrakhan and The Nation of Islam: Another Message to the Black Man in America.* Detroit: Press Toward the Mark Publications.
> A Black Christian critique of four notable speeches by Louis Farrakhan in 1995 and 1996.

Dolbeare, Kenneth, and Murray Edelman (1979). *American Politics,* 3rd ed. Lexington, Mass.: D. C. Heath.
> An American government textbook using the elite model.

Dollar, Creflo (1999). *Total Life Prosperity: 14 Practical Steps To Receiving God's Blessings.* New York: Thomas Nelson.
> A guide to Christian spiritual development.

Douglass, Frederick (1962; originally published 1892). *Life and Times of Frederick Douglass, Written by Himself.* New York: Macmillan.
>   Frederick Douglass's autobiography, covering his early life.

Dred Scott v. Sandford. U.S. 393 (1857).
>   United States Supreme Court decision that legally defined African Americans as property with "no rights that a white man was bound to respect."

Drewy, William (1971). "The Southampton Insurrection." In John Durr and Peter Mitchell, eds., *The Nat Turner Rebellion.* New York: Harper & Row.
>   An essay arguing that slavery was not the evil that provoked Nat Turner, but that he was a religious fanatic.

DuBois, W.E.B. (1965). *The Suppression of the African Slave Trade.* New York: Russell and Russell.
>   A comprehensive study of the chattel trade in Africans, including the economic and political ramifications of the slavery system.

———. (1969). *Black Reconstruction in America.* New York: Meridian Books.
>   The first full-length study of the role African Americans played in the post–Civil War era, using a modified class analysis.

———. (1989). *The Souls of Black Folk.* New York: Penguin.
>   A selection of social and political essays that define a new agenda for African American political liberation at the beginning of the twentieth century.

Dyson, Michael Eric (1996). *Race Rules: Navigating the Color Line.* Reading, Mass.: Addison-Wesley.
>   A collection of essays addressing the problem of racial division in America and exploring divisions within the Black community.

Easton, David (1965). *A Systems Analysis of Political Life.* New York: John Wiley.
>   A work that elucidates an empirical theory for analysis of political behavior.

Edley, Christopher (1996). *Not All Black and White.* New York: Hill and Wang.
>   A study of affirmative action programs and their future during the Clinton administration.

Estell, Kenneth (1994). *Reference Library of Black America,* vol. 2. Detroit: Gale Research, Inc.
>   A reference encyclopedia on African American life.

Fairclough, Adam (1987). *To Redeem the Soul of America: The Southern Christian Leadership Conference and Martin Luther King Jr.* Athens: University of Georgia Press.
>   An examination of the organization that arose around Martin Luther King Jr. as he emerged as a national civil rights leader.

Faw, Bob, and Nancy Skelton (1986). *Thunder in America.* Austin: Texas Monthly Press.
>   An analysis of the presidential campaign of Jesse Jackson in 1984.

Fishel, Leslie, Jr., and Benjamin Quarles, eds. (1967). *The Negro American: A Documentary History.* Glenview, Ill.: Scott, Foresman.
>   A history of African Americans through primary documents from the 1700s.

Foner, Eric (1990). *A Short History of Reconstruction.* New York: Harper & Row.
>   An abridged version of *Reconstruction: America's Unfinished Revolution,* the comprehensive study of the aftermath of the Civil War.

———. (1996). *Freedom's Lawmakers: A Directory of Black Officeholders During Reconstruction.* Baton Rouge: Louisiana University Press.

Foner, Philip (1970). *The Black Panthers Speak*. Philadelphia: Lippincott.
A collection of primary documents of the California-based Black Panther Party.
A census of more than 1,500 black office holders during Reconstruction, along with leader profiles.
Foner, Philip, and George Walker, eds. (1979). *Proceedings of the Black State Conventions, 1840–1865*, vol. 1. Philadelphia: Temple University Press.
The historical records of African American state political conventions in several states, including New York, Indiana, Maryland, Illinois, Kansas, Virginia, South Carolina, Louisiana, and Missouri.
Foster, William (1974). "The Garvey Movement: A Marxist View." In John Henrik Clarke, ed., *Marcus Garvey and the Vision of Africa*, 415–427. New York: Vintage.
A Marxian class analysis of the Garvey movement.
Franklin, John Hope (1995). "Race and the Constitution in the Nineteenth Century." In John Hope Franklin and Genna Rae McNeil, eds., *African Americans and the Living Constitution*. Washington D.C.: Smithsonian Institution.
An essay focusing on how race underlay much of the change the U.S. Constitution underwent in the nineteenth century.
Franklin, John Hope, and Alfred A. Moss (1994). *From Slavery to Freedom*, 7th ed. New York: McGraw-Hill.
A comprehensive history of African Americans covering social, political, and cultural elements of African American life in the United States.
Frazier, E. Franklin (1974). *The Negro Church in America*. New York: Schocken Books.
A sociological history of Black church in the United States.
Garfunkel, Herbert (1959). *When Negroes March: The March on Washington Movement in the Organizational Politics for FEPC*. New York: Free Press.
An analysis of the grassroots organization developed by A. Philip Randolph that led to the establishment of the Federal Employment Practices Commission.
Garrow, David J. (1978). *Protest at Selma: Martin Luther King Jr. and the Voting Rights Act of 1965*. New Haven: Yale University Press.
A history of the struggle led by Martin Luther King Jr. that resulted in the enactment of Voting Rights Act of 1965.
———. (1981). *The FBI and Martin Luther King Jr.* New York: Norton.
A historical documentation of the FBI surveillance of Martin Luther King Jr. and the abuse of government power.
———. (1986). *Bearing the Cross: Martin Luther King Jr. and the Southern Christian Leadership Conference*. New York: William Morrow.
An analysis of the ideology and strategies of Martin Luther King Jr. and the SCLC.
George, Carol V. R. (1973). *Segregated Sabbaths: Richard Allen and the Emergence of Independent Black Churches, 1760–1840*. New York: Oxford University Press.
A history of Richard Allen and the emergence of African American churches, especially the African Methodist Episcopal Church.
Glantz, Oscar (1967). "The Negro Voter in Northern Industrial Cities." In Harry Bailey Jr., ed., *Negro Politics in America*, 338–352. Columbus, Ohio: Charles Merrill.
An analysis of the political role of Blacks in electoral politics in northern cities after the Great Migration.

Gosnell, Harold (1935). *Negro Politicians: The Rise of Negro Politics in Chicago.* Chicago: University of Chicago Press.
    An analysis of elected African American politicians in Chicago after the Great Migration.
Grant, Joanne (1998). *Ella Baker: Freedom Bound.* New York: Wiley.
    A biography of Ella Baker, a civil rights leader active in the NAACP, SCLC, and SNCC.
Groh, George (1972). *The Black Migration: The Journey to Urban America.* New York: Weybright and Talley.
    An analysis of the African American migration from the rural South to the urban North early in the twentieth century.
Grovey v. Townsend. 295 U.S. 45 (1935).
    The Supreme Court upheld the right of political parties, as private groups, to exclude African Americans, since this action was not compelled by the state.
Guinier, Lani (1994). *The Tyranny of the Majority.* New York: Free Press.
    A collection of essays addressing voting rights and theories of representation.
Guinn v. United States. 238 U.S. 347 (1915).
    The Supreme Court ruled that the "grandfather clause" was unconstitutional because it violated the Fifteenth Amendment, which guarantees the franchise.
Gutman, Herbert (1976). *The Black Family in Slavery and Freedom.* New York: Vintage Books.
    A history of African American families from the early days of slavery until after the Civil War.
Hacker, Andrew (1992). *Two Nations.* New York: Macmillan.
    An analysis of continuing racial disparities in American society in the post–civil rights movement period.
Hamilton, Charles V. (1972). *The Black Preacher in America.* New York: William Morrow.
    An analysis of Black clergymen in political leadership.
———. (1991). *Adam Clayton Powell, Jr.: The Political Biography of an American Dilemma.* New York: Atheneum Press.
    A biography of Adam Clayton Powell Jr., the Harlem congressman.
Hamilton, Charles, ed. (1973). *The Black Experience in American Politics.* New York: Capricorn.
    A collection of essays revealing the political thought and participation of Black Americans.
Hamilton, Donna Cooper, and Charles Hamilton (1997). *The Dual Agenda: The African American Struggle for Civil and Economic Equality.* New York: Columbia University Press.
    A study of social welfare policymaking from the New Deal to the 1990s.
Hampton, Henry, Steve Fayer, and Sarah Flynn (1990). *Voices of Freedom: An Oral History of the Civil Rights Movement From the 1950s through the 1980s.* New York: Bantam Books.
    Interviews with participants in the major events of the civil rights era, with introductory essays and background material for each era.
Hanks, Lawrence J. (1987). *The Struggle for Black Political Empowerment in Three Georgia Counties.* Knoxville: University of Tennessee Press.

An analysis of African Americans in rural politics in three Black counties in Georgia (Hancock, Peach, and Clay) during the period 1960–1982.

Harding, Vincent (1969). "Religion and Resistance Among Antebellum Negroes, 1850–1868." In A. Meier and E. Rudwick, eds., *The Making of Black America*, vol. 2. New York: Atheneum Press.

An essay that documents the dual role of religion as a force of submission and as a wellspring of African American protest.

———. (1983). *There Is a River*. New York: Vintage Books.

A comprehensive history of African American resistance to racial oppression.

Harlan, Louis R. (1972). *Booker T. Washington: The Making of a Black Leader, 1856–1901*. New York: Oxford University Press.

Volume 1 of a comprehensive biography of Booker T. Washington.

Harris, Sheldon (1972). *Paul Cuffee: Black America and the African Return*. New York: Simon and Schuster.

A biography of Paul Cuffee, an early exponent of repatriation of Blacks to Africa.

Harrison, Roderick (2001). "Numbers Running." *Crisis Magazine* (May/June): 14–17.

An essay on the major racial shifts in population revealed by the 2000 census.

Hearn, Kimberly, and Lisa Jackson (2002). "African Women and HIV Risk: Exploring the Effects of Gender and Social Dynamics on Behavior." *African American Research Perspectives*. An Occasional Report. Vol. 8, no. 1, 163–173. Ann Arbor: University of Michigan Press.

A study of the effects of gender and the risk of HIV infection.

Held, David (1996). *Models of Democracy*, 2nd ed. Stanford: Stanford University Press.

An exposition of democratic political thought and practice.

Higginbotham, A. Leon (1980). *In the Matter of Color*. New York: Oxford University Press.

Details the role of the law in the subjugation and enslavement of African Americans.

Higginson, Thomas Wentworth (1971). "Nat Turner's Insurrection." In John Duff and Peter Mitchell, eds., *The Nat Turner Rebellion*. New York: Harper & Row.

An essay interpreting Nat Turner's rebellion.

Hine, Darlene (1979). *Black Victory*. Millwood, N.Y.: KTO Press.

A history of the white primary in Texas and its ultimate demise in court.

Holden, Matthew, Jr. (1973). *The Politics of the Black Nation*. New York: Chandler.

A comprehensive analysis of African American political behavior and theory in the context of the general American political arena.

Holt, Thomas (1977). *Black Over White*. Urbana: University of Illinois Press.

A history of African American political leadership in South Carolina during Reconstruction.

———. (1984). "The Lonely Warrior: Ida B. Wells-Barnett and the Struggle for Leadership." In John Hope Franklin and August Meier, eds., *Black Leaders of the Twentieth Century*, 39–62. Urbana: University of Illinois Press.

A historical essay on the leadership of Ida B. Wells-Barnett, a feminist civil rights activist and antilynching campaign organizer.

Hornsby, Alton, Jr. (1997). *Chronology of African American History.* Detroit: Gale.
A timeline of African American history from 1492 until the late twentieth century, with narrative articles on certain themes.

Hutchinson, Earl Ofari (1972). *Let Your Motto Be Resistance: The Life and Thought of Henry Highland Garnet.* Boston: Beacon Press.
An analytic history of the life and thoughts of Henry Highland Garnet.

Jacques-Garvey, Amy (1986). *Philosophy and Opinions of Marcus Garvey.* New York: Atheneum Press.
The collected speeches and writings of the famous proponent of Black Nationalism, Marcus Garvey.

Jakes, T. D. (1999). *Maximize the Moment: God's Action Plan for Your Life.* New York: Putnam.
A book detailing Jakes's fundamentalist Christian message.

Jaynes, Gerald, and Robin Williams Jr., eds. (1989). *Common Destiny: Blacks and American Society.* Washington, D.C.: National Academy Press.
A collection of papers and research notes from a four-year study of the status of African Americans in the 1980s.

Joint Center for Political Studies (1976). *National Roster of Black Elected Officials.* Washington, D.C.: Joint Center for Political Studies.
A census of Black electoral participation in the 1970s, including a list of office holders and an expanded section on women.

Jones, Mack (1972). "A Frame of Reference for Black Politics." In Lenneal Henderson Jr., ed., *Black Political Life in the United States,* 7–20. San Francisco: Chandler.
A theoretical model for the analysis of the impact of white racism on African American politics.

———. (1976). "Black Political Officeholding and Political Development in the Rural South." *Review of Black Political Economy,* vol. 6, no. 4 (Summer): 375–407.
An essay assessing the significance of the dramatic increase in Black elected officials in the rural South.

Jones, Rhett (1973). "Proving Blacks Inferior." In Joyce Ladner, ed., *The Death of White Sociology.* New York: Vintage.
An essay examining genetic theories of African American inferiority.

Jordan, Winthrop D. (1968). *White Over Black: American Attitudes Toward the Negro.* Chapel Hill: University of North Carolina Press.
An investigation into American racial attitudes toward African Americans and the historical impact on the development of a racialized society.

Kaplan, H. Roy (1977). *American Minorities and Economic Opportunity.* Itasca, Ill.: Peacock.
An investigation into the minority employment situation in the U.S. economy.

Keech, William (1968). *The Impact of Negro Voting: The Role of the Vote in the Quest for Equality.* Chicago: Rand McNally.
This study examines the impact of the new Black voters after the Voting Rights Act of 1965.

Kellogg, Charles (1967). *NAACP.* Baltimore: Johns Hopkins University Press.
A history of the NAACP from its origins through the 1960s.

Key, V. O., Jr. (1949). *Southern Politics.* New York: Knopf.
An analysis of racial politics in the former Confederate states.

————. (1955). "A Theory of Critical Elections." *Journal of Politics,* vol. 17: 3–18.
An essay elaborating a theory of "critical elections."

King, Barbara (1995). *Transform Your Life.* New York: Perigee Publishers.
A book of spiritual inspiration showing how prayer can transform personal lives.

Kinder, Donald, and Lynn Sanders (1996). *Divided by Color: Racial Politics and Democratic Ideals.* Chicago: University of Chicago Press.
A critical study of public opinion about race in the United States.

Klein, Michael (1991). *The Man Behind the Sound Bite: The Real Story of Reverend Al Sharpton.* New York: Castillo International Publishers.
A biography of the Reverend Al Sharpton, a New York–based clergyman-politician.

Kraditor, Aileen (1969). *Means and Ends in American Abolitionism.* New York: Pantheon.
An analysis of the abolition movement.

Krislov, Samuel (1967). *The Negro in Federal Employment: The Quest for Equal Opportunity.* Minneapolis: University of Minnesota Press.
A study of the role of the federal service as an avenue for African American employment.

Kryder, Daniel (2000). *Divided Arsenal: Race and the American State During World War II.* New York: Cambridge University Press.
An analysis of race and the mobilization of human resources for World War II.

Ladd, Everett C., Jr., and Charles Hadley (1975). *Transformations of the American Party System.* New York: W. W. Norton.
A study of political parties in the United States from the New Deal to the 1970s.

Lee, Chana (1999). *For Freedom's Sake: The Life of Fannie Lou Hamer.* Urbana: University of Illinois Press.
A biography of Fannie Lou Hamer, the Mississippi civil rights leader and orator.

Legette, Willie M. (2000). "The South Carolina Legislative Black Caucus, 1970 to 1988." *Journal of Black Studies,* vol. 30: 839–858.
An article on the development and activities of the South Carolina Legislative Black Caucus in the post–civil rights movement era.

Levy, Peter B. (1998). *The Civil Rights Movement.* Westport, Conn.: Greenwood Press.
An introduction to the civil rights movement and its development, issues, and leaders. It analyzes the crucial aspects of the movement and assesses its legacy.

Lewis, David Levering (1970). *King: A Biography.* Urbana: University of Illinois Press.
A comprehensive biography of Martin Luther King Jr.

————. (1994). *W.E.B. DuBois: Biography of a Race, 1868–1919.* New York: Henry Holt.
Volume 1 of the comprehensive biography of DuBois, covering his early life through the founding of the NAACP and World War I.

————. (2000). *W.E.B. DuBois: The Fight for Equality and the American Century, 1919–1963.* New York: Henry Holt.

The second volume of the comprehensive biography of DuBois, chronicling his life from his break with the NAACP to his death in Ghana.

Lewis, John (1998). *Walking with the Wind: A Memoir of the Movement.* New York: Simon and Schuster.

An autobiographical account of the life of this civil rights activist, SNCC chairman, and member of Congress.

Lewis, Rupert (1988). *Marcus Garvey: Anti-Colonial Champion.* Trenton, N.J.: Africa World Press.

A biography of Marcus Garvey.

Lincoln, C. Eric (1994). *The Black Muslims in America,* 3rd ed. Trenton, N.J.: Africa World Press.

A religious history and social study of the Black Muslims.

Lincoln, C. Eric, and Lawrence H. Mamiya (1990). *The Black Church in the African American Experience.* Durham, N.C.: Duke University Press.

A comprehensive religious history of the Black church in American history and culture.

Lipsky, Michael (1968). "Protest as a Political Resource." *American Political Science Review,* vol. 62 (December): 1144–1158.

A theoretical essay on protest as a form of political resource acquisition.

Logan, Rayford (1972). *The Betrayal of the Negro.* New York: Collier.

A history of the Reconstruction betrayal of African Americans.

Logan, Rayford, and Michael Winston, eds. (1982). *Dictionary of Negro Biography.* New York: W. W. Norton.

An encyclopedia of biographies of important African Americans.

Loury, Glenn (1995). *One By One From the Inside Out.* New York: Free Press.

A collection of essays and reviews on race relations.

Lynch, Hollis Ralph (1967). *Edward Wilmot Blyden: Pan-Negro Patriot 1832–1912.* New York: Oxford University Press.

A biography of Edward Wilmot Blyden, the African nationalist.

Lynch, John R. (1913). *The Facts of Reconstruction.* New York: Neale.

A history of Reconstruction in the state of Mississippi.

Lyons, Thomas T. (1971). *Black Leadership in American History.* Menlo Park, Calif.: Addison-Wesley.

A history of African American political activity with biographies of leaders.

Malcolm X, with the assistance of Alex Haley (1965). *The Autobiography of Malcolm X.* New York: Grove Press.

The autobiography of the Black Muslim leader, Malcolm X.

Malcolm X (1969). "Racism: The Cancer That is Destroying America." In John Henrik Clarke, ed., assisted by A. Peter Bailey and Earl Grant, *Malcolm X: The Man and His Times,* 302–306. Toronto: Collier Books.

A speech on racism and its destructiveness to general American society.

Marable, Manning (2000). "The Gary Black Political Convention of 1972." In Jonathan Birnbaum and Clarence Taylor, eds., *Civil Rights Since 1787: A Reader on the Black Struggle,* 635–640. New York: New York University Press.

An analysis of the Gary "Black Political Convention" of 1972 and its impact on the movement for a Black political party.

Marinelli, Lawrence (1964). *The New Liberia.* London: Pall Mall.

A historical survey of Liberia.

Martin, Robert (1967). "The Relative Political Status of the Negro in the United States." In Harry Bailey Jr., ed., *Negro Politics in America*, 13–33. Columbus, Ohio: Charles Merrill Publishing.

An essay detailing empirical changes in Black political status and participation through voting and office holding in the civil rights era.

McAdam, Doug (1982). *Political Process and the Development of Insurgency, 1930–1970*. Chicago: University of Chicago Press.

A social movement analysis of the civil rights insurgency.

McFarlin, Annjennette (1976). *Black Congressional Reconstruction Orators and Their Orations, 1869–1879*. Metuchen, N.J.: Scarecrow Press.

A collection of speeches by Black Reconstruction congressional politicians.

McKinney, George C., et al., eds. (1997). *The African American Devotional Bible*. Grand Rapids, Mich.: Zondervan Publishing.

A selection of theological devotions for Black Christians.

McMillen, Neil (1990). *Dark Journey*. Urbana: University of Illinois Press.

A history of African Americans in Mississippi.

McNeil, Genna Rae (1983). *Groundwork*. Philadelphia: University of Pennsylvania Press.

A biography of Charles Houston, the "father" of the NAACP legal strategy for racial change.

McWhorter, John (2000). *Losing the Race: Self-Sabotage in Black America*. New York: HarperCollins.

An argument that racism's legacy is self-defeatism in Black America, in academic pursuits.

Meier, August, and Elliott Rudwick (1966). *From Plantation to Ghetto*. New York: Hill and Wang.

A concise analytic history of African Americans in the United States.

———. (1973). *CORE*. New York: Oxford University Press.

A history of the ideology and tactics of the Congress of Racial Equality, a nonviolent civil rights group that organized the Freedom Rides.

Meyer, Michael, ed. (1984). *Frederick Douglass: The Narratives and Selected Writings*. New York: Modern Library.

A collection of essays by Frederick Douglass.

Miller, Floyd (1975). *The Search for a Black Nationality: Black Emancipation and Colonization, 1787–1863*. Urbana: University of Illinois Press.

An analytical history of African American emigration from the late eighteenth through the nineteenth century.

Miller, Jake (1978). *The Black Presence in American Foreign Affairs*. Washington, D.C.: University Press of America.

An analysis of African American diplomats.

Million Man March Organizing Committee (1995). *The Million Man March—Day of Absence Mission Statement*. Chicago: Third World Press.

A collection of essays on the Million Man March organized by Louis Farrakhan.

Mills, Kay (1993). *This Little Light of Mine: The Life of Fannie Lou Hamer*. New York: Dutton.

A biography of this Mississippi civil rights leader.

Missouri ex rel. Gaines v. Canada. 305 U. S. 337 (1938).

Supreme Court decision that ordered desegregation of the University of Missouri Law School. It presaged the *Brown* decision, which completely outlawed school segregation.

Moore, Jesse, Jr. (1981). *The Search for Equality: The National Urban League, 1910–1961.* University Park, Pa.: Pennsylvania State University Press.

A history of the National Urban League.

Moore, Richard (1974). "The Critics and Opponents of Marcus Garvey." In John Henrik Clarke, ed., *Marcus Garvey and the Vision of Africa,* 210–255. New York: Vintage.

An examination of Marcus Garvey and his chief critics.

Morgan v. Virginia. 328 U.S. 373 (1946).

The Supreme Court outlawed segregation of buses involved in interstate commerce.

Morris, Aldon (1984). *The Origins of the Civil Rights Movement: Black Communities Organizing for Change.* New York: Free Press.

A social movement analysis of the civil rights movement.

Morris, Aldon, Shirley Hatchett, and Ronald Brown (1989). "The Civil Rights Movement and Black Political Socialization." In R. Siegel, ed., *Political Learning in Adulthood.* Chicago: University of Chicago Press.

A discussion of the civil rights movement as a vehicle for African American political socialization.

Morris, Milton (1975). *The Politics of Black America.* New York: Harper & Row.

A textbook on African American politics.

Morrison, Minion K. C. (1987). *Black Political Mobilization, Leadership, and Power.* Albany: State University of New York Press.

A study of African American mayors in rural politics in Mississippi in the post–civil rights era.

———. (1989). "Racial Violence and Racial Mobilization in the United States (1960–1980)." In Sophie Body-Gendrot and Jacques Carr, eds., *Ville et violence dans le monde anglophone,* 97–114. Clermont-Ferrand, France: Université Blaise-Pascal.

A study of violence as a strategy for political mobilization in the United States in the 1960s.

———. (2002). "Prologue: Who Is J. Milton Turner and Why Is His Story Important?" In Hanes Walton, Jr., et al., eds., *Liberian Politics: The Portrait by African American Diplomat J. Milton Turner.* Lanham, Md.: Lexington Books.

An essay on the political development of J. Milton Turner in the context of Reconstruction partisan politics.

Morrison, Minion K. C., and Joe Huang (1972). "The Transfer of Political Power in a Bi-racial Mississippi Town." *Growth and Change,* vol. 4, no. 2: 25–29.

An analysis of the first Black chief executive in a biracial Mississippi town, Fayette, since Reconstruction.

Moynihan, Daniel P. (1965). *The Negro Family.* Washington, D.C.: Government Printing Office.

A government report on the historical causes and effects of poverty among African American families in the United States. It was controversial because of its assertion that family breakdown was the source of the problems.

Myrdal, Gunnar (1944). *An American Dilemma.* New York: Harper & Row.

A comprehensive investigation into race relations in America noting the disparity between the espousal of equality and the perpetuation of unequal treatment of African Americans.

National Advisory Commission on Civil Disorders (1968). *Report of the National Advisory Commission on Civil Disorders.* New York: Bantam Books.

A federal government report, known as the Kerner Commission, on the social and political conditions that led to racial strife and civil unrest during the 1960s.

Nelson, William, Jr., and Philip Meranto (1977). *Electing Black Mayors: Political Action in the Black Community.* Columbus: Ohio State University Press.

A comparative analysis of Black mobilization for mayoral elections in Cleveland, Ohio, and Gary, Indiana.

Newberry v. United States. 256 U.S. 232 (1922).

The Supreme Court ruled that since political parties are private organizations they could bar African Americans from membership and subsequent participation in the primary elections of those parties.

Newman, Richard, et al., eds. (2001). *Pamphlets of Protest: An Anthology of Early African American Protest Literature, 1790–1860.* New York: Routledge.

A collection of essays on the history of African Americans from 1790 to 1860.

Nixon v. Herndon. 273 U.S. 536 (1927).

The Supreme Court ruled that states could not make rules barring African Americans from primaries.

Nobles, Melissa (2000). *Shades of Citizenship: Race and the Census in Modern Politics.* Stanford: Stanford University Press.

An analysis of the role of race in census taking in the United States and Brazil.

Omi, Michael, and Howard Winant (1994). *Racial Formation in the United States from the 1960s to the 1990s.* New York: Routledge.

A theoretical analysis of racial formation processes and their consequences for the political participation of racialized groups in the United States.

Oppenheimer, Martin (1989). *The Sit-In Movement of 1960.* New York: Carlson Publishing.

An analysis of the civil rights sit-in movement of African American students in the southern United States.

O'Reilly, Kenneth (1989). *Racial Matters: The FBI Secret File on Black America, 1960–1972.* New York: Free Press.

A book detailing how political loyalties, priorities, and prejudices turned the FBI into an adversary of civil rights.

———. (1995). *Nixon's Piano: Presidents and Racial Politics from Kennedy to Clinton.* New York: Free Press.

A study of presidential relations with African Americans from Kennedy to Clinton.

Painter, Nell (2000). "Rodney King, Police Brutality, and Riots." In Jonathan Blaustein and Clarence Taylor, eds., *Civil Rights since 1787,* 645–649. New York: New York University Press.

A study of police violence and abuse, using the southern California beating of Rodney King as a case.

Parenti, Michael (1970). "Power and Pluralism: A View from the Bottom." *Journal of Politics* (August): 504–519.

An elite theory critique of the pluralist theoretical model in political science.

———. (1978). *Power and the Powerless*. New York: St. Martin's Press.

A critique of power relationships in American government using the elite theory model.

Park, Robert (1950). *Race and Culture*. New York: Free Press.

Volume 1 of the collected papers of Robert Park on the sociology of race.

Parker, Freddie (1993). *Running for Freedom: Slave Runaways in North Carolina, 1775–1840*. New York: Garland.

Focusing on North Carolina, the book explores the stories of Blacks who ran away from plantation slavery.

Patterson, Charles (1995). *Social Reform Movements: The Civil Rights Movement*. New York: Facts on File.

A discussion of the major civil rights movement events in the twentieth century, with details about their evolution and achievements.

Peake, Thomas R. (1987). *Keeping the Dream Alive: A History of the Southern Christian Leadership Conference from King to the Nineteen-Eighties*. New York: Peter Lang.

A comprehensive history of the organization, including changes after the death of Martin Luther King Jr.

Pease, Jane H., and William H. Pease (1996). *They Who Would Be Free*. Urbana: University of Illinois Press.

An analysis of northern Blacks within the abolitionist crusade against enslavement.

Perry, Huey (1990). "The Evolution and Impact of Biracial Coalitions and Black Mayors in Birmingham and New Orleans." In Rufus Browning et al., eds., *Racial Politics in American Cities,* 117–136. New York: Longman.

An essay focusing on biracial coalitions in Birmingham and New Orleans.

Perry, Huey, Tracey Ambeau, and Frederick McBride (1995). "Blacks and the National Executive Branch." In Huey Perry and Wayne Parent, eds., *Blacks and the American Political System*. Gainesville: University Press of Florida.

Perry, Huey L., and Wayne Parent, eds. (1995). *Blacks and the American Political System*. Gainesville: University of Florida Press.

A collection of essays analyzing the achievements of Blacks and their political allies in the American political system.

Pinderhughes, Dianne (1987). *Race and Ethnicity in Chicago Politics*. Urbana: University of Illinois Press.

An investigation into the nature of race in the pluralist politics of a major American urban city.

———. (1988). "The Articulation of Black Interests by Black Civil Rights, Professional, and Religious Organizations." In Lorenzo Morris, ed., *The Social and Political Implications of the 1984 Jesse Jackson Presidential Campaign*. New York: Praeger.

An essay examining the varying ways Black organizations influence the formation of policy positions, focusing on Jesse Jackson's 1984 presidential campaign.

Pitkin, Hanna (1967). *The Concept of Representation*. Berkeley: University of California Press.

A investigation of the concept of representation in European and American political theory.

Plessy v. Ferguson. 163 U.S. 537 (1896).
Landmark Supreme Court case that enunciated the doctrine of "separate but equal," legalizing racial segregation.

Plissner, Martin, and Warren Mitofsky (1988). "The Changing Jackson Voter." *Public Opinion,* vol. 11, no. 2: 56–57.
An examination of the evolution of voter support in the Jackson campaigns.

Ploski, Harry A., and James Williams (1989). *The Negro Almanac: A Reference Work on the African American.* 5th ed. Detroit: Gale Research, Inc.
An encyclopedic reference book about African American life.

Powell, Adam Clayton, Jr. (1971). *Adam by Adam.* New York: Dial Press.
The autobiography of Adam Clayton Powell Jr.

Price, Frederick K. C. (1999). *Race, Religion, and Racism: Perverting the Gospel to Subjugate a People.* New York: Faith One Publishing.
The author's exposition of his vision of Christianity for contemporary living.

Putnam, Robert (1993). *Making Democracy Work.* Princeton, N.J.: Princeton University Press.
An institutional analysis of the role of civic community in Italian politics.

Quarles, Benjamin (1969). *The Black Abolitionists.* New York: Oxford University Press.
An account of the Black participants in the abolitionist movement.

———. (1982). "A. Philip Randolph: Labor Leader at Large." In John H. Franklin and August Meier, eds., *Black Leaders of the Twentieth Century.* Urbana: University of Illinois Press.
A concise historical study of the grassroots leadership of Black labor union founder A. Philip Randolph.

Raboteau, Albert (1978). *Slave Religion.* New York: Oxford University Press.
The history of Christianity among Black slaves.

Redkey, Edwin S. (1969). *Black Exodus: Black Nationalist and Back-to-Africa Movements, 1890–1910.* New Haven: Yale University Press.
A historical study of African American nationalist thinkers and emigration to Africa.

Reed, Adolph, Jr. (1971). "Marxism and Nationalism in Afroamerica." *Social Theory and Practice* 1 (Fall): 1–39.
A comparative study of Marxism and nationalism among African Americans.

———. (1986). *The Jesse Jackson Phenomenon.* New Haven: Yale University Press.
A critical study of Jesse Jackson, the 1984 presidential election, and African American politics.

Reeves, Keith (1997). *Voting Hopes or Fears: White Voters, Black Candidates, and Racial Politics in America.* New York: Oxford University Press.
An examination of racially polarized voting focusing on white voters' attitudes toward Black candidates.

Reynolds v. Sims. 377 U. S. 533 (1965).
The Supreme Court ruled that each elected state legislator should represent substantially equal populations.

Rivers, Eugene (2001). "Faith in Politics: Beyond the Civil Rights Industry." *Boston Review* (April/May): 5–7.
   A study of religion in politics.
Robinson, Cedric (1983). *Black Marxism*. London: Zed Press.
   An investigation into how Marxism has been used in the African American struggle for freedom in the United States.
Robinson, Randall (2000). *The Debt*. New York: Penguin Books.
   A call for reparations to African Americans for 246 years of slavery, by the leader of the Pan-African lobby group, TransAfrica.
Rosenstone, Steven J., and John M. Hansen (1993). *Mobilization, Participation, and Democracy in America*. New York: Macmillan.
   A study of mobilization for political participation in the United States.
Salzman, Jack, et al. (1996). *Encyclopedia of African American Culture and History*, vol. 5. New York: Macmillan.
   A comprehensive alphabetical reference on the African American experience from 1619 to the present.
Scher, Robert (1997). *Politics in the New South: Republicanism, Race, and Leadership in the Twentieth Century*, 2nd ed. Armonk, N.Y.: M. E. Sharpe.
   A discussion of the rise of the Republican Party in the post–civil rights movement South.
Scott, James (1985). *Weapons of the Weak: Everyday Forms of Peasant Resistance*. New Haven: Yale University Press.
   An analysis of peasant resistance in Malaysia.
Scruggs, Otey (1977). "We the Children of Africa in This Land: Alexander Crummell." In Lorraine Williams, ed., *Africa and Afro-American Experience: Eight Essays*, 77–95. Washington, D.C.: Howard University Press.
   A biographical essay on Alexander Crummell, nineteenth-century Black clergyman and scholar.
Sears, David, et al. (2000). *Racialized Politics: The Debate About Racism in America*. Chicago: University of Chicago Press.
   A collection of essays by social scientists from various disciplines exploring the current debate surrounding racism in America, particularly in relation to white public opinion.
Sellers, Cleveland, and Robert Terrell (1973). *The River of No Return: The Autobiography of a Black Militant and the Life and Death of SNCC*. New York: William Morrow.
   The autobiography of Sellers and biography of some key leaders of SNCC.
Seraile, William (1998). *Fire in His Heart: Bishop Benjamin Tucker Tanner and the A.M.E. Church*. Knoxville: University of Tennessee Press.
   A biography that discusses both his life with the church and his role in politics advocating racial equality.
Shaw v. Reno. 509 U.S. 630 (1993).
   The Supreme Court ruled that determining the boundaries of an electoral district on the basis of race constituted racial gerrymandering in violation of the Fourteenth Amendment.
Shelly v. Kramer. 334 U.S. 1 (1948).
   The Supreme Court ruled that racially restrictive covenants were unenforceable.
Shick, Tom W. (1980). *Behold the Promised Land : A History of Afro-American Settler Society in Nineteenth-Century Liberia*. Baltimore: Johns Hopkins University Press.

A history of African Americans who resettled in Liberia during the nineteenth century.

Shingles, Richard (1981). "Black Consciousness and Political Participation: The Missing Link." *American Political Science Review,* vol. 75: 76–90.

This article discusses the impact of Black consciousness on African American political participation.

Shklar, Judith (1991). *American Citizenship: The Quest for Inclusion.* Cambridge, Mass.: Harvard University Press.

A study of what constitutes American citizenship.

Siebert, Wilbur (1968). *The Underground Railroad from Slavery to Freedom.* New York: Arno.

An analysis of the Underground Railroad.

Skinner, Elliott (1992). *African Americans and U.S. Foreign Policy Toward Africa, 1850–1924: In Defense of Black Nationality.* Washington, D.C.: Howard University Press.

A history of the role of African American diplomats in the formation of policy toward Africa.

Skocpol, Theda, et al. (2001). "Patriotic Partnership: Why Great Wars Nourished American Civic Volunteerism." In Ira Katznelson and Martin Shefter, eds., *Shaped by War and Trade: International Influence on American Political Development.* Princeton, N.J.: Princeton University Press.

An essay arguing that big wars have been surprisingly good for American civic voluntarism.

Smith v. Allwright. 321 U.S. 649 (1944).

The Supreme Court outlawed the white primary.

Smith, Charles Spencer (1922; reprint, 1968). *A History of the African Methodist Episcopal Church.* New York: Johnson Reprint Corporation.

A history of the African Methodist Episcopal Church from 1856 to 1922.

Smith, Jean, and Carrell Horton, eds. (1995). *Historical Statistics of Black America.* Detroit: Gale Research.

A compilation of more than 2,300 tables of statistics describing Black American life from 1619 to 1975.

Smith, Robert (1990). "From Insurgency Toward Inclusion: The Jackson Campaigns of 1984 and 1988." In Lorenzo Morris, ed., *The Social and Political Implications of the 1984 Jesse Jackson Presidential Campaign.* New York: Praeger.

Comparison between the Jackson campaigns of 1984 and 1988 along seven dimensions.

Smith, Robert C. (1996). *We Have No Leaders: African Americans in the Post–Civil Rights Era.* Albany: State University of New York Press.

A comprehensive study of African American political leadership and its deficits.

Smith-Irvin, Jeannette (1989). *Marcus Garvey Foot Soldiers of the Universal Negro Improvement Association (Their Own Words).* Trenton, N.J.: Africa World Press.

A biography of Marcus Garvey and the UNIA.

Southern Exposure (2000). "The Mississippi Freedom Democratic Party." In Jonathan Birnbaum and Clarence Taylor, eds., *Civil Rights Since 1787: A Reader on the Black Struggle,* 517–520. New York: New York University Press.

A study of the independent Black organization, the Mississippi Freedom Democratic Party.

Spady, James G. (1985). *Marcus Garvey, Africa, and the Universal Negro Improvement Association: A UMUM Perspective on Concentric Activity in the Pan African World.* New York: Marcus Garvey Memorial Foundation.

> An study of Marcus Garvey and the UNIA.

Stanley, Harold, and R. Niemi (2000). *Vital Statistics on American Politics, 1999–2000.* Washington, D.C.: Congressional Quarterly Press.

> A collection of general statistical data on American politics.

Steele, Shelby (1991). *The Content of Our Character: A New Vision of Race in America.* New York: HarperCollins.

> A collection of essays that critique liberal analyses of the origins of the conflict in race relations.

———. (1998). *A Dream Deferred: The Second Betrayal of Black Freedom in America.* New York: HarperCollins.

> A critique of liberal American policies and attitudes toward race.

Stoper, Emily (1989). *The Student Nonviolent Coordinating Committee: The Growth of Radicalism in a Civil Rights Organization.* New York: Carlson Publishing.

> A history of the civil rights movement and SNCC.

Strickland, Arvarh (1996). *History of the Chicago Urban League.* Urbana: University of Illinois Press.

> A history of the Chicago Urban League from its founding in 1916 through the early years of the civil rights movement in the 1960s.

Stuckey, Sterling (1972). *The Ideological Origins of Black Nationalism.* Boston: Beacon Press.

> A history of African American nationalism from enslavement.

Swann v. Charlotte-Mecklenburg County Board of Education. 402 U.S. 1 (1971).

> The Supreme Court sanctioned busing as a means of achieving school desegregation.

Sweatt v. Painter. 339 U.S. 629 (1950).

> The Supreme Court ruling that outlawed the avoidance of the desegregation of the University of Texas by the creation of a separate, inferior law school for African Americans.

Taeuber, Karl, and Alma Taeuber (1969). *Negroes in Cities: Residential Segregation and Neighborhood Change.* New York: Atheneum Press.

> A study of residential segregation and processes of neighborhood change in cities.

Tate, Katherine (1991). "Black Political Participation in the 1984 and 1988 Presidential Elections." *American Political Science Review,* vol. 85: 1159–1176.

> The political context of Black voter turnout in the 1984 and 1988 presidential elections is examined, focusing on the attitudinal and demographic variables associated with Black electoral participation.

———. (1993). *From Protest to Politics.* Cambridge, Mass.: Harvard University Press.

> An analysis of electoral politics in the post–civil rights era, focusing on the Jesse Jackson campaigns.

Thernstrom, Abigail M. (1987). *Whose Votes Count? Affirmative Action and Minority Voting Rights.* Cambridge, Mass.: Harvard University Press.

> An analysis and critique of African American politics in the context of affirmative action policy.

Tragle, Henry, ed. (1971). *The Southampton Slave Revolt of 1831.* Amherst: University of Massachusetts Press.

A documentary account of the revolt, with newspaper stories, letters, diaries, and trial notes.

Truman, David (1951). *The Governmental Process*. New York: Knopf.

A pluralist analysis of public opinion and American politics.

Tushnet, Mark (1994). *Making Civil Rights Law: Thurgood Marshall*. New York: Oxford University Press.

A chronological narrative history of the legal struggle for civil rights led by Thurgood Marshall and the NAACP Legal Defense Fund.

Valelly, Richard M. (1993). "The Puzzle of Disfranchisement: Party Struggle and African American Suffrage in the South, 1867–1894." Paper prepared for the Workshop of Race, Ethnicity, Representation, and Governance. Center for American Political Studies, Harvard University, January 21–22, 1993.

A longitudinal study of southern disfranchisement of Blacks after Reconstruction.

Verba, Sidney, and Norman H. Nie (1972). *Participation in America*. Cambridge, Mass.: Harvard University Press.

An analysis of political participation in the United States, focusing on political democracy and social equality.

Voter Education Project (1973). *Black Elected Officials in the South, 1973*. Atlanta: Voter Education Project.

Statistics on Black elected officials in the South.

Walker, Jack L., Jr. (1991). *Mobilizing Interest Groups in America*. Ann Arbor: University of Michigan Press.

An analysis of the role of interest groups in mobilization politics.

Walker, Robert (1976). "Society and Soul." Ph.D. dissertation, Department of Sociology, Stanford University.

A sociological analysis of African American popular music from the 1950s forward.

Walters, Ronald (1988). *Black Presidential Politics in America: A Strategic Approach*. Albany: State University of New York Press.

An examination of Black involvement in presidential politics, assessing the balance-of-power politics and independent and dependent leverage strategies.

Walton, Hanes, Jr. (1969a). *The Negro in Third Party Politics*. Philadelphia: Dorrance.

A study of African American affiliations with third-party efforts through American history.

———. (1969b). "Blacks and Conservative Political Movements." *Quarterly Review of Higher Education Among Negroes*, vol. 37 (October): 3–10.

A study of conservative movements among African Americans.

———. (1971). *The Political Philosophy of Martin Luther King, Jr.* New York: Greenwood Press.

A systematic analysis of the foundations of the social and political thought of Martin Luther King Jr.

———. (1972a). *Black Politics*. Philadelphia: Lippincott.

A textbook on African American politics using a developmental analysis.

———. (1972b). *Black Political Parties*. New York: Free Press.

A historical and political analysis of independent African American political parties.

———. (1975). *Black Republicans: The Politics of the Black and Tans.* Metuchen, N.J.: Scarecrow Press.

A study of the Black Republicans from 1854 to 1972, covering their origins and accomplishments and the forces that led to their decline.

———. (1985). *Invisible Politics: Black Political Behavior.* Albany: State University of New York Press.

A textbook on African politics critiquing the behavioral approach in American political science.

———. (1988). *When the Marching Stopped: The Politics of the Civil Rights Regulatory Agencies.* Albany: State University of New York Press.

An analysis of civil rights enforcement through the regulatory agencies since the passage of the Civil Rights Act of 1964.

Walton, Hanes, Jr., et al. (1983). "Henry Highland Garnet Revisited via His Diplomatic Correspondence: The Correction of Misconceptions and Errors." *Journal of Negro History* (Winter): 80–92.

A critique of two books on the Black abolitionist and diplomat Henry Highland Garnet.

Walton, Hanes, Jr., et al. (1997). "African American Political Socialization: The Protest Resignations of Councilpersons Jerome Woody and Renee Baker." In Hanes Walton Jr., ed., *African American Power and Politics: The Political Context Variable,* 113–128. New York: Columbia University Press.

A case examination of political socialization strategies employed by local African American political leaders.

Walton, Hanes Jr., and Robert Smith (2002). *American Politics and the African American Quest for Universal Freedom,* 2nd ed. New York: Longman.

A comprehensive analytic textbook on African American politics.

Warshaw, Shirley A. (1996). *Powersharing: White House–Cabinet Relations in the Modern Presidency.* Albany: State University of New York Press.

A historical overview of the relationship between presidents and their cabinets from Nixon to Clinton.

Washington, Booker T. (1967). "Atlanta Exposition Address, 1865." In Leslie Fishel Jr. and Benjamin Quarles, eds., *The Black American: A Documentary History,* 342–345. Glenview, Ill.: Scott, Foresman.

Washington's speech asserting that Blacks should seek not political equality but vocational education. It was widely seen as an accommodation to the southern disfranchisement of Blacks.

Washington, James E. (1968). *The Essential Writings and Speeches of Martin Luther King, Jr.* San Francisco: HarperCollins.

A collection of the writings, speeches, interviews, and autobiographical reflections of Martin Luther King Jr.

Watson, Denton (1990). *Lion in the Lobby: Clarence Mitchell Jr.'s Struggle for the Passage of Civil Rights Laws.* New York: William Morrow.

A biography of the widely influential NAACP Washington lobbyist for civil rights.

Weisbrot, Robert (1994). *Marching Toward Freedom, 1957–1965: From the Founding of the Southern Christian Leadership Conference to the Assassination of Malcolm X.* New York: Chelsea House.

A history of the civil rights movement from 1957 to 1965.

Weiss, Nancy (1974). *The National Urban League.* New York: Oxford University Press.

A history of the National Urban League from 1910 to 1940.

Wesberry v. Sanders. 376 U. S. 1 (1964).

The Supreme Court established the "one man, one vote" principle as the standard for apportioning congressional districts.

Wesley, Charles (1944). "The Participation of Negroes in Anti-Slavery Political Parties." *Journal of Negro History*, vol. 29: 32–74.

An essay on the participation of African Americans in political parties that sought the abolition of slavery by political action.

Wesley, Dorothy Porter, ed. (1969). *Negro Protest Pamphlets*. New York: Arno Press.

A compendium of written protests by Black Americans on a variety of themes.

———. (1971). *Early Negro Writing, 1760–1837*. Boston: Beacon Press.

Selected writings by African Americans in books, pamphlets, broadsides, and as parts of books between 1760 and 1837.

Wharton, Vernon (1947). *The Negro in Mississippi, 1865–1890*. Chapel Hill: University of North Carolina Press.

A history of Blacks in Mississippi Reconstruction politics.

White v. Regester. 412 U.S. 755 (1973).

The Supreme Court decision that multimember districts were impermissible because they diluted the votes of racial and ethnic minorities.

Wilkins, Roy (1994). *Standing Fast: The Autobiography*. New York: DaCapo Press.

The autobiography of a longtime NAACP executive director.

Williams, Armstrong (1995). *Beyond Blame: How We Can Succeed by Breaking the Dependency Barrier*. New York: Free Press.

A Black conservative perspective on African Americans in American society.

Williams, Eric (1961). *Capitalism and Slavery*. New York: Russell and Russell.

An economic history of American slavery.

Williams, Juan (1987). *Eyes on the Prize: America's Civil Rights Years, 1954–1965*. New York: Viking.

A chronicle of the events in the first eleven years of the civil rights movement.

Wilson, James Q. (1960). *Negro Politics*. New York: Free Press.

A study of African American urban leadership and politics.

IU(1961). "The Strategy of Protest: Problems of Negro Civic Action." *Journal of Conflict Resolution* 5 (September): 291–303.

An analysis of African American political protest in large Northern cities.

Woodward, C. Vann (1955). *The Strange Career of Jim Crow*. New York: Oxford University Press.

A history of southern segregation and race relations.

Wynn, Daniel W. (1974). *The Black Protest Movement*. New York: Philosophical Library.

A history of the protest and civil rights movements in the United States.

Young, Andrew (1998). *An Easy Burden: The Civil Rights Movement and the Transformation of America*. New York: HarperCollins.

A memoir of the civil rights movement by this clergyman aide to Martin Luther King Jr. who later became a cabinet member and mayor of Atlanta, Georgia.

About the Contributors

Editor	Minion K. C. Morrison Professor of Political Science University of Missouri–Columbia Columbia, Missouri
Chapter One	Minion K. C. Morrison
Chapter Two	Hanes Walton Jr. Professor of Political Science University of Michigan Ann Arbor, Michigan
Chapter Three	Lawrence J. Hanks Associate Professor of Political Science Indiana University Bloomington, Indiana
Chapter Four	Byron D'Andra Orey Assistant Professor of Political Science University of Nebraska–Lincoln Lincoln, Nebraska and Reginald Vance Assistant Professor Southern University Baton Rouge, Louisiana
Chapter Five	Minion K. C. Morrison and Richard Middleton, IV Visiting Assistant Professor of Political Science University of Columbia–Missouri Columbia, Missouri
Chapter Six	Minion K. C. Morrison

Index

385